T-FORCE

Also by Sean Longden

To the Victor the Spoils
Hitler's British Slaves
Dunkirk: The Men They Left Behind

T-FORCE
THE RACE FOR
NAZI WAR SECRETS, 1945

SEAN LONGDEN

CONSTABLE • LONDON

Constable & Robinson Ltd
3 The Lanchesters
162 Fulham Palace Road
London W6 9ER
www.constablerobinson.com

First published in the UK by Constable,
an imprint of Constable & Robinson Ltd, 2009

This paperback edition published in 2010

A copy of the British Library Cataloguing in
Publication Data is available from the British Library

ISBN: 978-1-84901-297-3

Printed and bound in the EU

1 3 5 7 9 10 8 6 4 2

Contents

Acknowledgements

There are two men whose hard work and eager assistance were fundamental in my writing of this book. These men, Ken Moore and Michael Howard, offered documents, support and guidance, giving a personal touch that went far beyond anything to be found in the reams of documents publicly available on this subject. Indeed, it was their knowledge that allowed me to make sense of the official documents – most of which are somewhat confusing when viewed in isolation.

Ken Moore fought in Normandy with the Royal Artillery before being posted to the 5th Battalion of the King's Regiment, which formed part of the infantry element of T-Force. As the editor of the unit's newsletter, *Freelance*, during 1945 and 1946, Ken Moore had a broad knowledge of this unusual unit. During the 1990s he resurrected *Freelance* as the newsletter for the '5th King's/No.2 T-Force Old Comrades Association'. The formation of the association was entirely due to Ken's drive and enthusiasm to ensure the work of the unit was not forgotten.

As an organization, T-Force first came to my attention in 2001 when I was researching my book *To the Victor the Spoils*, a social history of the British Army in the last year of the Second World War. Ken invited me to a reunion in London where I listened to the tales of a number of veterans, including Tommy Wilkinson, Norman Farmer, Len White, John Longfield and Ken himself. Some of these interviews were used within *To the Victor the Spoils*, leading Ken to make contact with me again.

Our discussions over my book resulted in his suggestion that I should consider telling the complete story of T-Force. The more I examined the subject, the more I realized this would cover a vast unknown story of the Second World War, a story that, if I did not write it now, would be lost forever. In the months that followed Ken provided me with vast numbers of documents and contact details without which I could never have completed my book.

Included among these were elements of the story of T-Force's bomb-disposal engineers as collected by Daniel Kington. Mr Kington's grandfather, Edward Kington had served in No.19 Bomb Disposal Company. Quotations within my text from Fred 'Sapper' Tapper are taken from Mr Kington's research. Fundamental to my research was *The T-Force Story*, produced by 5th King's/No.2 T-Force Old Comrades Association. This was privately printed by the association and formed the starting point for my research.

Since then I have attended two more reunions and travelled to the port of Kiel with a delegation from the Association. Tony Hibbert MC kindly spared four hours of his time to tell me his life story. His experiences in Germany during the 1930s, then at Dunkirk and Arnhem Bridge, gave me a great understanding of his eagerness to reach Kiel as swiftly as possible. Among others who have kindly given up their time to be interviewed by me include: Tom Pitt-Pladdy, Harry Henshaw, Tommy Wilkinson, Jack Chamberlain, Vic Woods (now deceased), Harry Bullen, Bob Brighouse, Ron Lawton, David March, Ted Tolley, Willy van der Burght and John Longfield. Through Ken I was also able to make contact with Reg Rush, a veteran of 30 Advanced Unit, Royal Marines, who worked alongside T-Force during 1945. I have also made use of an interview with the late Ken Hardy that I carried out for my book *To the Victor the Spoils*. At the time I had not heard of T-Force, nor realized the relevance of elements of his story.

Whilst Ken Moore was essential for establishing contacts among veterans of No.2 T-Force, Michael Howard played a similar role for No.1 T-Force. During 1946 and 1947, as a rather young captain, Michael had run the Intelligence Office for No.1 T-Force. Without his input my study of the postwar period would have been seriously hampered. Not only did he provide me with introductions to his former comrades but he offered advice and guidance on documents and his own clear memories of the period. His studies of T-Force activities in the Ruhr, carried out over many years, both enlightened me and shaped my final chapters. Numerous email exchanges also helped to clear up many areas of confusion and I have liberally quoted from Michael's messages. Michael also introduced me to other veteran officers including Tony Lucas and John Bendit, both of whom had served as subalterns at No.1 T-Force. Michael also kindly put me in touch with Julia Draper (formerly Jean Hughes-Gibb) who was the first civilian on the staff at T-Force HQ and shared both her wartime and postwar memories with me.

I have also been fortunate enough to receive assistance from Jane Weston, the daughter of Admiralty scientist John Bradley, who kindly provided her father's photographs and letters detailing his experiences as a scientist attached to T-Force. In exchange, I was able to offer her information on her father's role with T-Force, about which she had previously known little. Mrs Ruth Lambert, widow of Major George Lambert MC, kindly provided photographs of her husband and a copy of his written memoirs. My thanks must also go to Renate Dopheide of the Kiel archives whose own book on the events in Kiel in 1945 provided a valuable German perspective. I must also thank Margrete Thorsen-Moore, Ken Moore's wife, for providing me with a translated copy of Renate's book.

Unless otherwise stated, the quotations used within the text come from interviews I carried out with these veterans of

T-Force or the correspondence supplied to me via veterans of the unit and their families.

I must also offer thanks to my editor Leo Hollis and my agent Andrew Lownie, both of whom have offered support throughout this project. My thanks also go to Sam Evans and Hannah Boursnell at Constable for their hard work on my previous book, *Dunkirk: The Men They Left Behind*, and to the Constable sales team for helping make that book a success. As ever, thanks to Beth and Bethan at MGA for all their efforts to ensure effective publicity.

List of Illustrations

Soldiers of the 5th Battalion, The King's Regiment, at Sword Beach on the morning of D-Day. Photograph, 1945. © *Private collection, Lt-Colonel Percy Winterton / Courtesy of Peter Winterton.*

T-Force reconnaissance armoured car. Photograph, 1945. © *Courtesy of 5th Kings/No.2 T-Force Old Comrades Association.*

Signpost at the German border. Photograph, 1945. © *Courtesy of 5th Kings/No.2 T-Force Old Comrades Association.*

Officers of the 5th Battalion. Photograph,1945. © *Private collection, Lt-Colonel Percy Winterton / Courtesy of Peter Winterton.*

C Company of the 5th Battalion in Denmark. Photograph, 1945. © *Courtesy of Ron Lawton.*

B Troop of 30 Advanced Unit, Royal Marines in Germany. Photograph,1945. © *Courtesy of Reg Rush.*

Jeep of B Troop, 30AU, Royal Marines at Minden, Germany. Photograph, 1945. © *Courtesy of Reg Rush.*

T-Force Royal Navy investigator John Bradley with Commander Dunstan Curtis of 30AU. Photograph, 1945. © *Private collection, John Bradley / Courtesy of Jane Weston.*

T-Force evacuating equipment from a factory in Köln (Cologne). Photograph, 1945. © *Private collection, John Bradley / Courtesy of Jane Weston.*

German Type XVIIB U-boat. Photograph. © *Courtesy of the National Archives.*

An experimental glider bomb at the 'Walterwerke' in Kiel. Photograph.
© *Courtesy of the National Archives.*

Dr Walter's 'Cleopatra' anti-beach defence weapon after wartime tests. Photograph. © *Courtesy of the National Archives.*

The *Admiral Hipper* in Kiel harbour, 'captured' by T-Force. Photograph, 1945. © *Courtesy of Vic Woods.*

The bomb-damaged Naval Academy. Photograph, 1945. © *Courtesy of 5th Kings/No.2 T-Force Old Comrades Association.*

Dr Helmut Walter, detained by T-Force. Photograph, 1945. © *Courtesy of the National Archives.*

The 'Walterwerke' factory. Photograph. © *Courtesy of the National Archives.*

Men of the 5th Battalion listening to Churchill's VE Day broadcast in Kiel. Photograph, 1945. © *Courtesy of 5th Kings/No.2 T-Force Old Comrades Association.*

Soldiers of T-Force retrieving experimental torpedo combustion chambers from a bomb crater. Photograph, May 1945. © *Courtesy of the National Archives.*

German mini submarines under investigation by 30AU, Royal Marines at Eckenforde, Germany. Photograph, 1945. © *Courtesy of Reg Rush.*

German scientists on the Blankensee ferry after being detained by T-Force. Photograph, 1945. © *Private collection, John Bradley / Courtesy of Jane Weston.*

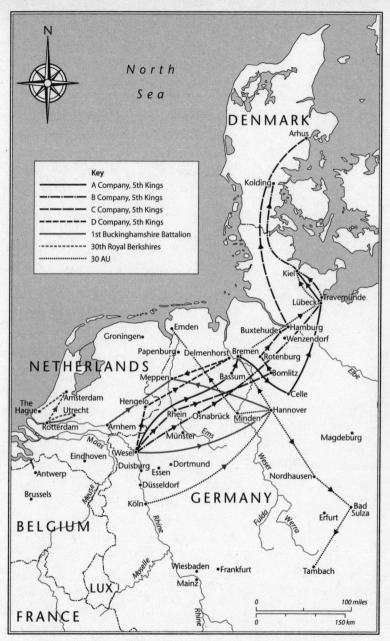

Key Expeditions by the T-Force Units, March to May 1945

Introduction

Headquarters of 8 Corps,
outside Hamburg, Germany,
5 May 1945

The major was in no mood for waiting. The war may have been drawing to a close but he was eager to move his men forward. In fact, despite the inactivity around him and the 'Stop Order' issued to all British units in Germany, he had specific orders to advance. They came directly from the Allied High Command – he had his instructions and intended to follow them.

Major Tony Hibbert was a man of action, a former commando who had been at the head of the beleaguered 1st Parachute Brigade during the doomed operation to snatch the bridge at Arnhem, and, if he had learnt anything from the failure of Operation Market Garden, it was the desperate need for speed. Now, however, the dangers were very different. It was not only the Germans who were the enemy. The Allied High Command was already looking to the future and had passed on instructions that would determine the future of Europe.

However, down in the frontlines, no one else realized the sense of urgency. After six long years, the war was coming to an end – the ceasefire had been signed and the field commanders were not about to take any chances with their men's lives. The moment General Miles Dempsey, commander of the British 2nd Army, had heard the news that a ceasefire was about to come into effect, he had issued an order for the four corps under his command to stand fast on the line between the towns of Dömitz, Ludwigslust, Schwerin, Wismar, Neustadt, Bad Segeberg, Wedel, Stade, Bremervörde and Bremen. His personal order went out: 'No advance beyond this line to take place without orders from me.'

Dempsey's order to halt was confirmed throughout the army and at Hamburg the commander of 8 Corps refused permission for anyone to advance beyond their current positions. Despite this, Major Tony Hibbert had no intention of waiting. He was a veteran of Dunkirk and Arnhem, had just over 500 men under his command and his target was over 60 miles away. He had been warned there were two SS divisions ahead of him – converging on the road he would be using – and that he would be advancing towards a city firmly occupied by over 40,000 German soldiers and sailors. Still Hibbert refused to wait. The Germans were not his concern and his authority came from way above the Corps commander.

The High Command believed the Russians were intending to advance on Denmark, which would make the Baltic a Russian sea. Fearing that the Russians would stop at nothing, Hibbert's brief had been simple: he had received the order 'get to Kiel before the Russians' and was going to follow it. As far as he was concerned, it did not matter that a Corps commander had refused him permission to advance. Nor was he worried by the messages from General Dempsey's HQ. His orders came from the very top and if the Allied Supreme Commander General Dwight D. Eisenhower believed Kiel needed to be occupied, he and his men were going to do it.

Major Hibbert needed just one signature to move through the frontlines and advance on Kiel. Returning to the 8 Corps HQ, with the seconds ticking away and a bottle of whisky, just one strategy remained – to ply the officer with liquor. In the hours that followed, Hibbert poured out glass after glass, ensuring his companion consumed the lion's share of the bottle. It was not a quick operation, but Hibbert was nothing if not persistent and finally he had what he wanted – one very drunk staff officer and the written permission to advance.

Now it was time to go. At 7 a.m. on the morning of 5 May 1945 the men of T-Force climbed into their vehicles and headed out on the road towards Kiel. Among their targets that morning was the Walterwerke factory and, within it, its founder – Germany's foremost expert on hydrogen peroxide rocket engines, Dr Hellmuth Walter.

In the spring of 1945 as the Allied army advanced into German there was one objective paramount for the vast majority of its troops – the prompt defeat of the Germans on the battlefield and the swift restoration of peace. However, there was one unit in and around the frontlines whose aim was very different. Unlike their frontline colleagues, these men were actively discouraged from engaging with the enemy or indulging in heroics. The truth of the matter was that these soldiers, surging across northern Germany in vehicles marked with a simple 'T' sign, were not actually fighting the same war.

As the men of T-Force sat in the spring sunshine, excited but nervous as they awaited their orders, few of them understood exactly what they were doing. They were not actually engaged in the final surge against Nazism but were unwitting players in the overture to the next great conflict of the era – the Cold War. All they knew was that they had been given a target and that they would soon be getting into their vehicles to head off into the unknown. It was a simple routine but very few of them understood the significance of the orders they were being given. The fact was that, at that moment and for much of 1945, the future security of the western democracies hung in the balance and, had the men of T-Force failed in those tasks, the entire future of the western world might have been very different.

There is little doubt that the Nazis had been victorious on the technological battlefield of the Second World War. With the world's first operational jet fighters, ballistic missiles, high-speed submarines, rocket planes, infra-red gun sights, new chemical weapons such as Sarin and Tabun, flying bombs and even guns that fired around corners, German scientists had provided the blueprint for military development in the postwar years. By May 1945 the drawing boards of these scientists were covered with designs for a variety of new weapons, all of which the competing former Allies were keen to exploit. In the years after the war, these designs resurfaced on the world's battlefields in the form of Cruise missiles and Stealth fighters, among others. During the Cold War, the US used radar systems developed from German wartime designs as part of its worldwide 'early warning' system. Unforgettably, it was German rocket scientists who eventually put man on the moon while German aviation researchers even provided the impetus for the development of Concorde.

However, in spring 1945 no one in the West knew the truth about the Nazi's atomic research programme; nor did they know the realities behind the rumours of deadly new military gases under development within Germany. What they did know was that even as the Allies advanced Nazi scientists were still hard at work at their desks and drawing boards and what they might achieve could still be significant. These were the same men, after all, who had brought the new weapons to the battlefield. While the Third Reich was collapsing, who could tell what horrors they might still inflict upon the world, what secret weapons they could have already passed on to their Japanese allies or what other potential enemies could do if they got hold of this technology?

The western leaders had no choice but to seize these weapons, find the scientists, uncover their research, and put them to work before someone else did. And for that they needed a special force – an 'elite unit' in the parlance of the postwar world – one that could secure the factories and research establishments of Germany, detain their research scientists and ensure the western Allies could profit from their knowledge.

With this in mind, in July 1944 General Eisenhower issued a secret order from the Supreme Headquarters Allied Expeditionary Force (SHAEF) to raise a 'Target-Force'. This force was so steeped in secrecy that its role has all but disappeared from the histories of both the Second World War and the Cold War. Yet, despite this secrecy, the British Target-Force – most commonly known as T-Force – was the least assuming of all the 'elite forces'.

This was not the SAS, and few among its number were commandos or paratroopers. Nor were they the 'spit 'n' polish' Guardsmen, so adored by tourists visiting London. Instead, they were ordinary infantrymen, pioneers and engineers from unglamorous regiments – the 5th Battalion of Liverpool's King's Regiment, the 1st Buckinghamshire Battalion, the 30th Battalion of the Royal Berkshire Regiment, the Pioneer Corps and the Royal Engineers. They had come from hospitals, some physically wounded, others mentally wounded by shellshock. Some were hardened infantrymen, who had landed on D-Day in the first waves and had seen the horrors of war in the frontlines. Others were 'surplus' artillerymen, whose units had been broken up to supply desperately needed reinforcements for an army depleted by the vicious slog through Normandy. Elsewhere among them were ex-landing craft crews, men who had braved enemy fire to deliver the infantry to Normandy on D-Day. They were joined by teenagers just out of training depots, who had been rushed to the continent, ready for the advance into Germany. Unfashionable as it might seem, these 'waifs and strays' were the soldiers who made sure the western Allies were prepared for the Cold War.

In the final months of the conflict in Europe and the first years of peace, these soldiers were responsible for one of the war's most unlikely success stories – the securing of military and civilian technology now estimated to be worth around £10 billion at today's prices. Nuclear scientists, gas technology, advanced submarine engines, jet-fighter technology – all passed through the hands of T-Force as the Allied armies occupied the ruins of Germany. In the years that followed, the western powers used the military technology they seized to ensure their future safety.

Despite the groundbreaking research carried out by German scientists, and the importance of their work for postwar development, the story of how this most unlikely of elite forces helped secure these men and their work is all but unknown. The creation of this secretunit remained forgotten for many years. Yet this was the unit that, in the final weeks of the war, had entered Germany to secure nuclear scientists, rocket research, chemical weapons production plants and U-boat designers, ensuring they did not fall into the hands of the Russians. Furthermore, T-Force made the British Army's final advance of the war in Europe, reaching Kiel to secure the city's naval research facilities.

It is no surprise if all this sounds like something from a James Bond novel. One of the influences behind T-Force operations was the author Ian Fleming. He was the driving force behind the creation of 30 Assault Unit, a unit of Royal Marines which provided the model for T-Force operations and served alongside it during the advance into Germany. Fleming also sat on the committees that provided the intelligence targets and determined the priority for T-Force operations.

CHAPTER I

The Birth of an Idea

'From very early in WWII there was a belief amongst the Allies that the Germans had a technical superiority in their armaments . . . As the ultimate entry into Germany itself began to be planned, the Allies started to consider what could be done to uncover German technological secrets.' [1]

Arriving at the Admiralty early one spring morning, Ian Fleming, a 34-year-old commander in the Royal Navy Volunteer Reserve, was just one of thousands of young men and women travelling to Whitehall. Amidst teeming government offices, this was the beating heart of Britain's wartime government. Each day thousands of civil servants and military personnel, in the uniforms of all the services and of every nation of the Empire and Commonwealth, arrived at their offices to play their part in orchestrating the functioning of the state and its vast military machine. Every one of them played a vital role in the war effort, but for some these roles would have a long-lasting impact upon the world's future.

In April 1942 Fleming entered Room 39 of the Old Admiralty Building for another day's work as the personal assistant to the Director of Naval Intelligence (DNI). It was there, in the white-walled, half-panelled room, complete with marble fireplace and increasingly packed filing cabinets, that he had formulated so many plans to gather intelligence on behalf of the Royal Navy. Some had been outlandish and were abandoned;

others had been accepted and carried out. However, what was of primary importance was that the Commander had shown himself as hard-working, meticulous in the detailed planning of his operations and possessed of a quick mind. Often at his desk by 6 a.m. and working long into the night, the Commander had displayed all the necessary credentials to be appointed as Admiral John Godfrey's assistant. As such, the Commander was the ideal man to take over the Admiral's latest project.

So it was that Admiral Godfrey telephoned through to the room adjoining his office and asked for Commander Fleming to join him to discuss an idea he had for gathering naval intelligence. The Admiral wasted no time. In a scene that would later be repeated so many times in Commander Fleming's works of fiction, the senior officer gave the younger man a no-nonsense outline of what he wanted.

Commander Fleming listened as the Admiral explained his plan. From studying reports of German activity during the Nazis' advance into Greece and the daring capture of Crete in 1941, he had learned that the Germans had employed 'intelligence commandos'. In particular, they had used forward field teams of intelligence troops to enter HQs and seize documents, moving just behind regular assault troops, or sometimes even in front of them. This role had included taking part in assaults on ports and moving into the Royal Navy's command facilities to gather any available intelligence, in particular codebooks and signals intelligence.

Commander Fleming took in the details: his task was to review these German operations, with a mind to working out how the British could learn from the experience. Over the next few weeks Commander Fleming closely studied the German methods. This was exactly the sort of task he relished, an opportunity to plan for genuine commando operations and throw himself into the fighting war. Subsequently, Fleming presented the Admiral with his plan for an 'Offensive Naval

Intelligence Group'. In July 1942 Admiral Godfrey reported to his superiors on the results of Fleming's work: 'I have prepared plans for using the German organization as a model in connection with naval intelligence requirements on future raids on the continent or in Norway, and which would operate in the event of a major offensive.'[2] At this stage what was envisaged was a small elite group, but it was to become both a blueprint for intelligence-gathering and a key component of the future T-Force unit.

Commander Fleming was then called to present his ideas to the War Office. As a representative of the Admiralty, Fleming explained the urgent requirement for personnel who could be intensively trained to carry out special naval intelligence duties. He pointed out that the Admiralty had been the first to ascertain the need for such a unit and emphasized 'the now increasingly urgent need for a permanent body to which this type of naval intelligence work could be entrusted.'[3] This principle was generally agreed at the meeting. Fleming also suggested that a single platoon of Royal Marines would be sufficient to carry out the task. It was a vast underestimation of the eventual force that would be used to gather intelligence: from the seeds of Fleming's plan for an intelligence commando unit grew a military force numbering thousands.

In September 1942, having earlier received the support of the War Office, Admiral Godfrey formally authorized Fleming's plan for the creation of a 'Special Intelligence Unit', whose task would be to undertake covert operations, infiltrate behind enemy lines and seize intelligence material that might be of use to the Royal Navy. There was considerable debate around what this new unit would be called, although at the time of its creation some in the Admiralty had suggested naming it '30 Intelligence Unit' as 'their role is an intelligence one rather than an assault one'.[4] Prior to the unit's formal creation, it was referred to as an 'Intelligence Assault Unit' or IAU. However, some of the other descriptions of the unit at this time were less complimentary, with a November 1942 memo referring to it as: 'a force of armed and expert authorised looters'.[5]

Despite the Royal Navy's enthusiasm for the scheme, elsewhere it was less well received. The plan had called for a combination of Royal Navy, Royal Marine and Army elements within the force and was put forward to the Joint Intelligence Committee in this form, only to be opposed by both the RAF and the Army, who felt the new unit would encroach on the roles of the RAF Regiment and Field Security Police respectively.

Undeterred by this resistance, Admiral Godfrey urged Commander Fleming to press ahead with the plan. Eventually, they secured support from both the Joint Intelligence Committee and the Chiefs of Staff. Thus, the new unit was formed, under the command of the Chief of Combined Operations, with the cover name of the 'Special Engineering Unit' of the Special Service Brigade. This name was chosen to disguise its true purpose after Hitler's famous 'commando order' which stated that all prisoners from commando and sabotage units should be executed, making it vital that its men were not seen as commandos by the enemy. However, it was soon renamed No. 30 Commando, for no other reason than it was the brainchild of Fleming, whose secretary worked from Room 30 at the Admiralty. The '30' element of the name would follow the unit through to 1945.

With the plan formally agreed, Commander Fleming and the staff of the DNI started to create a team that would be set to work in the Mediterranean. The Royal Navy element that formed the basis for the unit, which was again renamed to become the 30 Assault Unit (30AU), came from volunteers for hazardous service within the Royal Navy Volunteer Reserve (RNVR). 30AU's first commanding officer was Commander Robert 'Red' Ryder VC of the Royal Navy and his second-in-command was Major W.G. Cass, the senior representative of the unit's Army element. Others appointed to the unit included a group of energetic officers who remained with it for a long period, including Lieutenant Commander Quintin Riley, an experienced polar explorer, and Commander Dunstan Curtis, a veteran of the St Nazaire and Dieppe raids and the youngest commander in the entire Royal Navy.

Even at this early stage part of 30AU's role, and one which would be refined with the eventual creation of T-Force, was to take part in assaults: 'proceed with the 2nd or 3rd wave of attack into the port and make straight for the various buildings etc where the booty is expected to be found, capture it and return'.[6] In its early incarnations the officers and men of the unit were given training in assault and commando-style street-fighting. They were all proficient in small arms including mortars, hand grenades, mines, booby traps and explosives. Their training also covered enemy vehicle recognition, parachuting, handling small boats, recognition of documents, safe-breaking and lock-picking. Another intended duty was to gain information on enemy technology. Teams were trained to enter U-boats in dock and photograph the instrument panels in order to provide intelligence on the submarine's capabilities. In preparation for this role, Royal Navy officers received training in intelligence aspects of German sea mines, torpedoes, electronics and submarine detection systems. As training progressed, additional targets were specified, including torpedo fire systems, U-boat propulsion systems and handbooks on harbour boom defence equipment. The target lists grew as planning developed, with intelligence on enemy mining techniques, rapid-fire anti-aircraft weapons for use at sea, naval gun predictor sights and information on German military intentions all being itemized.

Even before 30AU was sent overseas to begin work, it became clear that not everyone understood or accepted the unit's methodology. There were concerns that commanders 'on the ground' would refuse to cooperate with what would appeared to be a raiding party. In fact, as early as December 1942, Admiral Sir Andrew Cunningham recognized the difficulties of launching such missions when he wrote: 'their work is not likely to be fully understood by the military authorities'.[7] However, while admitting the likely pitfalls of such innovative operations, he made genuine efforts to assist the 30AU missions by requesting they be issued special passes in order to facilitate their work. It was a simple idea but one which would later play a major part in the future successes of T-Force.

30AU's first opportunity to prove itself came during the final stages of the Allied advance in North Africa in 1943. In Tunisia the fledgling unit was put to work with 'S-Force', an ad-hoc unit which had been formed to gather intelligence during the occupation of the country's port facilities. However, the partnership was not a happy one, with the seemingly cumbersome nature of S-Force being seen as having held back 30AU by as much as 24 hours. It was a concern the unit was never to fully escape, and one that influenced both their later thinking and the eventual form of the T-Force operations in northwest Europe.

Ironically, while those inside 30AU saw its small size as an advantage, during the early operations in North Africa others were becoming concerned that the unit was so small there was a risk a single burst of machine gun fire could undermine an entire operation. The concern was such that it prompted Louis Mountbatten, as Chief of Combined Operations, to suggest the unit be withdrawn from North Africa, returned to the UK, and once there bolstered with volunteers from the Royal Marines.

After an uncertain start in North Africa, the unit soon began to gel during operations in Sicily and Italy, and the results of their intelligence-gathering operations were impressive. The unit discovered German charts for use by U-boats attempting to avoid detection in the Straits of Gibraltar and camouflage recognition sheets in use by the Italian fleet. The homing-beacon codes used on Italian airfields were also uncovered and put to immediate use by the RAF, whose bombers used the beacons to carry out bombing raids, cratering runways and putting enemy aircraft out of action. In addition, a map showing the location of similar navigational beacons within Germany was discovered and put to use by the RAF. The unit, however, did not only seize information, they also detained a leading pro-German Italian Fascist who had been in charge of the organization of German administration in the Bay of Naples.

There were also discoveries in the field of industrial research, including documents relating to German orders from Italian companies and the supply of raw materials to the German Navy. The Royal Navy was particularly interested in torpedo research carried out in Italy and 30AU obliged the Admiralty with samples of numerous torpedo designs, including remote-controlled devices. In addition, the Admiralty received detailed intelligence on sea mines as well as a new design of depth charge with a 50-day delayed firing mechanism that had been created for use in the sabotage of harbour facilities. In total, they discovered information on no less than 14 varieties of torpedoes and mines, including some previously unknown models.

Following these successful operations, the unit's officers requested more transport and the provision of armoured cars as they had previously been prevented from moving forward by having only unprotected vehicles at their disposal. As one officer later reported, it was suicidal to attempt their duties in soft-skinned vehicles and during one assault they had been forced to abandon their vehicles and approach on the backs of tanks in order to reach their targets promptly. The officer reported it had been quite unfair to the tank units for his men to use their vehicles as a taxi service.

During the Italian operations, they even collected charred documents that they hoped might still include important intelligence. However, one of 30AU's greatest successes in the Mediterranean was its role in uncovering the German 'Enigma' code machines. The Allies had a certain amount of intelligence on these machines but their knowledge was incomplete. To fill these gaps, 30AU was given instructions to search for examples of the machines and the related codebooks. Secrecy around these targets was such that 30AU personnel were forbidden from taking any notes during briefings. Operations by the unit in North Africa actually resulted in the capture of a previously 'unbroken' code machine. The machine's capture resulted in Allied intelligence being able to read German radio signals in the area for a period of six weeks. Related investigations also uncovered German documents about their attempts to break Allied codes.

During 1943 the Director of Naval Intelligence wrote to the head of Combined Operations to inform him of the importance of 30AU and the future potential of such intelligence-gathering units. Confident of the benefits gained from its work, he stated that: 'units of this type should take a permanent place in our basic establishment requirements for war.'[8] These successes also gave 30AU an opportunity to request an increase in their numbers. It was stressed that, had a larger force been available at Cape Passero in Sicily, they might have been able to prevent the destruction of technical information and equipment at the radar station and the looting of equipment by both Italian civilians and Allied troops.

The early operations carried out by 30AU had been a steep learning curve. In some locations their zeal had put them ahead of the Allied infantry and led to them being shelled by both sides. In addition, there was nothing in the training of Staff Officers that dealt with the seizing of vast archives of military and political intelligence. As such, they were still learning from their own mistakes.

It was during the Italian campaign that it was decided that combat troops of the intelligence unit should enter a target city just behind the assault formations. Being totally mobile, they would seize targets and hold them while specialist investigators were brought up from the rear. This method would become the model for T-Force. However, there were still some lessons to be learnt. Despite the early successes in Sicily, once in Italy 30AU had again been forced to operate alongside designated S-Force units. These were international in character and in the main they were made up of ad-hoc units, rather than a force specifically gathered for its purpose. In Florence the S-Force consisted of one company of American infantry, a group from 30AU, three Field Security sections, some Italian engineers and a platoon of US Military Police.

These new intelligence- and equipment-gathering units were learning as much by their mistakes as by their successes. There was often little control over the sifting of captured documents as some investigators simply rifled through boxes of papers and files of index cards, throwing away whatever was of no interest to them. As a result, vital documents were discovered to have been scattered into the streets of Rome by investigators. One witness reported them going through an office: 'like a storm, literally destroying and disrupting files'. Seeing the haphazard way in which documents had been treated, the same witness recommended that archives should be sealed and only examined when sufficient staff were available to examine them scientifically. His final comments were also to prove vital in the later development of T-Force: 'I hope that in the future we will avoid such a destruction.'[9]

Once the importance of the discarded information had been realized – and such damning reports had been read – orders were issued to curtail the uncontrolled sifting of documents. In their defence, the offenders pointed out they had been searching for intelligence that related to immediate military operations and such intelligence had to take priority over everything else.

What these soldiers failed to realize was that, as well as reports relating to the current conflict, the archives they were searching also held documents that might prove vital in the postwar world. These included notes on the relationship between the Catholic Church and the Franco government in Spain and reports on Italian activity in India, Iran, the Middle East and Thailand. There had also been documents which named pro-fascist individuals in Egypt and Iran who could have been a threat to British interests in those countries. That was not all: other documents threw light on international personalities believed to be pro- or anti-fascist. The intelligence material seized and examined in Italy also included reports on Italian propaganda carried out in the UK during the 1930s, Italian Foreign Ministry papers on international fascist groups, the supply of war materials to Spain during the civil war, the treatment of Indian POWs in Italy and secret details on the effect of Allied bombing on Berlin and Munich. As the writer of one classified report put it: 'When we are able to get hold of the other archives transferred to northern Italy by the Fascist republic government, it will give us the complete history of the tremendous international network of Italian and German propaganda.'[10]

However, not everyone was impressed by 30AU's practices. Some reports claimed the unit was withdrawn from Italy as a result of the methods they employed in intelligence-gathering operations. There were observers who described them as a private army of looters who failed to follow orders and whose dress standards left much to be desired. Even the unit's supporters reported how it was vital for discipline to be increased in order not to upset senior Allied commanders, with the lax dress standards and 'piratical' appearance of some being noted by critics. As one such critic scrawled in the margins of an official document, they were 'technical thieves'.[11]

With their work in Italy completed in late 1943, 30AU returned to the UK to begin preparations for the next phase of operations – the inevitable assault on 'Fortress Europe'. The unit also acquired a naval wing whose technical officers selected the targets, assessed information and then passed it on to the Admiralty. This was another approach the larger T-Force would later follow. These men were protected by the unit's Royal Marine wing whose role was to fight to capture targets, protect the Naval officers, and then provide guards and transport for targets. As the Director of Naval Intelligence wrote: 'The functions of each Wing are therefore equally essential to the success of the unit as a whole – i.e. without the RN Wing there would be no purpose in the unit; without the RM Wing the RN Wing would not long survive in the field.'[12]

The Mediterranean operations had revealed the value of such operations. 30AU's swift arrival in Italian towns and military facilities had provided both useful military intelligence and political documents. However, it was also increasingly acknowledged that the unit was too small for the task and its methods might not be suited to the situation in Germany. The Italian campaign had also shown that creating ad-hoc S-Forces was not a solution to the problem. Relying on whoever was available in the area did not provide the required continuity of experience. The days of competing agencies scattering documents on office floors while they searched for the information they needed had to be brought to a swift end. What was needed was cooperation, not competition; a unit that could learn by experience, adapt to new challenges and provide intelligence of genuine value – which could then be distributed fairly to whoever was interested in it. What Commander Fleming had set in motion was now to be examined in detail and would provide the inspiration for what would be part of the greatest intelligence- and technology-gathering exercise in modern history.

Whatever form this new force was to take, it would need infantrymen to seize, search, secure and defend its targets, and transport both to ensure its men reached their targets quickly – before too much damage could be done – and to remove whatever materials had been seized. It would need bomb-disposal engineers to defuse any booby traps they found and labour to dismantle any technology needing to be removed. With this in mind, the senior Allied planners began preparing for the days ahead. But first they had more pressing matters in hand. They would need to land safely in France before they could prepare to exploit the ruins of Germany.

CHAPTER 2

Normandy and Beyond

'I have been asked many times what my feelings were on approaching the French coast. I can only describe it as a sort of dry fear (which means, being interpreted, bloody frightened), mixed with a kind of mind numbness that allowed one to know and realize very fully what was going on – the intense shelling and mortaring, seeing landing craft being hit and sunk on either side, soldiers flung into the water – while at the same time having a fixation and rather automatic sleep-like sensation of doing the job that one had to do.'

Lieutenant Ken Davenport, 5th Battalion,
The King's Regiment.[1]

Sword Beach, 7:25 a.m., 6 June 1944

Sheltering deep beneath the walls of the landing craft, the officers and men of the 5th King's Regiment listened as the heavy guns of the Royal Navy pounded the coast of Normandy. Elsewhere the hideous whine of rocket batteries filled the Kingsmen's ears as they unleashed a barrage of high explosive on the French coast. Their senses were assaulted by the sights, smells and sounds of total war. Their ears were filled with the shouts of sailors, the whizz and clang of incoming machine-gun fire as it bounced off the thin walls of the landing craft, the splashing sound of near misses – enemy shells and mortar rounds that sent plumes of water cascading over the soldiers. Wrapped in a terrifying blanket of noise, their landing craft cut through the surf towards the coast of France.

In those final moments before the boat's ramp crashed down, Vic Woods contemplated his situation. A Merseyside-born jeep driver, serving in his hometown regiment, he was part of a 'Beach Group' − an infantry battalion whose role was not to assault the enemy's defences but to consolidate the beachhead, clearing the way for other units to drive inland. He knew he was deeply frightened, but couldn't understand whether he was frightened of death or just frightened of fear itself. He just desperately hoped he could carry out his duties. What concerned him most of all was what would he do on the beach? All he knew was that he had to drive his jeep to a specific location and remove the waterproofing − after that he would be alone and without orders. He thought to himself, 'I don't know where the hell I am going to go or what I am going to do.'

As the ramp finally lowered, Woods looked out at the beach. Before him were a number of fortified houses and from his left came a stream of incoming machine-gun fire and mortar bombs. As the last vehicle off his craft, Woods followed behind a Flail tank as it weaved through the mines on the beach. Looking to either side, Woods realized that his jeep seemed to be the first wheeled vehicle on to Sword Beach. Then, 'The tank had only got 20 yards off the craft when it got a direct hit. It disappeared in a cloud of flame and smoke. It really shook me − ten minutes before I'd been talking to them.'

Finding the position to which he was supposed to deliver the jeep, Vic Woods parked it and began to strip off the waterproofing. As he worked he noticed an ominous sign reading 'Achtung Minen' planted in the sand beside him. Rather than being occupied with fighting, Woods had nothing to do except shelter from incoming artillery, mortar, artillery and sniper fire. He soon found an outlet for his tensions: 'I was left in limbo.

I was waiting in the sand dunes a few minutes after landing. A platoon of infantry came up and they knew exactly where they were going. They were attacking a defence dug out. So I went with them.'

Although Woods was not supposed to be one of the assault groups, anything was better than sitting around waiting for something to happen. He knew that if he was active he would not have time to think about dying. Taking his Sten gun, he followed the infantrymen. Reaching a concrete bunker they began the attack, with Woods firing on the position and throwing grenades into the trenches around the bunker. All the time his mind was occupied by one simple thought: 'If I don't do it, they'll do it to me.' Within minutes the attack had proved successful and he watched as improvised white flags emerged through the bunker's firing slit. As the stunned prisoners filed out of the bunker, the infantrymen handed them over to Woods. Then, leaving him on the beach, they moved off to their next objective. The invasion of 'Fortress Europe' had begun.

Despite the reservations of some senior commanders, 30AU had produced impressive results and learned vital lessons in Italy. To those intimately involved in the project, men such as Admiral Godfrey and Commander Fleming, it was a vindication of all they had argued for and proof that such a force was essential if the Allies were to fully exploit all that might be discovered in the months ahead.

It was no surprise, therefore, that 30AU would be deployed again in the intelligence war against the Nazis or that such a successful project was to be refined and expanded to meet the changing needs – both military and political – of the western Allies.

The Admiralty began planning as soon as the Royal Marines returned from Italy and, in advance of Operation Overlord, the

Naval Intelligence Directorate had established a new branch, 'NID30', which would be responsible for all aspects of 30AU's work in the field. The control of NID30, based in Room 30 at the Admiralty, was passed to Commander Fleming, who had played such an active role in the unit's establishment.

It was proposed that 30AU undertake some very specific functions both on D-Day and during the campaign in France. So Fleming and the officers of 30AU set about preparing reports and collating all available information on the naval targets in the region. Unlike other Allied planners who were busy making sure every aspect of the coming invasion was bound together in a web of interconnecting orders, movements and support directives, NID30 made sure 30AU retained the spirit of independence that had been so vital to their initial creation and they had so carefully guarded. Effectively, in the run-up to D-Day the group worked autonomously, creating their own orders for their role in the forthcoming invasion.

Their instructions were clear. The unit was to search for code ciphers that could be of immediate use when intercepting enemy communications. They would also capture enemy equipment for use in mine-sweeping that could be used immediately to open up the ports and dock facilities which were vital for the logistical needs of the advancing Allied armies. They would be responsible for some elements of clearing ports ready for naval use, in particular carrying out anti-sabotage operations in ports and liaising with resistance groups whose duties would include hampering German sabotage.

To facilitate this work, a group of volunteer officers – experts in fields such as radar, underwater weapons and U-boats – were attached to 30AU before the invasion. All received weapons training prior to their deployment. One particular duty, that was later to be restated for T-Force, was that 30AU would proceed to Germany: 'to lay hands on all the weapons, documents etc required by Admiralty departments either for the prosecution of the war against Japan or to prevent the recrudescence of the German Navy'.[2] It was also made clear to the officers that speed was essential since, in the aftermath of the Great War, it was discovered that the Germans had hidden information and equipment that was later used to rearm the Third Reich.

Joining 30AU during this period was Reg Rush, a Royal Marine from Lincolnshire who had earlier avoided military service since, when war broke out, he had been working at a farm attached to a mental hospital in Staffordshire: 'I was old enough to be called up when war broke out. But being a youngster of 18 I had no interest in it at all. I thought those who caused it should fight the war.' His attitude was soon to change. One night there was a heavy air raid and, standing outside, he watched as a flare landed just yards from him, lighting up the hospital with an eerie glow. Concerned that the hospital might be the target of the raid, Rush decided to head to the local pub. As the all-clear sounded he returned to the hospital. What he saw as he headed back shocked him: 'From the bank up on the hill I could see right across the Midlands. I looked south and from Coventry to Birmingham everything was ablaze. It was the night they bombed Coventry.' Entering the staff room, he turned on the radio and listened to a broadcast by 'Lord Haw-Haw'. 'He did his usual bit about bombing civilians. I thought "What the hell am I doing here!" I felt embarrassed. I knew I'd got to go and do my bit. So when the time came to renew my exemption, I didn't bother. I got my call-up papers straight away after that.'

Being called up into the Royal Marines, Rush spent some time in various duties – including being selected to train as aircrew – before his refusal to accept promotion meant that he was transferred to 30AU. It was an unexpected move but one that pleased him, recalling that: '30AU was the happiest unit I ever served in.' He enjoyed the specialist training, including using explosives to blow safes, and was excited to realize he had been sent to a 'special intelligence' unit, even if the marines were given little idea of what they were actually looking for.

Yet before 30AU could begin the long advance on Germany, there was one outstanding issue. Nothing could happen before the Allies had achieved their principal aim – to gain a foothold in France. For this to happen, the Allies were not dependent on small teams of independently minded commandos working behind the enemy lines but on the combined efforts of millions of men and women, all working to orders that had been pulled together to create the most carefully planned operation in military history. And for this to succeed and allow such elite units as 30AU to begin their work, plenty of unspectacular units would face extreme danger and make sacrifices in pursuit of victory.

Included in that group of men preparing to make that very sacrifice were the 5th Battalion of the King's Regiment. Despite the regiment's illustrious history, the 5th Battalion had had a reasonably quiet war. While other battalions had travelled to Burma, Greece, North Africa and Italy, the 5th had remained in Britain preparing for the eventual invasion of Europe and by June 1944 only 5 per cent of its men had ever been under fire.

It was these men, among them Vic Woods, who attached himself to an assault unit to attack the enemy's positions, who landed on Sword Beach on the morning of D-Day. As the enemy positions were overrun, the Kingsmen set about their primary tasks. They set up defensive positions, ready to ward off any enemy counter-attack. They cleared pockets of enemy resistance from buildings around the beachhead and established safe areas for the storage of the supplies that were soon coming ashore. It may not have seemed a particularly glamorous role, but nevertheless it was vital to the success of the campaign.

Officers of the 5th King's were among the first casualties of the landings, with one being shot in the foot as he landed on the beach at 'H-Hour' and the battalion signals officer being wounded when caught by mortar fire. Despite the casualties, A and C companies of the 5th King's carried out their tasks while under a tremendous crossfire from machine guns positioned in the houses overlooking the beach. Among that morning's most heroic actions was that of Lieutenant Scarfe, who attempted to clear a strongpoint on Queen Beach. On landing Lt Scarfe noticed one of his men had been wounded and, despite the incoming enemy fire, went to the man's assistance, only to be shot. Although in pain from his wound, he gave orders to Sgt Cross of A Company to take up position and give covering fire. Then, scorning the hail of German fire, he went forward alone to deal with the position. Before finally falling mortally wounded, he accounted for several Germans in the position. His platoon completed the capture of the position.

The 5th Battalion were not the only Kingsmen who landed in the first waves on D-Day. A few miles to the west, reconnaissance parties from two companies of the 8th Battalion of the King's Regiment – known as the 'Liverpool Irish' – had also landed, disembarking from landing craft on Juno Beach at 7:35 a.m. Landing alongside them were assault companies of the Canadian Royal Winnipeg Rifles. Due to the rough seas they had no armoured support in those vital first minutes. As they waded ashore from their landing craft they were greeted by heavy machine-gun and artillery fire from the German defences. Nineteen-year-old Bob Brighouse recalled the landing: 'I were dropped into water up to my neck – in full kit, holding my rifle above my head. We were still getting shelled, mortared, machine-gunned and bombed. All your pals were around you, so you weren't on your own, but you saw people getting wounded. So the faster you could get off the beach the better.'

Despite the difficulties, both the Canadian assault troops and the Kingsmen advanced across the beach and pushed inland to secure their objectives. As the Canadians pushed ahead, the

Kingsmen sent anti-sniper patrols into the surrounding area, bringing in 14 prisoners. As on Sword Beach, they took immediate casualties, with the detachment's two senior officers wounded by incoming mortar fire. In the hour that followed, Company Sergeant Major Bilsborrow assumed command until an officer became available to take over.

With the beaches cleared, the Kingsmen on both Sword and Juno beaches began to organize the beach exits, while continually under a hail of mortar and shell fire. As Bob Brighouse later recalled: 'I was worried to death – we'd done exercises doing beach landings, but this was different. It wasn't something to laugh about. It was chaotic, there were dead bodies laying about, and wounded people getting treated. We just went up into the sand dunes to get organized.'

Behind Juno Beach, the Kingsmen found themselves helping to bridge two large craters in the exit route. Despite being under constant rifle fire, they found a horse and cart that was quickly commandeered to carry logs and stones to help fill the craters. With the exits secured, the 8th King's then sent patrols inland in an attempt to neutralize pockets of defenders left behind during the Canadian advance. They also searched the slit trenches and bunkers in the sand dunes, throwing hand grenades into each emplacement since they were forbidden from entering for fear of setting off booby traps.

As later waves of troops landed on Sword Beach, Vic Woods watched as they fired at non-existent targets ahead of them. It seemed they did not realize the buildings ahead of them were already occupied by British troops. The troops were nervous and were firing just to make themselves feel as if they were doing something positive. Woods saw the commandos begin landing, ready for the advance inland to take key positions: 'I can remember Lord Lovat and his commandos coming ashore with the piper playing the bagpipes. Myself and the others who were already on the beach thought

"Shut Up! You are just attracting attention." There were still snipers about.'

Snipers were not the only threat. On Sword Beach, two men of the 5th King's were killed when a German plane dropped a bomb among the disembarking troops. Sad as every loss was, the greatest shock came when contact was lost with the battalion's commanding officer, Lt Colonel D.V.H. Board. The CO went missing when he went off to 'recce' the beach. An anxious search was made of all the dressing stations and aid posts, but he could not be found. Some of the men on the beach noted their CO had been carrying a baton – an obvious sign of rank. They believed he had been targeted by snipers to whom it was obvious he was a senior officer. That evening men from A Company, clearing up on the beach, discovered the bodies of Lt Col Board and his batman, both of whom had been killed by machine-gun fire. In total the 5th King's lost 38 men killed or wounded that day.

As dawn broke on the second day of the invasion the Kingsmen were shocked to witness the scenes around them. The bodies of British and German soldiers still covered the beach and were being removed by the medical teams who interred them in hastily dug graves above the high water mark. Abandoned vehicles littered the shore. These twisted and scorched wrecks were being moved to enable the incoming troops and vehicles to cross the beaches.

The grim burial duty was soon shared by the Kingsmen. It was an unforgettable experience, as Vic Woods remembered: 'It was depressing. We had a "beach cleaning" day, collecting all the bodies. Some of the memories are awful – seeing the men floating around in the water. Some had been drowned. And I saw one body of a man I knew. It was peculiar but you just carry on.' He drove a 3-ton lorry along the beach as his comrades loaded bodies into the back. As he worked he thought to himself: 'There but for the grace of God go I'. Though not a religious man, Woods used to tell himself that his wife was his guardian angel and was looking over him: 'The intensity of the situation – bullets and bombs flying around – probably stopped me feeling anything. I had to become immune to the sights of suffering. I saw the dead – both British and German – and just thought "that was some mother's son."'

With the clear-up underway, snipers concealed in seaside houses in Lion-sur-Mer continued to fire on the beach, with anyone coming into their vision at risk. The next day put them in even greater danger. The troops noticed how the Germans seemed to deliberately time their artillery and mortar fire to coincide with high tide, hoping to catch as many ships and landing craft around the thin stretch of beach. On 8 June German bombs hit a ship on the beach. Instantly there was a holocaust of flame, with a fireball leaping 30 metres (100 feet) into the air and spreading out to trap several vehicles. The flames destroyed everything in their path, engulfing the HQ of the 5th King's. The flames then swept into an ammunition dump where explosions continued for hours. Members of B Company worked fearlessly to move some of the ammunition away, thus saving around half of the supplies. Sergeant Bob White was awarded the Military Medal after braving fierce artillery and small-arms fire to unload jeeps full of bombs and ammunition from a burning ship. Captains Thompson and Erdal were both killed while fighting the fire.

The Beach Groups – working under almost constant artillery and mortar fire, sometimes being machine-gunned from the air and sniped at from across the River Orne – helped consolidate the beachhead. They established supply dumps, set up anti-tank defences, fought off enemy patrols and searched out hidden snipers. Two officers of the 5th King's received the Military Cross for their actions in the days that followed. Disregarding his personal safety, Captain Bobby Fachiri, who had brought ashore a troop of anti-tank guns on the morning of D-Day, received a medal for his determination to maintain the position of his guns. Ignoring the threat of constant sniping and penetration by enemy patrols, Fachiri and his men manned the guns in the village of Hermanville-sur-Mer for six days.

At least he was able to deploy his guns. When the anti-tank gunners of the 8th King's landed they were told they were to defend the beaches as best they could. Their officer later wrote: 'Golly! What a chaos the beach is in. I've never seen so much junk lying around . . . Where do I put the guns then? . . . there's absolutely no field of fire . . . Up and down the beaches I go and can't find a spot anywhere for one gun, let alone six'.[3] The following day the officer's platoon lost 14 of its 39 men when a German aircraft bombed the landing craft they were unloading.

To counter the threat of enemy snipers, observers were sent to positions in a tower overlooking the enemy and mortar crews were established in the town in order to fire on enemy pillboxes across the River Orne. The men inside the pillboxes were driven off, helping to reduce the fire coming into the beachhead. One elusive sniper had taken up a position in a church tower that remained impervious to rifle and mortar fire, so a heavy field gun was called up from an artillery battery. A single shot blew away the top of the tower and the sniper with it.

As the days wore on, there was little decrease in the tension around the beaches. When Captain (later Major) George Lambert arrived at the battalion HQ a few days after D-Day his first impression was of how tired and grey all the officers looked. Although the frontline had moved on, the beaches – as the main supply point – continued to be the target for the enemy and Vic Woods experienced the threat of living under constant shellfire. One night he found himself driving a lorry of petrol to a supply dump. All he could think of was whether he was on the right road and whether it had been cleared of mines: 'I suddenly panicked – I felt I couldn't get my breath.

Then I realized it was just me – it was fear – I'd been holding my breath! So I sighed and let it all out, then I was okay again.'

As the frontline infantry battled to advance through Normandy, the heavy losses they endured had to be covered. Beach Groups like the 5th King's and its sister battalion the 8th were soon plundered of all spare personnel, who were swiftly transferred to under-strength frontline battalions. Some volunteers from both the 5th and 8th King's were quickly transferred to the depleted 6th Airborne Division, who had taken heavy casualties when they had been scattered through the countryside in the early hours of D-Day. Bob Brighouse remembered their arrival: 'Two officers came from the airborne. They said "Any volunteers for the paratroops?" So we said "Do we go back to England for training?" They told us they couldn't tell us anything about what would happen to us. They just wanted volunteers. My dad had always told me to never volunteer for anything, so I didn't go with them. But two or three of the other lads went.'

On 24 July, 5 officers and 360 other ranks were transferred from the 8th King's, joining the 2/5th Lancashire Fusiliers and the 2nd East Lancashire in detachments of 180 men per battalion. Much depleted, the remaining troops were transferred to Port-en-Bessin to guard fuel facilities. Having avoided volunteering for the airborne, Bob Brighouse found himself in a draft that joined the Lancashire Fusiliers: 'We were put on transport and sent to the frontline. It was done en masse, my whole platoon went but when we got to the Lancs we were broken up into various platoons. I often wondered if I would have been better off going to the airborne. Someone told me the blokes who went did go back for training and never saw any more action.'

On 15 August the 8th Battalion were further depleted when 100 men from the HQ and support company were transferred to units of the 49th Division. The following day, 4 officers and

40 other ranks were transferred to the 1/6th Queen's Regiment. Next to leave were the stretcher-bearers who were transferred to the Ox and Bucks Light Infantry, while the battalion's adjutant was transferred to the 49th Division, joining the Hallamshire Battalion, which had been hard hit in the Normandy fighting. One company-sized draft of former Kingsmen went on to form D company of the 4th Battalion Royal Welsh Fusiliers, later being referred to as the 'King's Company' by the battalion's officers. By mid-August, just 8 officers and 167 other ranks of the 8th King's remained.

The 5th Battalion suffered the same depletions as the military campaign moved away from the Normandy beaches. By the end of August the battalion's strength was 405 men below its designated figure. As George Lambert recalled, there was a sense of deep sadness as the remaining officers said farewell to the men they had trained over many years and taken to Normandy, only for them to be transferred to the frontlines with unfamiliar regiments. To compensate for this, on 31 August the 8th Battalion was finally put into 'suspended animation' and the remaining men were transferred to the 5th King's. The two battalions, which had played such a vital role on D-Day, had effectively become one.

While the Kingsmen had been fighting and dying on the beaches of Normandy, 30AU had been preparing to land in Normandy ready to continue the work they had begun in the Mediterranean. With the beaches secured, they were ready to land, exploit the chaos and seize their initial targets. On D-Day, 6 June 1944, 30AU was divided into two sections: one with the British, whose target was the radar station at Douvres, and the other with the Americans, heading to Cherbourg, where an assault was planned for eight days after D-Day. In Cherbourg 30AU were detailed to target the naval headquarters and the marine arsenal.

Having landed in France almost as soon as the beaches were secured on the morning of D-Day, the first 30AU section had hoped to make an independent assault on the Douvres facility, but finding it too heavily defended the marines instead sought assistance from Canadian units in the area. Unfortunately, the nearest Canadians had suffered such heavy losses during the landings that their battalion had been reduced to just 80 men and could offer no assistance. With no troops to spare from any source, 30AU took up positions around the target and waited. They were delayed for a week so it was assumed that the Germans would destroy all technical intelligence in the meantime. When the assault finally did take place, 30AU entered the radar station and, indeed, found little of importance.

Much of the exterior equipment had been destroyed during bombardment, although some elements of interest to the RAF were discovered buried in the grounds around the station. There was, however, one particularly interesting find – a lorry full of documents the Germans had failed to destroy but, before 30AU could secure it, the lorry was pinched by some unidentified British soldiers. Despite that setback, the work did provide one absolutely vital piece of intelligence: a set of wheels for an Enigma machine and a cipher pad with various workings written on it, all of which were vital to the codebreakers of Bletchley Park.

In the end, the failure to capture much intelligence from Douvres proved of little importance as 30AU quickly managed to acquire similar material at other locations. Radar stations at Arromanches and Pointe du Raz provided a wealth of technical data that is believed to have helped fill the gaps in the Admiralty's knowledge of German coastal radar and both the radar systems and transmission receivers carried by German ships. The RAF was also pleased to receive technical manuals on German radar sets. Even the valves used in German equipment were of interest to scientists who wanted to keep up-to-date with all technical developments.

However, once again, as in Italy and Sicily, it was noted that serious looting had taken place before 30AU had reached the radar station at Douvres. As one Royal Marines officer noted, he had done all he could to prevent looting short of arresting the British officers who were responsible. While a guard had been present at the target, with instructions not to allow anyone entry without a special pass, it seemed these same passes were readily available and large numbers of officers had been able to enter and strip the station of anything they desired. Commander Dunstan Curtis reported that he believed valuable intelligence had been lost and the work of his unit prolonged by the antics of the looters who had simply emptied intelligence documents on to the floor when they stole furniture.

During this period all documents or intelligence deemed to be of importance was rushed back to the Admiralty. Not trusting outsiders, the Royal Marines insisted that, whether by despatch rider or by truck, the consignments would be under the care of 30AU until they were personally handed over in London. On one occasion, this careful method put the safety of Whitehall under threat. Having uncovered a consignment of experimental high explosives, 30AU needed to deliver it to London. Upon reaching Whitehall the driver could not locate the Admiralty building and pulled into a sidestreet to ask directions. Upon noticing a commotion, the driver got down only to find a crowd had gathered around, fretting about the arrival of a lorry full of potentially unstable explosives. Then he noticed the cause of their concern: he had parked in Downing Street, just yards from the Prime Minister's home.

The delayed advance on Cherbourg had meant the 30AU detachment had to find other duties until Cherbourg was ready for the final assault. Along with the sections originally planned for the Douvres operation, they undertook intelligence-gathering at a number of locations on behalf of the RAF, assisting technical officers sent from the Air Ministry. It was the beginning of a type of cooperation that later developed during the advance into Germany.

Meanwhile, with heavy fighting continuing throughout Normandy, the Royal Marines found themselves embroiled in typical infantry action, rather than the specialist duties they had been trained for. Serving in B Troop of 30AU, Reg Rush recalled those days:

> It was frightening. It was my first time in action. My first impression was 'My God – Am I going to survive?' But thanks to Lord Haw-Haw's words I was really enraged when I went to France. So it wasn't difficult to fire at the Germans. You accept the fact that you have to protect yourself. The Germans would fight up to the very end. Sometimes we would go in the front of a house as they ran out of the back. Everyone reacts differently under fire. Some people revel in it – especially if they've had a tot of rum. Others were literally shitting themselves with fear. You get into a certain state of mind. You are living for tomorrow – you are a very different person when you are serving in the field.

Back at the beachhead on D-Day plus four, a young Royal Navy lieutenant commander, who would play a vital role in the unit's activities, arrived on Utah Beach. An expert skier, an outstanding self-taught yachtsman and trained diver, with a strong command of languages and a fearless nature, Patrick Dalzel-Job was the perfect choice to join 30AU. The son of one of the many victims of the Battle of the Somme, Dalzel-Job had been brought up in England, had lived in France for a number of years and then spent some time sailing around Norway while also working as a journalist for a yachting publication.

As an expert on the coastline of Norway, he had been active in the Norwegian campaign in 1940 and had later served in the flotilla of Royal Norwegian Navy motor torpedo boats that had patrolled the waters of the country while under occupation.

There, he put his prewar knowledge to good use. He had gathered intelligence on German activity in Norwegian waters – living for weeks in a one-man observation post. In addition, he had trained on midget submarines and was a qualified paratrooper. Dalzel-Job seemed typical of the type of man who would volunteer for 'special and hazardous service'.

His efforts had earned him a decoration from the Norwegian king and the recognition of the Directorate of Naval Intelligence, who saw his potential for carrying out 30AU's mission in France. Most notably, as a skilled sailor, active winter sportsman, brave fighting man, capable leader of men and someone who was able to live a solitary existence as he gathered intelligence, he had caught the attention of Ian Fleming who, in later years, claimed he had modelled the legendary literary creation of James Bond on him.

Indeed, the literary Bond's wartime history included undercover work in Norway, just as Patrick Dalzel-Job's had. Further evidence that Dalzel-Job may have been the model for Bond was provided in *Moonraker* (1955) where Fleming described Bond's wartime experience with X-Craft – the very same miniature submarines in which Dalzel-Job had trained. Dalzel-Job himself was less convinced and, somewhat modestly, he later remarked he believed it unlikely that the literary 007 had been based on him, pointing out that he was not a drinker and had only ever loved one woman.

Patrick Dalzel-Job advanced into France with a clear idea of how he wished to operate. With his two companions, Marines Bill Wright and 'Lofty' Fraser, he pushed as far ahead of the advance as possible. In the early stages of the campaign his patrols consisted of just one Scout Car, a jeep and a despatch rider on a motorcycle. With Dalzel-Job leading in the jeep – loaded with spare fuel, captured German machine guns, a folding motorcycle and plastic explosive – the marines attempted to seize the initiative. If the Americans were advancing in one area, he attempted to find an alternative route, moving swiftly through the country lanes of Normandy and Brittany in the hope of bypassing the enemy's main defences to begin his search for naval intelligence.

When they believed their column was being watched by the enemy they used a clever ruse. A man in the rear vehicle would beckon to a non-existent vehicle behind him. This had the effect of causing the enemy to hold their fire until all vehicles were in view but, before the Germans realized they had been tricked, Dalzel-Job and his men would speed into the distance. In fact, the dashing spirit of the unit was perfectly captured when Dalzel-Job took to pointing out directions while standing in his jeep, wielding a fencing sword.

Early targets for 30AU included the V1 rocket sites, including one which they reached via a gap in the German frontline. In Caen, they entered the city by jeep while the fighting was still going on, penetrating into the city centre to gather intelligence from the German naval headquarters. Despite, such ingenuity, for most of the time the frontline in Normandy remained impenetrable. Any advance could only be won at a heavy cost in lives.

During these early raids, Dalzel-Job was joined by another notable postwar personality – Captain Charles Wheeler of the Royal Marines. Later famous as a long-serving BBC foreign correspondent, Wheeler had come to France to act as a translator and interpreter. As Wheeler noted, Dalzel-Job was 'marvellously equipped – mentally and mechanically – to do his own thing in the war'.[4] One of his operations with 30AU was to gather intelligence from a badly damaged German boat that was half submerged in a basin at Blainville. He found a small cork raft and paddled out to the boat, which was then searched for intelligence – all under the gaze of the enemy who were dug in just 1,000 metres (3,300 feet) away. There was so much of interest on the craft that it took Wheeler and Dalzel-Job over four hours to complete the search. This gave the enemy sufficient time to bring up an artillery piece and shell the boat, prompting a swift withdrawal. Their haul was quickly loaded into a raft, covered in a waterproof sheet, and paddled to safety before the Germans could notice their movement and correct their fire.

When the Americans broke out from the Normandy bridgehead, 30AU were finally free to roam the countryside in the manner that had originally been planned by Commander Fleming and his team at the Admiralty. During the Cherbourg assault the unit helped the Americans capture the German naval headquarters, with General Karl-Wilhelm von Schlieben making his surrender jointly to an American colonel and Captain Hargreaves-Heap of the Royal Marines on 26 June. While the officers were handling the surrender of the port, a detachment from 30AU was sent to investigate tunnels beneath the naval base. Unknown to the investigating marines, an unidentified gas had been released in the tunnels, causing some of them to collapse. One was pulled out, apparently dead, and dumped on a trailer with other corpses. However, one of his comrades noticed a flicker of movement and the man was rushed away to be revived and given treatment. Unfortunately, though he survived, his lungs never fully recovered from the trauma, plaguing him with chest problems for the rest of his life.

It was around this time that Commander Fleming made his sole wartime visit to France. The rest of the time he controlled the unit – who he called his 'Red Indians' – from Room 30 of the Directorate of Naval Intelligence. The reason behind his visit was that the unit was often not being used in its correct role. Instead, the marines were being employed as infantry. As Reg Rush recalled: 'He came out and played hell with the American generals.'

Soon enough the marines were free to pursue their own objectives. Moving fast, they avoided both the retarding influence of

Allied armoured columns and the bands of Germans – many of whom were eager to retreat towards their homeland. Working behind enemy lines and in open countryside, and sometimes getting caught up in skirmishes with bands of retreating German troops, 30AU had to adapt where necessary. Captured German oil was used to keep their vehicles mobile, but it took a toll on the engines, leaving some in need of replacement.

The marines were eager to reach the Breton ports in the hope of investigating what had been left behind by the occupation forces. However, they were prevented from reaching their targets in Brest when it was discovered that many German military personnel had withdrawn into the city, effectively creating an impenetrable fortress. Instead, 30AU aimed for smaller targets, investigating around 20 sites in Brittany. They also took many prisoners, including a haul of 64 officers and men who were captured in a joint operation with a group of fighters from the French Resistance.

Dalzel-Job later admitted he could not have achieved such successful operations in France had it not been for the close cooperation of the French Resistance. The usefulness of the Resistance during these operations in open countryside was explained by one of the marines: 'We had contacts for the French resistance. We would go to their homes and give a special, secret knock on the door. They would let us in and they would tell us what to do – this was when the Germans might be at the end of the street. So they would say "don't go this way, go that way" because they knew where the German positions were.'

Despite the obvious success of 30AU's operations in France, and the RAF's use of its findings, the Royal Navy continued to be the only arm of the British military which believed a designated organization had a role to play in dedicated intelligence-gathering. Their next major aim was to exploit intelligence that

might be found within Paris. Although the French capital fell
into the American sphere of operations, NID30 made represen-
tations for the Royal Marines to be allowed to play their role in
the advance on the city. As a result, a 'Target-Force' was
formed for the Paris advance, which followed hot on the heels
of the combat troops who raced to secure the city. For the Paris
operation, 14 inspection teams – mainly consisting of officers
from the British and American armies and navies – were
attached to the American 12th Army Group. A total of 115 military officers and specialists, including Lt Colonel Lord
Rothschild, the head of MI5's Counter-Espionage department,
were flown into France ready for the advance on the city.

Of particular interest to those heading for Paris were intelligence documents relating to French politics. It was clear to the
Allies that cooperation with liberated French politicians would
be easier if they knew exactly what the individuals had been up
to during the years of occupation. Although there was a designated American force fulfilling the Target-Force functions,
30AU made a specific request to be freed from their command
and pursue their own targets without interference. This was
agreed following the intervention of Commander Fleming, who
used his influence with the Director of Naval Intelligence to
press the Americans for clearance.

30AU's situation was complicated by the fact that, as they
advanced towards the French capital, no one seemed to have
any clear information where the American Target-Force was.
Most of the Military Policemen they asked had never heard of
such a unit. When 30AU and Target-Force finally met up, a
number of details were agreed upon. The British agreed not to
remove any intelligence without the agreement of the
Americans, while the Americans agreed to guard all the targets
on the British lists.

For the Paris operation, 30AU's contingent was known as
'Woolforce' after its commander Lt Colonel A.R. Woolley of

the Royal Marines. Their move into the city was made alone, after it was decided that advancing with French General Philippe Leclerc's armoured division would be too costly. Instead, they advanced along open roads, on a route devoid of German opposition. Among the targets within the capital were French scientists who were believed to have played a role in the development of the next generation of German rockets, the so-called V3.

Finds included torpedo storage facilities at Houilles, cipher equipment, radio transmitters, a new design for powered aircraft gun turrets, new types of high-tensile steel and experimental 8-bladed torpedo propellers. At the Houilles torpedo store – the intelligence for which 30AU had uncovered in Italy – they discovered components including a list detailing the complete issue of torpedo tubes to the German navy. Elsewhere they visited fuel research centres and television research facilities. Of particular interest was intelligence related to an aircraft-delivered, high-speed, jet-propelled torpedo. However, little information on the weapon could be found as it transpired the Germans had eliminated all Frenchmen known to have had access to it.

Operations were also hampered by the fact that many of the people the American Target-Force and 30AU wished to interview were Frenchmen who had been working for the Germans. As such, the locals considered them to be collaborators and many were arrested by the French authorities – with some, it appeared, facing swift justice. One such 'target' had worked in naval salvage on German craft but before 30AU could find him he had been placed under arrest. When efforts were made to trace him in jail it transpired he had 'disappeared' following his incarceration. Evacuation efforts at the torpedo store were also hampered by the French. Rivalries between the Gaullist and Communist factions within the Resistance had left parts of Paris on the verge of civil war. The area around the factory was under the control of Communists who insisted that only men who had not worked there under the Germans should be employed. This meant that no local staff who had a useful knowledge of the plant were available to assist in the investigations.

Lessons for the future were learned during the Paris operation. 30AU did not have sufficient personnel to guard prisoners taken during the Paris operation and reported how they had handed over Germans to the French, who then paraded them through the streets. Considerable numbers of the prisoners succumbed to sniper fire from French civilians. To the observers from 30AU it seemed not only unfair to shoot prisoners, but it also threatened the loss of vital intelligence that might have been obtained through interrogation. As a result, requests were put in for an increase in personnel to carry out guard duties. The requesting officer even admitted that 'Marine pensioners' could be used for guard duty if it meant that combat troops were available for leading the investigation operations. Furthermore, they reported that 30AU had insufficient clerical staff to deal with recording their finds and arranging for transportation to the UK. All these problems would have to be overcome if similar successful operations were to be carried out in Germany.

Another problem noted by 30AU's investigators was that some of the intelligence they had been acting on was misleading. It seemed that targets were marked as 'Naval Headquarters' regardless of whether the building was a U-boat operations room or a quartermaster's store. Again, it was clear that more accurate intelligence would be needed if operations within Germany were not going to be hampered by searching irrelevant locations.

Finally, the operation in Paris showed how important it was for the unit to have sufficient time to conduct their searches. Diligent searches of premises had paid off, with 30AU uncovering vital codebreaking documents in offices where cipher work had taken place. They found documents pushed behind desk drawers, in the ashes of fires, on blotting pads and even hidden beneath a doormat. However, it transpired some of the unit in Paris had left prior to the completion of investigations. They had moved to the Pas-de-Calais to take part in operations there, despite the fact Paris was known to house considerably more important targets. As one Royal Naval officer wrote in complaint, 'the Unit must be prepared to carry out diligent searches in a known area rather than undertaking new and more spectacular operations.'[5] This illustrated the need for control of intelligence operations and to curb the swashbuckling desires of some of the Royal Marines.

After the capture of Paris, other cities became targets for what were increasingly referred to as 'Target-Force' operations. In Rouen, and then in Brussels, Target-Forces were formed from engineer, signals and intelligence units, including those whose previous roles had been in deception and camouflage. Although lessons had supposedly been learned from S-Force operations in Italy, these later operations were not entirely successful as there was little intelligence on the targets and what there was arrived too late.

Regardless of these operations, 30AU continued to operate independently throughout late 1944, making investigations in France into subjects such as metallurgy, with scientists wishing to look at the German programme for the recovery of the chemical element vanadium from scrap alloys. Their investigations identified locations in Germany and the Netherlands in which usable vanadium was being extracted from slag. The reports were of importance due to the knowledge that this product was being used by the Germans for the production of synthetic fuel. 30AU's work also continued with the investigation of U-boat manufacturing plants, in particular with metallurgists studying the welding used for the construction of the craft.

The operations carried out by 30AU in France provided a wealth of intelligence. Signalling manuals and equipment discovered in France had allowed the Allies to build up a clear picture of all communications procedure in use within the German military. 30AU found documents allowing naval intelligence to finally build a complete picture of the capabilities of certain models of U-boats, providing valuable information for Coastal Command on how best to attack these craft from the air. They found maps of channels that the Germans had swept through minefields and documents relating to the organization of the German navy. In total, 30AU found around 12,000 important intelligence documents.

By early 1945 intelligence captured by the unit had already been put to use in trials of captured U-boats and E-boats. As the Admiralty's Director of Torpedoes and Mining reported in February 1945, 30AU had made a 'remarkable achievement' in discovering designs for German torpedoes not yet fully in production: 'It is likely that this capture may have reaction in our own design, if not on countermeasures.'[6] Similarly, the Director of Anti-Submarine Materials noted that 30AU's capture of a German 'Gnat' torpedo had led to British improvements in their torpedo 'foxing' system. At the same time, the Admiralty's Director of Radio Equipment reported: 'It is considered most desirable that this flow of intelligence should be maintained at the highest possible level.'[7]

While 30AU had been roaming through the American zone, scouring for targets along the coast of Normandy and Brittany, the rest of the British Army had been embroiled in an altogether different type of war. In the fields and hedgerows of Normandy, infantrymen in slowly advancing armies were engaged in a vicious war of attrition. Daily, they fought pitched battles to control anonymous farms and villages. Scores of lives were lost to control hilltops or to cross rivers that were little more than streams. Each day the gun crews of the Royal Artillery fired thousands of rounds of high-explosive to support the infantry, flattening villages and laying waste to hundreds of acres of land, only to advance a couple of miles and begin again the next day. It was a world far removed from the mobility of 30AU's careering jeeps and rapid-firing machine guns.

For soldiers barely out of school, like John Longfield, a teenage Bren gunner in the King's Own Yorkshire Light Infantry, the brutal slogging match of summer 1944 was a vicious introduction to modern warfare. He had joined the army on a whim in early 1943, when he was called into his headmaster's office to be reprimanded about his membership of the National Fire Service as a messenger. When the headmaster told Longfield he should concentrate on his studies rather than spending his nights at the local fire station, the pupil replied, 'Don't you know there's a war on?' Astonished, his headmaster hit back 'If that's how you feel you should join the army.' Acting on impulse, Longfield asked for permission to use the headmaster's telephone, leaned over the desk, called his father and asked if it would be okay if he joined the army. With his father's permission secured, Longfield left the school and headed to the nearest recruiting office. The next day he returned to school to tell his pals, 'I'm a private now.'

Just over a year on from that fateful interview Longfield found himself in Normandy. From his first sight of dead bodies – the corpses of German soldiers who appeared to have had their throats slit – to his first patrol in which he was mistakenly left behind, the entire experience seemed designed to test him to his very limits. He recalled some of the moments that shaped his evolution from Yorkshire schoolboy to battle-hardened veteran: 'I came across an enormous bomb crater. Sat on the edge was a German, his arms resting on his knees. I was about to shoot him when he heard me, looked up and raised his arms. There were no hands on the end of his arms.'

In another sickening incident, Longfield was detailed to bury some corpses. When he went to pick the first one up by the arm, it simply came off the body.

Longfield also experienced the horrors of seeing his comrades be killed in battle: 'I found the youngest lad in the company lying on his back in front of a hedge, his tin hat over his face. I lifted his helmet up. The front of his head was missing and there was a grey mash of brains mixed with blood. The poor lad was only 17 years old and I felt protective of him. He had got into the army by falsifying his age. What a dreadful waste.' In another senseless waste of life, Longfield watched as his section corporal slumped into a slit trench with his entire face blown away, courtesy of his own hand grenade; the corporal had thrown the grenade but forgotten to duck.

Such intense experiences shaped his behaviour. When he saw reinforcements joining the battalion he was amazed at how young and naive they seemed, often telling the more experienced men they didn't believe they could kill anyone. In an attempt to make them see sense, Longfield implored them to change their mind, telling them that once in battle it would be kill or be killed. Unlike some of these reinforcements, Longfield had no compunction about killing. In one bitter encounter he found himself alone in a slit trench, with just the corpse of a comrade – whose death he had witnessed – for company: 'A bullet went in one side of his helmet and out of the other. He began to go into violent convulsions, shaking very rapidly but making no sound. I pushed him on to his side. He looked at me then both of his eyes turned inwards until the irises vanished and only the whites of his eyes were visible. Then the convulsions stopped. He was dead and once more I was on my own.'

The incident that followed just seconds later reinforced Longfield's understanding of the harsh realities of war. An SS man appeared in front of him. Lifting his weapon, Longfield pulled the trigger only to hear a dull click – the gun was empty.

Raising his rifle, the German smiled and pulled back the bolt – chambering the round with which he was going to kill the defenceless Longfield. With just a split second to react, Longfield hurled his empty weapon at his would-be killer: 'I thought the bastard was going to enjoy killing me. That really made me wild. If I hadn't thought that I wouldn't have been so violent. I wouldn't have had the strength to throw the gun at him with such force.' As the stunned SS man recoiled from the impact, Longfield grasped his dead comrade's Bren gun and opened fire, blasting the German with bullets: 'I realized that no mercy was expected – so I wasn't going to surrender.'

By the time the battle for Normandy was over the greatest surprise to Longfield was that he had survived, even though he knew his luck could not last forever. What was less surprising was that he had started smoking and had become an atheist.

Also in 'the thick of it' was Bob Brighouse who had been transferred from the King's Regiment to serve with the Lancashire Fusiliers. He was put in the same section as his former corporal and a couple of others from his old platoon. On his second night with the new unit, he went on a fighting patrol to snatch a prisoner. They blackened their faces and tied up their equipment to stop it rattling: 'Coming to the target there was an explosion. Someone had set a mine off. Corporal McAndrew was killed and another 5 chaps were wounded. One was an ex-Kingsman. I had to dress his leg and help him back.' Withdrawing under machine-gun fire, Brighouse got the man back safely and helped load him on to a jeep to be taken away for treatment: 'He shook my hand and said "Well Brighouse, I never thought you had it in you." And I never saw him again.'

The following night they went into another attack. Brighouse recalled that it was a grim experience. His new corporal was killed, making it two corporals in two days. Next, his sergeant got shot between the eyes by a sniper. He was replaced by another ex-Kingsman, who was next to be shot. After that, there were so few men remaining they had to be 'folded' into another platoon: 'There were only five of us left.'

The extreme pressure experienced by the infantrymen during this period was explained by Bob Brighouse: 'Inside, you were in turmoil. When men got wounded they would be screaming. Some screamed for their mother – others just couldn't go on. It fills you with horror and sticks with you all your life. When we were advancing, I used to wet myself. I just couldn't stop myself. It would be dripping like a tap that needed a new washer. I couldn't help it.'

Just four days after arriving at the Lancashire Fusiliers – having already seen so many of his comrades killed or wounded – it was Brighouse's turn to be hit. Advancing behind Sherman tanks during a night attack, his platoon came under fire: 'All hell let loose – machine guns were firing, mortar bombs were landing, the tanks were firing back – I was as close as possible to the tank – for protection I thought.' They had got no more than 100 metres (300 feet) when Brighouse blacked out. The tank he was sheltering behind had been hit, exploding with a tremendous force that set him flying through the air and crashing to the ground. His comrades continued to advance, leaving behind what they believed was his battered corpse:

> Next thing I knew I woke up in casualty clearing station. I couldn't remember anything. I was bleeding a bit from my arm and from my side and my body ached, but I felt alright. Within a week they signed me off and sent me back to the Fusiliers. When we got to the platoon they said 'Brighouse, where have you come from? We thought you were dead.' But I have never remembered anything about it. I was completely knocked out.

Just behind the 'poor bloody infantry', as they are often known, there were plenty of soldiers whose role was only just less dangerous. Beloved of the infantrymen, to whose operations they offered support barrages, were the gunners of the Royal Artillery. They were feted as the most technically proficient of all British Army units. Their guns were accurate and could deliver a furious rate of fire. Every man in the frontlines knew the relief that came from hearing supporting artillery fire racing over their heads towards the enemy. Making such barrages possible were thousands of officers and other ranks whose dedication had earned the respect of their comrades.

Among them was 26-year-old Lieutenant Tom Pitt-Pladdy, a former rugby league player for Wigan whose promising career had been interrupted by war. Pitt-Pladdy had been commissioned from the ranks and arrived in Normandy eager to display his professionalism. He soon learned that, in Normandy, the artilleryman's role meant more than just firing their guns. He was disheartened for a long time, feeling they 'weren't getting anywhere'. The Germans were a constant nuisance, attacking the artillery positions with mortar fire and sending out night patrols to harass them. It soon became clear to Pitt-Pladdy that the greatest threat to his efficiency was the lack of sleep: 'Going into an attack we would have orders at 3 in the morning, cross the start line at first light, then orders again at 9 at night. Then rations and petrol to organize – day after day. You weren't the brightest of bunnies after that.'

He further recalled the seemingly ever-increasing strain experienced by so many within the Normandy bridgehead, seeing his sergeant shot through the chest by a sniper as they were digging-in to make a command post. In addition to the day-to-day dangers, Pitt-Pladdy learned to cope with exhaustion. Tiredness took over and he thought of little else but when he was going to get some sleep. It was also a strain to witness the psychological traumas endured by others. He was disturbed to see an old friend from his rugby team. The man was obviously in a poor psychological state. Pitt-Pladdy could do nothing for him except hand over a bottle of whisky and hope this helped steady his nerves.

As the fighting grew increasingly bitter, Pitt-Pladdy found himself faced with the stark realities of war and the vicious price of advance when he was given the job of Forward Observation Officer following the wounding of a comrade by 'friendly fire'. He took over an observation post in a tank unit, operating his radio from the safety of the tank. In his first action he watched as two tanks disappeared in a ball of flame. The troop commander then said he was flanking to the left and disappeared, leaving Pitt-Pladdy alone. That night he attended an 'Orders Group' held by the colonel of the tank regiment who said 'What's the tank state?' The adjutant then replied 'We can muster 11 for tomorrow.' Pitt-Pladdy was shocked: 'That was out of 36 that had started in the morning.' He immediately offered his observation tank to the colonel and went into battle the following day in his unprotected jeep.

The everyday realities of war had taught the army many lessons, some of which had immediate implications for the future intelligence-gathering operations. Experience on the battlefield had certainly shown German military technology to be highly advanced. It had also shown that such technology would not only be under threat from destruction by the retreating Germans: if such technology was going to be secured and utilized for any future developments by the western Allies it would also need to be protected from the attentions of their own men who had thus far shown little respect for property. The scale of theft and looting had shocked the Army, resulting in desperate pleas from Military Police units for extra resources to cope with their workload. The army's own insurance assessors had also complained of their workload, with much of their time spent assessing claims for deliberate damage caused by soldiers rather than for the more acceptable damage caused in the heat of battle.

Although much of the damage had occurred in the fields, farms and villages of Normandy, the rural population were not the only ones to suffer. In 1944 a French scientist submitted a complaint to the military authorities on the behaviour of his liberators. He had returned to his laboratory to find it ransacked: doors had been broken down, drawers opened, documents scattered, tables overturned and valuable scientific instruments smashed or stolen. He wrote: 'I am sorry to report that I must use the same terms that I used when I submitted an account of the occupation by the German Army. Now, as then, the troops have behaved, not like men of culture in a sanctuary of science but like barbarians in a hostile country.'[8]

Such behaviour did not go unnoticed by the High Command. Many officers turned a blind eye to it, understanding the reasons why soldiers fresh from battle might behave in such a way, but those planning for the assault on Germany knew what might be lost if such behaviour was repeated in Nazi laboratories. As one report noted: 'The greatest menace to the security of targets will frequently be from the action, innocent or otherwise, of our own troops.'[9]

With most of France secured and the Allied armies advancing on Belgium, the High Command once again turned its attention to the opportunities that might arise once the German frontier had been breached. On 27 July 1944 Lieutenant General W.B. Smith, an American officer at Supreme Headquarters, issued a letter on behalf of General Eisenhower setting out the aims of the units to be created, with one attached to each Army Group. The letter instructed senior commanders that a force was to be raised to secure essential scientific and intelligence targets. They were told that the force would receive intelligence dossiers to guide them in their tasks and provide a briefing on the importance of each target. It also stressed that the closer the Allied armies came to Germany itself, the more important their targets were likely to become.

Furthermore, as they would 'assume particular importance in Germany itself, it is recommended that the personnel nominated to carry out these tasks should be placed under a single commander with a suitable staff and that they should be known as "T" Forces. All agencies interested in the search for intelligence targets should be made subordinate to the "T" Force Commander and should be under his absolute control and orders.'[10]

Lt General Smith went on to praise the success of similar operations in Italy and how the command structure had facilitated a smooth-running operation. He also stressed the need for flexibility, emphasising how some targets might need no more than a single section of Field Security Police to secure them. Again, it was pointed out that any T-Force should operate independently from the troops engaged in combat and occupational duties. At the same time it became clear to the High Command that the units which had been allotted to 'T' duties at Rouen and Brussels would no longer be available. Instead other units, those without prior commitments, would be needed.

So, in August 1944 serious planning for fully controlled and coordinated Target-Forces commenced. At the Supreme Headquarters Allied Expeditionary Force a simple instruction was prepared, laying out the brief for these new units: 'T-Force = Target-Force, to guard and secure documents, persons, equipment, with combat and Intelligence personnel, after capture of large towns, ports etc. in liberated and enemy territory.'[11]

CHAPTER 3

The Birth of T-Force

'Too often one associates the term "special forces" with a small group carrying out some clandestine mission having trained for years. Here instead is an unqualified Second World War success story, involving ordinary infantry regiments . . . carrying out an extraordinary task after a minimum of training.'[1]

What Ian Fleming had achieved with 30AU, first in the Mediterranean and then in France, did not go unrecognized. The unit had provided a wealth of vital information: technical intelligence on the latest U-boat designs; intelligence on the industrial dispersal of U-boat production; German maritime mine charts, detailing swept channels; and equipment reports for enemy ships. In August 1944, in an affectionate tribute to the unit's achievements, the Chief of Combined Operations wrote: 'this unit adopts somewhat unorthodox methods to gain its ends'.[2] In the same month, the Director of Naval Intelligence noted the effect Ian Fleming's 'Red Indians' had made upon General Eisenhower: 'SHAEF is understood to be thinking in terms of a force of some two divisions trained and manned on lines similar to No.30 Assault Unit . . . It should be noted that in the whole conception of this type of unit, the Admiralty has been a pioneer amongst the Allies.'[3]

With High Command finally acknowledging the true value of determined intelligence-gathering, they began to learn from these lessons. Clearly, 30AU had set the standard for future operations and, as one report detailed, 'the Admiralty has consistently led the way'.[4] As General Eisenhower and his staff began to prepare for future operations in Germany they looked to 30AU for inspiration for the creation of a unit dedicated to the search for intelligence documents and military equipment. There would be no more of the ad-hoc S-Force or Target-Force operations as seen in Italy and France. Instead, there would be freshly raised units, both British and American, whose sole task would be to secure targets within Germany, allowing teams of expert investigators to carry out immediate inspections.

Before any such operations could be embarked upon, it was necessary to determine intelligence targets. This task was put in the hands of the newly formed Combined Intelligence Objectives Sub-Committee (CIOS) whose task was to create 'blacklists' of targets within Germany. CIOS consisted of service personnel and scientists from the War Office, Admiralty, Air Ministry, Ministry of Aircraft Production, Ministry of Economic Warfare and Ministry of Supply, who were joined by corresponding American representatives. Among this group were some of Britain's foremost weapons experts, who worked with American specialists to gather intelligence material on the Nazi war machine.

CIOS took instruction from the Combined Intelligence Priorities Committee (CIPC) which was established in summer 1944 to determine the intelligence priorities for use in later T-Force operations. This sub-committee was initially headed by Brigadier General T.J. Betts, an American on the staff of SHAEF. There were also representatives from the US Navy, the US Army, the American Embassy in London, the Air Ministry, the War Office, the Ministry of Economic Warfare and the Admiralty.

Once again Commander Ian Fleming of the Admiralty made an appearance, representing the interests of the Director of Naval Intelligence. His role in the establishment of 30AU had made him a prime candidate for ensuring the style of their operations could be expanded to cover the vast number of German targets. From June 1944 onwards, Fleming played a vital role in deciding intelligence targets within Germany. These were the targets that would be fed to the British and American T-Forces, eventually leading to an immense haul of intelligence and scientific research that would serve the western Allies throughout the Cold War.

CIOS's main task was to coordinate all requests from British and US government departments for intelligence of military significance, excluding combat intelligence. Fleming's task, as a member of the priorities committee, was to help grade the intelligence and scientific targets. It was noted that the major technical intelligence targets were such material, personnel and military information 'either of great value to the Allies for operational purposes, or constituting a dangerous potential threat in the future, as justify urgent action on the part of the Allies in seizing them before and immediately after an armistice.'[5]

Commander Fleming worked closely with representatives of the US Navy, ensuring that their requests for intelligence were closely linked. As part of his work with CIPC, Fleming joined a subsection of the committee responsible for collating intelligence from documents and personnel captured from enemy headquarters buildings. Again, this role was ideally suited to Fleming since this was exactly the type of intelligence he had formed 30AU to gather. Another of Fleming's contributions was to propose that a sub-committee be appointed to investigate the methods by which investigation teams should be selected. This proposal was accepted, with CIOS looking closely into how best to combine the talents of investigators to ensure T-Force teams had immediate and effective support in the field.

As a result of Fleming's initiative, it was decided that all interested agencies should be approached to identify which investigators should be allocated to particular targets. Armed with their responses, CIOS was able to build up teams suitable to operate in specific areas. Fleming's plan played a major role in the creation and organization of Consolidated Advance Field Teams (CAFTs). These were teams of experts in various areas of science and technology – the so-called 'investigation teams' or 'assessors' – that would be central to all T-Force operations in Germany. It would be their role to accompany T-Force detachments into targets and to make the initial assessment of what they had discovered before calling forward the experts from the required area of industry.

Once collated by CIPC, the intelligence requests were transmitted to SHAEF in the form of target lists. Checks would also be made to ensure suitable specialist staff were available to carry out local investigations of these targets. CIOS would then disseminate intelligence to the relevant departments and dispose of technical equipment. Although CIOS would fall under SHAEF, it was to remain outside of that organization. In addition, the American and British elements of the operation would come under the auspices of the Joint Intelligence Committees (JIC) of their respective nations.

With the intelligence and scientific priorities decided, the first full meeting of CIOS was held on 1 September 1944. Again Fleming was central to the new sub-committee, which set about producing a vast 'blacklist' of military and industrial targets within Germany. For years, experts had been gathering information on what German targets needed to be destroyed to assist the Allied war effort. Now they were able to turn their collective minds to what might be of use to them in the future and which of their former targets should now be saved from destruction.

In addition, attitudes about Germany were charging and, while the military defeat of the Nazis was vital to securing future peace, there was little point in doing this if Germany was going to be thrown back into the type of chaos that had prompted Hitler's rise. It was a scenario the West could not allow to happen again. Although the defeated Germany was going to see its political leaders purged and its future placed into the hands of the victorious powers, this time the aim was to nurture the growth of a new, stable, democratic Germany.

A military government would be established in the immediate aftermath of the advancing armies to handle local government. However, to successfully achieve this it was important that the local infrastructure remained intact so normality could be quickly restored, as without power, transport, food and water there would be no new Germany. The tools for implementing social order were added to CIOS's list of targets, which made the lists longer and longer as they included such seemingly innocuous locations as telephone exchanges and post offices.

Such thoughts of ensuring Germany was able to rise from the ashes were far from the minds of the average soldier: the story of T-Force was far removed from the story of the rest of the British Army in 1945. Rather than purely ensuring that the Nazis were defeated, T-Force troops were entrusted with laying the path for Germany's rebirth.

With this in mind, in the summer of 1944 CIOS produced the definitive list of technology and military research establishments they wished to have searched and handed it, neatly contained in large black-bound books, to SHAEF. In these books were all known targets within Germany and other lands still occupied by the Nazis. The books, which inevitably became known as the 'blacklist' or the 'black books', became the 'bible' for all future T-Force operations.

The emphasis then moved towards developing a plan under which this intelligence could be acted upon. In order to comply with Eisenhower's orders to create a coordinated, comprehensive intelligence-gathering apparatus, the British Army began examining how the 30AU model could be

adapted to cover the myriad of targets they would find in
Germany. As a result, in September 1944, soon after the
arrival of the British 21st Army Group HQ in Brussels, planning began for the new-look T-Force.

There was one ideal, if unlikely, candidate to take on the T-
Force role. This was the Chemical Warfare (CW) branch of the
Army Group HQ, which was currently under-employed since,
strange as it seemed – for a nation whose leaders were happy
to gas innocent civilians – the Germans had not used gas on
the battlefield. At the head of the CW branch was Brigadier
G.H.C. Pennycook, formerly the head of the Army School of
Chemical Warfare. Although he had other responsibilities, such
as the use of flame weapons and tactical smokescreens, it
was clear he and his staff were in search of a greater role and
had the necessary resources available to create a T-Force.

As one of his staff later admitted, Brigadier Pennycook – a
rather shy and reserved man – had become something of a
joke among his fellow brigadiers at 21st Army Group HQ and
had become rather sensitive about it. T-Force, therefore, presented itself as the perfect opportunity for him to put the
branch to work. On 4 October 1944 Pennycook was informed
that his staff was to be increased and he and his senior staff
officer, Lt Colonel Ray Bloomfield, were to begin planning for
T-Force duties. The first question for the Brigadier, however,
was a simple one: where would he find the men to form the
new force?

Those who were about to embark on the creation of this new
unit had little idea of what lay ahead; Brigadier Pennycook
later admitted that he would have been astounded if someone
had told him he would eventually command a force of over
5,000 soldiers. Initially, they had no soldiers, no scientists and
no definite date for when their work would begin. All they did
have were their orders and reams of paper on the earlier efforts
made by 30AU in Italy and France. Not surprisingly, Brigadier

Pennycook and his staff were perplexed about what they were expected to achieve and so they decided to take the logical step of defining the *raison d'être* for T-Force – ready for when, and if, it became something more than a paper unit.

The Brigadier and his staff's statement of purpose became the basis for all planning in the months ahead:

1. The capture of large towns in enemy occupied and enemy territory involves the over-running or by-passing of war factories, research and experimental establishments, static military headquarters government departments and ministries, mines and fuel dumps and the like.

2. All of these will be of value, in varying degrees, to the further prosecution of the war. In particular, the examination by experts of certain information and documents, before their destruction or loss, may be of vital importance.

3. On the other hand, few of these targets will be of tactical significance in the course of normal operations. It will, therefore, be uneconomical to burden the armies in the field with the task of locating, securing and guarding such targets.

4. T-Forces are therefore considered to be required to perform the following tasks:

a) Moving in the wake of the assaulting forces.

b) Locating and securing intact the targets concerned.

c) Preserving them from destruction, loot, robbery and if necessary counterattack, until the completion of their examination by teams of experts or until the removal of the essential installation or documents.

d) In enemy territory, providing armed escorts for the expert investigators.[6]

Initially, the planning followed the pattern that had been used by 30AU, and some still believed that T-Force would operate in the way that Commander Fleming had proposed for the earlier unit – in effect acting as a kind of private army. Although this 'independent striking force' model had its supporters, especially within the Naval Intelligence Directorate, it became increasingly clear that the situation in Germany was very different to that in Italy. There, they had still been searching for the intelligence needed to win the war. However, once the Allied armies began to drive into Germany, it was a question of how the Allies were going to secure the peace.

As Pennycook recognized, any private army acting ahead of the main thrust might endanger both its own men and those in the main force. If a private-army-style T-Force struck out to seize a target with no tactical advantage they might find themselves losing men as they fought through the enemy lines and could even become surrounded. In these circumstances, troops that were needed to defeat the enemy elsewhere might find themselves being diverted to carry out a rescue mission for such a unit. Any such diversion from the main objective of defeating the German Army could not be contemplated. Quite simply, the British did not have sufficient manpower to risk hundreds of soldiers in such a swashbuckling manner.

As a result, a compromise was reached and Brigadier Pennycook laid down a new version of T-Force tactics. The unit was to advance just behind the main thrust of the armoured or infantry assault. As the tactical objective was achieved it would be T-Force's responsibility to secure and investigate any targets within the area. At this point the message was clear – T-Force targets were so important that whatever units were allotted to the task of securing them would have to forego any notion of winning any spectacular battle honours. Their war would not to be about glory but about practicality and making sure their mission was achieved.

The significance of the casualties sustained by surrounded troops was of more than a passing interest to one of the officers on Brigadier Pennycook's staff. During late 1944, the fledgling

T-Force HQ greeted a new appointee as GSO2 on the HQ staff: Major Brian Urquhart, formerly an intelligence staff officer at the HQ of the Airborne Corps. Urquhart had become notorious as the officer who had warned General Frederick 'Boy' Browning of the presence of German armoured units in Arnhem prior to Operation Market Garden. His persistence had led to him being sent on sick leave, supposedly suffering from stress. To his critics' shame, Urquhart's claims about German strength in Arnhem proved to be well-founded – as the 1st Airborne Division discovered to its cost.

Urquhart's fall from grace meant that 21st Army Group had been asked to find a new home for him. When he arrived at the headquarters of T-Force, he seemed less than impressed with his new position. It was clear the organization's offices in Brussels were far from central to the Allied war effort. As he later wrote, it was the 'backwater of back-waters'.[7] However, Urquhart was soon fully engaged in planning for the advance into Germany. There were intelligence dossiers to prepare, hundred of photographs to study and a myriad of units to contact regarding their future roles in the organization.

At this point, Urquhart requested that he should be given a roving role once operations began, allowing him to move around between detachments of the unit's infantry element. Pennycook quickly agreed and set about acquiring a second GSO2 – a Canadian officer – who was to fulfil the same role within the T-Force attached to the Canadian 1st Army.

While planning for the British part of the T-Force role continued, other organizations remained fully involved in developing their own roles. By the end of 1944 CIOS had already despatched 197 expert investigators to 115 targets in the aftermath of D-Day and uncovered a wealth of technical intelligence, including exhaust-driven engine superchargers, a swept-wing for use in rocket-powered fighter planes, a new design of bomb-torpedo for use against ships and production information on propellants for long-range weapons. Naval investigators had studied designs for high-pressure steam piping while British tank designers had examined German production and assembly methods in order to guide their own methods. During late 1944 and early 1945, 30AU had remained active, advancing with US units into Strasbourg and Mulhouse to search for naval documents.

As the long-awaited advance into Germany came ever closer, a detailed outline of T-Force's operational responsibilities was distributed. Targets were split into three distinct categories: military research and development facilities; static military headquarters, government departments and ministries; and factories and industrial plants employed in the manufacture of all types of military equipment. The key aim was to prevent the loss of equipment and documents, the destruction of facilities by Allied troops and the disappearance of key personnel. Targets were further classified into two groups: those to be seized intact which were of value to the ongoing prosecution of the war; and those which were important to the preservation of postwar security. Although no one troubled to define postwar security, it soon became clear it actually meant ensuring the western Allies retained the military and technological advantage over the creeping threat from the Soviet Union and its burgeoning empire. These classifications were to be used to ensure T-Force directed its energies towards only the most pressing targets.

Seeing the results of the investigations of late 1944 roll in, Brigadier Pennycook and his staff continued to work on their own directives, learning from both the successes and failings of the various operations. A list of instructions was prepared for all incoming officers setting out the structure and role of T-Force HQ and how it related to their own duties. Junior officers, in effect those who entered target locations, were told that their first priority was bomb disposal and the removal of booby traps.

Following on from experiences in other campaigns, they were instructed that the greatest danger to their targets would actually be Allied troops, so they were to be kept away from targets. In fact, other Allied troops would only be allowed inside targets for 'urgent operational reasons' with the approval of a brigadier or higher commander. All targets were to be boldly signed 'Out of Bounds' in British areas or 'Off Limits' in the zones of American operations. Most importantly, they were informed that 'It must be assumed that all Germans are hostile, untrustworthy and treacherous.'[8]

For these early operations it was highlighted that Japanese intelligence targets were 'of vital importance'. All follow-up investigations were to be handled by staff who would be appointed by SHAEF. It was also stated that all Japanese persons were to be detained, with officers being told to test anyone with a request to say 'Hullo' as it was noted that 'The Japanese are physically incapable of pronouncing the letter 'l' and will therefore say "Hurro".'[9]

However, despite all the planning and detailed instructions, Brigadier Pennycook still had not been assigned an infantry contingent. In fact, what was supposed to be a highly mobile force was at this point no more than a paper formation. Even if he did have troops, he had no transport for them. However, the solution was found close to home. Under his command were six companies of Pioneers whose task was to create smokescreens – and this group had a generous allocation of transport, including 48 lorries and trailers. It was therefore decided that, following the completion of the smokescreen needed to shield the Rhine crossing, these Pioneers would jettison their generators, unload their smoke supplies and take onboard the equipment and men of T-Force.

So Pennycook had a plan, as well as both logistical and technical support, but he still had a problem. As one staff officer later commented: 'the problem was all too clear that "T-Force" wasn't a Force'.[10] What Brigadier Pennycook and his staff really needed were some men to command.

Where would Pennycook find the troops necessary to carry out the unit's vital duties? In fact, this question vexed all senior commanders throughout late 1944 and early 1945. Following a visit to 21st Army Group HQ in December 1944, a senior officer from SHAEF reported to CIOS: 'the manpower situation of the 21 Army Group is at present so strained that . . . the residual effort available for securing intelligence targets of the types in which CIOS is interested is strictly limited'.[11] As he pushed British forces towards Germany, Field Marshal Bernard Montgomery had to balance the overall limitation of resources with the desperate need to secure intelligence targets; as a result, the role of T-Force would fall to some unlikely individuals.

Although initial casualties in the D-Day landings had not been as high as expected, considerable casualties had been sustained in the days that followed, resulting in serious troop shortages. While the outside world celebrated the Allied victory, the true price of it was only really known to those on the battlefield, where the toll of men killed and wounded had delivered a heavy blow. With hospitals and cemeteries full, there was a shortage of able-bodied men available to fill the gaps in the frontline infantry battalions. As a result, two full divisions, the 50th and the 59th, were broken up allowing thousands of men to flock to the dreary barracks of retraining camps and holding units across Belgium.

The Allies had reached the bottom of the barrel. Whole artillery regiments were broken up and sent forward as infantry reinforcements. Military prisons and detention camps were being scoured for men whose sentences could be suspended so they could be sent up to the front. Cooks, drivers, tailors and clerks – many of whom had previously been considered unsuitable as frontline infantrymen – were now receiving brief courses in infantry training, ready for new tasks. The situation was such that one Army company commander even recalled having two men under his command who proudly wore RAF pilot's wings on the breast of their battle-dress. Surplus RAF aircrew, Royal Marines and a vast new call-up of men previously deemed too old for military service found their way to holding camps in Belgium, where they awaited the call to join their units ready for the push into Germany. The irony was that many of these men would eventually become part of the supposedly elite T-Force.

Among the new infantrymen were vast numbers of former gunners whose regiments had supported the advance of the two divisions. With their artillery role finished, the gunners faced the ominous challenge of adapting to a new task. Tom Pitt-Pladdy was among them. When his regiment was broken up he expected to remain with his colonel – as a result of having worked closely with him to 'acquire' extra kit in the days before the invasion. It was not to be. Instead he found himself in a pool of replacement officers for the infantry. Though he would have preferred to remain in the artillery, there were now limited choices for Pitt-Pladdy:

> I went to see the Medical Officer and he said that the colonel had told him I had already done enough and that he should keep me out of the infantry lark. I said, 'That's all very nice, but how am I going to walk out of here knowing I'm not going into the infantry but the gunners I've just brought in with me are having to be infantrymen? That's not on.' So he let me go to the infantry.

What T-Force needed now was an established unit, with a combination of experienced, responsible soldiers and able commanders. Where could they find such a unit without withdrawing one of the desperately needed battalions from the frontline action? Across northern France and in Belgium were a number of well-trained, long-established regiments who had already played a vital role in the campaign but were no longer being employed at 'the sharp end'. Among this group, was the 5th Battalion of the King's Regiment, the unit that had played such a vital role on D-Day. The contribution of the Kingsmen had not gone unnoticed, with Montgomery himself writing to their commanding officer: 'No one is more fully aware than I of the magnitude of the contribution made by you and the officers and men of your command to the success of this operation.'[12]

Following the death of Lt Colonel Board, the 5th King's had needed a new CO and his replacement, Lt Colonel B.D. Wreford-Brown, arrived on 11 June 1944. Originally with the Royal Berkshire Regiment, Wreford-Brown had served as the second-in-command of the 8th Battalion of the King's Regiment on D-Day.

In mid-July the 'Beach Groups', including the Kingsmen, had been transferred to the 'Lines of Communication', effectively meaning they were no longer employed anywhere near the frontlines. Although it was clear his new command seemed destined to remain in the rear, Wreford-Brown believed the battalion deserved a role better suited to its illustrious history. Hoping such a role would eventually arise, Wreford-Brown was determined his troops should be battle ready. In July he sent a selection of officers and men to frontline battalions for 'battle training'. They returned 'Tired, weary and covered with mud but they had many exciting tales to tell.'[13]

Many officers and men had died or been wounded in D-Day and, in the weeks that followed, Wreford-Brown had seen his top-grade infantrymen transferred to units depleted in the vicious battles fought across Normandy. The same thing had happened to the 8th Battalion whose remaining men had been folded into the 5th Battalion. Lower category reinforcements came to the 5th King's in September, but Wreford-Brown continued to tell them that he hoped they would continue to perform to the same standards as the men who had served with the unit on D-Day. It was clear, however, that some of the incoming men were not even up to guard duties and routine tasks. More than 100 of the new reinforcements were posted back to the Regimental Holding Unit as they were medically unsuitable for duty.

In October, the battalion was used to protect pipelines and guard railway tunnels, and November saw them having to remove the Beach Group insignia of the 2nd Army and adorn the Lines of Communication insignia instead. It was a blow to the morale of the commanding officer and the remaining men who had proudly served in the first waves on D-Day.

During this period, however, the troops got used to life behind the frontlines – in particular the benefits of black market trading. As Vic Woods recalled:

> From D-Day until I was demobbed I never drew any of my army pay. We had cigarettes, coffee and soap. Everything could be traded – even blankets. The civilians made clothes out of them. These things were currency, you could barter for anything. You'd be driving along and would even see a priest standing by the roadside trying to sell a gold watch. Some fellows did well out of it. I bought a Longines watch from one of our interpreters – they were top quality, expensive watches – he seemed to have a vast supply of them to sell.

The following months saw a continuing decline in the battalion's fortunes. Between September 1944 and February 1945 the King's Regiment continued to receive drafts of soldiers who had been medically downgraded following service in Normandy. Some were men who had suffered wounds, debilitating sickness and 'battle fatigue' – the newly coined name for shellshock. The incoming men came from all types of backgrounds. For some it was pure chance that they arrived at the 5th King's.

One of these new arrivals was David March, who had fought in Normandy with the North Staffordshire Regiment. After the 59th Division had been broken up, March had been transferred to the 50th Northumbrian Division, serving in Holland until fate saw him transferred again. One morning his platoon sergeant told him there would be a full kit inspection the next day: 'That was after fighting all the way from Normandy! So we said "We're going sick in the morning." And seven of us did.' March was lucky to be sent to see a specialist: 'My ears had been damaged when we'd been firing our two-inch mortars in support of a stranded patrol. The fire that came back from the Germans was the worst I'd ever known and my ears were damaged by blast. So when I went sick they put me down to see a specialist. The rest of the blokes were being sent back to fight with the Gloucesters.' Due to an administrative error, March never reached the hospital. Instead, he found himself transferred to the King's Regiment: 'I was clapping my hands in joy – I was out of the line!'

Another of the new arrivals was John Longfield, the Bren gunner who had left school early to join the King's Own Yorkshire Light Infantry and survived some of the most vicious battles of the entire war. Lightly wounded, Longfield had spent time in hospital where a doctor noticed his varicose veins and broke the news that he was to be medically downgraded.

Not all of these new arrivals were in unfamiliar territory. When Bob Brighouse's battalion of Lancashire Fusiliers was disbanded he was found to have an infected toe and missed the draft to the East Lancashire Regiment. Sent to a holding camp, he was soon posted back to his original regiment, along with others from the regiment's home city of Liverpool, as a reinforcement for the 5th Battalion: 'I was thankful for that bad foot. Otherwise I'd have been straight back into the frontlines with the East Lancs!'

Other new arrivals included a number of soldiers who had served with the artillery in Normandy. Born in 1925, Gunner Ken Moore had been working in an antiquarian bookshop in Norwich when he was called up in 1943. Having arrived in Normandy as a replacement gunner, he served in a regiment of 105mm self-propelled guns: 'The first night in Normandy I was sitting on the top of my slit trench and watching the tracer fire come lazily through the sky towards me. I thought "Aren't they pretty!" I didn't realize there were three or four rounds between each tracer bullet.' He had soon learned the real dangers of such fire: 'I was shot at and shelled. I'd never messed my pants but I'd been close to it – you really shake like mad.' Despite quickly adapting to his new situation, learning when to take cover and to control fear by keeping occupied, Moore experienced one brief low period: 'About a week after landing I became extremely homesick. It was terrible. I walked away from the guns into another field and had a good cry. I finished crying, got up and went back to the guns and never felt anything like that again until the end of the war.'

At the end of the Normandy campaign Moore's regiment was broken up. As they were told at the time, there was a shortage of shells for their 105mm guns and therefore the continuation of the regiment could not be justified. When the selection day came, Moore and his colleagues had little idea of what to expect. As he recalled, they were simply called out and told: 'Right, you, you and you – on to the lorries – tomorrow you are going to the infantry.' It was the beginning of a journey that would eventually see Moore joining the 5th King's. However, for the moment he was little concerned about what might happen: 'It's difficult to explain why I wasn't bothered. I can't explain why I felt like that. We just thought we had a job to do – basically you did as you were told.'

The reinforcements that joined the 5th King's before the push into Germany came from all backgrounds and each had a different story, having come to the regiment through a combination of circumstances. There were men like Ron Lawton, who had operated a landing craft on the D-Day beaches. Born in Stoke in 1925, and called up in 1943, Lawton had elected to join the Royal Marines 'on a whim'. His landing craft had broken down in mid-Channel on D-Day, thus missing the most dangerous period of the landings. Having been pulled out of Normandy just weeks after D-Day and given leave, Lawton and his fellow marines received the shocking news that they were being transferred to the army: 'We were disappointed. We used to say "Once a Marine, always a Marine." We were annoyed.' To Lawton and his colleagues, it seemed a bizarre waste of resources to give them elite marine training only to retrain them as infantry after just a couple of weeks in France.

Elsewhere were fresh-faced teenage recruits. Some were recent conscripts, like Harry Henshaw and Harry Bullen, who were not yet aged 20 and easily recognizable to the 'old hands' since their fresh faces did not show the strain of war. Others, soldiers like Tommy Wilkinson who had signed on aged 17, were volunteers:

> I'd volunteered – signed on for seven years. I did twelve years in the end. I was a young lad and both my brothers were in the army. I was enthusiastic and I wanted to do my bit for the war effort. So as soon as I was old enough I volunteered. I thought it would be all 'bang, bang, bang' with your rifle. When I was sent to the King's I didn't know what to expect.

Newcomers among the officers included men from a similarly wide variety of backgrounds. They were a mixture of hospital cases, men from units that had been disbanded and those who had suffered from battle exhaustion. Among them was

Lieutenant Ken Hardy from Thornton Heath in South London, a 21-year-old who had experienced the sharp end of the Normandy battlefields. From June 1944 until February 1945 he had served almost constantly in the frontlines and had long sensed he would not survive the war. His worst experience had been the day he lost 13 men of his platoon in a matter of minutes. Eventually, he had succumbed to battle exhaustion:

> It was the most ghastly time of my life. It was humiliating, awful. I was already in a pretty bad way and I knew it wasn't going to take much to send me over the edge. I arrived in a Dutch village and the Germans 'stonked' it with mortars. After that, I don't remember a thing for five days . . . I'd reached a point where I could never have gone back into action. I'd used up whatever reserve of courage I'd had. I think anybody who'd gone all the way from the beaches had had enough by then.

One thing Hardy was certain about – he knew that he no longer had the mental strength to undergo the rigours of prolonged combat. As a result, he found himself transferred to the 5th King's to join the intake of ex-hospital cases, former gunners and lower grade soldiers who were about to be given a new and important task.

Lt Colonel Wreford-Brown made strenuous efforts to demonstrate that his new men could still play an offensive role and contribute to the defeat of the enemy. Finally, his campaigning paid off and, in February 1945, his battalion was sent to Antwerp to be deployed as a mobile reserve. The region was hard-pressed for manpower, as much of the main force was fighting through the Reichswald Forest towards the Rhine. The additional units needed for the crossing of the Rhine and the later exploitation of the bridgehead were being rested, retrained and re-equipped ready for the drive into Germany. After a short time outside Antwerp the Kingsmen were moved to another zone in which troops were needed to hold the line. During the advance through France the Army had made a conscious decision not to assault ports whose reopening was not vital to the campaign. As a result the town of Dunkirk had remained in enemy hands. Quite simply, any assault would have cost lives they could not afford to lose.

Instead, the town was ringed by Allied troops who patrolled the area to prevent a German breakout. In March 1945 it was the 5th King's Regiment's turn to man the Dunkirk perimeter. It proved to be a location that was less than popular with the troops. As Private John Longfield remembered, it was a 'not too healthy place'. However, despite the miserable winter weather, at least he was no longer in the frontlines: 'The Germans had their guns pointed inland and they knew every inch of the ground. We just held positions in farmhouses and were told not to make ourselves visible.' Instead, they listened for German activity, bringing down artillery fire on any movement: 'The only excitement was when we were shelled by the enemy. One bloke did a bunk and three blokes were killed in one of the farmhouses.'

Commanding A Company, Captain George Lambert recalled the situation around the town:

> The Germans did a lot of patrolling over wide areas and they were determined to make as much nuisance as they could. It was reported to us when we took over the sector that there was a mad major in the German lines opposite to us. This major was apt to lead patrols right up to and through our lines. We would know when he was about by the smell of his whisky, which he always carried with him. I was very proud of my men, who responded very well to the conditions and maintained a high standard of patrolling.

While the Kingsmen were patrolling the sodden ditches and fields around Dunkirk, Brigadier Pennycook of T-Force remained troubled by having a force that existed only on paper. With the Brigadier so desperate for troops to join his fledgling force and Lt Colonel Wreford-Brown searching for an active role for his troops, it was not long before their paths crossed. Despite their employment in France, Wreford-Brown was delighted at the thought of his regiment getting the chance to move forward into Germany. After all, there was nothing more dispiriting for a battalion commander than realizing he was going to spend the rest of the war guarding supply lines or POW camps. The meeting with Pennycook offered an opportunity that was not only new and exciting, but would play a vital, if unheralded role, in shaping the future of Europe.

With the Kingsmen finally given their new role in T-Force, George Lambert, who had previously been an instructor at divisional battle school, was given the task of getting the battalion ready for the tasks ahead. As one of these new arrivals later recalled to his wife, it was the efforts of Captain Lambert that ensured they were prepared to return to active service. For six weeks he gave them basic infantry training and took them out on exercises to get the new officers used to handling men in the field. Eager to ensure his motley collection of new troops would be ready for action, Wreford-Brown sent some of the men away for specialist training. Included among them was David March:

> We'd moved up to prepare for T-Force and a notice went up asking for volunteers to join the sniper section. Guess who joined? I was stupid. I was attracted by the extra money. I was sent to do a sniping course – right there at the front. It was a dangerous job – but I never gave it a thought. I was a silly so and so, just 18 years old. When I returned to the Kings I was sent to the HQ company as a sniper.

It was not only the infantrymen, however, who were to undergo training before the move into Germany. In February 1945 some of the Admiralty scientists who were to join 30AU as their investigators were also sent for a course to acclimatize them to life in the field. The training was carried out by Patrick Dalzel-Job, the officer who had played such a vital role in the unit's investigations in France. John Bradley, a metallurgist who had worked for a railway company prior to secondment to the Admiralty, was among them. His training began with a run that left him with stiff ankles for a week. That was followed by digging slit trenches and then having live ammunition fired above their heads:

> One amusing incident occurred during a supposed skirmish. Some of us had to charge a supposed enemy placement while covered by a Bren. We had fired all our live ammunition and after waiting for the Bren to stop we got going. I slipped on jumping down an embankment on to a sunken road and came a hell of a crash on my left side; simultaneously someone on the Bren fired a single shot with the result that Job thought I had been shot.

After the arrival of the 5th King's at T-Force, Brigadier Pennycook received the next batch of troops, the 1st Buckinghamshire Battalion of the Oxfordshire and Buckinghamshire Light Infantry, who had already had an active war. Originally raised as a prewar Territorial Battalion, they had been divided into two battalions at the outbreak of war and had served in France during the retreat to Dunkirk. The 2nd Battalion had been all but wiped out as part of the rearguard force holding the town of Hazebrouck, while the 1st Battalion had returned to the UK where it had remained until D-Day. Like the 5th King's, the 1st Bucks were employed as part of a 'Beach Group', landing on Sword Beach and helping to clear the Germans from the port of Ouistreham. Following the invasion, like the King's, the battalion had been slowly stripped of its first-rate infantrymen who were sent as reinforcements to hard-pressed frontline battalions.

After the advance into Belgium, the Bucks and Ox had been employed as garrison troops for Brussels and remained there until they were released to join Brigadier Pennycook's burgeoning force. After months of providing security patrols and guarding the detention facilities housing drunks and other miscreants who had overindulged themselves on leave in Brussels, the Buckinghamshire battalion was ready for a change. However, the way in which they received the unofficial news of their imminent deployment at the front was cloaked in mystery. Towards the end of February 1945 Lt Colonel Wreford-Brown breezed into the Bucks office at St Jean Barracks, carrying an enormous sheaf of papers. These he declared to be highly secret and confidential, and asked the adjutant to keep them locked up while he had tea.

Knowing that Wreford-Brown's battalion was currently tied up patrolling the Dunkirk perimeter, the Bucks officers were intrigued by the sudden display of intense security and pressed the colonel for details. Obviously confident that the officers knew nothing of what was afoot, Wreford-Brown asked them, 'Haven't you heard?' In what was later described as his 'best cloak and dagger style', he asked the officers where they might be able to talk without being overheard. They swiftly made their way to the commanding officer's room where Wreford-Brown finally relaxed, sunk his hands into his pockets and whispered 'T-Force!' His words meant nothing to the assembled officers who did their best not to appear perplexed. Fortunately for them, however, the excited Wreford-Brown didn't hesitate and spent the next 20 minutes informing them about the new unit.

Although he could make no specific promises, Wreford-Brown whetted their appetite when he told them there was a chance they might soon form part of this mysterious new force. It was noted in the battalion war diary that 'It sounds a good job but no details are to hand at present,'[14] but, as one of the officers who had already grown bored of life in the Brussels garrison later wrote, 'Hope had been born anew.'[15]

Official confirmation of their reassignment came on 28 February 1945 when the commanding officer, adjutant and company commanders of the Buckinghamshire Battalion were informed they were to attend a meeting on 2 March at the headquarters of the 5th King's. There was a general sense of excitement surrounding the new role and the officers left the meeting with their heads filled with fascinating facts and their arms full of paper – including maps, reports and the famous 'black books' containing their future targets.

With so much work to do, and so little time to do it, the Bucks set about focusing their efforts. Realizing intelligence would be the hub of the unit they started building up their intelligence section. One of the sergeants began constructing large mobile map boards, while others 'acquired' drawing desks, shelves and drawers – all of which were to be carried from location to location, allowing the battalion's Intelligence Officer to carry out his duties of mapping the location of targets and keeping track of the position of each detachment. They also created hundreds of wooden signs and the battalion's signallers tested their wireless sets to pinpoint the range to which they would be effective. While all this work was going on around him, the Intelligence Officer began putting his new map boards to good use, briefing the company and platoon commanders as to exactly which targets they would be securing once the crossing of the Rhine had taken place, and plotting the route for the proposed line of advance.

There were also local exercises conducted by each company, in which troops practised taking over empty factories, securing the grounds and ensuring their communications equipment was effective. As one officer later recorded: 'It was now a question of polishing off final details and waiting for the starter's pistol.'[16]

With troops now available and the transport question solved, T-Force's next task was to acquire enough engineers to deal with the mines, booby traps and demolition charges they expected to find at their targets. One of the units chosen was No. 19 Bomb Disposal Section, Royal Engineers, a unit which had been raised in 1940 in response to the Luftwaffe's attacks on British cities. Many of the soldiers in the unit, which was under the command of Major W.S. Harris, were in the low medical category, including a number who were married with young children. After years of overseas service, including in Egypt, Sicily and mainland Italy, the unit had returned to London in 1944 where it served during the German flying bomb campaign against targets in southeast England. From there, the engineers had moved through France and Belgium into the Netherlands. On 29 March, the unit's officers were gathered together to hear the news that they were being assigned to the new T-Force unit.

On 2 April, Major Harris received further orders to report to Lt Colonel Wreford-Brown at Gescher near Düsseldorf and learnt that his sappers would be attached to the Kingsmen. They arrived on the next day, ready for the move into Germany. Some of the sappers were given particularly interesting training. Knowing they would be needed for opening safes in German HQs and research establishments, bomb disposal personnel were sent to the UK to learn the art of safe-cracking. They were sent on courses at prisons where experts in the art gave lessons to the soldiers. Following one such cloak-and-dagger course one of the attached officers reported he was now able to open the safe in his own company office in just five seconds.

While official records indicate that the engineers all learned their new trade from safe-breakers incarcerated in British jails, some soldiers were told a different story. Tom Pitt-Pladdy was surprised to find that some of the engineers really were expert safe-breakers who had been released from prison to assist the war effort. Though closely watched, their sentences were suspended to allow their skills to aid the war effort by blowing safes for T-Force.

As the weeks passed T-Force continued to grow. It was no longer just a paper unit, but an ever-increasing formation. Sixteen interpreters, mostly NCOs and other ranks originally from a variety of regiments, arrived. Most were foreigners serving with the British Army; all of them spoke both English and German, and some were also fluent in Russian. They were closely followed by a group of Dutch interpreters who had been recruited from the newly formed Netherlands Army and chosen for their knowledge of German.

Even with T-Force growing at an almost daily rate in advance of the move into Germany, there was still one concern for Brigadier Pennycook. He had his infantrymen, engineers, drivers and lorries, but he still needed experts to escort into Germany. The first step was to establish a camp at which the scientists and technicians could be based. So without any official 'paper' establishment, a 'T-Force Investigators Transit Camp' was formed in the Dutch town of Venlo, staffed entirely from personnel held in the 5th King's Reinforcement Holding Unit. By the end of March 1945 this camp was ready and could hold up to 100 investigators passing through at any one time.

While facilities to house the teams of scientific and industrial experts were being established, the T-Force officers faced another worry. They knew the assessors would be experts in their field, but their aims and expectations remained a mystery. As one officer later wrote: 'The thought of assessors had haunted us since the first conference. Our ideas had been rather hazy on the whole, would they be professors with longish beards? Would they have any kit?'[17]

Unfortunately, some of the soldiers concerns about potential problems would be justified, even if their initial impressions of their new scientific colleagues were positive: 'We viewed them from a first floor window: no beards at any rate and all were dressed in one of the three coloured uniforms generally associated with His Majesty's Services; so far so good. Masses of baggage appeared too, including we noticed with joy in our hearts, bedrolls. We almost beamed. Things obviously were not going to be as grim as we imagined.'[18] However, despite the military appearance of the assessors, it soon became clear most were unprepared for the realities of life in the field.

Arriving at 8 a.m. the assessors were told their transport would not be leaving until 11 and, since there was nowhere for them to wait, they would have to sit on their kitbags. Such arrangements were typical in the army, but clearly unacceptable for the newly arrived civilians:

> Angry noises were raised at once complaining bitterly that it did seem a lot of damned nonsense getting them up at 6 o'clock to report here at 8 o'clock to move off at 11 o'clock. Several harsh words and phrases were directed at the general army administration and the difference between what they had been told would happen in the United Kingdom, and what was actually happening seemed difficult to accept. Things were not going too well really. After a further loud explosion when they were asked to travel in a 3-toner, and a lot more patient listening to how they had been definitely promised staff cars etc, we managed to hustle them in, put up the tailboard and yelling at the loading driver – one must take it out on someone after all – we gave the order to move off.[19]

The soldiers might have thought their problems were over but there would be more to come in the days ahead.

If T-Force was to achieve its objectives one thing was clear, the soldiers whose task it was to secure targets needed to be able to do so without the interference of other units in the area. Many of the targets known to be on the 'blacklists' were desirable locations. If the target happened to be in a hotel used by German intelligence, for example, they needed to be certain that it was not being taken over by a formation commander in search of a comfortable billet for his HQ. It was also essential that targets were secured against any soldiers who were intent on rifling through desk drawers in search of souvenirs.

As a result, Brigadier Pennycook came up with the idea of issuing a document similar to one previously used by 30AU which had read, 'The bearer of this card will not be interfered with in the performance of his duty by the Military Police or by other military organizations.' He requested that a pass be issued, giving all his men the right to prevent unwanted intruders from entering targets. The plan was agreed and Major General Freddie de Guingand – Field Marshal Montgomery's highly respected Chief of Staff – issued a pass giving unusual powers to even the lowliest private in T-Force. It read: 'The holder of this card is entitled on my authority, to deny any member of the forces entry or access to the building or area which he is guarding.'

30AU was to have more influence on the future of T-Force than the wording of a pass. It became the final unit to be brought into T-Force. Having spent the period from D-Day onwards almost constantly engaged with searching for German military research, 30AU wereideally placed to offer expertise to the recently established force. From November 1944, 30AU – which now numbered 400 personnel – had come under the command of Colonel Humphrey Quill, a regular Royal Marine officer with a background in intelligence. Although working with an organization as large as T-Force was against the ethos under which 30AU had been established, and anathema to many of its officers, the decision had been taken.

From March 1945, 30 Advanced Unit, as 30 Assault Unit had been renamed, joined T-Force. Although given a relatively independent role, from this point on the marines would – on paper at least – no longer be free to roam wherever they chose. One forward team was attached to T-Force in the Canadian area of operations and two forward teams were attached to the 2nd British Army. Under the new instructions all liaison work was to be carried out through T-Force HQ, which was in charge of all movements, operations and intelligence investigations. T-Force HQ was also designated as the location through which the Royal Marines would gain permission to switch from one Army Group area to another. However, it was stressed that all documents seized by the marines found to be solely of naval interest were to be cleared with T-Force and then sent to the Admiralty. Those documents of mixed interest were to be processed through T-Force and sent to SHAEF. Any documents of no interest to the Navy were to be left for other investigation teams to follow up.

The treatment of documents uncovered during operations needed to be regularized. It was decided that all documentation should be held in situ and not immediately evacuated. This would ensure all technical information would be retained with the machinery to which it related. Furthermore, administrative records would be required by the Allied military government after the end of hostilities. The only exceptions were to be documents of immediate operational importance, which were to be sent to the relevant intelligence HQ, and particular documents that had been requested by agencies in the UK. Furthermore, only investigators were to be allowed to remove documents, ensuring a careful record was kept of their nature, the circumstances of removal and their destination. The only other exception was the removal of documents from scattered locations within target sites to a central gathering point, thus reducing the requirement for guards.

As the required troops began to assemble, it became clear that the original notion of how T-Force might operate was no longer feasible. Even if the German forces did not collapse following the crossing of the Rhine, it was obvious the war would become increasingly mobile. Intelligence estimates of the total number of troops available to the German High Command showed that, with the Rhine breached, there would no longer be a continuous frontline and the Germans would attempt to hold a series of vital locations. As a result, the decision was taken that each of the three armies under the control of Montgomery's 21st Army Group would have a separate T-Force detachment attached to it: General Miles Dempsey's 2nd British Army and General Harry Crerar's 1st Canadian Army would have permanent T-Force detachments, while General William H. Simpson's 9th US Army would make units available, using the methods previously employed in Paris and elsewhere.

In essence, the British T-Force was going to be a highly mobile force capable of sub-dividing into self-contained teams available to cover all necessary targets within their zones of operation. These would then work within the areas of operation of each Corps. In a move designed to prevent the Corps HQs from being burdened with the planning of 'T' operations, it was also decided that two staff officers should be trained to act as planning officers for the operations, with one being allotted to each of the armies.

As the planning continued there emerged an understanding that Brigadier Pennycook's role as an adviser to the Army Group General Staff on chemical warfare was far less important than his new position. Realizing that 'T' operations could only be fully successful if he was able to give operational orders, he pressed for a change in status. In his advisory role he would be forced to always turn to the General Staff – who would usually have more pressing matters to deal with – and request they transmit orders. Although usually a reserved character, Pennycook successfully pressed Major General de Guingand for full recognition of his newly expanded role. As he later described it, he began to 'wear another hat' as 'Brigadier General Staff T', directly responsible to the General Staff for all 'T' matters.[20]

As the time for the crossing of the Rhine came nearer, 21st Army Group HQ moved forward from Brussels to set up camp near the western banks of the river. Brigadier Pennycook and his staff went with them, setting up their HQ in an empty lunatic asylum. From there they continued their planning and took the opportunity to run a test of planned procedures. The vast headquarters of a German steel company, Deutsche Edelstahl Werke, was in the nearby town of Krefeld and entering the steelworks they discovered – to their relief – the retreating Germans had not sabotaged the machinery. However, it was clear the factory had been thoroughly looted of anything movable. It seemed this looting was the work of the slave labourers who had been employed there. Fortunately, the newly freed slaves had not destroyed any of the most important machinery, which had been too large to be of any interest to them.

With the steelworks secured, T-Force began to set in motion its plans for the investigation of targets. For this 'rehearsal', they notified the rear SHAEF HQ that a CIOS target had been secured and arranged for the reception, accommodation and transport of the teams of investigators. Within days the first team arrived. Much to the surprise of T-Force HQ, the investigators – though dressed in army uniforms – had been sent by the Admiralty. Even more surprising was the excitement generated when the investigators saw a number of 'creep testing machines' – used for testing metal equipment used at high temperatures – which they discovered in a basement. Within days, 12 of these machines had been dismantled, crated and sent on their way to the UK.

It was in these final days before the advance into Germany that Lieutenant Tom Pitt-Pladdy joined the 5th King's. The

former artillery officer, who had chosen to join the infantry in
a show of solidarity with his men, was not shocked to see the
vast changes the infantry had undergone as it attempted to
recover from the Normandy campaign. As he recalled, he had
been sent to command an artillery observation post in a tank
and discovered his driver was not even a tank driver but, until
the day before, an ambulance driver. Despite the pride Colonel
Wreford-Brown showed in his battalion, Pitt-Pladdy saw little
sense of regimental identity among those who had been scraped
together to reinforce the King's:

> None of my platoon were 5th King's Regiment, except the ser-
> geant. When I got to the King's they had a lot of below grade
> people who were being released. So I had to go to the
> Reinforcement Holding Unit to pick up a platoon's worth of sol-
> diers. They said they couldn't give me any NCOs. By luck I
> recognized three anti-tank gunners who I knew had been lance
> bombardiers. So I took them as my section commanders. So I
> never knew much about the King's Regiment.

As he later recalled, among the men collected from the holding
unit were former Royal Army Service Corps drivers and even
a former member of the Merchant Navy.

Pitt-Pladdy was confused as to why the T-Force job had not
been given to a unit better placed to accept the role. He
thought, 'Why the hell didn't they pick an artillery regiment to
do this?' After all, an artillery regiment would have had more
NCOs, its own communications and its own transport. He
recalled, 'Instead they started off with the wreck of a battalion,
with only a few people left in it.'

Even if he didn't agree with throwing a battalion together
from 'odds and sods', Pitt-Pladdy soon recognized that, despite
the inauspicious start, many within the King's were keen to
cement their role within T-Force: 'The colonel was hell bent on

retaining the 5th King's name – and everything had to be sub-
sidiary to that. To me, 5th King's was just a cap badge. Some
of the "old and bold" from the regiment didn't want to know.'
When he first arrived at the King's, Pitt-Pladdy's company
commander looked at him with obvious disfavour and then said
his first (and almost his only) words to the new arrival: 'My
company works perfectly well under the sergeant-major and I
don't want you people interfering with it. You can go off and
do your T-Force business but leave my company alone'. As
Pitt-Pladdy later recalled: 'That was ok because we went off on
our own. We were free.' This sense of independence followed
Pitt-Pladdy right through his time with the unit and he even
risked the wrath of his commanding officer by continuing to
wear a Royal Artillery cap badge.

As this new, and somewhat uncertain, unit began to assemble for the task ahead, the troops had little idea of what was
expected of them. All they knew was that they were soon to
advance into Germany to seize industrial locations. Whether
they would be expected to fight their way in was not yet clear.
Despite knowing their unit was called T-Force, the meaning of
their role was still uncertain. In A Company of the
5th King's, Bob Brighouse befriended a new arrival, 18-year-
old Harry Bullen, who had arrived on the continent just weeks
before. Bullen recalled, 'We'd been told nothing at all – not a
thing. I was just a kid, with all these blokes who'd been through
Normandy but they never really spoke about it. We were
expecting to go straight into action.'

Yet, if the troops had little idea of what their duties would
entail, they would not have been mollified to realize that their
officers, and even T-Force's most senior commanders, were just
as puzzled as everybody else. As Tom Pitt-Pladdy later admitted: 'Do you know – I don't think anybody ever did tell us what
it was all about! Except in very broad terms.' Not only did the
junior officers have little idea about operations but it was clear

the confusion was shared with senior officers throughout the army, as Major George Lambert, commanding A Company of the 5th King's, recalled: 'T-Force was so secret that many High Ranking officers had not heard about it and hence did not always realize how important it was to give T-Force officers information about the troops likely to take a certain area.' Similarly, the Buckinghamshire's war diary noted: 'it is now left to us to work out how we do it.'[21]

As the final replacements joined the 5th King's – and the scientists and specialists got ready to join T-Force on the advance into Germany – others within the ever-expanding organization continued with the process that had begun in Normandy. Detachments of 30AU operated in their intelligence and research gathering role, working alongside the US Army during the advance on the Rhine. Admiralty metallurgist John Bradley accompanied Patrick Dalzel-Job on his 30AU investigations. It was an unfamiliar world for a man more used to research laboratories than slit trenches and heavily armed jeeps. Indeed, since Normandy, Dalzel-Job had added an additional machine-gun to his vehicle – a captured German gun fixed to the bonnet in order to increase its fire power. They spent most of their time in forward areas, with Bradley writing to his wife to admit: 'The sound of American shells winging their way overhead was rather strange.' For an entire week Bradley slept in his uniform and was hardly able to wash. It was normal for the average British infantryman but was far from a regular experience for Admiralty scientists.

The team travelled through towns like Düren, which had been all but destroyed following almost two months in the front-line. Another day saw them in Jülich, a village that Bradley noted 'no longer exists'. At Hellenthal, their progress was blocked by the wreckage of a King Tiger tank and they could hear the chatter of machine-gun fire from positions less than a mile away. Elsewhere they had to divert from their chosen route after jeeps were 'shot up' by Germans on the opposite bank of the Rhine.

At Mannheim 30AU's B Troop carried out investigations at an aircraft factory. Although the area was little more than a heap of rubble, they discovered the factory had remained operational since most of its work was carried out underground. Reg Rush recalled leaving the factory with his mate Jimmy and staring out across the waters of the Rhine. As they stood chatting atop the rubble they noticed a concrete bunker on the opposite bank:

> We were chatting away – you don't hear the shot that gets you but you hear the one that just misses you. You hear the whizz as it passes – then you hear the shot. We didn't hear this one. It just hit the bricks next to us. We immediately dropped to the ground. Then we pumped fire into the slit of this bunker. But we had just been stupid – we had exposed ourselves and they had fired.

While 30AU continued with their investigations inside the American area of operations, the main body of T-Force waited for the start of operations in the British zone. Most target dossiers had been received, and the Kingsmen were waiting in their trucks for the signal to advance. The battalion may have been a strange mixture of D-Day veterans, teenage 'virgin' soldiers, ex-Royal Marines, former gunners, soldiers returning straight from hospital and shell-shock cases, but they were about to embark on a journey that would have enormous repercussions for the postwar future of the whole western world.

CHAPTER 4

Operation Plunder and Beyond

'As soon as we crossed the border I halted the convoy, really to check my route with the map. The CO came forward to ask why I had halted. I said "After 5 years of war I thought the men might wish to relieve themselves on reaching German soil".
"Very good idea, George," said the colonel.'

Major George Lambert MC, commander of
A Company,
5th King's Regiment.

On 23 March 1945, 21st Army Group, under the command of Field Marshal Montgomery, began one of the largest military operations of the entire war and crossed the Rhine to the north of the Ruhr. The name chosen for the operation was to have great significance for the soldiers of T-Force – 'Operation Plunder'. While average soldiers connected the word 'plunder' with any personal loot they might acquire in the weeks ahead, in T-Force plunder was the very purpose of their existence. Their role may have been the rigorously organized removal of technology and equipment from Germany – planned and authorized by the High Command – but for many it still felt like looting.

The Rhine crossing employed vast resources. Although Germany appeared to be just weeks from defeat, Montgomery took nothing for granted. The river was broad and fast running, its waters swelled by both the thaw of winter snows and spring downpours. As in all his operations, 'Monty' used every resource he could lay his hands on. Heavy bombers pounded German towns to the east of the river; smokescreens obscured the riverbanks from the Ruhr to the central Netherlands. The same area was pounded with artillery fire – much of it acting as a diversion, leaving the Germans confused as to where the assault would come. There were landing craft crewed by sailors of the Royal Navy, thousands of aircraft and gliders to drop airborne troops directly on to German positions and searchlights to create artificial moonlight for the night crossing. In addition, the Allies had amassed vast stockpiles of temporary bridges, hundreds of miles of telephone cables and millions of rounds of ammunition of every calibre. And on top of that, the thousands of men – in tanks, carriers, lorries and on foot – waited to advance into Germany and bring five years of war to an end.

The crossing was a great success. The airborne forces suffered heavy casualties, which was the one major regret for the Allied commanders, but nevertheless achieved all their objectives. Bridges were swiftly assembled and 21st Army Group began to pour across the river for the final drive eastwards. Behind them came the men of T-Force, who were ready to start their work as the Third Reich collapsed around them.

However, before they were sent forward there was one final hiccup. On the evening of 28 March the commanders of the T-Force infantry battalions were summoned to 21st Army Group HQ for an urgent conference. The British 2nd Army was moving swiftly eastwards, necessitating T-Force to join them immediately. The Buckinghamshire battalion should have moved at this point, but they were still committed in Brussels. Since the King's Regiment was free to move, it was given the task and the Buckinghamshires were switched to take over duties with the Canadian 1st Army. Feverish activity occupied the staff of both T-Force detachments as 'black books' and

maps had to be swapped over. This mix up left the senior officers of the Buckinghamshires 'hopping mad'[1] since they had
foreseen such a situation weeks before when they had failed to
be swiftly relieved of their duties in Brussels. The confusion,
combined with the overall difficulty of finding sufficient transport, led one officer to note: 'We hope for the best but expect
the worst.'[2]

The switch over was further complicated by the heavy workload envisaged for the 2nd Army in Germany. As a result, the
decision was made to hand over two companies of the
Buckinghamshires to the 5th King's Regiment, with the Bucks'
second-in-command – Major H.C. Le Neve Foster – taking the
role of detachment commander. These two companies – 'B'
under command of Major Kershaw and 'D' under command of
Major Marshall – would remain with the King's until the end
of the war.

Thanks to the seemingly miraculous work of the bridge
builders of the Royal Engineers and Pioneer Corps, the advancing detachments of T-Force made safe – and dry – crossings of
the Rhine. As the detachments advanced along the dusty, pot-
holed roads they became aware that every bridge, however
small, had been demolished by the retreating enemy but now
had been replaced by one of the ubiquitous Bailey bridges of
which the Royal Engineers were so proud.

Moving amidst the vast, snaking queues of military transport,
they could see that their safe passage had been won by hard
fighting. The towns and villages along the riverside were
scarred with the signs of battle. Further east the troops drove
past fields strewn with the wrecks of the gliders that had
delivered the airborne forces. There were fields full of dead cattle and the hastily dug graves of the victims of the battle.
However, it was not just the dead who were waiting by the
roadside. The further the T-Force trucks moved east, the more
they were greeted by crowds of released prisoners of war of all

nationalities. Clad in tattered clothing, the ex-POWs cheered at every passing vehicle.

In the days that followed the crowds would be joined by thousands of civilian slave labourers, soon to be known as 'displaced persons' – or DPs – whose existence would come to complicate the lives of the T-Force detachments. In Hannover Major Brian Urquhart uncovered a group of Russian DPs who had forced their way into an underground store of alcohol. They had smashed open vats of wine and spirits so that the floor was deep in a vicious cocktail and knelt down to drink themselves into a stupor. Overcome by their indulgence, many had collapsed and drowned in the liquid as their comrades continued to drink around them. One Kingsman recalled seeing the reaction of slave labourers to their new found freedom: 'The labourers just went crazy after they were liberated and started smashing up valuable equipment. Although I perfectly understood why they were doing it, it was quite an annoyance to T-Force at the time.' The soldier also noted how, in contrast, the German population behaved in a manner that actually aided them: 'The German love of keeping things in a good order helped us immensely because they seemed loathe to make a mess and destroy what they were working on.' It crossed his mind that the Germans may have expected the Allies to let them continue their work as soon as the war was over.

In the midst of this chaos, the various detachments of T-Force – along with more than 150 target investigators – began to fan out, ready to commence operations. In their first two days east of the Rhine the Kingsmen covered more than 220 miles. Noting the destruction and chaos, Tommy Wilkinson recalled the uncertainty of the T-Force role. Unlike the rest of the army, which knew it would move forward day after day in pursuit of the enemy, T-Force seemed to move all over the front: 'You didn't know what to expect. You were on the move so much, you didn't know where you were going or what you were going to do next. You'd be told you were going to wherever – but you would not really know where it was. You'd just pack your small kit and be off.'

In this world of high-speed military operations, the officers and men of T-Force once again became aware of the difference between their expectations and those of the investigation teams attached to them. Brian Urquhart recalled the first investigation teams being rushed forward from Brussels and appearing in 'bedraggled batches'.[3]

When the Buckinghamshire battalion paused to establish its HQ, its officers were immediately assailed by aggrieved assessors who were still hopeful of being put up in hotels and given unlimited transport: 'More trouble came bounding up the road, in the shape of our old friends the assessors. Where, they would like to know, were they expected to sleep? What about some food? Who was going to look after them? No one seemed to care as far as they could see. They had been here half an hour now, and nothing, absolutely nothing, had been done.'[4]

Seemingly resigned to their situation, the assessors shrugged their shoulder and quietened down. It appeared a truce had been reached until one of their number asked, 'What about my trousers?' Sharply, the officers retorted, 'What about them?' only for the assessor to complain loudly, 'These are my service dress trousers and they are simply covered in coal dust from sitting in that 3-tonner.' That did it. The officers 'let themselves go', telling the assessor that they had far greater concerns than his trousers.

Their outburst seemed to do the trick. When the situation calmed down the assessors were informed that everything that could be done was being done and they finally settled into their quarters for the night. As one officer later wrote: 'At 2300 hours we turned in, feeling that it had been a trying day.'[5] These sentiments were echoed by John Longfield, who had arrived at the 5th King's Regiment following his hellish experiences in

Normandy with the King's Own Yorkshire Light Infantry, later recalling of the investigators: 'They had no conception of war at the sharp end.'[6] One Buckinghamshires' officer found a simple method of calming the assessors. He acquired a number of bogus requisition forms and drew unauthorized, additional kit to be issued to them.

Despite the reported conflict and comedy of having civilians attached to a military unit, there was a real sense of seriousness about their role. Jack Heslop-Harrison, a specialist in radar serving in the Royal Army Service Corps, was summoned to Brussels and then forward to T-Force to examine German radar facilities. He later wrote of the instructions his party received from an American major, who told them that there should be no confrontations with German scientists and that they were to be treated with respect. He was also warned that, although most German units were expected to comply with ceasefire orders, there was a definite threat from the 'Werewolves' – the groups of diehard Nazis who were expected to attack the occupation forces in Germany.

As soon as the orders were received it became clear there would be certain limitations to their work. The scientists understood that initial investigations would have to be carried out swiftly. In-depth examinations were out of the question. Furthermore, although they were specialists in their own field, they were not necessarily in possession of sufficient technical information to know the importance of some finds. As Heslop-Harrison later wrote: 'We had little or no advance knowledge of how much was already familiar to British intelligence.'[7]

Once over the Rhine, a standard pattern of T-Force operations began to develop. From this day onwards the 5th King's was no longer a cohesive battalion; rather, it was divided into detachments and scattered around northern Germany. Though companies were allocated to various corps, the companies themselves were further subdivided to take in any number of small targets. In the weeks that followed, T-Force began one of the war's genuine – if unheralded – success stories. The combination of strong intelligence, careful planning, a spirit of independence and troops who displayed both dedication and determination allowed the seizure of all the planned targets – and many more besides.

The basis of planning for 'T' operations started with an up-to-date analysis of the operations of each individual corps. Detachments were then allotted to the corps in ratio to the size of the targets in the area. As plans were made for occupying targets, T-Force staff officers liaised with their counterparts at Corps HQ to advise on the targets. The information was then passed to individual divisions in order that they too might be aware of their responsibilities in relation to targets. Once the relevant information had been given to each division, arrangements were then made for the accommodation of 'T' detachments within the divisional area. All of this was done by the T-Force General Staff Officer 2, working from his desk in Army HQ.

Then, in the final hours before the advancing troops reached the targets, officers liaised with the commanders of individual brigades and forward units. The final assessment of the targets was made using town plans showing the location of targets and aerial photographs which helped give the detachment commanders a clearer idea of the expected size of the target they were expected to secure.

T-Force was unleashed into a violent and uncertain world. At times they moved in the wake of the assaulting infantry, at others they advanced into towns side by side with the assault formations. In some locations they found themselves moving immediately behind the forward tanks, with even the assault infantry behind them. However, in a few locations, T-Force strayed ahead of the advancing army, arriving at target locations before attacks had commenced. Fortunately, in such instances, they found their targets undefended or in the hands of Germans who were willing to surrender. More often than not, T-Force detachments found themselves heading towards targets across open countryside – often less than certain which side controlled the area. Given this freedom of movement, the dangers increased but it also meant that they were able to seize and examine a number of 'targets of opportunity' that arose on their travels.

Under the command of Major John Langdon, B Company headed straight into Osnabrück to deal with targets. In this constantly changing situation, and with communications uncertain, individual detachments moved forward hoping to meet up with the assault units. Caught up in the organized chaos, a small group of T-Force bomb disposal engineers made their way to 8 Corps Headquarters to join an infantry company that was heading for Osnabrück. Unable to locate either the HQ or the assault troops, the engineers moved into the town hoping to catch up with the advance units.

Upon entering the town they found the streets eerily deserted. Not bothering to find the infantrymen, they moved straight to their first target, the main telephone exchange. Finding it in ruins and hardly worth protecting, they moved on to a copper and aluminium factory that was on the target list. After driving out a group of DPs who had begun looting the establishment, the engineers posted guards and considered their next move. As they did so, a fighting patrol from 4 Commando Brigade swept into the town, carefully making their way through the streets in search of the enemy. Both groups were shocked: the commandos had expected to be met by German soldiers rather than bomb disposal engineers, who themselves were amazed to see the spearhead of the advance entering the town they had unwittingly captured. With the town safely in Allied hands, T-Force was able to move on to the remaining targets including a plant in which new metallurgical processes were found to have been developed. One of the unit's finds was a submarine 'Schnorkel' with a radar unit attached, the first of its type to be uncovered.

The fluid situation was illustrated during the first night in Osnabrück. Former marine Ron Lawton, serving in C Company, was awoken by gunfire. He was swiftly sent to set up his Bren gun by the backdoor of the house they were occupying. It was soon discovered that the firing had been one of the Kingsmen shooting at two lost German soldiers who had wandered into the gardens.

For John Longfield, serving in A Company of the 5th King's Regiment, travelling by truck through the countryside as it enjoyed the first awakenings of spring seemed like luxury after months of foot-slogging through Normandy. Early targets such as factories were also a welcome relief from the dull days of winter around Dunkirk. Longfield was relishing a sense of freedom after surviving the Normandy battles: 'I wasn't worried about it. We had loads of transport. We had all sorts of people attached to us. It was great fun! It was a mad rush from place to place. We went haring through these places – taking things. Not that we had any idea what a lot of them were.' On Sunday 8 April they took control of the Gestapo HQ in Osnabrück: 'I broke into a couple of safes, which proved to be empty. I didn't see much else except a few typewriters, draughtsmen's instruments, and numerous pornographic pictures presumably taken by the Gestapo in their recreation time. They were a bit of an eye-opener.'[8]

The typewriters were later given to civilians in the Dutch town of Hengelo. No record was kept of what happened to the pornography. Despite the troops' interest in the photographic finds, the T-Force assessors found more substantial items to attract their attention. At the Kupfer und Drahtwerke factory they uncovered submarine parts for which new metallurgical processes had been used. It was a fitting introduction to a

period in which significant military research developments
would be uncovered.

These early operations gave the attached scientists an
opportunity to inspect German equipment, helping them to
build an understanding of what they could expect to find during investigations. On his journey east, Jack Heslop-Harrison's
team were offered a chance to examine an 'opportunity target' in Osnabrück. Amidst the scenes of destruction in the
station's goods yards, the team came across a consignment of
aviation radio equipment that had spilled out from a wrecked
freight wagon. It gave Heslop-Harrison his first chance to
examine German electronics in detail, and he was impressed
by the design and qualityof the equipment. In particular, he
noted the use of magnesiumaluminium alloy that had resulted
in savings in size and weight. The downside of the handiwork,
he noted, was the elaborate construction methods this
entailed.

As operations got underway D Company, under Major
Jimmy James, was allocated to the 43rd Division and sent north
– alongside a battalion of the Dorset Regiment – to deal with
targets at Hengelo in the Netherlands, initially targeting a factory producing anti-aircraft and naval firing gear. The factory
was fully occupied by 3 April, with all the heads of department
having been detained for interrogation by the investigation
team. Of particular interest to the investigation team was a new
type of anti-aircraft predictor, only two examples of which were
believed to be in existence. Assessors described the find as of
the 'utmost importance'.[9]

Major Frank Denton's C Company joined 12th Corps and
headed for the town of Rheine at the junction of the River
Ems and the Ems-Weser canal. As they reached the town,
some elements of the force – including the transport staff, engineers and investigators – had yet to catch up with them. Also
on the way to join the company was No.4 Film Production

Unit of the RAF whose role was to make films of an airfield of interest outside Rheine.

Even targets that had been all but destroyed by the retreating German forces could not be ignored. At Rheine the main telephone exchange was discovered to have been blown-up with hand grenades. Despite the damage, a detachment was left to guard the exchange since it was one of just 20 such offices throughout Germany, playing a vital role in countrywide communications. Only by securing, then repairing, such establishments would the Allies be able to ensure the smooth running of military government and the return to order in the postwar period.

While many of the Germans that T-Force came into contact with were eager to cooperate, some deliberately obstructed the investigations, as Tom Pitt-Pladdy found on his first T-Force operation. He took the men of 13 Platoon, C Company, 5th King's, into Rheine on foot, since the only river crossing was allocated solely to designated infantry and armoured units. The platoon entered the Takke Fabrichen factory, which made gearboxes for U-boats, and noted that around 20 Mauser pistols had been kept in metal boxes fastened to posts in the work areas. These had been used to keep the slave labour force in order. It was a stark reminder of the nature of the regime that T-Force was helping to demolish.

As Tom Pitt-Pladdy remembered: 'Their chief designer was someone we'd been told to get our hands on. He was a Czech – a Sudeten German – and a Nazi fanatic.' Evidence of his obstinate resistance to the British troops became obvious as it soon transpired that the man had locked all his safes and sent his wife to throw the keys into the River Ems. Not prepared to be outwitted by the Nazi designer, Pitt-Pladdy asked one of the investigators, Mr Good, to interrogate him and also sent for his safe-breaking team, the former inmates of Wormwood Scrubs prison: 'The orders were that nobody was allowed to be in the room with the safe-breakers, but I thought that didn't include me. I'm glad I did that, because in Hamburg we took one million Reichsmarks out of a safe. I shudder to think what would have happened if I hadn't been watching over them.'

Unable to break through the man's defences, Mr Good suggested a new course of action. He sent the man upstairs and told Pitt-Pladdy to blow the safes: 'There was a ruddy great "Whoomf!" A dense cloud of fine sand permeated the building and seeped through every crack including into the upstairs office. It certainly had the effect of breaking the nerve of the designer who decided to be a little more cooperative.'

Pitt-Pladdy was eager to move on and reach his next target but needed someone to watch over the designer until more investigators arrived. He soon found a unit who were happy to oblige: 'I found this anti-tank regiment. I told them I needed this chap guarded. So they sent an M10 tank destroyer.' The commander of the gun crew found a simple way to subdue the designer. The vehicle was driven up to his house, and its high-powered gun was forced through the window into the middle of the room: 'We said to this bolshie Czech chap, "You stay here quietly, if you don't you've lost the house!" I don't think that was strictly within the rules, but who cared at that time?'

Aside from the contents of the safes, there was another immediate reward for T-Force's work. Beneath the factory were three cellars full of ball bearings. Realizing the importance of these finds, assessors were soon despatched from T-Force HQ to investigate, with estimates putting the value of the haul at £2,000,000.[10] As Pitt-Pladdy recalled, these were urgently required for evacuation, since a British ball-bearing manufacturer had recently been bombed, halting production: 'We flew out three Dakotas full of ball bearings, from Rheine airfield to the UK. It was an immediate turnover.'

As the Kingsmen headed north, the two-company detachment of the Buckinghamshire Battalion was attached to the 9th US Army advancing on Hannover. As they prepared for the move, the Bucks became acquainted with some new arrivals. Having previously carried out similar operations in Italy and France, 30AU of the Royal Marines was now attached to T-Force for operations in Germany. For some among the marines, who had been pioneers in this type of operation, their new home seemed a restrictive environment. Along with the loss of the earlier, more martial, name, they felt their swashbuckling instincts were being tamed as they shared their duties with rather unglamorous infantry units rather than fellow commandos.

However, 30AU did not have the necessary manpower for the task ahead. Such was the scope of operations within the Reich that the task was beyond their limited capabilities. Instead, T-Force had the transport, back-up and wherewithal to look after a force of scientists and specialists. Previous operations carried out by 30AU, where the primary focus was on intelligence rather than on technology, had not necessitated such a developed infrastructure. The Royal Marines had been equipped with fast-moving jeeps and were heavily armed, acting in a commando role – hardly suitable for taking a team of middle-aged metallurgists across the plains of northern Germany.

The first arrivals from 30AU were Lieutenant Commander Mitchell of the Royal Navy and Lieutenant Commander Lambie, attached to the unit from the United States Navy. In the weeks ahead these and other members of the Naval detachments forged a strong bond with T-Force, yet all the time retained a sense of independence that betrayed their earlier involvement in the campaign. As one Buckinghamshires' officer later recalled, the question was often asked of 30AU, 'Where are they now?'[11] This question, he later discovered, would remain relevant at almost any given point during the campaign.

It was later noted that 30AU appeared to spend much of their time either behind enemy lines or scouting around the Allied frontlines. In the words of Tom Pitt-Pladdy: 'They didn't want to have anything to do with us. You'd say you were going somewhere and would meet them there, but they'd end up thirty miles away.' When asked whether he considered this dangerous, one of the Royal Marines officers agreed, then stated plainly, 'The trouble is no-one can tell us where the enemy are. One simply goes on until an unfriendly incident occurs.'[12]

While T-Force was specifically established to ensure the equitable sharing of intelligence and research information, there were serious concerns that the independence of spirit earlier demonstrated by 30AU would prevent vital documents being shared between the Allies. During initial operations in the American 12th Army Group zone, the teams from 30AU felt their work was hampered. They were restricted to targets that had already been heavily shelled, which meant they were unable to move on targets with the speed they had grown used to in Italy and France. Later reports stressed how the Americans had thwarted many of their activities, believing them to be a 'private army' engaged in the removal of intelligence material for its own nefarious purposes. Part of the difficulty was that the Americans were uncertain over the correct handling of documents. They wanted everything sent via SHAEF while the marines insisted that all naval intelligence discovered within 21st Army Group's area of operations – regardless of whether the local units were British or American – belonged to the DNI. The marines stressed that it was for the DNI to share intelligence with its US equivalent. In March 1945 Brigadier Maunsell at SHAEF noted the American concerns about the flow of intelligence and sought to allay their fears: 'I think we can take it that, unless 30 Advanced Unit start playing tricks, all will be well.'[13]

In one instance a compromise was agreed under which 30AU removed naval intelligence while the remaining documents were left for inspection by CIOS teams. However, at one location 30AU protested that documents were left without guard but this went unheeded by the Americans. As a result they were left in the building and were all burned by the next unit to be billeted in the facility. Such experiences did little to endear the various T-Forces to the Royal Marines.

Despite these restrictions, a group under the command of Lt Commander Dalzel-Job continued to push forward beyond the Rhine. Metallurgist John Bradley again accompanied Patrick Dalzel-Job, later writing home to describe the first target he visited after crossing the river. It was a lubricating oil factory on the outskirts of Duisburg: 'The destruction round about was pretty terrific, but now one was becoming rather accustomed to it. We did not spend long at the works as the Germans had earlier that day been putting long-range shells into the place, one of which wounded a colonel and killed two other ranks of T-Force.'

What really counted was reaching Köln (Cologne) and carrying out investigations of the targets around the city. To the north of the city, 30AU captured an 'opportunity target' which was not on the 'blacklists' but was a source of vast intelligence. The factory was producing equipment for use in guided rocket systems, jet- and rocket-propelled aircraft, and chemical fuels. They even discovered a suitcase full of papers relating to similar work being undertaken throughout Germany. One female member of staff, evidently a devout Nazi, fainted when she saw the nature of the documents seized by the marines. This intelligence coup was later described as one of the most profitable operations carried out by 30AU. Just ten days after the operation the Admiralty produced a 300-page book of translations of the seized documents.

In the final days of March, Dalzel-Job's detachment headed into Köln itself. Bradley wrote, 'You have no idea of what a devastated city looks like until you have seen Köln. There is literally nothing left but rubble until you get to the extreme outskirts.' The reason for the destruction was not lost to Bradley: 'Two German shells came over in rapid succession and burst only 50 yards away. They made a noise like an express train and were certainly too near for comfort. We and some nearby GIs beat a rapid retreat.'

30AU examined targets at the Wilhelm Schmidding works where, fortunately, the works manager was accommodating and offered no obstacles to the detachment. The factory staff had been ordered to carry out sabotage of the plant, but the manager had issued a counter-order, telling them no destruction should take place. Among the intelligence they discovered was research on torpedoes with a design of warhead known as 'Dynal'. This warhead was constructed of layers of papers, compressed and held together with resin. However, the assessors soon discovered the German research had been wasted and none of the torpedoes had ever been used operationally.

Another area of research was a torpedo 'pistol' mechanism that was found to be under development. The staff of the factory knew little about the mechanism but one revealed that an example had been used as a paperweight in one of the offices. However, an Allied soldier had already smashed it and, despite investigations, none of the parts could be found. Of more interest was a new and unfamiliar type of torpedo casing, about which even the German staff appeared to know little, not realizing that a new type of power was to be used to propel the torpedo.

The criticisms of the restrictions put on 30AU by the Americans were understandable, but, happily, the situation was to improve when 30AU came into closer contact with the British T-Force. Despite orders from SHAEF that T-Force elements were not to advance beyond the forward combat elements, it was soon discovered that 21st Army Group interpreted this order most liberally, allowing them 'almost absolute freedom of movement'.[14]

On 11 April, the detachment from the Buckinghamshire Battalion, led by armoured cars in a reconnaissance role, moved towards Hannover and into the American 84th Division's area of operations. It was a fine spring morning as they sped along the dusty autobahn towards the city, which US forces had reached the previous day. Entering the city, moving through the rubble-strewn streets, past shattered houses and still burning buildings, the Bucks and 30AU set up HQ in an abandoned Wehrmacht barracks. In the hours that followed the HQ became a hive of activity. Additional assessors began arriving – doubling their number from 10 to 20 – ready to be rushed to their targets. At the same time, reports began arriving from platoons that had secured their objectives. The good news was that many of the targets were in reasonably good condition, with just a couple burnt out; however, many were in the process of being ransacked by gangs of DPs desperate for loot. At the telephone repeater station, near the main railway station, a vast network of tunnels had to be cleared of DPs who had hidden underground while the battle had raged in the streets above them.

Unfortunately, the American signals staff responsible for ensuring the station was in working order had no idea how to operate the equipment. Instead, an officer of the Pioneer Corps rounded up the German technicians and forced them to work under an armed guard. As work continued to get the repeater station up and running, the British guards came under almost constant sniper fire.

At a post office sorting depot T-Force discovered all the mail sacks had been broken open and their contents had been strewn across the ground, covering an area of 30 metres by 10 metres (100 × 30 feet). After forcing out a gang of Italian labourers at bayonet point, all they could do was seal the area and hope that the post would eventually be sorted. This situation was repeated throughout the city as gangs of former slave

labourers and released POWs ignored the curfew and roamed
the streets, mostly in a state of intoxication. As Brian Urquhart
later reported, the city was gripped by the celebrations of the
displaced persons and one of Germany's biggest wine cellars
was completely consumed in three 'Hogarthian' days.[15]
Elsewhere, they ransacked shops, throwing looted goods out
into the streets to the crowds waiting below. The men of
T-Force watched these displays of lawlessness with a detached
interest. After all, Hannover was the American's responsibility
– it was their job to keep law and order. The city could burn
down around them so long as the T-Force targets were secure.

However, the looting carried out by Allied personnel sometimes did have an effect on T-Force operations. Assessors
pinching cars for themselves, and thus increasing the available
transport, was acceptable, but looting from targets was not. In
one instance it was found that staff of the military government
had taken models of German ships to decorate their offices.
These models were actually required by the teams of assessors
attached to T-Force by the Admiralty. The military government teams were informed that if they did not comply with
T-Force orders on the handling of equipment they would be
removed from the offices.

The prized target within Hannover was the headquarters of
the local Wehrkreis, or military area. No.16 Platoon, under the
command of Lieutenant Pethick, arrived to find that its previous occupants had just departed, leaving half-finished meals on
tables, plenty of heavily braided uniforms in cupboards and
fresh spring flowers on their desks. As the very heart of the
local military command structure the offices were soon scoured
for intelligence documents. This task was only fully realized following the arrival of a documents team whose labours were
greatly aided by the work of No.19 Bomb Disposal Company.
As they worked, the air was rent with the sound of explosions
as safes were blown open. One particular safe caused problems

for the officer in charge, entailing one hour's labour and defying the effects of three explosive charges. Still he endeavoured until one of the sappers began playing with the lock. After a few idle seconds of fiddling with the lock he stumbled upon the correct combination and the doors swung open, revealing the documents within.

As well as intelligence targets there were plenty of economic sites to be secured. The vast Hanomag truck factory was found to be divided into three separate sections and was far larger than could be guarded by the single platoon that had been given the task. All that could be done was to put a guard on the front gate and maintain search platoons throughout the premises. It was three days before they discovered that a group of Italian labourers were actually on one of the factory's upper floors.

Once the investigators were able to start their work they soon found plenty to interest them. As well as producing half-tracked vehicles, the factory had created mechanical parts for radar equipment. In addition, the metallurgists were fascinated to see that the Germans had been using sintered iron (created from heat-treated powder) as a substitute for copper in the production of driving bands for artillery shells.

At the factory of Maschinenfabrik Niedersachsen the investigators made further discoveries. The plant specialized in infra-red technology, which the Germans were developing for use in night-fighting. They discovered telescopes, large lamps and filters which the scientists believed to be all part of the same equipment. Within days the equipment was packaged up and flown back to the UK for rapid assessment. It was not just industrial concerns that were targeted. Professor Hase, a physicist specializing in infra-red technology and the head of the city's Technical Institute, was held for investigation for his work on measuring temperatures in gun barrels.

Elsewhere in Hannover, T-Force evacuated samples of altimeters and discovered a light metals factory that had been sharing its processes with the Japanese. A full guard was put on the factory, which was relatively undamaged, allowing proper investigation by experts in Japanese industry, called forward from SHAEF, who were able to interrogate the heads of departments.

Of particular interest was a Doctor Max Kramer, an aviation scientist who was located by an RAF team attached to T-Force. He had been placed on the 'blacklists' as the inventor of the Fritz X, a radio-controlled rocket bomb, and the Henschel 293, a radio-controlled glider bomb. The investigators soon discovered details of his latest projects. These were the X4 and X7, which were rocket projectiles for use against both air and ground targets. Under questioning, Dr Kramer revealed that flight of the projectile could be affected by lines that were spewed out in spools behind the rocket as it was in motion. He also revealed that some of his research work had been buried to keep it away from the Allied investigators. Such was the interest in his work that Dr Kramer became one of the first German scientists to be evacuated to the UK for further investigation.

At the city's Continental Gummiwerke the preliminary report of the assessors was 'extremely favourable'.[16] Specialists were called over from the UK to assess the finds, which included the development of synthetic rubber cable covers to be used at low temperatures and new designs to be used for aircraft tyres and fuel tanks. Also among the new processes discovered was one for softening synthetic rubber. Like all such new technology, samples were swiftly evacuated to the UK. Other finds included a process by which pure aluminium could be recovered from secondary aluminium scrap.

Throughout T-Force investigations discoveries were made that indicated a deliberate policy of concealing military research facilities. One investigation team was directed by an informer to a private house where they discovered a model torpedo testing-tank hidden under straw in the attic. They also found the results of tests including photographs taken with underwater cameras. The firm which had hidden the testing-tank was found to be engaged in research on hollow-charge projectiles used to project a cone of shrapnel at a target aircraft, thus negating the need for a direct hit.

While large-scale investigations proceeded in Hannover, the main body of T-Force continued to advance. As 21st Army Group progressed across northern Germany, the deployment of T-Force detachments became an increasingly polished art. The methods employed changed according to circumstances. For some priority targets T-Force used small reconnaissance parties who moved forward with the lead units, ready to exploit the situation and take their target. In more routine operations the detachment followed the lead divisions on to their targets. In all cases, once targets had been secured, both the troops and the assessors scoured the area for further 'targets of opportunity'.

At Buxtehude, T-Force led the British forces into town, along with the advancing armour of the 7th Armoured Division – the legendary 'Desert Rats'. Although the history of the 7th Armoured Division shows they captured the town, the reality was somewhat different. With targets in the town including the rear headquarters for the German Navy, T-Force moved ahead of the infantrymen whose task it should have been to clear the town of its defenders.

Officers of the Desert Rats told the Kingsmen they had enough tanks ready to take Buxtehude but did not have enough infantry. When T-Force offered to provide infantry cover, the Desert Rats agreed to advance on the condition they would leave immediately afterwards. With the defenders subdued and the targets secured, T-Force set about investigating the naval HQ. Rather than finding a hive of activity they were greeted by an ageing German admiral, who appeared limping on his stick. It turned out he was the only German man in the place. The rest were women from the German version of the Wrens. Tom Pitt-Pladdy soon received a message about the situation at the HQ: 'The first I knew of it was when I picked up a message from the commander of the detachment. I thought he was panicking. He said, "I must have reinforcements." It turned out the women were tearing the place apart. He placed sentries on the door but the women just pushed the sentries aside. Eventually he just opened the doors and told them to go home.'

When operating away from the main axis of advance, T-Force units were the first to enter many German towns. Tom Pitt-Pladdy explained how the tactics developed once T-Force was active within Germany: 'We were supposed to work behind the infantry and tanks. But because of pressure on the roads I chose to use the side roads. It didn't matter where the infantry were – I wasn't interested. But sometimes it didn't make me too popular with some of those at the HQ.' T-Force entered Bomlitz and Delmenhorst in this way. However, in the latter, the T-Force detachment occupied a Focke-Wulf factory, only to be forced to withdraw when enemy troops counterattacked the town.

While most T-Force detachments were fortunate not to have to fight for their targets, they were not taking part in some safe 'swan' through the countryside. It was a tense time for the men of T-Force as they left the safety of the main advance and drove into uncharted territory. Quite simply, the assault troops went wherever the German defenders were to be found while T-Force ignored the defenders and went to wherever a target was to be found.

Such was the fluid nature of the fighting during this period that T-Force operated in areas where the frontline seemed irrelevant. John Longfield recalled the experience of racing around northern Germany in a landscape that often seemed deserted: 'We were supposed to go ahead of the infantry alongside the tanks, but, as far as I could see, it seemed to be a load of chaos.

We were fired on – but usually only by these fanatic youngsters. Everyone else ignored us. We turned up in towns that hadn't even been captured. We just went into targets and took them over – otherwise, we had no idea what was going on.'

The sights encountered during the advance left an indelible impression on the infantrymen. One of the recent arrivals surveyed the scenes in the town of Münster:

> As we were passing through – snaking our way through the rubble – over to my right, about two hundred yards away, in the midst of all this desolation, was a young lady in her early twenties. She seemed to me to be immaculate in a pretty dress, as is ready to go to a party. I never took my eyes from her as she watched us disappear in the dust, and I wondered whether she was glad to see us, or was her heart full of hate?[17]

As they advanced, many of the T-Force detachments came under attack. Fortunately, some of their attackers were less than enthusiastic about continuing to resist the Allied advance, as Tom Pitt-Pladdy remembered: 'We ran into trouble at a German officer cadet school. But all they wanted to do was surrender. They came across a field at us and fired one volley – then they surrendered.' While Pitt-Pladdy attempted to find someone to hand his prisoners over to, he ordered that there was to be no looting: 'When I left all the Germans had been wearing black leather gloves. But when I came back I noticed something funny – all my men were wearing the Germans' gloves. But what could I do?'

While 'veteran' infantrymen like Longfield had plenty of experience of war, and an understanding of the extreme behaviour inspired by the psychological trauma of battle, others were experiencing the situation for the first time. Metallurgist John Bradley had to get used to passing through areas in which piles of dead soldiers lined the roads. He also witnessed the looting of civilian homes by Canadian troops and was surprised how their behaviour compared unfavourably with that of the British troops, despite the Canadians not having experienced their own land under attack by the Nazis. He later wrote home to describe the world he had entered: 'A party of Royal Engineers had been shot up by civilians . . . as a reprisal – questionable practice or not – they had blown up and set on fire most of the houses in Sogel itself. The village presented a striking contrast to what it had been when we first passed through.'

In Friesoythe a few days later Bradley saw the results of a further incident in which the Canadians had taken their revenge on the local population: they had set fire to the town. It transpired the troops had used flame-throwers after their colonel had been killed by a civilian. In the days that followed suggestions were made that the Canadians had deliberately destroyed the village in order to produce sufficient rubble to fill bomb craters in the local roads.

Despite the careful planning, the ever-changing situation ensured that no two operations were the same. In most cases the investigation teams were on hand to give a rapid assessment of the value of targets. In other cases, targets had to be kept occupied until specialist teams could be brought over from the UK to assess the finds. For targets selected by branches of the military, T-Force simply had to hold the target until the relevant units could move forward to take possession. Examples of such operations were the seizure of communications stations which were rapidly handed over to detachments from corps or division signals, while local government records were handed over to detachments from Civil Affairs or Military Government.

In the weeks following the crossing of the Rhine, T-Force spread out across the countryside, with each detachment heading into the unknown to reach its targets. One officer recalled driving 250 miles in a single day in order to deliver reports to

T-Force HQ. Priority was given to targets within Germany, with Dutch targets being all but ignored for the time being. It was a period of fluid movement with no settled frontlines. Everywhere across northern Germany, towns were bypassed by the main attack as the British advanced. Some towns and villages were surrendered without resistance, while elsewhere bitter battles were fought for possession of a single farmhouse. After miles of advancing unopposed, British units found themselves held up by determined teenagers armed with anti-tank rockets. For those brave enough to resist the advance the end was usually bloody – after five years of war few among the British soldiers were prepared to take any chances. For those at the spearhead of the advance, any notion of war as a gentlemanly sport had long since been abandoned.

As T-Force began to spread out across northern Germany its HQ became preoccupied with the question of administration. Unlike other formations within 21st Army Group, T-Force detachments could be deployed anywhere within the British area of operations. Rather than make demands upon the individual corps to which detachments were attached, T-Force supplied itself with food, petrol and ammunition, thus ensuring it did not become a burden on its hosts. By working independently, although making plenty of work for the drivers whose job it was to distribute fuel to the various detachments, T-Force was able to remain self-contained and self-reliant – and ready to head to any target at a moment's notice.

For all the careful planning and controlled allocation of investigators, the duplication of target assessment became a thorny issue. This situation was encountered by the detachment of the Buckinghamshire Battalion while in Hannover. It soon became clear to the military commanders that there was little coordination of effort between the various assessors. As a result, the precious transport resources were being used to ferry individual scientists from location to location. Furthermore, much of their work was also wasted as assessors made repeated visits to targets that had already been investigated. To counter this, each morning a conference was held to coordinate activities. This gave the scientists the opportunity to read earlier reports on any targets they might have an interest in, thus avoiding unnecessary duplication.

In addition to making best use of the limited transport available, the T-Force detachment commanders also took further action to alleviate the shortage of trucks and jeeps. Instead of waiting for official transport, they began to acquire civilian cars. Although unauthorized, such individual acquisitions became commonplace within a country on the verge of defeat. Some cars were simply pinched from their owners, others were acquired by soldiers who swapped them for scarce supplies such as soap, coffee and cigarettes. After all, those Germans who owned cars had little use for vehicles since there was no petrol.

Furthermore, many officially sanctioned investigators arrived at targets to find that others – who they referred to as 'witches' since they 'flew over everyone's heads on broomsticks' – had got there before them. It seemed that some of the agencies who had sponsored investigations wanted them to reach the targets first, ensuring that other interested parties did not receive the relevant information. This competition, entirely outside the spirit of T-Force operations and reflecting the chaos that had been seen during some operations in Italy, made life difficult for Brigadier Pennycook and his staff. Investigators began rushing to targets, ever mindful that someone else might reach them first. Elsewhere, they arrived at targets only to discover the relevant technology had already been spirited away in what Pennycook later described as 'semi-piratical expeditions'. To deal with this the Brigadier made it clear that all searches were to be carried out only on behalf of CIOS, following their lists and carried out under the auspices of T-Force. The threat was clear: all teams not passing through official channels were to be arrested and expelled from the theatre.

Despite T-Force's early successes, the unit had not been working at its full strength. It was not until well after the commencement of operations that T-Force finally acquired all of its allotted vehicles. Only on 19 April – almost a month after the Rhine crossing – were the lorries of the smokescreen companies finally free to join the advancing detachments. As one Buckinghamshire Battalion officer later noted: 'We felt like patting each one on the bonnet, so long had we waited for them.'[18] To aid T-Force's progress, its vehicles were often marked with official 'Priority T-Force' signs and gave the designation of the Corps to which the unit was attached.

The list of targets in every town was staggering – post offices, power stations, factories, railway control offices, electricity sub-stations, telephone repeater stations, Nazi Party offices and research laboratories all had to be searched. The list of successes continued throughout April. The town of Papenburg revealed complete records for all the concentration and labour camps in the area, while in nearby Embsen a nitrogen fixation and nitric acid plant was secured, with samples of the fuel evacuated quickly to the UK for further investigation by rocket propulsion specialists. While the fuel was being examined other specialists arrived in Germany to examine the rocket fuel tanks that had been found within the plant. At Delmenhorst, D Company of the King's Regiment secured a helicopter factory, telephone repeater station and a Focke-Wulf aircraft factory.

Elsewhere, investigations at Nienburg revealed a radar assembly plant while at Twistringen diesel submarine engines, radar equipment, range finders and periscopes were all uncovered. At Starkshorn the assessors set to work at a naval depot where they found a new style of marine mine that could be ejected from a submarine torpedo tube.

Both economic and military targets competed for attention from the overworked T-Force soldiers and scientists. At Bentheim a natural gas field, capable of producing 340,000 cubic metres of gas each day, was secured. This plant had previously been used to provide the power for a synthetic rubber production plant in the Ruhr. Fortunately, the wells had been sealed with mud and destruction of the plant had been prevented. Such targets would soon play a vital role in re-establishing German industry in the postwar period.

With the investigators hard at work assessing the vast number of targets, there came the question of ensuring their reports were typed up, collated and despatched to the correct locations with the utmost speed and efficiency. However, there were too few clerical staff available to type up reports. As a result, after a long day riding across the countryside in the back of an open lorry, many investigators found themselves having to hammer out reports on typewriters looted from their targets. All the reports needed to be indexed and duplicated, keeping the nine men of the HQ's intelligence section fully employed all day at typewriters and copying machines, completing around 50 reports each day. As they worked, they were interrupted by an endless stream of assessors and specialists, all bringing in new reports or asking for copies of their earlier efforts.

If that were not enough, the intelligence office at T-Force HQ soon became home to a weird and wonderful collection of equipment that had been collected from various targets. Many of these were supposed to be swiftly packaged and sent to eager recipients back in the UK. The only problem was that many of the assessors were uncertain of who was supposed to receive particular items. As a result, the office took on the appearance of a store for second-hand industrial equipment. It was a situation that was only resolved as the system for despatching equipment was refined and improved. Despite these improvements, there was no relief for the intelligence office staff, who continued to work day and night to keep up with the vast number of reports.

The burden of administrative effort was not the only thing with which the teams of 'civilian' assessors had to cope. Despite the opening difficulties, the teams sent from the UK had no choice but to adapt to life in the field. John Bradley recalled having to spend a night in a farm building, being offered the choice of sharing bed space with either the cattle or the pigs. Instead, he chose to sleep outdoors. Elsewhere, he found himself struggling to fall asleep as he listened to the noise made by the rats that were occupying the rafters above him. He also recalled how the changing circumstances of the operation meant that he did not have sufficient clean clothing.

However, the discomfort of life in a war zone was nothing compared to the experience of being right at the front. Bradley later recorded how he had spent one night sleeping just 70 metres (230 feet) away from a gun battery and at one location his arrival had been greeted by the sound of incoming mortar rounds that fell just 30 metres (100 feet) away. He also noted how his team were actually further advanced than the Germans' target, an HQ where casualties were inflicted by the mortar rounds. They were even told not to use wireless sets, to prevent the enemy picking up their signals and targeting their positions. Unlike some of the other scientists and members of investigation teams, he was able to make light of his less than comfortable situation, writing home to his wife: 'C'est la guerre!'

Despite the best efforts of Brigadier Pennycook to organize the positions of his units, the situation in Germany was too fluid to allow for all movements to be controlled. With no single frontline, every movement of troops was fraught with danger. Not only did they face the continual threat of German resistance, the trail of destruction that was forged by the advancing armies left whole areas in ruins. Detours had to be made to bypass locations where bridges had been destroyed. Whole routes were determined by the needs to avoid pockets of resistance or cratered roads and the rubble that awaited the arrival of British bulldozers.

Since the plains of northern Germany were the traditional training grounds of the German army, it was little wonder that the area through which the British were advancing included a significant number of military research facilities. One of the most interesting targets was the Rheinmetall-Borsig research establishment at Unterlüss, near Munster. This was one of the foremost small arms research stations in Germany. Technicians and designers were all seized by T-Force and held ready for interrogation.

At Meppen T-Force took control of a vast military–industrial complex. This was the testing and proving range for Krupps, the German steel giant which was responsible for the production of so many of the Wehrmacht's field guns. On 9 April one platoon from C Company, 1st Buckinghamshire Battalion, alongside one section of bomb disposal engineers and a squad of armoured cars, were sent to occupy the site. The town had earlier been reported clear of enemy troops by an armoured patrol which had entered the previous evening and met no resistance. Yet T-Force was forced to enter the town under sniper fire. Fortunately, the local 'Home Guard' who had been detailed to defend the town swiftly surrendered, leaving the Buckinghamshires to carry on with their investigations.

It soon became clear that this was a target which could not be investigated hastily, nor one that could be successfully investigated by such a small detachment. John Bradley, who was detailed to help with the investigation, later wrote home to describe the approach to the site: 'We reached Meppen in the early afternoon after a journey on some of the worst dirt roads I have been on. At one place some vehicles were bogged down for an hour . . . All the traffic had to come over one appalling stretch of road as by now we were in the narrow confines of the spearhead and the better roads had not been cleared.'

Little sabotage had taken place at the facility. Dauntingly, the site was home to various research centres and even a testing range which allowed the firing of projectiles up to 36 miles. At the range were found practically every type and calibre of shell, cartridge case and propellants used by the Germany army and navy. In addition, investigators found a selection of experimental shells, including some that were rocket-assisted, others that were skirted and some that contained a specially shaped propellant charge for use in naval guns.

Closer inspection also revealed the Germans to have been developing a new design for a 16-inch gun and super-heavy anti-aircraft weapons. The finds were swiftly crated ready for evacuation on instruction from assessors who found the equipment to be of 'extreme technical and scientific interest'.[19] Three tank hulls that carried a new 7.5-inch gun were also uncovered, suggesting that the Germans had been working on a new, super-heavy tank. These immediately attracted close attention, leading investigators to report: 'the knowledge obtained may well save Britain and the US more than years of research and costly experimental work'.[20]

As well as laboratories and a full complement of staff there was a meteorological research station and a further research unit found to be investigating flying conditions at stratospheric altitudes. Elsewhere within the plant were found documents and equipment relating to at least ten new types of 'radiosounds' – balloons with radio sets attached which were used for transmitting data. Most importantly, investigators located documents indicating the type of equipment that had been sent to Japan.

During investigations of the facilities, John Bradley encountered at least one German who was honest in his feelings towards those occupying his country: 'This chap was at least honest; he admitted to being a Nazi, was proud to be one and said he hated our very guts; he said the war had taken a bad turn for them but thought that it was only temporary and that they would win in the end. He did not say if it was to be in this war or the next!'

With so many targets to be investigated, D Company of the Kingsmen were also sent to Meppen. Once in place they searched a factory producing naval firing equipment and aiming equipment for anti-aircraft guns. While some parts of the establishment were in ruins other areas were fully intact, yielding positive results for the investigation teams. They discovered technical documents for the production of anti-aircraft predictor equipment that aided the firing of shells against target aircraft. The predictor equipment itself was soon discovered and was found to be of the utmost importance since there were only two known examples in existence. Along with the equipment, T-Force also secured the technicians who had worked on the predictor, holding them until a specialist could arrive to debrief them.

While at Meppen, the troops of T-Force were given the additional task of securing and investigating the network of slave labour and concentration camps in the area. Large amounts of documentation were found by the troops, who were given tours of the camps in order to acquaint themselves with the gruesome details of life for the enemies of the Nazi regime. At Neuengamme, where the main camp records had been destroyed, other records were uncovered showing the entire system by which slave labour was exploited in the area. This was of interest to economic investigators who hoped to find information about assets held by the SS.

The realities of the system of slave labour and concentration camps was noted by John Bradley who witnessed the scenes at one camp after his column took a diversion from the main line of advance: 'Most of the inmates were living skeletons and a more shocking sight I have rarely seen.' As another officer noted, exposure to the crimes of the Nazi regime 'had the right effect on the men, and made enforcement of the non-fraternisation rule unnecessary'.[21]

No stone was left unturned. As a result of investigations, the most unlikely locations were found to contain items of interest – often at 'targets of opportunity' that had not been mentioned in the original 'blacklists'. It was a policy that was to produce positive results in the weeks ahead. Near Bassum, outside Bremen, investigators discovered that naval equipment had been dispersed around the area and hidden in cottages, barns and farmhouses. Included among the finds were complete sets of gun control apparatus for battleships. The policy of industrial dispersal meant that T-Force investigators even uncovered parts for Tiger tanks being produced in a bicycle factory. Another example of industrial decentralization, discovered when John Bradley's team went to look for alcohol in a distillery, was the use of the distillery's cellars for the storage of aircraft parts.

As investigations continued, the soldiers of T-Force began to become increasingly familiar with the weapons of war that had blighted their lives for almost six years. When the Blohm + Voss aircraft factory at Wensendorf was occupied, the troops found they had taken possession of an aircraft plant in which Messerschmitt Me 262 jet fighter aircraft were assembled. The fighters – high-speed and in advance of any Allied fighter aircraft in service at the time – were just the latest in a long line of highly advanced Luftwaffe planes. With the plant safely under British control the troops could rest easy that no more fighters would leave the production line. As well as valuable technical documents, five directors of the company were detained, ready to be interviewed by experts from the RAF. Meanwhile, at Hesedorf, T-Force took control of the vast GAF ammunition dump, with its six-mile long perimeter fence.

Within the facility they discovered an improved version of the HS293 glider bomb that was soon evacuated for analysis.

The hectic work continued throughout April, as one veteran recalled: 'Most of the time I didn't have a clue what we were doing. Everything was rush, rush, rush.'[22] Sitting in the backs of lorries, moving through a landscape devastated by war, seemed odd for the troops. Sometimes they found themselves in towns where dead bodies were strewn in the streets and buildings were still ablaze; elsewhere, they found themselves driving rapidly through the countryside, along roads and country lanes seemingly untouched by war.

The youngsters who had only recently arrived from the UK were given a slightly unreal introduction to war. Many were nervous, uncertain of what might happen next, yet conversely some of them were eager for action. The 'old-hands' – men who had seen more than enough action in the months before – were able to approach this period with a sense of calm. They were unaffected by dead bodies and unmoved by the sight of shattered buildings. After the bitter fighting of Normandy just to move along roads in relative safety was a bonus.

As the Kingsmen continued to advance across the plains of northern Germany, 30AU undertook further 'T' duties within the US zone of operations. During April the marines received permission to enter the US zone to search for enemy naval intelligence personnel in the Bad Sulza area. At one target building, the team made detailed measurements and scale drawings so that they could search the interior for any hidden rooms. Teams went from room to room systematically tapping walls, opening all doors and measuring the internal spaces. The investigations bore fruit, leading to the discovery of a boarded-up cellar. Among the documents discovered were the home addresses of some of the most important members of staff in German naval intelligence. Other documents indicated the methods that had been used by the Germans to gather intelligence on the navies of the Allies.

Following up on the intelligence found during the search, 30AU moved on to inspect the Schloss Tambach, which contained probably the unit's most notable intelligence haul. Within the target were the entire archives of the German navy from 1850 to 1944. There were copies of the log books of all German U-boats and surface craft, copies of High Command orders and minutes of naval meetings. In all, it was a complete picture of the German navy during the Second World War. As a bonus, they even located some of the historical research staff who worked at the site, who helped 30AU to make sense of all the documents.

As the advancing army moved forward, not all of the marines went with them. Instead, 30AU continued the vital work of searching for those documents and research facilities that had not been examined during the earlier phase of operations. In the French zone the unit met some resistance from the French authorities. At one location the team came across a German naval gunnery research station, with its ranges, laboratories and archives intact. However, the French refused them access to the site since it adjoined the Mauser rifle manufacturing plant. The French insisted the site be kept entirely at their disposal so they could use the plant for manufacturing rifles for their reforming army. So 30AU made requests via the American T-Force that the naval research plant be put under guard, passing on information to all the relevant agencies that the plant contained research that might prove vital in the continuing war against the Japanese. However, due to a signals mix-up, it was a full two months before any detailed evaluation of the plant was made.

The process of following up on documents already seized bore fruit for 30AU during this period. At the Daimler Benz works, a Royal Marine discovered documents relating to secret engine research that had been carried out locally. This led to a quarry in which experimental aircraft engines had been tested and stored.

What Patrick Dalzel-Job discovered during this phase of
operations was that the methods he had employed in France
were not applicable to the situation in Germany. It was clear
there was no way of getting ahead of the main Allied formations. The notion of swanning around behind enemy lines was
not valid – there was simply too much hard fighting to be
done to make such a move possible. Despite the changing situation, the marines of 30AU found plenty of opportunity to
confront the enemy. On 13 April Dalzel-Job's unit discovered
there were two farmhouses full of German troops 'on the star-
board bow' near the town of Bakum. The marines
dismounted their vehicles with evident enthusiasm, eager for
an opportunity to put their training into practice. They carried out a textbook assault on the enemy positions, resulting
in the capture of 13 prisoners, who were quickly interrogated
by 30AU's officers.

During the advance into Germany, the Royal Marine commandos of 30AU had to come to terms with being a part of
T-Force. For some among them this was unacceptable. Their
lack of enthusiasm was strongly expressed by Patrick Dalzel-Job
in his memoirs in which he described T-Force as 'cumbersome'
and a 'retarding influence'. He was also critical of T-Force's
methods: 'It was indeed quite satisfied to enter its targets
behind the troops, and its function was to look after whatever
documents and material remained at that stage, rather than
attempting to forestall removal or destruction.' The criticism
continued: 'T-Force usually arrived too late to do much good
and (like most non-fighting soldiers) their guard-troops were
often more interested in private looting than in securing enemy
intelligence.'[23] As many in T-Force later observed, how could
Dalzel-Job have even known what the rest of T-Force was
doing? When 30AU were tearing around the countryside
uncovering their targets they were seldom in contact with the
Kingsmen, or even T-Force HQ. Even individual company

commanders often had little idea of what was happening at platoon level – so how could outsiders have known?

At the same time as the marines were being critical of the rest of T-Force, 30AU's own faults were being assessed at T-Force HQ. Writing in an official report, Brian Urquhart related how relationships were not as smooth as should have been expected: 'Their dislike of doing guard duties or of following the most simple routine channels for evacuation of documents, information or equipment, made them stimulating but somewhat uneasy companions, and their exact relationship to our own naval investigators was always somewhat of a mystery. Their predilection for small armoured sorties in front of the main advance showed admirable daring but was sometimes a little difficult to fit in to the general plan of T-Force activities.'[24]

It seemed there was little chance of the two factions coming to a mutually acceptable operational methodology. Patrick Dalzel-Job's attack on the soldiers of T-Force – right the way down from Brigadier Pennycook to the lowliest infantrymen, pioneers or engineers – was unjustified. Throughout the advance into Germany there were numerous occasions when the men of T-Force took their lives in their hands to ensure they reached their targets in time. Every time their lorries drove off from the main axis of advance they were entering uncleared territory – effectively going behind enemy lines. This was exactly the tactic that Dalzel-Job had been so proud of doing in Normandy.

In many ways his Royal Marines – all fully trained commandos – were doing exactly what they had volunteered to do, but for those in the rest of T-Force, the situation was very different, which made their achievements all the more remarkable. For while most 'special forces' – the fabled commandos, paratroopers and SAS – were made up of volunteers who were possessed of a drive and a determination to see through their missions, the soldiers of T-Force were a somewhat different breed. Rather than being volunteers filled with a sense of daring, they were ordinary infantrymen, pioneers, engineers and ex-gunners who had never expected to be given such a vital task. Some, of course, were volunteers but in the main they were conscripts from a range of backgrounds who had been thrown together to form a uniquely British 'special force'. Though few realized it at the time, the future potential of the West's military research was placed in the hands of a unit in which some of the men were deemed unfit for frontline service.

April 1945 was a chaotic month for all in Germany. As the advance moved inexorably forward, pockets of German troops were inevitably left behind. With no definite frontline every mobile unit found itself in danger of attack. Thrown into this volatile equation were liberated POWs, who had surged from their camps in the hope of a rapid journey home, and vast numbers of former slave-labourers who had been let loose into the German countryside. On 13 April, T-Force had received the order that all personnel below medical category A2 were to be replaced by A1 reinforcements, with just administration staff of the lower categories being retained. In T-Force the decision was taken for those being withdrawn to be redeployed to the unit's transit camp.

Among the latest batch of reinforcements who joined the King's at Bomlitz was the teenage ex-gunner Ken Moore:

> There were really two versions of the 5th King's Regiment. There were the old pre-war Territorial Army men and then there were the youngsters – like me – who joined as part of T-Force. I was in a batch of 92 A1 men who joined at that time. We were never told anything about T-Force duties – we were just told to get into the 3 ton truck and we went off to Rodenburg. There we spilled out into a field and they counted us out – so many into A Company – so many into B Company – so many into HQ company.

Moore was immediately sent to the HQ Company where he was attached to a liaison officer, 'Jock' Lawson, whose job it was to travel between the headquarters and the forward detachments. Moore acted as the Bren gunner on the officer's armoured car and found himself 'tearing around here there and everywhere'. At one moment they might be at the front, liaising with a Corps HQ to stop firing long enough for T-Force to move on a target. The next, they might be at a target discussing what had been found. Effectively, the liaison officer was fully employed attempting to keep HQ informed of where a detachment was working at any given time. On Moore's very first day with T-Force he found himself visiting a slave labour camp attached to a target factory – it was a clear indication of what they were fighting for. The first people he met were prisoners from the Channel Islands, a couple and their child who had been forced to work as slaves for the Nazis.

Despite the arrival of the replacement troops, there was one final task for some of the old hands before they would be withdrawn: Lieutenant Tom Pitt-Pladdy found himself embroiled in battle outside the town of Bomlitz with a group of lower-graded infantrymen from C Company of the 5th King's. Pitt-Pladdy and 13 Platoon were examining the Wolff shotgun factory, which had been used for making V2 rocket propellant and a product named 'DIGL', a substitute for nitro-glycerine – considered by assessors to be 'of special interest'[25] – when Pitt-Pladdy was ordered to report to his company commander. At company HQ Major Frank Denton informed Pitt-Pladdy of his next task. An escaped French officer had reported that a dozen German marines were holding a nearby farmhouse, having just looted the wreckage of a bombed train. Within the farmhouse were 20 civilians, believed to be Displaced Persons, who the Germans were holding as hostages. As Pitt-Pladdy remembered: 'I was given the job. They gathered together a scratch party or thirty or so chaps – they were all B and C grades who were on their way back to the holding unit. But it wasn't like an ordinary infantry platoon. I wouldn't say they were a rabble, but they were just 30 odds and sods.'

Given just these infantrymen and three Humber armoured cars, Pitt-Pladdy was told to capture the German position. Pitt-Pladdy was astounded that he had been ordered to attack a well-protected farmhouse full of German marines with these lower-grade infantrymen. Even first-rate assault troops would have been offered either artillery or armoured support to achieve their objective. Despite his concerns, and the fact that he was not even an infantry officer, Pitt-Pladdy realized he just had to get the job done. Fortunately, his training had equipped him for the task: 'I wasn't worried about leading the patrol because earlier in the war I had been to battle school and had been a sergeant-instructor, teaching Bren gunnery. So I was a first-class Bren gunner.'

After a quick drive, Pitt-Pladdy prepared his men for the attack: 'We got there and found that dug across the road was a machine-made channel – about nine feet deep and ten feet across. So nobody was going up that road.' Held up by the anti-tank ditch, he ordered the infantrymen to deploy in woods overlooking the farmhouse and then took the armoured cars down a small lane to another position overlooking the farmhouse. Having stopped to open a gate, allowing the armoured cars to advance, Pitt-Pladdy recalled what happened next:

> They drove like a bat out of hell up the road and opened fire on the farmhouse. It was a bit of a blunder really because the Germans weren't in the farmhouse, they were in the other building sorting out their loot. After closing the gate, I went back to my car to find the gunner laying on the floor with his hands over his ears. My first two cars opening fire on the farmhouse brought the Germans out of the stables only about 30 to 40 yards away – they were blazing away with sub-machine pistols.

As the German marines left the stables they were actually behind the first two armoured cars. The British gunners attempted to turn their turrets and deploy their weapons, and Pitt-Pladdy's car joined in: 'Bringing up the rear, I caught them in the open so I fired the Bren gun at them – as they turned round and fired at me. They were sitting ducks and were treated accordingly . . . one or two ran away, the rest threw down their guns or lay on the ground. Three of the marines were dead, two slightly wounded, the other three stood hands held high.'

The prisoners were taken back to C Company HQ where they made a stupid mistake. Upon being handed over to the company sergeant major, the prisoners gave the Nazi salute. The Company Sergeant Major was not amused – he was a Liverpool man whose family had been killed during the Blitz. As a punishment he found a metal bust of Hitler that had been on display within a local factory and, giving the prisoners a hammer, he told them they would remain outside in the pouring rain until the bust had been destroyed. The two wounded prisoners were more fortunate: they were told to bury the dead marines and then instructed to make their way to their homes in Hamburg. As Pitt-Pladdy later admitted: 'I couldn't do anything else with them.'

CHAPTER 5

To the Bitter End

'I was a member of an official looting party.'

Steve Wallhead, 5th King's Regiment.[1]

Passing through the large ornamental gates, decorated with eagles and swastikas, the soldiers looked around at their latest target. Like so many others, it was virtually deserted. The staff had either fled or were in hiding, fearful of the reaction of the British soldiers. Looking around, the soldiers had little idea of what the numerous buildings might contain. Still, they all needed to be secured and searched. Section by section, they began to make their way through the office blocks. Some offices were still neat and tidy; others were strewn with documents and chemical equipment. One room soon caught the soldiers' attention. Numerous photographs had been thrown on the floor. Crouching down to look at what they had found, many of the images were dull – photographs of laboratories, test tubes and beakers. Then something else struck them: photographs of people. Not just anybody, but people with haunted looks in their eyes and hideous marks on their skin. Their cropped hair and gaunt faces marked them as the inmates of concentration camps. Those same gaunt faces were inflamed with blisters and lesions. They were 'guinea pigs' in a cruel programme of military experimentation. As detailed later in this chapter, T-Force had just seized the German army's main chemical research and production plant.

As April progressed, T-Force moved through swathes of the
north German plain. This was the area that had traditionally
been the training grounds of the German army. As a result,
the area was also home to numerous factories and
military–industrial research centres, all of which had been central to the technological advances that had taken the Nazis to
the brink of world domination. From tanks and small arms to
rockets and jet fighters, all had been designed and built in this
region. Not only that, but new weapons continued to roll off
the drawing boards and production lines even as Hitler's
regime collapsed around him. It was little wonder that the
'blacklists' produced by CIOS were teeming with targets to be
occupied. In the final days of the European war the soldiers
and investigators of T-Force would be astounded and
impressed by what they found.

One of the locations that was home to many such targets was
the town of Celle. Close to Bergen-Belsen, where the British
uncovered the hideous concentration camp in which the Nazi's
enemies had perished in their thousands, Celle became the
focus of attention as the entire world was stunned by evidence
of quite how depraved the Nazis had been. For a moment it
seemed that everything else had lost importance as shocked soldiers surveyed the scenes. As Vic Woods remembered: 'We
could see the people – they were just walking about. It was
unbelievable.' Despite being witnesses to these horrors, the soldiers of T-Force had little opportunity to examine the situation;
instead, they had numerous targets to investigate.

These scenes of horror were not confined to the concentration camps. For the men of 30AU the true nature of the Third
Reich was revealed when they entered the rocket production
facilities at Nordhausen, where slave labour had been employed
to construct the weapons that Hitler believed might turn
around Germany's descent towards defeat. For men like Reg
Rush, the scenes left an indelible impression:

We went underground where they had been working on these engines. There were bodies piled up – the smell never leaves you. To see it was indescribable. There were survivors there but there was only a handful of us, there was nothing we could do. We had our job to do, we did it and carried on to the next one. If you were there, you'll never forget it. If you were not there, no words can ever describe it. Nightmares still bring these things back to you. I could not believe that human beings could do that to other human beings.

Under orders from their officers, the men of the Buckinghamshire Battalion set up noticeboards showing photographs of the liberation of Belsen. They also went on tours of the slave camps. Officers noticed that these tours caused their men to feel increasingly bitter towards the German population, making them more than willing to turn locals out of their homes without any 'tender thoughts'. One of the officers noted: 'This is as it should be and is encouraged officially. Some of the men turned quite green when they saw some of the emaciated bodies and sights in these camps.'[2] As one officer later noted when a German family complained about being forced from their home, insisting the British should find some Nazis to make homeless: 'Before we told them to stop arguing and do as they were told, we pointed out that since we had arrived in their blighted country we had not found a single self-confessed Nazi but everyone had taken great pains to impress on us that they were non-Nazi.'[3]

While some British units searched Celle for supplies to feed and clothe the pitiful survivors of Belsen, T-Force had other concerns. Outside the town, the unit made some startling discoveries. After travelling through deep, dark woodland, they reached a gated perimeter. Beyond it was the entrance to a tunnel. With some soldiers left to guard the entrance, others – including experts attached to the unit by the RAF – moved in to search the facility. What they found was a vast underground aircraft factory belonging to the Focke-Wulf company, whose fighters had earlier plagued the skies of Europe. Entering the premises the soldiers were shocked to uncover two miles of underground passages in which the aircraft were constructed. Such discoveries started to reveal to them how Germany had been able to continue producing aircraft and military equipment despite the nightly pounding of their cities by the Allied bombers. At a nearby aircraft factory, an RAF unit attached to T-Force seized the premises while the firm's directors were in the middle of a conference to discuss how the plant should be evacuated.

As a number of aviation targets were seized by T-Force, the RAF became increasingly interested in what had been located. To investigate these aircraft a number of specialists were despatched from the Royal Aircraft Establishment (RAE) Farnborough, to assess the finds. Among them was Captain Eric 'Winkle' Brown, a highly experienced Fleet Air Arm test pilot. During his work as a test pilot at Farnborough he had specialized in testing captured enemy aircraft and eventually held the distinction of having been the only man ever to fly every major combat aircraft of the Second World War. His experience – in particular his involvement in test flying British jets and his knowledge of the German language – made him ideal to investigate the new designs of jet fighters under development in Germany.

Prior to travelling to Germany, Brown was already aware of the advances made in aviation by the Germans. They had jet fighters in operation, were employing rocket planes and had pioneered the use of ejection seats in combat aircraft. Scorch marks shown on reconnaissance photographs had first revealed the existence of rocket-powered planes, and the British were eager to find out as much as possible about German research before it fell into the hands of the Russians, French or Americans.

Captain Brown flew into Germany on 19 April, landing at Fassburg near Lüneburger Heide (Luneburg Heath). Nearby were important T-Force targets including the Göttingen aeronautical research centre. He soon followed the advancing armies into Schleswig-Holstein where T-Force reports indicated the discovery of Messerschmitt Me 262 jet fighters and Me 163 rocket planes at Husum airfield. It did not take Brown long to fully appreciate the qualities of the Me 262, noting it as having colossal firepower and being 'the most formidable aircraft of WW2'.[4] Despite his vast experience, test flying the Me 262 was Brown's first encounter with a swept-wing aircraft, a design that would later dominate aircraft design. In tests he discovered that it could reach speeds of up to 914km/h (568mph), a full 196km/h (122mph) faster than the latest version of the Spitfire. The tests also revealed that the immense speed of the jet fighter meant that, by the time it came into the range of enemy bombers, it had just two seconds in which to carry out its attack. After those two seconds, the Me 262 sped past the bombers and into the distance.

The uncertain nature of the time was shown by a number of incidents around Celle. While units of T-Force remained in the town to investigate the targets, the rest of the army moved swiftly on – driving across northern Germany in the race to defeat the enemy. However, with no definite frontline, danger was never far away. David March recalled the fluid nature of the fighting, as his section was sent to investigate a bridge north of Celle:

We parked up nearby and walked up the road. Suddenly we noticed two Germans laying flat on their bellies in the road – ready to fire. But the interpreter called out to them to surrender. They stood up – they were covered with ammunition belts and hand grenades – they could have picked us off but luckily they didn't bother. We got them on the vehicle and were driving

back. As we were going along I saw movement in the woods so
I let off a burst of fire, just to scare them off. So that was
another lucky escape. It was a tense time.

In addition to the standard military weapons under development in the region, there were scientists working on projects
that were far more chilling. At Celle, T-Force made one of its
most important discoveries. As the 5th King's Regiment's
Intelligence Officer Lieutenant Ken Davenport remembered,
'My intelligence office had reports from Combined Intelligence
Objectives Sub-Committee (CIOS, or CHAOS as we fondly
termed the organization) that a silk factory in Celle was being
used as a cover for an interesting physics laboratory.'[5] When
the facility was studied it seemed to be of particular interest –
one whose work would prove to be of significant importance in
the months that followed.

Although his role was that of HQ liaison officer, Brian
Urquhart took to roaming around the target areas accompanied by his batman Stannion, a former poacher from Norfolk
whose first name is not recorded. The two men entered the
German silk factory, which was not on the official CIOS lists,
but was simply an 'opportunity target' – just one of so many
that was searched in the spring and summer of 1945. Urquhart
was alerted to the target by Stannion, who had been searching
for loot and identified the factory as a lucrative source of silk.
As Davenport later recalled, the entrance to the cellar was
found by the two Kingsmen who were 'on the look-out for "a
bit of silk for the missus"'.[6]

Touring the factory in the company of the manager, there
seemed to be little of interest for them until Urquhart came
across a locked steel door which was to lead to the discovery of
something of far greater importance than rolls of fabric. The
manager was ordered to unlock it but refused, telling the British
soldiers he did not have the authority. Stannion then suggested

that they should shoot the lock out, something that his officer thought sounded ridiculously cinematic. Despite his better judgement, Urquhart unholstered his pistol and fired at the lock. Immediately the door opened, not as a result of the shooting, but because it had been unlocked from within. A white-haired man appeared and asked Urquhart, in perfect English, what he wanted. Explaining that they wished to discover what was going on within the facility, they were ushered inside and descended into two hidden rooms which they soon realized was a sophisticated research laboratory. The man soon identified himself to the two British soldiers. What he told them was virtually meaningless: 'I am Professor Groth and I am doing research on isolating isotopes of uranium.' Also secured at the facility were two other scientists, Suhr and Faltings. As was noted in official T-Force records kept at the time, the team had been working on a 'de-atomisation bomb'.

Uncertain of what this might mean, Urquhart passed the message on to headquarters where the equally baffled Lt Colonel Ray Bloomfield sent a routine report to SHAEF about who – and what – Urquhart had discovered. He later wrote of the response: 'Within an hour a very excited officer was on the telephone to me. I was asked to transfer our conversation immediately to the BGS scrambler telephone; I was then told that Groth must be sent to London immediately for interrogation, escorted by an officer of field rank.'[7]

Urquhart knew for sure that this rapid reaction was proof they had stumbled on to a truly important discovery within the factory. On the following day, 22 April 1945, a group of British armoured cars arrived to escort Professor Wilhelm Groth to a nearby airfield. Several American military aircraft then landed, carrying American officers. However, as Brian Urquhart later recalled, their uncomfortable appearance in uniform betrayed the fact that they were really civilians – most likely senior scientists – who had been put into uniform for their trip to collect the professor. Some appeared to be familiar with the German and were soon engaged in dismantling his laboratory, which was crated and sent back to England under escort of Major Hill and Commander Welsh.

Dr Groth was not the only nuclear scientist that fell into British hands during this period. One of most valuable human 'targets' discovered by T-Force was Professor Otto Hahn, the head of physics at the Technische Hochschule in Hannover. Professor Hahn – described by T-Force intelligence reports as 'the consultant to OKW on infra-red applications and designs of small sensitive bolometers and thermo-couples for gun barrel temperature measurements' – was most famous for his discovery of fission of uranium and thorium in medium-heavy atomic nuclei. First published in 1939, his work was groundbreaking and he was widely known to be one of the foremost scientists working in Germany. Such was his status that he had even been awarded the 1944 Nobel Prize for chemistry.

Varying stories late emerged about the discovery of Professor Hahn, including his capture by French troops operating in southern Germany. However, according to witnesses in the 5th King's Regiment, Professor Hahn handed himself over to a soldier from the regiment. Private Henry Hilton of the intelligence platoon had just stopped his vehicle in a town centre when he was approached by a distinguished-looking gentleman. The man requested to be taken to the British authorities. When Private Hilton failed to react as expected, the man spoke again: 'Perhaps I should introduce myself; I am Professor Hahn, chief scientist for atomic research in Germany.' Although Hilton had no idea what the professor was talking about – words like 'atomic' and 'nuclear' were meaningless to him at the time – he agreed to assist Hahn and he was soon handed over to someone in authority. Thus, one of the most notable scientists of the period came under British control.

Although talk of atom bombs and isotopes of uranium meant nothing to the ordinary soldiers of T-Force, there were other weapons in the Nazi arsenal that all among them had good reason to fear. As sons of the generation that had been scarred by the use of gas on the battlefields of the Great War, the men of T-Force were well acquainted with the horrific effects of chemical warfare. For many, one of the great mysteries of the Second World War was why the Nazis never used battlefield chemical weapons. Both sides had openly employed such weapons during the Great War and both sides again had the wherewithal to unleash these terrible weapons upon their enemies. Yet neither side descended to those depths.

Despite the reluctance to utilize their gas stocks, the Nazis strode ahead in developing new and extremely dangerous gases that could have been employed at any moment. Quite appropriately for a unit whose structure was based on the British Army's own chemical warfare specialists, it was T-Force who led the British efforts to uncover Nazi gas research. In the final weeks of war T-Force and its investigators uncovered disturbing evidence of new military gases that had been developed by German scientists. As one later report described the gases, they were: 'more effective than those heretofore produced'.[8] On 29 June 1945 a report in *The Times* hinted: 'The Germans had a new gas in great quantity, with certain qualities more deadly than any yet used.'

Following the crossing of the Rhine a number of chemical weapons stores had been uncovered. At Espelkamp the British had expected to find an ordinary ordnance dump, but it transpired to be a newly constructed chemical weapons production and shell-filling plant, while at Walsrode they found an ammunition dump that included gas-filled bombs for use in Nebelwerfer mortars. On 6 April T-Force HQ received a message that two dumps of German gas-filled ammunition had been discovered at Frankenberg and Hunstadt in the US area of operations. Brigadier Pennycook rapidly despatched staff from the chemical warfare (CW) element of his command to obtain gas samples for evacuation to the British military's chemical weapons research facility at Porton Down. It was a fine example of why the 'CW' and 'T' duties sat so well under a single command.

After so long waiting for any chemical weapons work, suddenly Brigadier Pennycook's staff had plenty to occupy them. On 7 April two gas dumps were uncovered at Espelkamp and Rehden. Again samples were swiftly evacuated to Porton Down. As quickly as T-Force could send samples back to the UK, the War Office fed back the results of tests on the sample weapons. Just two days after samples were despatched, a reply was received to inform the CW investigation teams that white rings painted on shells denoted the shell was filled with tear gas. More ominously, London reported that a green band identified a new, and previously unknown, gas. On 11 April the first example of a yellow-ringed shell was located and sent to Porton Down.

With the news that previously unknown gases had been uncovered, the staff at T-Force HQ found themselves hard at work. On 12 April an officer who had delivered shells to Porton Down returned to Germany with a file of additional information on the green-ringed gas shells. He was then despatched to Montgomery's HQ to report on the medical aspects of this new gas. On 21 April, 4 tons of chemical shells were crated and carefully despatched to the UK for closer investigation.

After so many years of speculation about the Nazi chemical warfare research programme, there was a genuine sense of excitement about what was beginning to be uncovered by T-Force. As noted in 'CW Intelligence Summary no.11', released on 18 April 1945: 'After years of fruitless search, stretching from the desert to the Rhine, Germany's stocks of gas ammunition have at last been uncovered.'[9] The writer was pleased to report that only one gas was not previously known.

Records showed the gas shells had never been sent west of the Rhine and that some – found in the US zone – had previously been in Poland. This was taken to mean the Germans had only ever intended their use on the eastern front. That said, the existence of shells painted a sand colour indicated that the gas shells had been prepared for, but not sent to, North Africa.

With the war drawing to a close, some of the German chemical warfare staff were eager to ingratiate themselves with the Allies. During early April the interrogation of Captain Schweckendien revealed that the chemical research facility at Spandau in the suburbs of Berlin had been relocated to Munsterlager – right in the line of the British advance. The captain explained that the facility was so crowded that he and other staff had been scattered around the area in whatever buildings were available. Such was the dispersal that the captain even had trouble locating his own laboratory on a map. Instead he stated it was 20 minutes walk from the railway station.

Despite some signs of openness, the investigators felt that Schweckendien was being deceptive. He denied all knowledge of some issues, only to admit his knowledge when asked a leading question. As they noted, he was eager to ingratiate himself with the Allies but was also keen to distance himself from any criminal behaviour in his gas research. It was an indicator of the mentality of so many of the scientists that fell into Allied hands during 1945 when Captain Schweckendien defiantly asked if the Allies would employ him to continue his research. He also asked for helping preserving his equipment, in particular his cherished Siemens electron-microscope that was vital to his research.

In the final week of April, T-Force's chemical staff set to work on what were possibly the most important chemical warfare plants in western Germany. The unit's first major breakthrough on gas research came on 22 April 1945 when they reached the German Army Anti-Gas Defence School in a location known as Raubkammer, or the 'Robber's Lair'. The vast plant, covering an area of 16 x 8km (10 x 5 miles), was situated just one mile outside the town of Munster. This area included both research facilities and areas of open ground on which gases had been tested, with all of the plants being referred to under the title 'Munsterlager'. As the T-Force teams spread out through the facilities they found 10km (6 mile) firing ranges, with protected positions used by researchers to examine the effects of chemical weapons. Some positions were constructed from thick concrete and sealed against chemicals. One of the shelters could accommodate up to 100 observers, while another was disguised as a windmill. Elsewhere, there were concrete gas-testing chambers, up to 27 metres (89 feet) high, and a 150mm artillery piece mounted on a 10-metre (30-foot) tower that was used for test-firing chemical-filled shells. Around the tower was a miniature railway that carried apparatus to record the effects of the gas.

Investigations revealed that Munsterlager was also the prime location for storing German gas munitions. One camp had around 100 underground bunkers, each with a capacity of 150 tons of chemical munitions. Most stocks in the plant had recently arrived from bases in eastern Germany, but orders had been issued that munitions should be dumped in the river Elbe rather than be captured. Subsequent interrogation of one German general showed that his troops had marked the gas stores and passed information to both British and German units fighting around Lüneburger Heide so that they could avoid accidentally damaging the chemical munitions. The orders not to enter the area did not apply to T-Force who had to secure the targets.

The gas school was located 20 miles north of Celle and just miles from the concentration camp at Bergen-Belsen. Entering the plant the troops found various storerooms and laboratories that appeared to have been hurriedly vacated; open notebooks

had been left out on desks, as if the staff had fled without warning. At first it seemed to the troops that there was little of
interest within the plant. However, one of the investigation
team, an American named Captain Kraus, noted that the floor
of a barn on the edge of the facility appeared particularly clean.
He searched the barn and discovered a trapdoor leading to an
underground chamber containing a laboratory filled with fur-
naces, rubber tubing and condensers.

At Raubkammer, where 800 German staff had been
employed, the T-Force teams found that bulk stores had been
evacuated and some documents had been burnt but fortunately
the laboratory and museum were intact and under guard.
Within days specialists from Porton Down arrived to investigate
the finds. The investigation teams found that Raubkammer was
not a research plant but a field testing station, where the
German military had tested its chemical weapons. This was
where the new German gases that had been developed at
Spandau were put through their paces as potential weapons.
The gases were tested on animals in a firing chamber in which
air was circulated by fans. Investigators also found that a larger
testing chamber was also under construction. Elsewhere, a gun
mounted on a 20-metre-high (65-foot) tower was used to fire
shells into the ground – simulating the arrival of an artillery
shell. After these tests had been carried out, live shells were
tested on the Raubkammer range. The T-Force teams also
found evidence of aircraft-mounted spraying devices – not
unlike those used for crop spraying.

Closer investigation of the facilities showed how far the Nazi
scientists had been prepared to go in their quest to discover
new methods of chemical warfare. Searching through the buildings the troops discovered photographic evidence that revealed
how inmates from the nearby concentration camp had been
used as guinea pigs. The photographs showed the effects of pro-
gressive exposure to the gases, leading one of the soldiers to

later write: 'It certainly appeared that we were winning the war not a moment too soon.'[10] The time spent guarding the facility gave Tommy Wilkinson a heightened understanding of why he was at war:

> The sheds that the staff had been working in were strewn with photographs. All over the place were photos of these people covered in blisters. So we had a clear idea what we were up against. They took in prisoners from the concentration camp at Belsen and experimented on them. We thought 'What sort of animals are we dealing with?' It made you realize you were doing the right thing. I was glad I'd took up arms.

At the chemical weapons field trials station, T-Force made further discoveries. Investigators noted that a gas-filling plant was still under construction, revealing how the enemy had continued research and development even as defeat loomed. Artillery shells containing new military gases were all found loaded on to a train in the sidings, indicating that it had been planned to evacuate them to be hidden elsewhere. In the days that followed intelligence suggested that gas stocks had been removed and hidden in disused mine shafts in the Harz mountains. Meanwhile, at Munsterlager, the Kingsmen experienced a gas scare, as recalled by Ron Lawton: 'It was bloody horrible. We suddenly felt we were having a hard time to breathe. We went to the guardhouse but it was full. Everyone's eyes were streaming. It was tear gas – a cylinder or shell had been damaged and the gas had escaped.' What was clear to the Kingsmen was that they were lucky it was a tear gas shell that had leaked rather than one of the more dangerous gas shells stored around the site.

Even as the specialists arrived at these plants, there was a genuine need to take care. The investigation of gas research facilities presented a new problem for the unit's sappers. When safes believed to contain documents relating to military gases needed to be opened there was the concern they might also contain gas samples. As a result, great care had to be taken to ensure gas was not released. Rather than blowing open safes, and risk spreading poison throughout the room, the sappers were forced to employ oxyacetylene cutters to remove the entire door.

Accidental unleashing of chemical warfare was not the only concern. At this point in the war the CW staff still feared that desperate Nazis might unleash chemical weapons on the advancing Allies. In addition, they feared that ammunition shortages might result in desperate German troops using chemical munitions in ignorance of what they contained. More worryingly for the British teams that carried out investigations at Raubkammer, the SS continued to be active in the woodland around the plant. The dangerous uncertainty of the situation was recalled by Tom Pitt-Pladdy: 'One group of scientists set off on their own and were held-up by German soldiers in the forest. I think they might have been deserters. They took the car. The scientists were very upset by that.'

In the days that followed the occupation of the Munsterlager facilities, T-Force was fortunate to locate some of the plant's staff. On 27 April, 32 members of staff, including a Lieutenant Colonel, emerged from the forest near the plant and handed themselves in to the troops guarding it. In the following days, the troops extended their searches for personnel by carrying out house-to-house searches in an attempt to find other research scientists and technicians who had remained in hiding.

With the British Army moving ever deeper into Germany, it became increasingly clear that the enemy was on the brink of defeat. Reaching Lüneburger Heide, where Montgomery would soon take the German surrender, detachments from T-Force were given tasks that would ensure the survival of the local infrastructure. At Rotenburg, C Company of the 5th King's

were instructed to occupy and hold the local telephone
exchange, ensuring it remained fully functional at all costs, as
Ron Lawton recalled:

> We were in the woods just outside the town when German mor-
> tars opened up, with their bombs falling all around us. They
> were very accurate. My mate Frank Preston − another ex-
> marine − had found a slit trench. I scrambled over and tried to
> get in but there wasn't room. He said − in no uncertain terms −
> 'There's another one over there.' I can tell you I reached it so
> quickly. It was a death trap where we were. The mortars weren't
> far away but the officer wouldn't let us go and sort them out.
> We had to get to our target.

Moving swiftly on, the Kingsmen took control of the telephone
exchange and occupied a well-furnished flat above the
exchange: 'We were there for a couple of days until a battalion
of Guards came along and captured the rest of the town.'

With the sites around Celle under close examination various
units of T-Force moved towards the next major target −
Bremen. In the middle of April, the British Army began ready-
ing itself for what was to be its final large-scale assault of the
campaign in northwest Europe. In preparation, A Company of
the 5th King's Regiment moved to the German town of
Bassum, 20 miles (30km) outside the target. Arriving there on
14 April, John Longfield recalled that they were fired upon by
local children who seemed eager to show their continued devotion to the collapsing Reich. Fortunately, the following days
were quieter, allowing the Kingsmen a chance to relax in
advance of the assault on Bremen. They were even able to play
football against the Royal Engineers and watched a Bing
Crosby film, courtesy of a mobile army cinema. However, as
John Longfield remembered: 'We came back to reality the following day when we took Eskel and were shelled by enemy

artillery.'[11] The Kingsmen were also joined by a detachment of Buckinghamshires who had previously been employed at the numerous Hannover targets. Arriving at the T-Force HQ in Bomlitz, Major Le Neve Foster, the commander of the Bucks detachment, took command of one-and-a-half companies of Kingsmen and two companies of Pioneers, and prepared to move into Bremen.

Despite a period of relative quiet prior to the attack on Bremen, some in T-Force found themselves fully employed. At Bassum a chance find of naval gear in a farm building led to the discovery of an elaborate policy of the industrial dispersal of numerous naval production plants, which had been relocated in cottages, farms and barns. While carrying out investigations in the area 30AU made the first discovery of the 'Lat' torpedo predictor and a complete fire-control apparatus for the use in the German battleships, the *Admiral Scheer* and the *Lutzow*. The torpedo predictor system was of primary importance since it was believed to have been sent to the Japanese navy.

In preparation for the move into Bremen, Major George Lambert found himself racing around behind the spearhead of the British Army – at one point getting caught in a 15-mile long traffic jam – switching between various Corps HQs in a desperate attempt to discover exactly where his company should be placed in order to advance into Bremen. He discovered that it was far from simple to get anyone to impart the necessary information. Only by producing his T-Force card, signed by Major General de Guingand, was he able to find out what he needed to know.

It was at this time that Lambert was introduced to an American liaison officer who was due to be attached to the unit as it moved into Bremen. The reason behind the attachment was simple. Following capture, the port was due to be handed over to the Americans to be used as their major German supply port. Since the British zone was to cover the country's only sea ports, the Americans desperately needed somewhere to resupply their forces.

As planning for the operation continued it was decided that, once T-Force had occupied the city's main police station, it would act as the main meeting place for all interested parties. Such parties included the Royal Marines, who would be responsible for all captured shipping, the incoming military government, the Intelligence Corps and the representatives of the American T-Force.

While T-Force waited to move into Bremen, the unit's sappers were given six days of specific training for underwater operations. Then on 17 April they moved forward to take their position for the assault. En-route they collected diving equipment, in readiness for any submerged demolition charges they might encounter in the vast U-boat pens, docks and shipyards. They were left in no doubt of Bremen's importance and of the need for its rapid handover to the Americans.

Also due to enter Bremen as part of T-Force was a detachment from 30AU under Patrick Dalzel-Job. With Charles Wheeler again acting as an interpreter, Dalzel-Job soon realized that the methods he had employed in France were no longer applicable. It was clear that the old roving style – finding gaps through the frontline and exploiting the local landscape with assistance from the population – might have worked in lightly occupied areas of France, but Germany was a different proposition. In many areas the fighting was simply too hard for such a team to travel unaccompanied. Elsewhere, the fluid situation allowed them to move away from the main advance into uncleared areas. However, Dalzel-Job was also convinced of the necessity for his unit to quickly reach the docks and seize intelligence. The Admiralty had made clear its desire for all intelligence and naval research to reach London swiftly, without first going through the official channels at SHAEF.

Waiting outside the city, the Kingsmen were told that German forces in Bremen had been warned that, if the city did not surrender, it would face the full fury of an RAF air raid. No such agreement was reached and RAF bombers were unleashed to reduce swathes of the city to ruins. As T-Force then moved forward to take part in the push, the RAF were once more called upon for support, as Harry Henshaw remembered: 'It was a dangerous time. One time we were going through a wooded area and there were SS tanks hiding in the woods. We couldn't get through. So they sent a squadron of Typhoons over and they saw the SS off.'

As the RAF pounded the city's defences prior to the infantry and tanks moving forward, T-Force's sappers dealt with demolition charges and booby traps around the nearby town of Etelsen. The assault on Bremen started on 24 April, with the men of T-Force – one company attached to each of the two divisions taking part in the assault – hard on the heels of the assaulting infantry of 156 Brigade, which moved towards the city at night.

The following day another platoon joined the assaulting infantry as they entered the city at 9 a.m. As the advance continued, Major Lambert brought forward a squad of 'recce' cars and another infantry platoon to exploit the targets within the city. Inside the city, the troops listened to the whistle of incoming enemy artillery, ducking down to avoid shrapnel. Fred 'Sapper' Tapper was also with the advancing T-Force units:

> There were German dead lying in the gutter . . . some of them hadn't been shot long. We moved up to the railway station but we were told there was a big park up ahead and there was an SS battalion up there. At that time we had hardly any armour with the infantry . . . the next minute the SS counter-attacked with mortars, and heavy machine guns . . . they pushed our infantry back towards the station and we had to move back. And

then our armour came up and pushed them back. That was
Bremen.

All over the city, pockets of resistance continued to hold out –
including the SS men who counter-attacked the British positions at the railway station. Despite the attentions of the SS,
T-Force moved forward to its principal target: the city's main
post office. It was just 200 yards from where the SS battalion
was making its last, desperate stand. Fred Tapper recalled the
situation inside the post office: 'I've never known so much mortar fire in all my life, really deafening it was.'

With tanks crashing through the rubble, slowly crushing
pockets of enemy resistance amongst the ruins, John Longfield
remembered the situation as A Company of the King's
Regiment occupied the post office: 'The Post Office itself was
relatively undamaged though snipers were very active, and
shells came uncomfortably close. However, wine and spirits
materialised from somewhere which helped to keep out the cold
and rain.'[12] Also taking cover within the post office was Harry
Henshaw, who recalled: 'There was a sniper in a tower on the
other side of the railway line. We couldn't see him but he could
see us. He had us pinned down – we couldn't move.' Although
they were able to take shelter others were not so lucky: 'There
was a bunker across the road and a little girl came out carrying a water jug. She was going to collect water for her family
in the shelter. She came running across the road and was shot
by one of the snipers.' Fortunately, the sniper was soon dealt
with. As the Kingsmen sheltered behind the post office walls,
an artillery shell whizzed over them and hit the building, sending the tower crashing to the ground: 'That was the end of our
problems.'

The surrender of Bremen was claimed by a number of units
within the city. According to 30AU's official history, the unit
was the first into Bremen and accepted the surrender of the city

from the acting burgomaster. This was recorded as having taken place on 26 April after Lt Commander Job's team had arrived two hours in advance of the main British force. A competing claim came from A Company of the 5th King's, as 18-year-old Harry Bullen remembered:

> We were in this big house, I think it had been a Gestapo HQ. We went outside and we saw this Jerry officer walking towards us. We don't know how he had got there because there was a big fight going on a couple of hundred yards ahead of us. He came up to us and handed over his Luger to my mate. Then he gave my mate this thing. I thought it was a dagger – I didn't know what it was. It turned out it was a Field Marshal's baton! So we took them to the sergeant and told him they wanted to see an officer. It turned out they wanted to surrender the city.

With the fighting drawing to a close, the soldiers began to take stock of what the assault had meant to Bremen. The blackened ruins of once grand buildings, some still burning, others smouldering, stood broken as the British troops moved around them. The stench of death hung in the air from the innumerable corpses that littered the streets – the smell combining into a sickening cocktail of odours as sewage seeped from shattered pipes. Amidst the chaos came the figures of innumerable surrendering German soldiers, who were joined by the lonely figures of distraught civilians, uncertain of what they should do or where they should go. More ominously, the streets were also filled with a less docile population, the released slave labourers, all of whom seemed intent on filling their bellies, guzzling alcohol or exacting revenge on their oppressors.

Yet the horrors and dangers of this shattered city were not the concern of T-Force. There were hardly enough troops available to seize and secure the main targets, let alone search for any 'targets of opportunity'. In keeping with the spirit of

30AU, Patrick Dalzel-Job decided that risks had to be taken if the U-boat pens in the shipyards were to be seized intact. Discovering that the area was to face a British artillery barrage as the precursor to an infantry operation to clear any final defenders from the area, Dalzel-Job wanted to find a way through and secure the area. Deciding he could not risk the entire troop, he moved forward with a single Scout Car. If there were any defenders left in the area this would draw their fire; if not, he might be able to secure a safe route into the shipyards. After encountering no opposition, but running out of petrol, Dalzel-Job abandoned the Scout Car, leaving its gunner and driver waiting at the dockyard gates. He then borrowed a bicycle and rode back to find the rest of the troop. Mounting their vehicles, they raced to the dockyards to secure the targets. Finding their quick action had prevented serious sabotage, they swiftly occupied the area and awaited the inevitable arrival of the rest of the assaulting force.

As the fighting around them subsided, the infantrymen and sappers of T-Force set to work, first within the post office and then throughout the ruins of Bremen and its port. The infantrymen secured target buildings while the safe-crackers set to work. In the three days following the surrender of Bremen a total of 95 safes were blown by the sappers. The haul was exciting, with one team of safe-cracking sappers uncovering a stock of nearly 4 million Reichsmarks – making a significant increase to the cash the infantrymen discovered in the tills of the post office's counters. A number of methods were employed for blowing the safes. There was no time for the refined arts of the expert safe-crackers, such as making skeleton keys or listening to the clicking of the combination locks. Instead, plastic explosives were employed. The sappers rolled the explosives into long, thin sausage shapes that were pushed inside keyholes before a detonator was inserted. These charges were sufficient to open 60 per cent of the doors. If this technique was not successful a condom was pushed into the hole created by the explosion and this was then stuffed with explosive which was detonated to force the lock. For stronger safes a mixed technique was employed, including the application of brute force. Firstly, the outer plates were blown off with plastic explosive, then the anti-drill and anti-cutting alloy plates were smashed with sledge hammers and plastic explosive used again on the final sheets of metal. It was hardly a subtle process – and certainly not one suited to cat-burglars – but it was successful.

In order to discourage any private investigations by soldiers keen to search for loot within, the sappers were put under direct orders from Brigadier Pennycook that safes could only be opened by an officer following direct instructions from investigators. Furthermore, the contents of each safe had to be recorded, with details of all money found within and the name of who had sanctioned the cracking of the safe. Despite these rules the scenes were somewhat chaotic, as Harry Henshaw remembered: 'The safe breakers with us, they blew the doors open. It was exciting – there were billions of Marks blowing all over the place. We couldn't carry that many – we had nowhere to put them.'

Regardless of the strict orders about handing the contents of the safes, one of the Kingsmen decided to fill his pack with Reichsmarks when they finally departed from the post office. His mates all laughed at him – what was the point in carrying around a pack full of money that was seemingly worthless. However, he had the last laugh when it was decided that the notes would remain legal tender in the immediate postwar period.

For T-Force, the targets within Bremen were of utmost importance. Before 25 April the unit had investigated a total of 94 targets. Then, with the port of Bremen occupied, investigators were faced with a further 31 initial targets – an increase of one-third from the total investigated across the rest of northern

Germany so far. Some were swiftly occupied only to discover
the entire factory had been transferred elsewhere. In other locations they discovered the jet engines they had hoped to seize had
been destroyed by bombing, forcing them to be abandoned.

Among the main targets for the incoming detachment were
the vast submarine pens of the Valentin bunker shipyard at
Bremen-Farge. More than 400 metres long and up to 25 metres
high (1,330 × 82 feet), these concrete monstrosities dominated
the riverside. Within this reinforced concrete structure – weighing more than 1.2 million tons – was a series of 13 assembly
lines, from which it had been planned to launch U-boat after
U-boat in the hope that these vessels might once more turn the
tide of war. The original planners had reckoned on a total
annual output of 150 new U-boats. These boats were to be of
the latest design, the Type XXI high-speed craft developed by
A.G. Weser.

As the soldiers entered the U-boat pens they marvelled at the
scale of the facility. Just one year earlier, this mighty concrete
fortress had been constructed using a workforce of more than
8,000 labourers from all over Europe. Among the labour force
had been Soviet prisoners of war and concentration camp
inmates, of whom more than 2,000 had died during the construction work, as well as foreign volunteers enjoying the wages
offered by the Nazis.

Despite the efforts of the labourers, only 90 per cent of the
construction had been finished and the fleets of war-winning
craft never sailed off into the North Sea to confront the Allied
navies. Instead, with no one left to produce U-boats, the whole
area was eerily silent. Hanging in the air 18 metres (60 feet)
above the heads of the T-Force troops, there was a 200-ton
steel crane, which had been built to lift the submarine sections
along the production line.

Elsewhere, 47-ton steel girders ran across the ceiling above
them. In some areas there were three storeys of workshops and

offices, and there were also turbines to supply emergency power. All of this was beneath a roof with a depth of more than 7 metres (23 feet) of solid, reinforced concrete. Around the entire site was a 15-metre-thick (50-foot) concrete wall, designed to protect both the factory walls and its foundations. Ken Moore recalled entering the U-boat pens: 'They were the most memorable places. It was like going into a cathedral. They were so huge – colossal. They stood out because, while a factory is a factory, the U-boat pens were something different.'

At the Deschimag U-boat assembly plant, 30AU and T-Force soldiers uncovered 16 submarines and a Narvick class destroyer all approaching completion. Initial investigations by T-Force's marine specialists showed that, although most documents had been destroyed, the craft had a number of constructional features of specific interest. Such was the importance of the finds that it was expected that the plant would need two complete months of investigation in order for it reveal its secrets. To assist with investigations, ten key personnel of interest to the Royal Navy were detained. The plant was of particular importance to the Japanese section at CIOS who believed material had been sent to Japan.

Within the city were a number of targets whose seizure was deemed equally important for the Japanese section. In the months prior to the end of the war in the Pacific nobody outside of the very highest echelons of the military and political elite realized that the world was about to reach the age of atomic warfare. Even those who would eventually have the power to make the decision to unleash nuclear warfare were uncertain whether the 'A bomb' would actually be used. Thus, the length of the war in the East could not be determined. As a result, it was deemed vital to seize any intelligence relating to the economic and military links that had been forged between Germany and Japan. There were many important questions that needed to be asked. What technology had the Germans passed to their eastern allies? What military secrets had they shared? And, most importantly, had the German scientists handed over any information that might help the Japanese create nuclear weapons?

Within Bremen the Allies hoped to begin to find the answers to these questions. Once again, the role of providing the answers fell to T-Force. One of the targets in Bremen was a factory producing Focke-Wulf aircraft engines that was known to have been in contact with Japan. More importantly, they were given the task of securing the Japanese consulate in Bremen and ensuring any secrets were made safe from destruction. The Japanese consulate was discovered within the office of a shipping firm. However, the property had been severely damaged by recent air raids. With little to be found at the target, T-Force extended their search as they attempted to find the location of the consul, F.H. Noltenius. Two other companies believed to have been involved in exports to Japan were also put under guard to await assessment.

In total, the initial T-Force operations within Bremen lasted for nearly a week. At the Borgward plant, which had been partly destroyed by bombing, they uncovered a production line for heavy lorries and samples of shell cases. In addition to the central post office, communications centres such as the trunk telephone exchange and a repeater station were put under guard, ready to be handed over to signals personnel. Collections of military records belonging to the Wehrmacht, including the pay records for units in the area, were also seized. Finance records and details of ordnance stored in the area were also put under guard, ready to be handed over to the Americans as soon as they set up their headquarters in the city.

The rivalry between the main sections of T-Force and the independent-minded representatives of the Royal Navy raised its head while they were holding targets in Bremen. The earlier agreement had been that 30AU would pass relevant intelligence to the Admiralty, but would also make it available to CIOS via T-Force HQ. At one location in Bremen all documents of interest were removed by the Royal Marines without making them available elsewhere. T-Force documents later recorded that efforts were made to retake them and make them available to all interested parties.

With Bremen under British control, and being prepared for handover to the Americans, elements of T-Force moved on to the next target. The vast port complexes at Hamburg had long been vital to the German war effort. Just two years earlier the British and American air forces had destroyed much of the city in an effort to bring the local industry to its knees. The firestorms that raged through the port had brought much heartache and misery to the local population, but the industrial targets had not been destroyed. Now the British land forces had changed their tactic. Instead of destruction, T-Force was poised to enter the city to seize, preserve and investigate more than 100 targets – many of them the same locations that had previously been targets for Allied bombers. With Germany all but defeated, the industry that had survived the firestorms was now needed for whatever conflicts that might arise in the future.

On the eve of the British Army's entry into the great port city, C Company of the 5th King's received one of those rude awakenings that were to become so familiar in May 1945. After weeks of driving around Germany in the backs of lorries, the company sergeant major, CSM O'Connor, decided his men needed to smarten up their appearance. Gathering the company together he told them: 'Tomorrow you lot are going into Hamburg, the eyes of the world will be on you. Now my bloody eyes are on you! Put him, him and him in the guardroom.'

Advancing on Hamburg, Tom Pitt-Pladdy could not help but notice the appalling scenes that reflected the pitiful state the German nation had been reduced to:

It was an odd situation. On the road in were thousands of refugees. Some of them were shell-shocked – one was walking along with a broken chair hanging over his head. It was chaotic. But I'd got used to it. Some of the towns were totally on fire. Just after we crossed the Rhine I saw a nun pushing a dead body along in a wheelbarrow, with the legs hanging over the sides. Death was routine, I'd got used to it after the first two weeks in Normandy.

While Bremen had been the scene of much hard fighting, Hamburg surrendered to the British after the outlying suburbs had fallen. As a result, T-Force was able to occupy its targets unopposed. High amongst its priorities was the city's radio station. Quickly taken under control by the Kingsmen, the station was preserved in working order and handed over to the Military Government. That night, the station was put to work, broadcasting instructions from the victors to the population of the occupied city. Ron Lawton recalled entering Hamburg:

We were the first into the city when it surrendered. The main body of troops hadn't got there yet. It was just rubble. I was going along a street and saw a barbed wire enclosure with all these DPs behind it. They were shouting at us and some of them looked angry. We didn't understand them – maybe they just wanted to get fags from us. We had to make straight for the U-boat pens. It was weird being on sentry duty in the U-boat pens. We didn't know if there was anyone in the subs. We just marched up and down the dockside, guarding them. It was a vast area. I also found myself guarding a room full of fully armed Germans. It was just me with my rifle. It was a bit tense.

As T-Force took control of its targets in Hamburg a strange sense of unreality set in. It seemed many Germans had accepted defeat and, even though the war was not yet over, they took little interest in the activities of the occupation force. When the Kingsmen entered Shell House – the base for the Royal Dutch Shell Company – they expected that those inside would react to their presence. However, when they announced to a room full of secretaries that the British Army was taking over the building they were greeted by only the briefest silence as the women looked up from their desks. The clacking of typewriter keys immediately returned as the secretaries continued with their work.

Another target was of far greater importance. The Phoenix Rubber works, in the southern suburb of Harburg, was famed for its innovative production of rubber for military use. The tanks of 131 Armoured Brigade had been detailed to occupy the facility but they were unable to carry out the move due to the large numbers of refugees blocking the roads. Instead, Tom Pitt-Pladdy's 13 Platoon, C Company, advanced alone. Their early arrival at the factory soon caused some consternation at 131 Brigade. The factory had been intended as Brigade HQ, but with the arrival of T-Force, their base was denied to them.

Ignoring such petty matters, T-Force set to work. Upon arrival they discovered the factory's 'Home Guard' unit already lined up, ready to hand over their weapons. Once inside, the finds became increasingly interesting, including the company's silver and the equivalent of £1 million in Reichsmarks that had been intended for wages payments. They also uncovered rubber submarine protectors as well as the key technicians involved with the development of the apparatus which was designed to make submarines invisible to the detection equipment in use by Allied navies. To the southeast of the city, the unit uncovered around 40kg (90lb) of platinum catalyst from a nitrogen fixation plant. This was believed to have a commercial value of around £30,000 and was immediately handed over to the Military Government.

In the days that followed, teams within Hamburg carried out numerous investigations. Targets included individuals such as Professor Habs, an expert in the treatment of malaria, and Dr Frick, a specialist with combined knowledge in X-rays, radar and submarine direction finding. Dr Groll, a research scientist believed to have made a breakthrough on thermo-dynamics, was also detained for interrogation. Factories included the Germaniawerke, whose periscope technology had been shared with Japan, and Electroacoustic, whose staff will-ingly provided a list of all German research shared with the Japanese since 1939.

Another Hamburg target successfully detained by T-Force was Herr Johannes Engeike, who handed over the blueprints for his photo-electric homing device used for guiding aircraft-to-aircraft missiles. There was also Dr Dohler, a physicist who had developed a spark-plug pulse generator considered to be in advance of anything available in the UK or US. Military inves-tigators believed this to have important applications for radio-controlled missiles and radar use. To their delight, he was found to be very cooperative.

More experimental research surfaced in the form of a small marine launch, propelled by a V1 power unit. When on full power the boat was raised fully from the water, apart from two supporting planes. When Dr Karl Badstein was inter-viewed he provided details of the design for 15cm guns which were to have been installed at St Omer in order to fire on London. This was a part of what later became known as the 'super gun' project, which was subject to significant interest in later years. As an expert in stabilized projectiles used in smooth-bore weapons, Badstein was of particular interest to artillery research teams; he claimed penetration for 75mm guns as being 210mm of steel at a range of 800 metres, a fig-ure suggesting a significant increase in power over guns in use by the Allies.

With Hamburg secured, T-Force ensured that one of the most vital parts of its brief was carried out: information on the economic and military relationship between Germany and Japan had to be established. As in Bremen, T-Force swiftly took possession of the Japanese consulate, detaining the consul and his staff. The consulate's records were swiftly examined to establish which firms had passed military equipment to Japan. These firms were in turn targeted to discover exactly how much information had been sent east. It was now vital for T-Force to discover if any records existed to indicate such a move.

For 30AU the main target within Hamburg was the Blohm + Voss shipyard where evidence was uncovered of submarine prototypes. On 3 May they found two craft that had been damaged by Allied bombing raids. Investigators immediately realized these were no ordinary submarines just from the shape of their hulls. As one of the investigation team later reported, these new submarines closely resembled a gigantic fish rather than a conventional submarine. The team under the command of Lt Cdr Jan Aylen set to work investigating the machines and found that the shipyard's bosses were reluctant to discuss any matters relating to the craft's highly efficient propulsion system.

As Hamburg came under British occupation other T-Force elements were hard at work in the surrounding countryside. The team of radar experts that included Jack Heslop-Harrison was once again sent to examine an 'opportunity target', this time a scientist who was believed to have important information relating to rocket guidance systems. The information came via a T-Force officer who had amassed a dossier of reports from civilians who had been eager to pass on information as proof that they had never been Nazis. First they attempted to find the man at his home address but discovered he had left the city and moved to the countryside. All the time fearing attack by 'Werewolves', the small team drove to the farm in question.

Arriving at the location Heslop-Harrison sent two men to guard the rear of the house in case their target attempted to make a break.

In the minutes that followed the operation descended into farce. As he approached the front of the house Heslop-Harrison spotted the scientist dashing away from the room he was seated in. Certain the man was attempting to escape, the team moved in swiftly to apprehend him. However, once safely inside it was revealed he had no intention of escaping. Instead, he revealed he had simply dashed from the room to get his jacket in order that he would be correctly dressed to greet his visitors.

Once the team was settled inside, the scientist took time to explain the system he had been working on. It was a pioneering rocket guidance system for surface-to-air missiles that involved the rocket being guided to its target riding on a radar beam. Directional control was through graphic vanes affixed to the missile which were in turn controlled by a rotating aerial which followed a guidance beam. The team were convinced by his explanation and the scientist was passed on to Hamburg for evacuation.

With some detachments in the thick of the final battles of the war in northwest Europe, investigation teams continued to assess the finds made during the initial advance. At Nienburg T-Force tracked down Dr Hermann Valde, a chief chemist from a chemical plant and a specialist in waxes. Investigators were swiftly despatched to carry out a full interrogation and assess the depth of his knowledge. The occupation of the offices of the Shell & Standard Oil Combine gave T-Force access to its directors who were made available for interrogation, along with the German government's controller of foreign oil. Meanwhile, the CWF Muller factory was assessed and found to be producing 2 million volt neutron generators, many of which had been provided to other research institutes. Closer investigation uncovered a 15 million volt prototype which had been dismantled. The same factory also produced X-ray tubes that were deemed of immediate interest to investigation teams and were rapidly despatched to the UK.

With elements of T-Force remaining in both Hamburg and Bremen, B Company of the 5th King's moved forward with the 11th Armoured Division, crossing the River Elbe and advancing on Lübeck. Rather than heading into the city, the armoured cars of the 5th King's reconnaissance platoon advanced northeast on Travemünde. Their instructions were simple: to safeguard T-Force interests in the area. Despite the apparent simplicity of such instructions, the truth was far different. Although it was clear to all that the war was almost at an end, there were thousands of fully armed Germans in the area – men whose intentions remained unclear. Under the command of Captain Bobby Fachiri, the nine Scout Cars advanced towards Travemünde with the aim of preventing the destruction of a Luftwaffe experimental research station and seaplane base.

The advance was a tense time for all concerned. Crossing the Elbe at lunchtime on 3 May, Captain Fachiri and the 5th King's armoured car platoon needed to move swiftly. His intention was to link up with the 11th Armoured Division, moving up just behind their forward troops. Receiving the news that the 11th Armoured were moving across the land ahead of them, Fachiri realized it was time to employ the signs that had been made to ensure T-Force could move quickly to their targets. Mounting the 'Priority T-Force, XXX Corps' sign on his armoured car, Fachiri found this had an immediate effect. Soon his column was moving through the lines of vehicles that made up the tail of an armoured division. Captain Fachiri noted that even the division's tanks had moved aside to let them pass, though, so he ensured the signs were quickly removed: T-Force needed to be close on the heels of the forward troops but it was certainly in no position to be in the vanguard in such a hostile environment.

Fachiri may have been reluctant to be in an overly exposed position in uncleared areas (he had already been unsuccessfully 'shot-up' by a German ME109 fighter plane), but the swift advance of 11th Armoured Division, and the gaps on it flanks, meant that T-Force had little choice but to move through areas as yet unpenetrated by British infantry. Fortunately, during their overnight move towards Lübeck, Fachiri's small detachment encountered no one – not even a single British or German soldier.

At Lübeck, elements of T-Force, including detachments from both the 5th King's and 30AU, occupied targets within the city. Attached to an SAS team, John Bradley reached the port in search of naval targets. He later recorded the scenes: 'never have I seen such chaotic and fantastic scenes. The streets were crowded with German soldiers making their own way to surrender; they were travelling on foot, in cars and in horse-drawn vehicles of many types. . .We had been seeing strings of German prisoners all the way up to Lübeck but in the city itself there were so many that the great majority were unguarded.' He also noted that amidst the columns of surrendered enemy soldiers were carloads of former POWs and displaced persons, many speeding along in looted vehicles with flags and signs proclaiming their nationality.

In the port, 30AU helped take control of an SS prison ship in which 6,000 prisoners were being held, having been battened down in the holds for 12 days without food. Following the capture of the ship, two of the SS guards were summarily executed. It was while investigating the Berliner Maschinenfabrik plant in Lübeck that T-Force made one of its most remarkable discoveries. The company's research teams had unearthed new ways of rifling gun barrels. One specimen evacuated was a gun with a curved barrel that had been intended for use from tanks, pillboxes and around corners in street-fighting. The weapon, a modified version of the German STG44 (itself the world's first assault rifle) combined its curved barrel with a prism-lensed sight that allowed the user to safely aim around corners without straying from cover. Back in the UK, the weapon was quickly assessed by researchers. They discovered it was reasonably accurate up to 100 yards when firing single shots but that in automatic fire it would be unlikely to hit a target at 50 yards.

While occupying a medical research facility within the city, Bob Brighouse witnessed an eerie collection of specimens: 'I went into this big room. All around the room were shelves, all covered with these glass jars filled with a clear liquid. In each jar was a baby, all in different stages of development, all different sizes. Each one still had its umbilical cord attached. They were all perfectly clear and fresh. That stuck vividly in my memory. I never found out what it was.'

While these teams occupied their targets, Captain Fachiri's reconnaissance section refuelled and prepared to join the advancing tank columns. At Travemünde, they found that the advancing British columns were moving out to the northwest. Though there was little fight left in the German army, the town was in chaos, packed as it was with thousands of refugees fleeing from the advancing Red Army. Ignoring the chaos, Captain Fachiri moved his unit on to the Priwall Peninsula, commandeering a local ferry whose operator had remained on duty.

At this stage in the war the high-speed mobile operations carried out by T-Force were vital to the success of the advance. By arriving before the main British force, T-Force caught German troops unprepared. Although many of them, by this stage, had given up any hope of victory, there were plenty of die-hard Nazis whose willingness to fight against the odds continued to cost the lives of Allied men. By surprising the Germans, arriving as if from nowhere, T-Force caught the garrison off balance. In such uncertain circumstances, most Germans seemed content to lay down their weapons. It was this that saved so many of the targets from destruction. Had the British been forced to fight – even against lightly defended targets – the advancing commanders would have happily brought down the full force of artillery, air support, tanks, mortars and infantrymen upon the hapless defenders. No amount of protesting by T-Force commanders could have stopped them: all that mattered was wiping out any opposition and saving the lives of the advancing troops.

At Travemünde the swift action of Captain Fachiri prevented any unnecessary destruction. Despite the presence of around 4,000 fully armed Germans and around 6,000 civilian refugees, mostly travelling in horse-drawn carts as they fled from the Russian advance, the reconnaissance platoon quickly settled the situation. German officers were happy to help organize the refugees – preventing the civilians or soldiers from clogging the roads needed by T-Force – while French POWs were given arms and sent to guard the facilities at the research station, where they remained until T-Force had sufficient resources to guard all their targets.

To bring the situation under control, Fachiri detailed one section of armoured cars to patrol the roads, rounding up civilians and soldiers. The rest of the cars were used to guard the aircraft at the airfield and to prevent unauthorized use of the ferry. Fachiri engaged another source of personnel, the civilian police, to ensure the situation on the peninsula was kept under control. The police were given the task of concentrating all the civilians in the Luftwaffe barracks and making them responsible for their behaviour. By carefully positioning his armoured cars and using German resources, Fachiri was able to prevent any fighting or serious damage as a result of looting.

Having secured the area using such precarious sources of manpower, Fachiri was pleased to see the main British force arriving in Travemünde. With the arrival of a battalion of the Northamptonshire Regiment, enough troops became available to help T-Force. The infantrymen guarded the targets, assisted by a T-Force armoured car, which allowed Captain Fachiri to move on to examine other targets.

With Travemünde secured, Fachiri and the reconnaissance platoon moved on to the Blohm + Voss flying boat factory, submarine repair and assembly works in the town. One of the investigators who later arrived at the extensive facility described it as having the air of a deserted city. Everywhere were the half-built carcasses and wings of giant flying boats, spread across the concrete areas outside the research hangers. One of these air-craft, discovered prior to having its engines fitted, was thought to have sufficient range to cross the Atlantic. Rumours soon spread that some of the flying boats had been intended for use by Adolf Hitler. Stories told by the plant's staff suggested that plans had existed for the Führer to escape from Germany, fly-ing north to take refuge in the snowy expanse of the Arctic Circle. There was little evidence to suggest any truth to the rumour but it proved a colourful and fitting use for the gar-gantuan but unfinished craft.

With just three armoured cars under his command, Captain Fachiri took the surrender of 30 German officers and 200 other ranks. As he entered the office of the German commander he found a clerk seated behind a desk waiting to type out the for-mal surrender of the establishment. Once the formalities were over, the German commander took the British detachment on a tour of the base, pointing out that within the hangars was suf-ficient material for the construction of 150 aircraft. Later investigations revealed four almost complete Type XXI sub-marines and a partly damaged Walter 250-ton closed cycle submarine. One of the completed U-boats was waiting on a slipway, merely awaiting torpedo fuses before it would be ready for service.

With insufficient forces available to guard the plant, Fachiri ordered the German commander to guard the entire area on the understanding that he would be held personally responsible if any damage was to occur. The orders were carried out without complaint. As the citation for Captain Fachiri's Military Cross read, he had carried out the operations with 'personal disregard for his own safety'. Thanks to his actions, another vital installation had been secured intact. Two days later the first representatives of the RAF and Royal Navy arrived to begin their investigations of the airfield and research station. With members of the RAF regiment guarding the aerodrome and sailorsin place at the seaplane base, Captain Fachiri and his armoured cars were free to continue their work, and rejoined the battalion on 8 May – VE Day.

As investigations continued in the Lübeck area, T-Force seized a number of opportunity targets. Among them was a mobile radio-transmitting station later described as one of the most remarkable finds of the period. They found 26 gigantic vehicles, believed to be worth several million pounds. When they arrived to investigate, the station's director sought protection on the grounds that demoralized German soldiers were about to loot and destroy the equipment. The director admitted that the equipment had originally been tested during the Spanish Civil War and that since then he had been standing by, with orders to put the station into operation during an emergency. With Germany all but defeated, he admitted he had somehow missed his cue.

While the main body of T-Force continued its work in northern Germany, some elements had moved into the Netherlands to investigate targets. Searching for naval targets was B Troop of 30AU under the command of Lt Commander Jim 'Sancho' Glanville. In the final days of the war Reg Rush was called out to take part in what his colour-sergeant suggested would be their last operation: 'He called out "C'mon Reg." We got in the armoured Scout Car. He didn't tell us where we were going but said "It's a special job. Keep your heads down boys. The war's almost over and with a bit of luck we'll be back in the UK in a month."' After driving for almost four hours, passing numerous surrendering German units, they reached a beach. They swiftly dismounted from their vehicles and approached a solitary house:

> It belonged to Lord Haw-Haw. We did our usual routine for searching such a place. We were all dropped off at a door and then someone went in at the front. I tried my door and it opened. It was a back getaway from the house. I went up the stairs, threw the doors open to find an empty office. There were all these gold-framed portraits around this room of all the German leaders and generals. Beside his desk was a large tropical fish tank. I was just about to open fire on it – I was so fired up because I'd heard this bastard on the radio over the years. Then I heard movement in the lock, I whipped round with my finger on the trigger, and it was my mate, Jimmy.

Relieved that neither had opened fire, they went into the next room, which was full of broadcasting equipment. It was a strange moment for the marines to look upon the large microphones that had broadcast Haw-Haw's hated voice into so many British homes. The irony was compounded by the fact that it was the sneering cynicism of Haw-Haw's broadcasts that had caused Reg Rush to leave his reserved occupation and 'do his bit' for the war effort. Now it had come full circle, as Rush recalled: 'We didn't know whether we had missed him by three minutes or three hours. That was my last operation of the war.'

As the war drew slowly to a close, T-Force investigation teams ignored the circumstances of the collapsing enemy resistance and continued their search for the secretive Nazi research facilities. At the start of May, John Longfield wrote home to his parents to explain something of the fantastic nature of T-Force's duties:

> It may interest you to hear that we are responsible for the capture of a rifle which (literally) fires around corners, of several two man submarines and long range subs. Gestapo documents dealing with espionage and fifth columns, plans of new V weapons etc, etc. The rifle has a curve of 30 degrees and does fire around corners. . .next thing will be a bullet which if it misses you will come back and take you prisoner.[13]

The team to which Jack Heslop-Harrison was attached was detailed to examine a German navy research station at Pelzerhaken on the Baltic coast to the north of Lübeck. Reaching the facility, Heslop-Harrison's team soon set to work. The senior scientist on site, Dr Östertag, was happy to cooperate with the team and readily expressed a desire to travel to the US or UK to continue his research. It transpired that in the final days of war most of the staff had fled, in particular the political appointees who had been little involved with the scientific research. What followed served to illustrate why T-Force's work had been so vital.

Prior to the arrival of the first British troops, liberated slave labourers had swarmed through the facilities. Though there had been little to interest them within the office and laboratories, they had struck a path of destruction, wrecking anything that stood in their way. Despite the destruction, the investigation team found plenty of interest. One example was the work of Dr Müller, an infra-red specialist who had been researching a detection system. Most of his research had been destroyed during the bombing of Berlin and he had been transferred to Pelzerhaken. Although none of the British team had sufficient knowledge to assess his description of his own work, it was clear that Dr Müller was sufficiently important to be sent to the UK for interrogation.

Of direct interest to the investigation team was the range of radar equipment – massive permanent installations that were directed eastwards, indicating they were part of a chain of radar stations protecting the Baltic coast. The largest of the radar aerials was some 25 metres (83 feet) across, impressing the scientists with the scale of the project. Given the timescale allowed for their investigations, the team could do little but make the briefest assessment of the equipment. In the surrounding area they discovered vast numbers of German radar systems, from the basic earlier models to the most advanced, as if it were some sort of informal museum of radar.

Concentrating on developments taking place inside the laboratories, it became clear that research had been focused on attempts to mask U-boat snorkels and conning towers. Dr Östertag told the team that the intention had been to find a way of reducing the reflectivity of the U-boat's steel hull by increasing its absorption of radiation from British radar. To test the system a mock-up of a U-boat had been erected outside the laboratory. This had been used for the application of various coatings, one of which was constructed from sandwiched layers ofbubble-filled plastic and perforated aluminium foil. Other experiments had been carried out with various paints that were intended to match the conning tower to the sea's surface, regardless of the wavelength of the light it was viewed under. This was so that the tower would be rendered less visible to infra-red detection systems.

Similarly, fabricated U-boat sections were also discovered within a large testing tank. The submerged sections were used to test various methods of masking the U-boats from the counter-submarine ASDIC echo-location systems used by the Royal Navy. Another interesting find was a 12-metre (39-foot) deep pressurized water tank. The tank had a ram at its bottom which could be moved up and down to increase water pressure, thus simulating deep-sea water pressure for use in tests of submarine equipment including sound generators and mine or torpedo fuses.

Despite the British Army having reached as far as the Baltic, T-Force's duties continued. Towns became easier to occupy, targets were reached without fighting through defence lines and the threat of attack diminished. However, this meant that there were simply more targets available to investigate. As a result, the final days of war saw plenty of activity for the men of T-Force – not all of which was in pursuit of their regular targets.

On 5 May, with the 'stand to' ordered, the sappers of 58 Bomb Disposal Platoon found themselves in an awkward position, one which demonstrated that, despite the ceasefire, the dangers of war had not quite abated. They advanced north from Bremen and reached the village of Winsen in Schleswig-Holstein, where the sappers encountered a group of Polish slave labourers – just one of the thousands of such groups tramping the roads of Germany that spring. An engineer, Fred 'Sapper' Tapper, approached the Poles, one of whom informed him that a group of fully armed German soldiers were occupying a large house nearby. Like so many of the situations faced by T-Force following the entry into Germany, it was not something for which the bomb disposal engineers had been trained. They had only the most basic training in infantry tactics but, despite the dangers, there was little choice but to confront the enemy.

Following a brief reconnaissance, Major Peter Davies called a group of his men together and explained what he wanted to do. The engineers were divided into two groups with one group approaching the house from the front while the others flanked the house and took up positions to the rear. 'Sapper' Tapper, who was approaching the rear of the house, heard his sergeant utter the ominous words, 'Now look, it's almost the end of the war. For God's sake don't get yourself killed.'

Eschewing such practices as establishing a base of fire to suppress the defenders of the house, Major Davies drew his revolver and led his men forward. In amazement, Fred Tapper watched as the engineers charged towards the house, shouting at the top of their voices as they ran forward, their fixed bayonets waving in front of them. Despite the unorthodox tactics, the sappers achieved the element of surprise and the Germans were shocked by what they saw. Stunned to encounter the British soldiers charging towards them, the German defenders fled through the backdoor – straight into the arms of the waiting bomb-disposal troops. One of the sappers reached out and caught a German by the throat while another let off a burst of Sten gun fire over their heads. Caught completely off-guard, the Germans immediately surrendered. Included among their prisoners were two German officers who, just like their men, had fled in the face of the defiant charge by the engineers.

This attack on a farmhouse, carried out by an unlikely group of soldiers, was one of the final incidents of the war in northwest Europe. However, despite the ceasefire coming into effect that night, it would not be T-Force's final action.

CHAPTER 6

Kiel – Into the Unknown

*'Take Kiel before the Russians can get there . . . immediate means
immediate.'*

Brian Urquhart to Tony Hibbert, 4 May 1945

The major took stock of his situation. He had less than 500 men
under his command. His target, the city of Kiel, was 60 miles
ahead of him and contained 40,000 German troops. Between him
and the target was the German frontline and two full SS divisions
were believed to be converging on the road he intended to use.

What else did he know? If he did not reach his target, then
the Russians might get there first. If that happened it would
threaten Danish freedom and the entire balance of power in
the Baltic. Furthermore, the Russians would acquire some of
the most important military scientists in all Germany.

His problems did not end there. He was not afraid of taking
risks: as a veteran of Dunkirk and Arnhem he had already
faced his share of danger. However, this time the stakes were
somewhat higher. It was not just his personal safety that was
the issue. Not only did he risk putting 500 men of T-Force in
mortal danger, he was endangering the safety of thousands
more. A ceasefire was in force and any further advance would
breach it. It was a terrible dilemma. If T-Force was to follow
its orders, though, there was only one thing to do: ignore the
ceasefire and capture the target.

There was no choice. The major had his orders. Nothing – not the 40,000 soldiers in his target city, not the terms of a ceasefire or the orders from the army commanders – could be allowed to endanger the future security of the western Allies. His mind was made up. Major Tony Hibbert gave the order for T-Force to advance on Kiel.

With the war all but over T-Force was set to embark on possibly its most audacious operation. So far it had advanced with the Allied armies into the towns and cities of the Reich. Sometimes it had struck out alone over short distances, attempting to seize secrets from smaller targets that were of no strategic importance to the Allied commanders. However, as it had moved across Germany, T-Force had always remained within the general limits of the Allied advance. Finally, with negotiations for the German surrender underway, the Allied armies stalled on a line that would mark the end of the dash across northern Germany.

At 18.20 hours on 4 May the German delegation arrived at Field Marshal Montgomery's HQ on Lüneburger Heide, where the act of surrender was signed. There was a tremendous buzz of excitement around the headquarters as the dour-looking German delegation arrived to put pen to paper and bring the bloodshed to an end. As the Germans put their signatures to the document, they surrendered all forces based in northwest Germany, Schleswig-Holstein, Holland, Denmark, the Frisian Islands, Heligoland and the garrison at Dunkirk: a total of almost one-and-a-half million men. To all intents and purposes the war was over.

At the HQ of the British 2nd Army, just ten minutes after the surrender was signed, General Miles Dempsey issued the order that all the four corps under his command were to stand fast on the line between Dömitz, Ludwigslust, Schwerin, Wismar, Neustadt, Bad Segeberg, Wedel, Stade, Bremervörde and Bremen: 'No advance beyond this line to take place without orders from me.'[1] It was a simple, unassuming order that perfectly reflected the man who had issued it. He was a general who cared about his men and had no intention that any should be endangered now that this long war was finally at an end.

This was a desire shared by the men under his command and the order was taken seriously. No one wanted to take any risks. With the German army collapsing there was no need to advance beyond the line ordered by Dempsey. Thus, the 2nd Army, which had slogged its way from the beaches of Normandy to Germany's River Elbe, finally came to a halt. The ceasefire and 'stand to' order then came into force in order for the German army to ready itself for the final surrender on 8 May.

Yet for some among those under Dempsey's command this long awaited order was to have little meaning. At Lübeck, the Kingsmen of B Company had been ready for an advance on Kiel but stood down upon hearing the news of the German surrender. They were joined at Lübeck by A Company, who had also been selected for the Kiel operation. Suddenly, for the first time, they received an order that reflected the 'gung-ho' spirit that had originally been intended for T-Force. Now was the moment they would finally charge ahead of the advance and head off into the unknown to seize their target: the port of Kiel.

The operation that followed left many of the senior officers involved uncertain of what had actually occurred. Brigadier Pennycook later described the events as deriving from 'a series of obscure and misunderstood telephone conversations' and that the T-Force commanders on the ground had been deluded when they later claimed they had been ordered to Kiel with 'all speed'.

The orders for this final advance came via a new face within T-Force, Major James Anthony Hibbert. Tony Hibbert was something very different for the unit, someone later described as 'engaging and enterprising' by Lt Colonel Bloomfield and as a 'maverick Staff Officer' by Brigadier Pennycook. Most of the other officers serving within T-Force had served with the 'ordinary' infantry and artillery regiments. Yet Major Hibbert was from another world and seemed the very epitome of the dashing young army officer. The son of a highly decorated Great War veteran (a winner of both the Military Cross while an infantry officer and a Distinguished Flying Cross following his transfer to the Royal Flying Corps), Hibbert had attended Marlborough public school and then spent nine months in Germany during Hitler's first year in power. What he experienced there – in particular seeing his hosts, boys in the Hitler Youth, doing theoretical exercises for a military advance on Paris – was enough to change his life. Abandoning his planned career as a wine importer, he instead returned to the UK to join the Royal Horse Artillery.

Following the debacle at Dunkirk, Hibbert volunteered for the newly formed commandos, finding himself in No.2 Parachute Commando. When the Parachute Commando evolved into the fledgling Parachute Regiment, Hibbert had gone with it and risen through the command structure, serving in Sicily and Italy before attending the Staff College. He had eventually found himself promoted to Brigade Major of the 1st Parachute Brigade. He had been awarded the Military Cross for his role at Arnhem Bridge during the doomed Operation Market Garden. Having first drawn up the plans for the Brigade's advance, he emerged as the final unwounded officer, commanding the paratroopers as they were finally surrounded. After Operation Market Garden, Hibbert had been taken prisoner but had escaped before making his way across the Rhine to safety.

Following his return to the Allied lines, Major Hibbert broke his leg in two places in a car accident. He was sitting on the bonnet of an overcrowded jeep as it raced away from the

Rhine, when it ran into the back of a lorry. When he returned to England for treatment he did not expect the accident to result in any long-term problems. However, he soon discovered it was not a simple break, requiring a steel pin to be inserted into his ankle, thereby immobilizing him. The break would eventually mean Hibbert would have to forego any hope of a sustained career in the army.

The accident put paid to any hopes of returning to an active role in the Parachute Regiment. He had once thought nothing of making parachute training drops dressed in the full dress uniform of the Royal Horse Artillery, complete with riding boots and spurs, but even he could not parachute with his leg in plaster. However, he soon found the army still had a use for him.

In March 1945, with his leg still in plaster up to the waist – the trousers split to the waist to get them on – he left hospital and was called to a meeting in London. There, he was appointed as the coordinating officer for a major airborne operation to seize the port of Kiel, reporting to General 'Boy' Browning's airborne army HQ. As early as December 1944, Eisenhower had requested that plans be drawn up for an operation to seize the port. He also emphasized that, whichever force was set to capture Kiel, it should have a T-Force attached to it. Eisenhower further stressed that, since so many of the targets were of a maritime nature, 'T-Force Kiel' should have a sailor as its second-in-command. In order to cover all eventualities, it was agreed that two sets of plans should be drawn up – one for a ground assault and one for an airborne landing. One of the tasks given to Hibbert was to bring together the various investigation branches – including representatives of Operation Alsos, the group that was searching for evidence of the Nazis' atomic research programme – to ensure all the necessary specialists would be in place to assess targets within the city.

However, with the ground war progressing so well the airborne operation was cancelled and instead Hibbert was appointed to a staff role at T-Force. Once at T-Force HQ, Hibbert had taken on a liaison role similar to that occupied by his friend and former colleague, Brian Urquhart, whom he knew well from his days with the Parachute Regiment. The two men had both been intimately involved in Operation Market Garden and Hibbert respected Urquhart for his stance over the launching of the operation. As Major Hibbert later noted, his friend was 'intelligent, and his fears for 1st Airborne's safety were justified'.

During this period Hibbert had been involved in the investigations at the silk factory in Celle in which Urquhart had discovered the nuclear laboratory. He had delivered a group of scientists to the facility and, while they carried out their investigations, explored the factory:

> There were all these bales of silk in the factory. I thought of all the Dutch people who had not only fed us while we were hiding, but had clothed us. So I loaded up the 3-ton lorry with silk and headed back to T-Force HQ. Just as we were passing through Ede, where all my Dutch friends were living, the load 'fell off the lorry'. So they were able to distribute it. That was the only time I did any looting. It was very much appreciated by the Dutch.

Soon, Major Hibbert won the brief to seize Kiel, but with just 500 men rather than the entire airborne division originally envisaged. With his broken leg still in plaster, Hibbert found himself ready to embark on his final wartime adventure – occupying a city believed to contain 40,000 armed German military personnel and 420,000 foreign labourers with just a tiny force under his command. He was expected to quell the local military forces, bring order to the city and still have time to investigate 150 targets – 50 per cent more than within the vast dockyards of Hamburg.

The genesis of the operation to seize Kiel remained shrouded in mystery since no one within T-Force, including Hibbert, received a written order. In a document written in 1945 it was stated that 21st Army Group had given authority for the move. However, the same document admitted that 8 Corps, acting on General Dempsey's directives from 2nd Army HQ, had ordered all units in the area to 'stand still'. Some of the accounts written in 1945 make clear that the order to advance had been given in error and that 'T-Force Kiel' acted outside of orders.

For others, there was absolutely no confusion. What later became clear was that on 1 May Hibbert was at T-Force HQ in Bremen when he received a verbal order from his fellow staff officer Brian Urquhart. What Urquhart told him was simple: take two companies of Kingsmen, some engineers, pioneers and experts, link up with the Royal Navy – in the form of 30 Advance Unit – and then charge 60 miles cross country to seize the targets in the port of Kiel. Once all the necessary units were in position, Hibbert was told the operation was to take place immediately. The detachment from the King's was to include Major John Gaskell, the battalion's second-in-command, and A and B Company under the joint command of Major George Lambert. As Lambert later recalled, T-Force were told to reach Kiel 'by hook or by crook'.

This was no ordinary operation. Hibbert received the usual 'blacklists' associated with T-Force operations but, more importantly, Urquhart gave him a separate brief – to head off the Russian advance on Denmark. He informed Hibbert that he was to expect the Russians to launch amphibious commando operations on the port. Urquhart's words made his mission clear. He was to 'take Kiel before the Russians can get there'. At this early stage in the proceedings Hibbert was told that his tiny force might face an entire Russian armoured division. When Hibbert queried the instructions to immediately advance on Kiel, Urquhart gave his answer in stark terms: 'immediate means immediate'.

For all the talk of solidarity there was little warmth between the western and eastern Allies. Urquhart had been told that Allied intelligence had picked up signals suggesting that the Red Army had little intention of halting at the agreed demarcation lines. Instead they were expected to attempt an advance through Wismar, Lübeck and Kiel, and then moved northwards into Denmark. The idea was simple: by taking control of Denmark the Russians could control the entrance to the Baltic. Furthermore, with control of Kiel, and the strategically vital Kiel canal, the Russians would win themselves a year-round, ice-free port on the Baltic with easy access to the North Sea. Simply by continuing Marshal Konstantin Rokossovsky's scything assault through the last German defences they might find the opportunity to snatch vast military and economic power.

Uncertain of where his orders had originated from, Tony Hibbert later made enquiries. He learned that on 4 April 1945 a radio signal from the Japanese Embassy in Stockholm to the Foreign Ministry in Tokyo had been intercepted and passed to the headquarters of the Danish Resistance. They had in turn forwarded the signal to General Eisenhower at SHAEF. As Hibbert was told, Eisenhower passed the intelligence on to President F.D.R. Roosevelt and Prime Minister Winston Churchill on the same day. According to this intelligence the Russians intended to fully disregard the Yalta Agreement and occupy Denmark. To prevent what would amount to a catastrophe for western Europe, a selection of British forces had been thrown forward. At 8 a.m. on 1 May, the 3rd and 5th Parachute Brigades were ordered to punch through the German lines and advance 60 miles to occupy Wismar. Having just completed an assault crossing of the River Elbe at Lauenburg, the paratroopers were immediately despatched north accompanied by an armoured escort squadron of Royal Scots Greys, the divisional artillery and an allocation of transport.

As the two brigades advanced on Wismar there was no time for contemplation. They plunged into unconquered territory, passing vast columns of petrified German refugees who were fleeing westwards in the face of the Russian threat. In some places bewildered enemy soldiers stood by the roadside, simply staring at the paratroopers as they sped past in their vehicles. Elsewhere, roadblocks and pockets of resistance blocked the route until they were swiftly destroyed by the guns of armoured cars of the Scots Greys.

By 9 a.m. the following day the troops reached the city, just in time to stem the Russian advance. There were tense stand-offs in the town as the lightly armoured British force faced down an infinitely stronger Russian one. Despite the dangers, the paratroopers held their ground and any further advance on Denmark was halted.

At the same time, a Royal Navy flotilla had been ordered to clear the enemy's minefields and steam to Copenhagen. The flotilla, consisting of the cruisers HMS *Birmingham* and HMS *Dido* plus four Z-class destroyers, was ostensibly sent to help disarm the German forces in Denmark. However, as was made clear to Major Hibbert, it had actually been sent as a deterrent to the Russians. On 4 May – one day before the ceasefire came into effect – they entered the harbour and liberated the Danish capital. Later that day, two squadrons of RAF Typhoon fighter-bombers landed at an airfield in the city, ready to provide a necessary show of force if the Russians advanced on Denmark.

Although the arrival of 3rd Parachute Brigade had effectively stalled the Russian advance, other concerns had gripped the minds of the High Command. T-Force had received the order for the advance on Kiel on 1 May, at the same time that Brigadier James Hill had been ordered to Wismar. On that day, A Company of the 5th King's

Regiment had been told to hand over all their 'targets' in Bremen in readiness for the Kiel operation. However, with Hamburg still defended by the enemy there was no immediate route to Kiel open. Only when Hamburg fell on 3 May was T-Force able to assemble ready for the advance. At that point, B Company was ordered to hand over targets in Lübeck to the infantrymen of the 5th Division.

To all intents and purposes the British arrival on the Baltic coast meant that the Russian threat was over but Major Hibbert's orders remained unchanged – he was still to rush forward and seize Kiel. This gained urgency when intelligence sources raised the threat of a Russian seaborne operation to capture the city and the Kiel canal. Major Hibbert was not told whether the Russians intended to hold the city or just to raid German naval establishments and seize the very same secrets coveted by T-Force. All he knew was that, ceasefire or no ceasefire, Kiel needed to be occupied as swiftly as possible. And so, at 6 p.m. on 4 May, just as the German delegation were putting pen to paper in Montgomery's tent on Lüneburger Heide, 'T-Force Kiel' began to assemble. There, still with just 500 men under his command, Major Hibbert prepared to advance into the unknown.

At this stage Hibbert had little idea of the nature of targets within the city. His concern was not the reasoning behind the interest in the Kiel targets but simply to get his force into position ahead of the Russians. The most important target was the Walterwerke factory and its chief designer, Dr Hellmuth Walter. Since March 1943 the Allies had received intelligence that Dr Walter was developing a U-boat capable of up to 30 knots while submerged; such speeds were unheard of and clearly the boat would be able to outrun Allied craft. Other reports stated that the boat ran on fuel believed to be hydrogen peroxide. To some, these reports had seemed laughable for their seemingly colourful descriptions of the research. As later investigations revealed, the reports had been essentially true and the craft was dangerously near completion.

However, before T-Force could move they needed to get authorization to pass through the forward positions of 8 Corps. At 11 p.m. on 4 May Majors Gaskell and Hibbert drove to the Corps HQ at Hamburg to seek permission for the move from the Corps Commander Lieutenant General Richard O'Connor. The events of that evening caused some consternation in the days that followed, as Major Hibbert explained:

> At 10pm I reported to the Duty Officer at 8 Corps headquarters and told him that my orders were to proceed immediately to Kiel with the forces I had. He told me flatly that the Corps commander had gone to bed early and he had given strict instructions that no one – not even a fly – would be allowed through the lines. I said it was going to be difficult and pointed to a map on the wall. I said 'The only route from Hamburg to Kiel runs through Neumünster and we've got two SS divisions converging on Neumünster. Unless we move at 3 a.m. at the latest we are not going to get through. That is contrary to my orders.' He told me he was sorry.

Although refusing to sign the order for the advance, the Duty Officer did telephone Brigadier Pennycook to tell him what Hibbert had requested. Pennycook replied by telling the officer that, although Hibbert was a 'bloody renegade', his orders were to advance on Kiel and he did not appreciate being woken in the middle of the night just to reiterate these orders. The same reaction came from Lt Colonel Bloomfield when a message came via 'Phantom' – a long-range signals unit – asking for permission for T-Force to enter Kiel. As Bloomfield later admitted: 'My rather cross reaction was that if T-Force was ready to go to Kiel what was there to stop them? And could Major Hibbert be told he need not have bothered to ask me?'[2]

Despite these assurances from T-Force HQ, the Duty Officer still refused to sign the movement order. He apologized but stressed it conflicted with his own instructions.

Many less determined men might have meekly accepted the situation, but Major Hibbert had never been an ordinary staff officer. What followed was certainly not conventional, as he later admitted: 'I did something for which I have been ashamed ever since and for which I was later deservedly punished.' He explained how the impasse was resolved:

> I went and got a bottle of 15-year-old Scotch whisky out of my jeep. I told him we might as well waste our time profitably together. This chap had already been on duty for about 40 hours and was getting very tired. After two or three slugs of this very nice single malt – I'd been pouring my glass away each time – he was getting very sleepy. I was perfectly beastly and said to him 'Do you remember that chit I showed you? Well, you were going to sign it for me.' So he signed it. Well, I helped him. It was a most disgraceful thing for me to do. It is the one thing I regret most of all. Except he wasn't a career officer, so it didn't ruin his career. But I got the signature. At 3 a.m. I left the HQ.

With the order signed T-Force were ready to move. At 7 a.m. A and B companies of the 5th King's – many of whom had been enjoying the temporary impasse that had arrived with the news that a ceasefire was about to come into effect – left Lübeck and drove towards the start line at Bad Segeberg. One of the officers who travelled from Lübeck that morning could not understand what they doing. Ken Hardy – who had already amazed himself by surviving to reach the end of the war in Europe – had listened on a looted radio to the broadcast announcing there were to be no further troop movements and questioned the order to move into Kiel: 'But the Major in charge wasn't going to put up with that. He said "My orders are that we go to Kiel and unless I hear personally from the commander, I'm still going – and you're coming with us." So we went. That was VE Day for us.'

Despite the misgivings of some of the soldiers, at 8 a.m. Major Hibbert finally gave the order to move and T-Force advanced. Major Lambert later admitted he had not even been aware of the 'stand still' order and was surprised to be moving through areas untouched by the British advance.

This scratch unit – 'T-Force Kiel' – was marked by a number of contrasts. This was an elite force made up of the glamorous and mysterious Special Air Service (SAS), the commandos of the Royal Marines – one of the most illustrious fighting forces in the British military – and two companies of infantry of the line. Also in the unit were representatives of the Special Boat Squadron, or SBS, the Royal Navy's equivalent of the SAS. Beside them were the Kingsmen. These infantrymen were the least specialized of all the special forces – a group of teenagers recently arrived on the continent, ex-gunners, wounded veterans of the Normandy campaign and victims of battle fatigue. As if to underline the contrasts, the commander, Major Hibbert, was a former artilleryman, commando and paratrooper – a veteran of Dunkirk, Italy and Arnhem. He, at least, seemed to have a foot in both camps – and one leg in plaster. It was this hastily assembled force that embarked on the British Army's final advance of the war in northwest Europe.

First to leave were a few jeeps from D Squadron of the 1st Special Air Service Regiment. As they departed, they sped past the Kingsmen seated within their trucks. Not wanting to be left behind in the race to occupy Kiel, the Kingsmen increased their speed. It seemed the Royal Navy was also keen to stake its claim on the city. As Brian Urquhart later reported, there were the members of 30AU who were 'straining at the leash' prior to leaving for Kiel.[3]

As the column departed, even Major Hibbert was uncertain how the Germans might react. He watched as the Germans looked towards his jeep in astonishment and then ran off to their positions. As the Kingsmen moved off, the troops were uncertain what to expect, as Bob Brighouse recalled: 'All we knew was that there was supposed to be a standstill and no one was supposed to move. Then half an hour later we were on the move. We went through the British lines, then we went through the German lines. Both sets of lads, British and German, were astonished. If the Germans had opened fire we'd have been finished. We had no defence at all.' Harry Bullen remembered: 'The Germans were still dug in at the side of the road. The tanks were in the forest. I saw one of the tank crews running towards their tank. They didn't know what was happening – nor did we.' As Tony Hibbert later recalled, the column was moving too fast for the stunned Germans to take any action.

Halfway to Neumünster, where Major Hibbert feared he might find themselves face-to-face with two SS armoured divisions, the jeeps of 30AU, complete with their White Ensigns fluttering behind them, raced past the convoy.

Reaching Neumünster the three elements of the T-Force column joined together. They may have avoided the SS columns rumoured to be in the area but they could not avoid the badly cratered road that had slowed the speeding jeeps. A contemporary report described the advance on Kiel: 'The drive from Bad Segeberg onwards was most eerie. We had left all signs of battle behind, no directional signs at the side of the road, no traffic or signs of traffic, no slit trenches and perhaps worst of all no white flags. One or two German soldiers, complete with kit, were straggling down the road, otherwise there were hardly any people about.'[4] As John Longfield remembered it: 'No slit trenches, no white flags, no signs of battle but a few German soldiers straggling down the road. We ignored them and they ignored us.' Major Lambert recalled that his driver noticed German soldiers darting into the cover of the woods. However, Lambert himself was so engrossed in map reading that he never noticed any enemy activity.

Also on the roads that morning was Vic Woods, acting as a driver for Major Gaskell. They however, were not travelling in the main convoy:

I was on Luneburg Heath with Major Gaskell and his batman. There were thousands of enemy troops standing around. There weren't enough British troops to guard them. Suddenly Major Gaskell said 'We've got to get to Kiel.' On the journey there were bands of DPs wanting us to stop, but we couldn't. Major Gaskell got his batman to fire into the air to clear them out of the way. When we saw German soldiers some would throw down their weapons, others would leap over hedges and get out of sight. Most just put their hands up. But our job was just to ignore it all. We drove past a German barracks but I don't know who was more shocked – them or us! Luckily no one fired on us.

As T-Force advanced, the men within the trucks and jeeps were able to get some idea of the area they were advancing through. This was a quietly bourgeois region, a land of villages and hamlets, with the countryside scattered with individual farmhouses and flat fields. Drainage ditches criss-crossed the land. Beneath them, the cobbled roads shook the soldiers as they sped through the dull and drizzly spring morning towards their target. The woods and copses that were liberally scattered across the countryside were forbidding –a potential lair for die-hard Nazis.

Where the trees cleared, the landscape was not unlike eastern counties of England – stretches of flat land interspersed with a gently rolling terrain of hedge-lined fields where cattle grazed the lower pastures and crops spread where the fields rolled upwards. For Lancashire-born Harry Henshaw, serving with A Company of the 5th King's, the scene was familiar. He looked around at the miserably incessant drizzle and thought to himself that this horrible morning was a 'home from home'.

Yet there was little time for sightseeing. Though all feared attack, their fears went unanswered. Instead, forlorn German soldiers sat by the roadside or were seen sitting slumped in ditches. Others among the stunned Germans spotted the convoy and went running to alert their officers or fetch their weapons. But the column was moving too fast – once they had returned the speeding column had passed them by.

German soldiers skulked in the woods rather than open fire on the convoy. Once these Germans had been part of a victorious army but now they could just look on as the spearhead of the Allied armies raced towards the Baltic. What little resistance that did appear was swiftly suppressed. The lack of a martial response was a great relief to the Kingsmen who felt – quite correctly – that their rear was dangerously exposed. One of the soldiers remembered seeing the German troops: 'A young sentry standing guard looked around helplessly, obviously in deep shock and hoping for someone to tell him what he should do, as the vehicles steam-rollered straight on past him.' Elsewhere, confused local farmers stood beside their tidy homes, the spring flowers of their gardens a stark contrast to the dusty vehicles and dirty brown battledress of the advancing armies.

In one area a large group of emaciated slave labourers appeared. As Bob Brighouse recalled, there were hundreds of them. He noticed how starved they looked, with their legs no thicker than the average arm. Many were openly weeping as they blocked the road, slowing the column to walking pace. The advancing column was forced to clear the way. It seemed heartless to ignore the plight of the starving victims of the Nazis but the column could not wait – their target was of greater importance than any individual, however great their suffering.

This land seemed so different to the world they had passed through in previous weeks. So often the only colour they spotted in gardens had been the vicious flames that licked from the windows of any building that had offered resistance to the advance. Now there were no more roadblocks, no shattered and blackened shells of German homes and no corpses. Nor was there any sign of the terrifyingly efficient handiwork of the RAF that had so dominated their vision of Hamburg.

Nearing the port, the Germans at the roadsides were replaced by greater numbers of displaced persons who waved and cheered as T-Force raced past them. From the back of his truck, John Longfield noted the contrast between the smiling DPs and the Germans who stared uncomprehendingly at the British vehicles and the men within them.

As 'T-Force Kiel' raced forward the sights on the roadsides were soon forgotten. At times the various factions seemed to be racing each other as if desperate to claim the port as their personal prize. Maybe somewhere in their minds was the feeling this would offer the war's final chance to grasp glory for their regiments. The glamour of the SAS, the long and proud history of the Royal Marines and the solid infantry pride of the Kingsmen all jostled for space on the roads. But this was no competition – it was no game and no time to let their guard down. One of the enemy's greatest ports lay ahead of them, as unstable and potentially dangerous as anywhere in the collapsing Reich.

As the men within the jeeps and trucks crossed their fingers and held their breath – hoping their luck would hold – enemy action was not the only danger they faced. Harry Henshaw recalled the situation:

> We had a race into Kiel with the Marine Commandos – part of the way there, there was a very nasty accident. One of the jeeps – with the Marines or SAS in it – began to overtake us. There

was a burning 88mm gun, still blazing in the road – it had been shot up. So we had to move over but that left no room in the road. So they ran off the road and drove smack into a tree. Their four bodies were hanging over the side. But of course we couldn't stop. I suppose their own people looked after them but I think they were dead.

As Henshaw remembered: 'You don't think about it – you do what you are told – it was just a job.'

By 10 a.m., with the morning mist beginning to clear, the convoy closed on its target. Across the flat landscape arose the vision of a city battered and bruised by the attentions of the heavy bombers of the Allied airforces. The first signs that they were reaching the city came in the form of the garden colonies, the suburban allotments that ringed so many German cities, allowing the city's residents a small taste of rural living. Soon they reached the fringes of the city proper. Despite the rain and the knowledge that the city had been thoroughly 'pasted' by Allied bombers, there was a sense of hopefulness in their advance. There was cherry blossom on the trees and the innumerable lime trees were in bud.

Major Hibbert, seated in the leading jeep, could see the arched steel spans of the bridge that would take the column into the heart of Kiel. As they mounted the bridge he cradled his driver's Sten gun, his mind fully occupied by the dangers that might be ahead of them. Reaching the crest of the bridge a view of the entire city emerged before them. To the right was the port with its seemingly endless miles of dockyards. Much of the port lay in ruins with an ominous pall of smoke rising into the sky. In the waters were the results of the RAF bombing: some ships were upside down, others had settled into the water with just their funnels visible, while a few were still burning. In total, nearly 40 per cent of the T-Force targets within the city had been completely destroyed in bombing raids.

Although there was a ceasefire in place, the T-Force advance had risked everything. The Germans who knew of the ceasefire did not expect to see the British in Kiel. Others, who most likely did not even know of the cessation, were shocked enough to open fire on the advancing British units. Their fire was soon suppressed. Those in T-Force's trucks were struck by the sight of one of their number lying prone on the bridge, firing into the city with his Bren gun. It was a stark warning that the German threat had not evaporated and that the ceasefire was fragile.

Travelling in the column was Royal Navy metallurgist John Bradley who was seated within an SAS jeep. He later claimed that his party had outstripped all others in the column and was the first to enter Kiel. He wrote: 'We drove straight up to the bridge but were refused permission to proceed by armed German sentries who maintained that it was an armistice and not a surrender. One silly marine nearly precipitated an incident by kicking one of the sentries.'

Regardless of who was first to enter Kiel, all shared a similar experience. What confronted them was a scene of utter devastation. The city's cobbled streets were filled with rubble, the remains of buildings were hanging at dauntingly precarious angles and spires of charred brick jutted skywards. On the horizon the tower of the battered town hall rose defiantly from amidst a sea of destruction. Over 80 per cent of the city had been destroyed. The cathedral was in ruins, its medieval splendour torn apart by high explosive. The main railway station was but a shadow of its former self: its roof had collapsed and its walls were pockmarked. All but a few of the homes in the city centre had lost their roofs and most were merely shells. As in so many other towns and cities across the Third Reich, the airmen had done their duty and torn the heart out of Kiel.

Despite his apprehension about forming the spearhead of the drive into enemy territory, Ken Hardy found time to enjoy the moment: 'It was absolutely hilarious, we rolled into Kiel and the German population – who thought the war was over – stood aghast as this mob marched in.' Another officer later wrote: 'It was a strange experience to stand in the centre of Kiel on a wet Saturday morning and direct our mere handful of troops to their various targets. The civilians stared very hard at us but we stared even harder when we saw that the German soldiers, sailors, policemen, firemen, etc, were still armed.'[5]

A German witness later recorded the scenes as the British arrived in Kiel:

> The streets in the city centre were dead, as slowly, even cautiously, a couple of military vehicles rolled across the City Hall square from the direction of the Holsten Bridge. As they came to a halt in front of the main entrance, there was suddenly a small group of people gathering around them. I felt uneasy watching from the window. The English smoked some cigarettes and threw the fag ends on to the ground, before they left their vehicles. This prompted sudden movement in the confounded group, as a struggle ensued for the stubs in the space around the cars.[6]

As the two companies of Kingsmen and the marines of 30AU headed for their targets, Major Hibbert drove along the water's edge of the Kiel Fjord and headed straight for the Naval Academy. It was not long before Major Hibbert reached his target, which had become the epicentre of the remaining power structure in the area. With around 12,000 fully armed enemy sailors and soldiers, and up to 40,000 unruly and unpredictable displaced persons in the city, Hibbert realized he would need to take control of the one location able to influence their behaviour. With just his driver/batman seated beside him, the jeep pulled up in front of the stern red-brick edifice of the academy. On one side, across the gardens, was the Kiel Sound, the waterway that had once been famed as a playground for Germany's yachtsmen. On the other side was the ominous sight of his target. Looking up at the pockmarked walls perched atop an imposing stone plinth, Hibbert was glad he had not needed to fight his way into the building. As he stepped down from the jeep, Hibbert had no idea of what sort of greeting he would receive.

Hibbert realized the ridiculousness of his situation: his leg was encased in heavily stained plaster, his uniform was damp, he was 60 miles (96km) behind enemy lines and, with just his driver as back-up, he was about to attempt to negotiate the surrender of a fully armed German city.

Looking up the steps towards the entrance, Major Hibbert realized he was about to find out the answer: 'There was this very smart naval officer standing there looking at me with some considerable disdain. I noticed he was pointing a Schmeisser at me. I was unarmed.' The situation called for some quick thinking:

> Because he was a naval captain and I was only an army major, I saluted him and said 'Guten morgen.' I pointed at his gun and told him in German he should not shoot me. I then said in English 'I have come here to help you end this bloody war and it won't do you any good to shoot me. So if you would be so kind as to help me up these steps and show me to your office I think we can get the matter settled.'

The German, whom Hibbert soon discovered was Kapitan Wilhelm Möhr, abandoned his look of disdain and roared with laughter before offering his hand to help Hibbert climb the steps up into the Naval Academy. Entering the building, Hibbert was ushered into an office in a ruined side wing, where the roof had caved in following Allied bombing. The German admitted it would be unfair to make the disabled British officer attempt the ascent to the first floor where his office was situated.

At first the Germans at the Naval Academy were unconvinced about the news they had received from Major Hibbert.
They had received no official news of surrender – why should
they believe a lowly British officer with just a couple of hundred
soldiers under his command? As Brian Urquhart later reported:
'The German Naval Commander was at first inclined to be
sceptical as to the opinion of the T-Force commander, backed
by 200 men, that the German nation had surrendered.'[7]

The situation was soon resolved. Kapitan Möhr put a call
through to Flensburg, the seat of the new German government
following the death of Hitler. Demanding to speak to the newly
appointed Führer, Admiral Karl Dönitz, Möhr received the
news that it was correct, the Germans had surrendered and
that he was to hand over the city to the newly arrived British.
It was also agreed that all ships of the German Baltic Fleet
would be ordered to return to Kiel and that there would be no
further movement of ships already within the port. The
dejected German officer then handed over his side-arm as a
gesture of surrender.

With Dönitz's order fully digested, the Germans set about
allowing the tiny T-Force detachment to take control of the
city. As Hibbert noted, 'Our frontline was 60 miles behind us
and we were out of communication.' The first thing was to
ensure order in the city; the local chief of police was summoned
to the Naval Academy and a proclamation was issued to allow
the police to continue to carry their weapons in order to maintain security in the city.

The targets within the city were an absolute priority for
T-Force. Setting up an HQ in a large bunker close to the main
submarine pens, Major Lambert ordered A and B companies
on to a total of 11 targets. Arriving alone, and still uncertain as
to whether the rest of T-Force had arrived yet, Vic Woods
drove Major Gaskell into the heart of the port:

I don't know who got to Kiel first – us or the main column. When we got to Kiel we drove right on to the dockside. There was a ship with a German sentry, complete with rifle, standing there on duty. And just the three of us turned up in this jeep. I was thinking to myself 'I hope he doesn't open fire.' Major Gaskell went on to the ship and told us that the ship's captain refused to surrender except to someone of an equal rank. The sailors refused to believe the war was over.[8]

At the same time, the Royal Navy team from 30AU – led by Dunstan Curtis and Jan Aylen, with attached American representative Captain Albert Mumma – made their way with haste to the Walterwerke factory. At the facility they were joined by a platoon of Kingsmen which Major Lambert had detailed to occupy the target, regardless of naval interest. Once again 30AU displayed the sense of independence that had characterized their earlier actions. As Brian Urquhart later reported, 30AU's interests 'fleetingly' but 'frequently' coincided with the rest of T-Force and noted that 'they became impatient with the pace and thoroughness of T-Force activities and became increasingly advanced and dispersed until in Kiel they disappeared from view altogether and have not been seen since.'[9]

This independent spirit was also shown by the unit's official records that offer an alternative version of events at Kiel, noting that the Royal Navy's contingent were the first to arrive in the city and claiming the honour of the official surrender. Contemporary Admiralty records showed Commander Curtis and Captain Pike going to the Flanderen Bunker which had become the operational HQ of the German Admiral commanding Kiel. There, Commander Curtis took the official surrender of the port from Rear Admiral von Gerlach.

As the commander of T-Force Kiel, Major Hibbert spent the next two days, as the *de facto* boss of an entire German city. Working from a ground floor office in the Naval Academy, surrounded by rubble, he issued the edicts that brought peace to the city.

While Hibbert concentrated on ensuring the German forces in Kiel surrendered as quickly as possible, the rest of T-Force went about their business with their usual efficiency. The Kingsmen set about securing the area of the port, a vast area of quays, wharfs and docks. Just yards from the main railway station, the port was the very heart of the city. For five years of war, the ships that sailed from Kiel had dominated the Baltic. For years, ferries had plied their trade across the sea to Scandinavia and more recently troopships had tied up at the quaysides as they took German troops to and from Russia. Yet the glory days of Kiel, as the home port of Germany's Baltic Fleet, had passed. As the soldiers arrived they were also met by concerned shipyard workers who seemed uncertain what they should do. They stood around nervously, staring at the soldiers until they discovered that the new arrivals were British rather than Russian. They made no efforts to conceal their relief at the news. As Lieutenant Jones' platoon arrived at a U-boat pen, they were astonished to find staff still hard at work constructing a submarine.

Among the vessels in the port were two of Germany's mightiest warships. The *Admiral Hipper* and the *Prinz Eugen* were the two most famous examples of the Kriegsmarine's 'Hipper Class' heavy cruisers. Armed with eight 8-inch guns, the *Admiral Hipper* had spent the war attacking Allied shipping in the Atlantic and the Arctic, sinking HMS *Glowworm* and seven merchant ships. Latterly, it had taken part in evacuations from East Prussia, rescuing trapped soldiers and civilians. The *Prinz Eugen* had been involved in more notorious actions, acting as an escort for the *Bismarck* and possibly helping to sink HMS *Hood*.

Despite the scenes of devastation and the scorch marks evident on the *Admiral Hipper*, the sailors in the docks appeared not to have conceded defeat. As the lorries containing the

Kingsmen arrived at the docksides they soon came under fire from sailors on the decks of the *Admiral Hipper*. The British troops swiftly dismounted and returned fire, their bullets hitting the decks and superstructure of the massive ship. As many remembered, they were fortunate that the sailors employed nothing larger than rifles to engage them. The ship's anti-aircraft guns alone, let alone its heavier guns, could have wiped out the tiny British force.

As John Longfield recalled, it was the only serious resistance he had experienced while with T-Force. He later wrote home to his father: 'The Boche sniped at us from a German Navy ship, so our platoon, which was the only one in the Krupps works, raided it and disarmed the crew.' Some of the soldiers recalled that the ship's captain insisted that a senior officer be called to accept his surrender. The soldiers laughed at the suggestion and told him that if he did not surrender the ship would be bombed and both he and his crew would be blasted into oblivion.

With the crew of the *Admiral Hipper* swiftly subdued, the Kingsmen raided another vessel on which they captured 43 fully armed U-boat crewmen. The British troops were in no mood to see the Germans continue their resistance to the occupation of Kiel, as John Longfield wrote to his father: 'We then got hold of some civvies and told them that if anything happened to us, the RAF was going to wipe what was left of Kiel off the map. This was passed on to the German troops who gave us very little trouble afterwards.'

In the days that followed, the two companies of the King's Regiment, under the command of Major Lambert, played a vital role in ensuring the security of the city and the surrounding area. Outside Kiel some of the Kingsmen had to go into the woods to hunt for SS men who were 'causing a bit of bother'. It was these tasks – combined with his bravery on the D-Day beaches and his work at Dunkirk, where his troops had occupied positions just 100 metres (330 feet) from the enemy defences, despite the fact that most of the men were 'nerve cases' – for which Major Lambert was to receive the Military Cross. As was noted on his citation: 'Through his coolness and confidence in himself, his force were complete masters of the town till arrival of further troops on May 10.'

At the ELAC factory, which just one year earlier had employed more than 4,000 staff, the Kingsmen were greeted by a bizarre sight. An Allied fighter bomber, most likely one of those that had participated in the final bombing of the port, had been shot down and had crashed through the factory roof. The troops looked on in wonder, hardly able to believe that the downed plane had somehow remained virtually intact on the factory floor. More importantly, they detained a group of researchers who were working on a mechanical calculator which was designed to estimate the altitude of enemy aircraft and deliver this data to anti-aircraft batteries. The designers completed their work and immediately handed it over to the British.

T-Force managed to create order from the chaos that surrounded them in Kiel. Under the terms of the ceasefire T-Force had no right to be there and, as a result, they had uncertain powers over the German troops in the area and needed to be careful not to antagonize the local commanders. As one of the bomb disposal officers who arrived on 6 May recorded, 'the situation was a little confused'. In the words of another officer, many German naval officers seemed not to accept the surrender and 'they could have blown us out of Kiel with one salvo.'[10]

Following the acceptance of the surrender of the naval garrison, Majors Hibbert, Gaskell and Lambert made their way to the city's police headquarters. At 2.30 p.m. they issued orders to the people of the city. German troops were initially allowed to retain their weapons, while the freed slave labourers, who considered themselves allied to the British Army, were forbidden

from carrying weapons. The proclamation to the foreign workers – written in French, English and German – informed them
that swift compliance with the British orders would ensure that
they would be returned to their homes as soon as possible.

In addition to these orders, it was decreed that any German
military personnel who attempted to hand themselves in to the
British were not to be treated as prisoners of war. Instead, they
would be directed to the nearest German unit. For the men of
T-Force this meant that they were not even allowed to search
the defeated Germans for loot such as watches – something that
was considered the rightful 'spoils of war' by many of the
British soldiers. Fortunately, for all concerned, the order did
not last for long. From 9 a.m. on 8 May, with the final surrender of Germany coming into effect, all weapons were to be
handed over to the victorious men of T-Force. From that point
onwards, only those in possession of a pass signed by Major
Hibbert were permitted to retain their weapons.

Across town, 30AU forged ahead to Hellmuth Walter's
Walterwerke (also known as H. Walter Kommanitgesellschaft
or HWK) at Kiel-Tannenberg. At Bremen they had discovered
two Walter-produced U-boats that had been badly damaged
due to Allied bombing. These were just two of the nine examples believed to be in existence, part of a new breed of
submarines far in advance of anything in production in either
Britain or America. Now 30AU wanted an intact U-boat that
could be studied by Royal Navy designers and they felt certain
the Walterwerke was the place to find one.

Their target was the factory itself and the thousands of staff
within, and specifically one man, Hellmuth Walter. According
to German reports, upon arriving at the Walterwerke the first
question asked by the British marines was 'Where is Herr
Walter?' At the same time, a detachment of marines arrived at
the home of Heinrich Heep, one of Dr Walter's top submarine

designers. He was immediately taken into custody and driven to the Walterwerke.

Born in August 1900, Dr Walter was a heavy, flabby-cheeked, black-haired man who had joined the Nazi Party in 1932 and was one of the most famous of all German engineers. In 1945 he had been awarded the prestigious Knight's Cross for his contribution to the Nazis' wartime research projects. His most famous work was on rocket motors designed for use in fighter aircraft and on revolutionary propulsion systems for U-boats. Upon being interviewed by the T-Force team, Dr Walter said he had been a weapons specialist all his life and now had a staff of 4,500, divided between the Kiel plant and an aircraft plant in areas already overrun by the Russians. During interrogation, he admitted that developing the high-speed submarine had been his primary aim. To achieve this, he had experimented with various oxygen carriers, including liquid oxygen, compressed oxygen and nitric acid. Eventually, he had settled on hydrogen peroxide.

The idea of using such a fuel system in submarines had first been planned as far back as 1911, when German submarine researchers began work on engines that would create a true submarine – a boat that could function fully underwater, rather than a boat that was capable of submerging. The essential problem of conventional submarines was the need to resurface in order to run their diesel engines and recharge their batteries at frequent intervals. Each time they did this they were vulnerable to attack either from the air or from nearby ships. In short, submarines were designed to operate on the surface, diving only to avoid detection. Yet with a closed-cycle engine they would be able to move at high speeds beneath the waves, re-emerging at a time that suited them.

The Walter submarine engines were special because they did not need oxygen to produce energy. As early as the 1920s, Dr Walter recognized that a submarine using a fuel already rich in oxygen would be free from the constraints of spending long periods on the surface. Instead of being fuelled by a petrol engine, the new system used closed-cycle propulsion. The engines were basically steam turbines in which the steam was generated by the chemical reaction achieved when hydrogen peroxide was mixed with diesel oil. The reaction caused an expansion of oxygen and steam producing sufficient pressure to turn a turbine. Dr Walter had also worked on introducing extra fuels to the chemical mix in order to produce a further surge in energy. At the age of 25, he had secured a patent for his invention and spent the next 25 years developing the system for military use.

From 1934 onwards Walter worked for his own firm, HWK, approaching the German Naval High Command with his proposals for U-boat engines. After initial scepticism, Walter was able to convince the head of the Kriegsmarine, Admiral Dönitz, of the value of his designs and won a contract to develop them. Between 1937 and 1939 he worked on his prototype, launching the V-80 in 1940. To the amazement of everyone except Walter, the craft had a submerged speed of 23 knots – twice that of any other submarine in service anywhere in the world. His 1938 tests with hydrogen peroxide allowed a speed of 26 knots – other submarines were still not able to match that speed in 1945. He spent the next five years attempting to refine the design by ensuring that the volatile hydrogen peroxide could be efficiently, and safely, harnessed. As was noted by many, it seemed Dr Walter was obsessed by the idea of high-speed submarine propulsion.

By 1945 it was clear to all involved in naval research that if such fuel could be effectively harnessed it would revolutionize the future of submarine warfare. Military losses in the latter stages of the war had made Germany's use of Dr Walter's high-speed and long-range U-boats an imperative; it was hoped that, if these submarines could successfully attack Allied ships which were reinforcing the armies on the continent, then this might buy the Nazis the necessary breathing space to stabilize the western front and hit back against the advancing Russians.

As had been made clear to Tony Hibbert, it was essential that the Russians did not get their hands on the technology before the Allies. Men like Dr Walter would be essential to ensuring the West retained the upper hand in military developments of the postwar period. The last three Type XVII U-boats left Kiel at the end of the war – passing through the Kiel canal just yards from Dr Walter's factory only a few hours before 30AU arrived.

While 30AU did locate a Type XVII testing submarine almost intact, much of the intelligence they were searching for was nowhere to be found. All documentation and 50,000 technical charts and drawings had been incinerated to stop them falling into Allied hands. It transpired that Dr Walter had spent the best part of four days burning documents on the orders of the German High Command. Fortunately, he had taken steps to ensure his research was not lost forever. Microfilm copies of the documents had been packed into six tin drums and Dr Walter had personally supervised their burial along the coast. Technical devices had been sunk into lakes and ponds while 300 tons of fuel had been emptied into pits.

Despite being keen to stress his credentials at these initial interviews, Dr Walter appeared reluctant to fully cooperate and discuss the finer details of his work. After the inspection teams arrived on the morning of 5 May they demanded that Dr Walter immediately reinstall his machinery, recover his microfilms and reopen the plant. It was only when the Royal Navy representatives explained to him that the British considered all oaths to the Nazi regime to be void that he began to unreservedly divulge the secrets of his research. Also 30AU's commanding officer visited Admiral Dönitz's Flensburg HQ and obtained his signature on a document reiterating that all research secrets were to be handed over to the British in Kiel. Upon seeing the document on 7 May, Dr Walter finally accepted that he should cooperate with his captors.

In the days that followed the fall of the port, a team of Royal Navy scientists, under the command of Commander Aylen, arrived to carry out detailed investigations of the intelligence within Walter's factory. After their interest had been sparked by the craft discovered at Hamburg, Aylen and his officers – consisting of Lt Cdr Haynes, Lt Cdr Carling and Lt Cdr Pearson – were eager to get to work and expand their knowledge of these revolutionary craft. As Major George Lambert later noted, the arrival of the teams of scientists meant he needed to look after an additional 200 men, all of whom also had to be fed and housed wherever possible.

The facility the Admiralty scientists had arrived to investigate was vast. The main premises, built in 1939, consisted of a four-storey building for the director's offices (complete with a panelled boardroom), drawing offices and records rooms. There were two large workshops, each 150 metres (500 feet) long. One was the machine shop and the other the U-boat shop, with cranes running the length of the roof. Between these two workshops was the torpedo assembly shop and 12 heavy concrete bunkers for testing torpedoes. The experiments were watched by the scientists from a safe location, with a periscope allowing them to remain undercover. Elsewhere, there were jet-engine testing rooms, chemical labs and welding shops. In the factory grounds were two large hydrogen peroxide storage bunkers that had been built partly underground with thick concrete, camouflaged walls. Within these were a total of ten 20-ton aluminium storage tanks.

Professor Walter's factory was not the only place of interest to the investigation teams that arrived in Kiel. The marine arsenal was found to contain large amounts of torpedo parts and

nautical instruments so it was soon sealed, with the commanding admiral placed in detention. At the ELAC plant Dr
Fischer, known to the investigators as an outstanding torpedo
designer, was taken into detention and held for interrogation
by the naval investigators. At a torpedo research station in
Eckenförde, where the entire staff were detained by T-Force,
interesting new developments were discovered. These included
acoustically guided torpedoes and zigzagging torpedoes, the
GNAT and the LUT. They were intended for use with a torpedo predictor that had been discovered in late April and was
already under investigation in the UK. Early investigations
showed that the torpedoes were designed to be fired in salvos
of three, making avoiding action by ships particularly difficult.

In the badly damaged Krupps Germania shipyard, T-Force
uncovered a complete Type XXIII submarine, while in the
Deutsche Werke establishment they discovered two almost
complete submarines and six small U-boats that were still under
construction. These were all exciting finds that soon received
trophy status, with sailors, marines and investigators posing for
photographs on the decks and in the conning towers. At the
Deutsche Werke, nine company directors were locked into an
office in the submarine pens and told they would soon be interrogated. In the end, they waited three weeks before the
investigators got around to visiting them.

Less imposing, but no less important, was T-Force's discovery of Dr Richter. The doctor was known as the leading
German authority on the Japanese economy and had been in
close touch with the authorities in Tokyo during 1944. He was
detained and handed over to the intelligence branch of SHAEF
where he was interrogated to discover what he knew about the
last remaining Axis power.

On 6 May, with the Germans within the city happily accepting the rules imposed by the occupying army, it was discovered
that to the north of the city, at a bridge crossing the Kiel canal,

there remained plenty of German soldiers in full fighting order
with little intention of accepting the war had finished. They had
been ordered to defend the canal, with some units retreating
from Hamburg to fortify the positions. On 4 May the order to
defend the canal had been reiterated, despite the fact that the
ceasefire was on the brink of being signed.

Despite the arrival of the British Army at the canal, the
defenders were reluctant to surrender or hand over their
weapons, leading to a stand-off at the canal bridge. John
Longfield was with the detachment sent to contain the
Germans: 'We were on the south side of the canal, they were
on the north side. Both sides were firing at each other, but it
was nothing exciting – if you saw someone you'd take a pot at
him, but usually you'd miss. The Germans had put a large
heap of explosives on the bridge and said they would blow it if
we advanced. We couldn't afford to lose the bridge so we
couldn't cross.'

With no one wanting to risk losing their lives now that the
war was all but over, T-Force remained in their positions on
the southern bank while negotiations continued, in the hope
that the Germans would realize that a ceasefire had been
declared. At one point a delegation of Germans attempted to
cross the bridge and approached a column of British armoured
cars at the southern end of the bridge. The German officer
later wrote:

> I slowly proceeded across the bridge towards its southern end;
> the two soldiers each had a machinegun . . . I carried my pistol.
> This was interpreted as an 'act of unfriendliness' by those at the
> front end of the [British] column, and we were immediately sur-
> rounded by officers, amongst them a German speaking
> lieutenant, and some soldiers all with pistols or machineguns,
> who made it crystal clear what would happen, if we proceeded.
> I could communicate my request for release, referring to the

armistice. The two submariners were relieved of their machine-guns and wristwatches and they were kicked, whereas I was left with my pistol and my watch and just received a blow to the head. We started back across the bridge and I ordered the iron gates to be shut.[11]

On 7 May the detachment holding the bridge were then confronted by an SS officer. He approached them insisting that he be allowed to destroy the bridge. It was only after the officer in command explained that there was an armistice in place, surrender was imminent and that Admiral Dönitz had ordered that the bridge should be preserved intact that the SS man withdrew. At the same time one German civilian noticed that two SS men and two Hitler Youths armed with a machine-gun had occupied a trench beside the canal in order to delay the English. They were driven away by a young woman who shouted at them: 'What are you doing here? Get out! The war is over!'[12]

Eventually the German commander agreed to hand over all his weapons to the British. Having collected them together that evening, he was perplexed to discover that the British had sent just three trucks to collect the 30 tons of arms he had gathered. It was quickly agreed that the British would return the following day to collect the rest.

With the situation resolved satisfactorily, the bridge was safely crossed. However, as John Longfield later recalled, the dangers had never been as great as he had believed: 'Years later I met the German officer who had been in command at the bridge. He admitted that the booby trap wasn't even real – there weren't actually any explosives.' Instead, the booby trap was an unexploded bomb that had been rolled to the centre of the bridge, with wires leading towards it, to create the impression of a deadly demolition charge ready to be detonated at a moment's notice.

Ensconced in the Naval Academy, with his soldiers and scientists spread throughout the now subdued city, Tony Hibbert was blissfully unaware of the stir he had caused when he had got a sleepy, drunken staff officer to sign the movement order and took T-Force into Kiel. In his mind, he had been acting firmly on the orders his friend Brian Urquhart had given him – to reach Kiel and take control of the port before the Russians arrived. This was the order that had come from SHAEF and, short of a direct message from the King or Winston Churchill, it was the highest authority. Yet by the reckoning of others, T-Force Kiel had disobeyed all standing orders. When the German authorities had made their way to Lüneburger Heide to surrender to Field Marshal Montgomery they had done so in good faith. The British had agreed to stand firm in their current positions – as identified in the orders issued by General Dempsey – until the surrender came into force three days later. As such, Hibbert and his men had jeopardized the ceasefire.

Apart from the potential danger of some Germans reacting to this apparent betrayal and reopening hostilities, there were other concerns. It seemed the Royal Navy felt that the occupation of Kiel was its right, considering it fitting that the German navy's Baltic base should be surrender to the 'Senior Service'. Possession of the city was also desired by the British Army. At 8 Corps HQ, where the tired and drink-sodden duty officer had signed the movement order Hibbert had presented to him, the Corps commander General O'Connor was irritated that someone had reached Kiel before him. His plan had been for a ceremonial entry into the city led by tanks of the 6th Guards Brigade, part of the Guards Armoured Division.

At 5.30 p.m. on 6 May the commanders of the T-Force detachment in Kiel received a visitor, Colonel Wreford-Brown, who passed on the news that it seemed they had acted in defiance of orders when they had advanced northwards. The move had breached 21st Army Group's orders and the actions of Hibbert, Gaskell and Lambert had put the entire ceasefire in danger. At a high level, there was concern that T-Force's action had risked an international incident. To many in T-Force, the news that they had acted against orders came as a surprise. Major Lambert was shocked to learn from his commanding officer that T-Force had potentially given the Germans an excuse to ignore the terms of the surrender and to fight on in Norway and other unconquered areas. The seriousness of the situation resulted in all T-Force officers and senior NCOs being called to a meeting to be advised that the troops were to do nothing to antagonize the Germans. At the meeting Wreford-Brown emphasized that each company of Kingsmen would be responsible for the defence of its own position and should fight to the 'last man and last bullet' if attacked.

Major Lambert was not the only officer concerned by the criticisms of the advance on Kiel. The Royal Marines of 30AU were also accused of having acted outside their orders in racing forward to Kiel. On 6 May Colonel Quill of 30AU wrote: 'The last few days have been most hectic, and our efforts to push forward have been grossly misinterpreted by many people as sheer piracy. My temper has shortened.'[13]

News of the British arrival in Kiel did not seem to have reached everybody within the city, and some of the population seemed to want to continue life as normal – despite having just been defeated in total war. On the morning of 7 May the men of T-Force stationed in the shipyards and factories were shocked to see local men arriving for work as normal. The troops shouted at the Germans to go away, trying to show them the facilities were now under British control. Crowds of shipyard workers stood around as if hardly able to understand what had happened. It appeared that many just wanted to go to work to earn enough money to feed their families, although at the time most of the British troops believed the Germans had failed to understand that their nation had been defeated. Eventually, the milling crowds wandered off to their homes to await the return of normality.

Later that day others were to be equally shocked by the presence of T-Force in Kiel. When the men of 8 Corps – led by the tanks of the Guards – finally arrived in the city they were also surprised to find it under the control of a handful of infantrymen, marines and scientists. The Guards' tanks, newly cleaned and crewed by correctly attired soldiers, moved through the streets in formation – a far cry from the piratical detachment that had arrived two days earlier. It seems they believed they would be the first British soldiers to enter the city and were perplexed to see groups of infantrymen already ensconced in Kiel. As one Guardsman later complained: 'We thought we were to be the first into Kiel, and there was f-ing T-Force signs on all the streets, and f-ing T-Force washing hanging out on the washing lines.'[14]

The men of T-Force were enjoying the moment, as Ken Hardy remembered: 'We were still having to work but no one was going to get killed. There was a wonderful sense of freedom. We had a party – we had lots of parties! It was all a bit childish . . . it was a lovely time. But there was a sense of anticlimax and sadness – it was all over and life was never going to be as exciting again.' John Longfield also recalled the light-hearted air that was moving through Kiel: 'It was a beautiful sunny day for a change, and some of the men who were not on duty explored the local area. They tried out their German by chatting up the local girls. The war may not be over but there seemed little point in being hostile to the Frauleins!' After T-Force had finished their celebrations a bemused naval officer arrived at A Company HQ to ask George Lambert whether he had witnessed the strange coloured lights over the sea. Lambert denied all knowledge and decided not to reveal that the 5th King's had fired all their mortar flares in celebration of victory.

Although some were able to joke about the matter, the situation for Tony Hibbert was far more serious. He had deliberately defied the orders of a corps commander and advanced way beyond the boundaries ordered by the head of the British 2nd Army. At best he realized he faced 'a rocket'; at worst he risked court martial. Hibbert recalls that while the Kingsmen were outside listening to Churchill speaking on the radio, Brian Urquhart entered his office and brought him up to date with the latest news:

> Tony, you are in a lot of trouble. General Barker has told me to put you under immediate close arrest. The trouble is, I have to get back to Bremen straight away. I can't leave an officer to guard you because you are the only officer here. So you'll just have to be under arrest. General Barker will be here tomorrow to deal with you. You are not the flavour of the month, personally. Nor is Brigadier Pennycook pleased with you since he is getting all the stick. You'd better smarten yourself up, I think the general will be displeased with your appearance.

Before he departed, Urquhart handed Hibbert a bottle of champagne to enjoy while 'under arrest'.

The next morning General Barker arrived, telling him: 'You are in considerable trouble. As a career officer, this isn't going to do you any good at all. You disobeyed an order.' Hibbert queried the claim that he had disobeyed an order, telling the general that his orders were to reach Kiel before the Russians. Presuming there was specific intelligence stating the Russians were going to send raiding parties from the sea to reach T-Force targets, Hibbert had thus not questioned orders from above. He told Barker: 'I did exactly as I was ordered and I understand that the orders had come from General Eisenhower.' His explanation seemed to work, with Barker telling Hibbert: 'Under the circumstances, and because you have done everything that I would have done had I been in Kiel, I will – on this one occasion – forget about it. Another thing, you'd better keep out of the way of Admiral Baillie-Grohman. He had been promised he would take the victory salute in Kiel. You've robbed him of it because everywhere in Kiel you see notices saying T-Force HQ.' General Barker's final words to Major Hibbert were: 'And please remember Hibbert, you are supposed to be a staff officer, not a bloody Commando.'

As a result, Major Hibbert spent VE Day under arrest for disobeying orders and carrying out what was the British Army's final advance of the war in Europe. Unknown to either General Barker or Major Urquhart was that there was a certain irony in Hibbert's arrest. On 3 September 1939, the day that war broke out, Hibbert had been sent by his commanding officer to collect an issue of alcohol for the officer's mess. While returning to their base, Hibbert had crashed his CO's car, wrecking it and smashing the bottles. As a result, he had been put under arrest. Thus he had been under arrest on both the first and the last days of the Second World War.

Elsewhere in the city, the men of T-Force gathered around wireless sets to listen to Winston Churchill's victory speech. Dispersed around the city, others just heard about it secondhand and watched as aircraft dropped leaflets which they were told were to inform the Germans of the news of surrender. John Longfield recalled the events: 'A few bottles of alcohol appeared from somewhere and at last we learned officially that the war was definitely over. It was something of an anticlimax and all the celebrating I did was to spend my evening trying to communicate, with some success, with a few Russians. It was just another day – there was no dancing in the streets.'

The following evening saw relaxed celebrations as Longfield and his comrades were sent to guard a German dignitary who was detained at the top of a tower. The British soldiers found bottles of wine from the cellar of a bombed-out hotel and shared them with civilians and the local policemen who were on hand to pass orders from the soldiers to the local population. As Longfield remembered, 'an inebriated time was had by all. The only fully sober man was the prisoner at the top of the tower.'

In the days immediately following the seizing of Kiel, as the city settled down to occupation, there were more new arrivals. Arriving by sea were hundreds of German soldiers, sailors and marines. Among them was teenage marine Jurgen Hakker. He was returning to his home city, from which he had first been evacuated as a result of Allied bombing, prior to being conscripted into the German navy as a marine. Having been evacuated from Stralsund by sea, first to Rügen then to Kiel, his homecoming was a moving experience. As he descended the gangplank and stepped ashore, he was greeted by a British soldier. The soldier stepped forward and told him he should throw away the spade he was carrying. It was a symbolic order for the young marine – the spades had been issued one between two and they had been told it would be used for burying their dead comrades. Then came a piece of even more direct news – the soldier told him the war was over.[15]

Despite the celebrations, there was a serious matter in the minds of all the soldiers in Kiel. As John Longfield recalled: 'Yes, the war in Europe was over, for which we were profoundly thankful, but military service was not, nor was the war with Japan. Those of us who had managed to survive all the way from Normandy to Kiel did not fancy a trip to the Far East, but at that stage it was very much on the cards.' Similarly, for Major Lambert the issue was unavoidable, so on VE Day he told himself: 'I am not going to think about

Japan for at least another day.' Lambert, Longfield and their comrades did not know that Japan would also soon be defeated; nor did they know that the work of T-Force would continue long after the end of the war. More importantly for T-Force, the UK and its western Allies were facing a new enemy – the Soviet Union – and a new conflict. They were soon to play their part in the first engagements of the forthcoming Cold War.

CHAPTER 7

Liberators – T-Force in Denmark and the Netherlands

'By the time I got there the shops were back to normal and it was good to see them full of cream cakes and other luxuries. Most of the locals seemed to ride bicycles and the young ladies did not seem to worry how high their skirts were blown up!'

Major George Lambert on arriving in Denmark.

VE Day came on a Tuesday, but for so long the days of the week had meant nothing to Ken Moore. Instead, each day had just blurred into the next:

> I tried to define what the end of the war meant. I felt it difficult to reconcile war with peace. During the fighting you thought of your family at home, but your focus wasn't very far ahead. You live for the moment – you didn't think a week ahead. So when it all finished, I felt let down. That might sound strange . . . when it came, in a sense we weren't prepared for it and frankly I don't think we knew what to do. To suddenly realize that you were reasonably safe and there was no more fighting, you didn't know how to handle it. We felt so lost. It overwhelmed me.

However, if Moore and the rest of T-Force thought their service would soon be over they had a shock coming. For instead of jubilant celebrations, the men of T-Force found there were even more targets still to be examined. Thus, the end of the war did not affect their workload and, for companies of the King's Regiment, this meant a rapid drive north through Schleswig-Holstein and into Denmark.

The move into Denmark, just like the decision to advance on Kiel, was based on the swiftly changing circumstances on the ground. The terms of the ceasefire stated that the Germans in Denmark had surrendered to Field Marshal Montgomery and, as such, it was the British who had authority over the German garrison, not the Danes. In an attempt to prevent any disturbances between the defeated occupation forces and the newly free Danish Resistance, the decision was made to rush T-Force into Denmark to bolster the small British force of paratroopers which had already flown into Copenhagen. Even including the Royal Navy flotilla and a squadron of RAF fighter-bombers that had been sent to Denmark, the British contingent was a token force. However, it was hoped that this would be enough to assert British control over the Germans remaining in the country.

T-Force detailed two separate columns to enter Denmark. Early on the morning of 7 May the first T-Force detachment crossed the border into Denmark, on their way to the town of Kolding. First came a Humber Scout Car, followed by jeeps and a column of trucks carrying the liberators. The soldiers standing in the open trucks were soon coated in a film of dust kicked up from the roads beneath them. Yet there was little time to be concerned with such matters. What mattered were the scenes around them. As T-Force advanced north, they became aware of other columns moving south towards them – long, dejected rows of German troops escaping Danish revenge. Ken Moore recalled the German columns he watched from the turret of his Scout Car: 'The roads were filled with men, young and old, wearing rags and tatters that once were uniforms, they were weary in mind as well as in body. Occasionally one of the young soldiers would find the strength to raise his arm and cry "Heil Hitler!" This was the death rattle of Nazi Germany, a state built by fanatics and in the end dragged down to the depths of the dark ages.'

It was not the defeated soldiers that stuck in the mind of Ron Lawton as his column advanced towards Denmark. Passing through Flensburg he looked out from the truck and noticed an old German man sitting on top of a pile of rubble: 'As we went past he raised his hat and waved his stick and said "Hello Boys." He spoke perfect English. We were all gobsmacked! We thought, isn't that fraternization? He was welcoming us. It always stuck in my memory.' A little later he had another encounter with Germans that summed up the sense of humanity that emerged to accompany the end of war. As his truck stopped at the roadside, Lawton walked down to a small river to fill his water bottle: 'I got down there and it was full of German soldiers who were making their own way back home. I had a drink as they all stared at me. It was probably the first time they'd seen a British soldier up close. I just looked up and winked at them! So they started smiling at me.' In a small celebration of peace, Lawton handed round some cigarettes and shared a smoke with his former foes.

After hours of driving along the roads north from Kiel, the column finally approached Denmark. The posts on the German side of the border were abandoned; whoever had been stationed there must have joined the columns moving homewards. The column continued until it reached the positions manned by Danish border guards and a detachment of British paratroopers who had been sent south after landing in Copenhagen. From the lead vehicle a letter giving permission to enter Denmark was formally presented to the border guards and the column continued northwards. Ken Moore recalled the scenes he witnessed around the Scout Car in which he was manning a Bren gun: 'It was as if someone had lifted a curtain; crowds of Danes flocked around us, shaking hands and pressing gifts upon us.' It was a shock to him: 'The Danes were crazy with happiness – I left the world of war and went into the airy-fairy world of peace. The Danes were fantastic. It gave you something to hang on to. If I'd stayed in Germany I don't know how I could have handled it.'

Commanding 13 Platoon of C Company, Tom Pitt-Pladdy assembled a column of troops to advance on Århus, outside Copenhagen. His detachment consisted of his jeep and driver, a camouflaged Opel car that had been 'liberated' from the Wehrmacht and fitted with a mounting for a Bren gun, three armoured cars of the 1st Royal Dragoons, four Mack trucks courtesy of the Pioneer Corps, the company ration truck, one amphibious DUKW truck that had previously been used by T-Force in the docks of Hamburg, and one other amphibious truck that had been taken against orders.

For Tom Pitt-Pladdy, the most notable scene at the Danish border was the large piles of suitcases. He soon realized the source. As Germans approached the border, hoping to cross back into their homeland, the Danish border guards were relieving them of their possessions – no doubt feeling that whatever the Germans were taking home had been stolen from the people of Denmark.

Every man in the British column was amazed by the scenes. The dejection of the withdrawing Germans they had been passing for the last few hours was in stark contrast to the local population who emerged from their homes to greet the liberators. At one town the column was diverted into the central market where they were forced to circle the square as the local population celebrated liberation. Charles Russell recalled the celebrations: 'At one place a young girl yelled "Hey! Tommy!" and threw a package up to my pal. He clapped his hands together around it. But he shouldn't have done that – the package contained newly laid eggs. That was bad luck – but it was well meant.'[1]

The day was celebrated by the newspaper of the Danish Resistance:

> Montgomery's brave men, we know you have fought and won, we know you have fought and suffered, and that you too have men that fell on the field of glory for their beloved country . . . Together we have fought the Nazidom which has desecrated the word man, through its bloody cruelty. Together, you and me will make part of the Allied front in times to come, and watch and guard around the peace and freedom we won. Blood and tears were the price of the fight, and happiness and right are to be made safe through the victory.[2]

Although they were feted as liberators, the men of T-Force faced a great deal of hard work. Arriving in the town of Kolding, their vehicles were immediately mobbed by joyous crowds. Everyone who could climb onboard the jeeps and trucks did so, clambering over the soldiers within. As the crowds grew larger – singing, dancing and throwing flowers – so the column grew slower. Eventually, they abandoned the vehicles, deciding it would be quicker walking to their target. When they reached the Staldgaarden, the former Gestapo headquarters, they quickly set about securing the archives and removing valuables from safes.

Arriving at Århus, the men of C Company – dirty and dusty from their long journey – were met by the local chief of police who led them to a hotel in the city centre where they were presented with a dining room laid out with silver cutlery and crystal glasses. That night they were billeted in a local school. At that point there were just 100 British soldiers in the city, while the German contingent numbered 8,000. The situation led to bizarre encounters such as when a British

Lance-Corporal accepted the very formal surrender of a four-gun German coastal defence battery. Tom Pitt-Pladdy recalled the overall situation:

> We had 8,000 German soldiers who were refusing to surrender to the Danes because they said they had surrendered to Montgomery. But the Danish resistance were busy hunting the Gestapo. That was causing a little bit of trouble. At first we left the Germans alone with their own guards fully armed. This was causing a problem with the Danes so we made the Germans move their guards back out of sight. Then we had a Danish liaison officer attached to us, so that helped. The Germans just wanted to get back to Germany, so we sent them back in groups of 200 at a time. Each column was accompanied by one truck to carry food and blankets for the prisoners.

In the days and weeks that followed, the Kingsmen were billeted with families around Danish towns and villages. There was fierce competition to allow the liberators into their homes. Night after night British soldiers were invited to parties and showered with gifts – in particular food and alcohol. They marvelled at the creamy Danish butter and the thick rashers of bacon that was almost constantly placed before them. After years of rationing and army rations it was like manna from heaven. A new favourite among the troops was *smørbrød*, an open sandwich with either fish, eggs, bacon, veal, ham or cheese on it. As Brian Urquhart noted in his official report on T-Force: 'a tremendous and stupefying welcome was, and still is, being extended to those fortunate detachments'.[3]

With the Germans disarmed and sentries in place at all important locations, there was little to do but to enjoy themselves. As the local newspaper in Århus reported, 'A walk around the sleeping quarters, formerly a classroom, one can gain the impression that a soldier's life is one of ease. But one must not forget that they have had tough times, in three months never sleeping in the same place two nights running so they are in need to rest out. Asked what they do with their time they answer "It's very nice to do nothing."' The newspaper also noted that the soldiers were particularly happy with the food in Denmark. Since the introduction of rationing in the UK there had been little bacon available except the strongly salted, fatty type favoured in North America. As one Kingsman told the paper: 'We had to win the war, if for nothing else, to get Danish bacon back on the table again.'4

In addition, there was a flood of evening invitations to formal dinners in which the British representatives found themselves plied with spirits, often leaving them barely capable of making their way home. By day, innumerable football matches were played between the liberators and the liberated. These often took place after a reception, again involving copious amounts of food and drink, as one man recalled: 'We were as pie-eyed as cuckoos.' Ken Moore's overriding memory of the football matches was getting drunk on schnapps and retiring to a hedge with Lieutenant Hardy where they lay down and slept off the drink. Other days were spent reviewing the local girl guides and playing cricket matches on a matting wicket against the local club. This overwhelming hospitality impressed the Kingsmen, leaving few in any doubt about Denmark. It was little wonder a number of relationships blossomed between the soldiers and local girls, as Ken Moore recalled: 'It was a very sorry day indeed when we got our orders to leave Denmark.'

Despite the good times enjoyed by T-Force, there was a serious side. They had a job to do. Among the targets in Denmark was a V2 rocket experimentation plant on the island of Fanø. The T-Force DUKW amphibious lorry came into use, ferrying teams to the island to carry out their investigations. Meanwhile, a detachment from B Company, under the command of a Canadian officer named Lt Keslick, was sent to

Høruphav with the task of guarding a group of German scientists and their families who had been held for interrogation.
The guards were necessary to prevent members of the Danish
Resistance taking revenge on their former oppressors. The
presence of the soldiers prevented any attempts to reach the
Germans and the detachment was able to pass its time in relative comfort. At Sæby one-man torpedo samples were found
and evacuated to the UK, while at Århus 12 midget submarines were also found. Elsewhere Danish resistance were
used to guard a dump of electrically charged rockets each
weighing 100 kilos.

One of the main T-Force targets was a novel system of
linked torpedoes that had been developed for harbour defence.
The system soon received close attention from the 'boffins' that
arrived to carry out an assessment. The teams also found harbour defence torpedoes, which could not be neutralized once
they had been set to 'danger', and shore-fired torpedoes controlled by a cable. Other examples of torpedoes included one
with a range of 80 miles (130km) that had earlier been
launched from Le Havre to attack shipping arriving at the
Mulberry Harbours off the coast of Normandy.

Once again, U-boats became the focus of attention. The
detachment at Århus was alerted that a U-boat was waiting
outside the port, uncertain of what it should do next. It
appeared that, while returning from the South Atlantic, the
captain had received the order that he should take his submarine past Denmark for the few short miles to Sweden and
surrender it there. With the possibility of losing out on acquiring a fully intact submarine, Lieutenant Pitt-Pladdy made the
decision to confront the U-boat's commander. Rushing to the
local yacht club, Pitt-Pladdy mounted the unit's amphibious
truck and sailed out to sea, approaching the submarine from
behind as it waited at the mouth of the harbour:

Because of the height of the boat's sides they couldn't see me. So I took out a large spanner and banged it on the hull. A scruffy red bearded submarine commander – a typical Hollywood version of a U-boat captain – popped his head out so I motioned for them to follow me into the dock. When we got back to the dock he said they had been sailing for three weeks and wanted his men to get some exercise. So I told him that one hour before dusk he could let them out on the docks.

Despite the British orders and the crew's willingness to accept Pitt-Pladdy's authority, the locals were less than happy. Once the crew were safely out of the U-boat they came under fire from snipers of the local resistance who were hiding among the dockside cranes. The gunfire sent the sailors rushing for the safety of their boat, raising the fear that they might sail for Sweden. Some of the British soldiers recalled U-boat crewmen returning fire from the cover of their boat. Earlier experience with T-Force had taught Pitt-Pladdy that U-boat technology was of the utmost interest to the scientists attached to the unit and he was determined that he would not risk losing a complete vessel. He took immediate action to prevent the hostile reaction of the Danes jeopardizing the smooth surrender of the boat and its crew:

So I went down in the armoured car to sort it out. I found the Danes up in a crane firing at the Germans. One of the Danes then came dashing out from behind a building firing a Sten gun. I was sat there with bullets hitting the front of my car. So I jumped down and really laid into him – flattening him. I wasn't at all happy. Then I looked down and one of his bullets had cut the strap off my gaiter. All I could think was, it wouldn't be very good to go all the way from Normandy only to be killed by a drunken member of the Danish resistance.

The Dane was lucky not to have killed Pitt-Pladdy and was sent on his way, but not before he had received a 'good thumping' from the British officer.

The Kingsmen were not alone in carrying out investigations in Denmark. One of the earliest British arrivals was Captain Eric 'Winkle' Brown, who flew in to carry out immediate investigations of captured enemy aircraft. He landed at a German airbase at Grove where he expected to meet the British Army. Instead, he was greeted by 2,000 German personnel. He bluffed the base commander by insisting a large British contingent was due to arrive, but the entire occupation force on that first night was just six 'boffins' and two British pilots. They were aided by the arrival of a contingent of drunken members of the Danish Resistance who surrounded their rooms to guard them from the Germans. One of the planes he tested while in Denmark was the Arado 234, an unarmed experimental reconnaissance plane. As Captain Brown noted, it was faster than any plane then in service with the RAF.

During this period, Captain Brown also flew to newly liberated Norway to carry out tests on a captured German seaplane. This was the giant, diesel-engined, Blohm + Voss 222 flying boat. The tests were carried out on the fjord at Trondheim, with Brown being given a captured German pilot to assist him with the take-off. For three miles they thundered along the water, but still he could not get the craft airborne. He then realized the German had locked the controls in an effort to frustrate Brown. The matter was resolved when Brown punched the German, knocking him out. He was then handed over to the Army and the test flight continued without incident.

It was not only in Denmark that the men of T-Force were in the vanguard of the liberation. The Netherlands also played host to T-Force units that were sent to uncover any military and scientific secrets left behind by the defeated German army.

In the days immediately following the crossing of the Rhine it had become clear that the bulk of the targets would be on the 2nd Army's front. With the 5th King's as the only fully ready T-Force unit, they had been switched from their original position attached to the Canadians and instead had been moved to join the 2nd Army. This move, which left the Canadians without a T-Force detachment for the initial period following the Rhine crossing, did not cause any particular problems. There were few targets on their front, apart from those expected to be found once the Netherlands was occupied. On 8 May 1945 the 30th Battalion of the Royal Berkshire Regiment finally became fully operational as part of T-Force, joining two companies of the Buckinghamshire Battalion preparing to occupy the Netherlands and secure targets within western Holland. On being transferred into T-Force, the Berkshires were informed they would be covering the entirety of the western Netherlands and had 8 category A targets and 140 category B ones.

The Buckinghamshire Battalion became the first T-Force units to move into the western Netherlands following the German ceasefire, advancing into the occupied zone on 7 May. They advanced into land which had been hit hard by war. Five years of occupation had resulted in thousands of men being forced from their homes to work as slave labourers in German factories. Bicycles, the common form of transport, had been confiscated by the occupation forces to prevent their use by the resistance, while the population had to endure terrible food shortages. It was little wonder the populace were ready for the arrival of the liberators:

> The triumphant entry into western Holland was a sight not to be missed. Crowds of rejoicing people lined the roads for mile after mile all waving and shouting and displaying hundreds of flags. Whenever the column stopped they swarmed all over every vehicle and as we approached Utrecht the vehicles were so bedecked

> with boys and girls it was dangerous to proceed at more than five
> miles per hour, chiefly because the driver could not see, but also
> lest the attachments might fall off and be hurt.[5]

One of the Buckinghamshire's vehicles reported having six children on the roof, two on the bonnet, three hanging off either side and others clinging to the wings.

Despite the carnival atmosphere, T-Force had serious work to complete. While other units came simply to act as a liberation force, T-Force had the task of securing facilities that were vital to the reconstruction of the Netherlands. By occupying such locations they could ensure the prevention of any further damage by the defeated Germans. At Utrecht a platoon from a smoke company were sent ahead to occupy the central post office and repeater station. They arrived to find the building occupied by a fully armed German unit. The officer in charge of the smoke company summoned the German commander and insisted he and his men hand over all their weapons. The German was shocked by the order and informed the British officer that under the terms of the armistice he and men were allowed to retain their weapons: 'In our best German we told him that, if he ever made another statement like that again, we would not only disarm him but would have him in chains.' The officer then told him: 'Armistice terms my foot . . . you take your orders from us, no argument!' The weapons were duly collected and locked in an empty room.

When a British signals officer arrived to take over the working of the repeater station, the T-Force officer explained why he was there and expressed his surprise at the arrogance of the German officer who had refused to hand over his weapons. He was shocked by the reply: 'He's quite right. Those are the terms.' It was a surprise to discover the Germans had the right to be armed; nobody had bothered to inform the liberators of the Netherlands of the rules for handling the defeated occupying army. Despite the revelation of the armistice conditions, the officer decided the Germans should remain unarmed, only allowing them to collect their weapons once they left the facility. As the officer later commented, 'We subsequently read the full terms in the *Daily Herald*. If only we could have got the daily papers a bit quicker we would not have fallen into those errors!'[6]

While in the Utrecht area the Berkshires were responsible for the discovery of a torpedo-firing pistol for use within midget submarines. This was handed over to representatives of the Royal Navy who expressed significant interest in the find. They also undertook work in a number of botanical laboratories specializing in moulds and fungus that were believed to be producing a penicillin equivalent, and called forward investigators to confirm this.

The move into the Netherlands continued with T-Force in the vanguard. At Haaksbergen, the 49th Division gave T-Force permission to forge ahead to reach their targets. Although the offer was made in good faith, it did little to ease their way. As the first Allied units to enter many Dutch towns, the T-Force detachments found themselves caught up in crowds that swarmed over their vehicles and slowed them to walking pace while 'brushing the children off the bonnets every mile or so'.[7] In one town just outside Amsterdam the armoured cars were forced, at the request of the local mayor, to make a diversion. He did not want the children of a particular school to miss out on the liberation and so T-Force was asked to drive past the school gates.

Outstripping the main liberation force, a detachment under the command of Captain Lowe of the Buckinghamshire Battalion became the first Allied troops to reach Rotterdam. Entering the town he made contact with members of the local resistance, the NBS.[8] His vehicles were directed to the group's local headquarters where its members were formed up around a square. As Captain Lowe arrived the resistance fighters presented arms and received a smart salute from the British officer. The formalities over, the troops asked for assistance to reach the target factories and set off under escort from the local men. It later transpired that the formal reception had actually been planned for a brigade commander from the Canadian Army who arrived minutes after the T-Force detachment had sped off to its original targets. As an officer of the Buckinghamshires noted: 'T-Force had beaten everyone to it once again . . . T-Force seems to have stolen a few chaps' thunder by infiltration tactics. We just move on our own in small packets . . . so Divs never really know when we are going to arrive'.[9]

With the Buckinghamshire Battalion and the attached smoke companies rushing forward to occupy targets, the 30th Royal Berkshires moved forward to join them, searching for and taking over targets in previously agreed areas. The battalion, in keeping with the T-Force tradition, found itself split asunder and sent in company-sized detachments across the country, with A Company heading for Amsterdam, B Company guarding targets in Utrecht, C Company occupying Rotterdam and D Company covering the Hague and a number of islands near the Hook of Holland. As the battalion commander later admitted, he had 'sent off companies into the blue'.[10] He soon realized he could only visit one detachment a day and that there were no telephone links to many of the targets guarded by his troops.

The battalion's A Company were proud to be the first British troops to move into the north of the country, where they soon occupied targets in Amsterdam and acquired a motor launch to patrol the many waterways of the region. While in Amsterdam, T-Force teams carried out investigations at a petroleum plant believed to be at the forefront of fuel research. The plant's staff explained that much of their research had remained hidden from the Germans. They had achieved this by consenting to carry out other work for the Germans, thus concealing the plant's most important research.

With the war finally officially over, a wave of assessors joined the forward units. In particular there were representatives of the Royal Navy – accompanied by members of 30AU – who arrived to study maritime facilities. Radar experts were soon fully occupied at targets that had previously acted as early warning against the fleets of Allied bombers that had bombarded the Reich for the past two years. Members of intelligence sections were sent forward with them to type out their reports. This speeded up the transit of reports from forward locations back to the T-Force HQ and then on to England. However, the workload in the Netherlands was greatly lightened by the discovery that there was little of interest left in the Netherlands. It transpired that much had been removed to Germany following the Allied airborne landings at Arnhem the previous year.

At Arnhem during April the Buckinghamshires had found they could reduce the force needed to search the town from a company to a platoon since the advancing army had requested the RAF to 'smash up' one of the main targets since it was 'a fortress and must be eliminated'.[11] The RAF continued to conspire against T-Force when a Typhoon fighter-bomber fired a rocket into a Royal Engineers equipment dump needed for constructing a ferry across the river, thus slowing the advance on the town. When they finally entered Arnhem the operation was further delayed by a German mortar bomb that put the leading T-Force armoured car out of action as they sped towards their target.

Despite the destruction and wholesale pillaging of Dutch industry, some discoveries were vital to the war effort. With the war in the Far East continuing, the teams had been briefed to locate documents relating to the Dutch East Indies – at that time still in the hands of the Japanese. They needed to search for maps and books containing topographical information that was not available elsewhere. In the university and municipal libraries at Groningen, Deventer and Wageningen more than 50 books were obtained that contained the necessary information that could be used to plan landings in the Japanese-controlled territories. And T-Force had some other interesting finds. At Utrecht the unit detained a Dr Strabismus, a scientist who had earned his place on the CIOS lists due to his research on perpetual motion. The doctor was an interesting find since he was last reported as working in Spain in 1944.

Of particular importance was anything that assisted the population of the Netherlands to return to a state of normality as quickly as possible after five years of oppressive occupation. At Leeuwarden T-Force uncovered complete minefield charts for Harlingen harbour, allowing mine clearance operations to be carried out swiftly and safely. The same office that revealed the minefield charts also contained plans for a treacherous new naval mine that had been designed to resemble a mooring buoy. Once at Harlingen, the Buckinghamshires uncovered 'opportunity targets' including a munitions plant and a barge loaded with the complete turbine equipment for a large ship. At Doetinchem they located the laboratory of a Dr Büttcher. According to former members of his staff who had gone into hiding to avoid being forcibly sent to Germany, he had been experimenting with splitting the atom with X-rays. The doctor, reportedly both a scientist and an officer in the SS, was required for interrogation but had already fled to Germany.

There was one target of particular interest, if not to the experts, to the men themselves. One company of the Buckinghamshire Battalion was moved to the town of Norden. Here the soldiers took over the radio transmitter that had previously been used to transmit Lord Haw-Haw's propaganda broadcasts to the UK. They were disappointed to find that the broadcaster was not at the location, since he had earlier been

Soldiers of the 5th Battalion, The King's Regiment, on Sword Beach on the morning of D-Day.

T-Force reconnaissance armoured car, Spring 1945. Part of a detachment from the 5th King's serving with the British 11th Armoured Division.

March 1945. A signpost at the German border warning British troops how to behave.

(top) Officers of the 5th Battalion, The King's Regiment, photographed in May 1945. Lt Colonel Guy Wreford-Brown is fifth from the right on the front row.

(middle) C Company of the 5th King's in Denmark, May 1945.

(bottom) B Troop of 30 Advanced Unit, Royal Marines in Germany, May 1945. The Troop commander Lt Commander Jim 'Sancho' Glanville is standing in front of the tree wearing a Royal Navy cap.

(above) A jeep of B Troop, 30AU, Royal Marines at Minden, Germany, May 1945.

(left) T-Force Royal Navy investigator John Bradley (left) with Commander Dunstan Curtis of 30AU. Bradley was a metallurgist who had worked in railway engine design before being seconded to the Admiralty.

(below) T-Force evacuating equipment from a factory in Köln (Cologne), March 1945. The photograph was taken by John Bradley, who had helped investigate the factory.

(above) A German Type XVIIB U-boat, salvaged from the waters of the Baltic, being prepared for despatch to the UK for further investigation.

(right) An experimental glider bomb being tested at the 'Walterwerke' in Kiel. This was just one of many new weapons developed by the factory's owner, Dr Walter.

(below) Dr Walter's 'Cleopatra' anti-beach defence weapon after wartime tests. The jet-powered boat was designed to be fired from the sea, before rising from the water and destroying beach defences.

(above) The *Admiral Hipper* in Kiel harbour, 'captured' by T-Force on 5 May 1945. Soldiers from 'A' Company of the 5th King's came under fire from the ship before boarding her and disarming the crew.

(below left) The bomb-damaged Naval Academy in May 1945. It was there that Major Tony Hibbert accepted the surrender of Kiel's garrison.

(below right) Dr Helmut Walter, detained by T-Force in May 1945. Walter (in hat) is seen here watching weapons tests at his factory.

The 'Walterwerke', the factory where so much of Germany's most advanced military equipment had been designed. Its output included high-speed submarines, V1 rocket launch systems and the engines for the V2 missiles.

Men of the 5th Battalion, The King's Regiment, listening to Churchill's VE Day broadcast in Kiel, 8 May 1945. They had arrived in the city on 5 May, having ignored the ceasefire and advanced 60 miles behind German lines.

Soldiers of T-Force retrieving experimental torpedo combustion chambers from a bomb crater outside Kiel. The equipment had been hidden there on the orders of Dr Walter.

German mini submarines under investigation by 30AU, Royal Marines at Eckenforde, Germany. Summer 1945.

German scientists on the Blankensee ferry after being detained by T-Force, September 1945.

Soldiers of No.1 T-Force with a German Panther tank. Detachments searched throughout the British zone for tanks that could be used for research purposes.

(above) Jean Hughes-Gibb at her desk in HQ T-Force. She was the first civilian to be employed by the unit and was responsible for organizing the collection of German scientists who were to be sent to the UK.

(right) Lt Colonel Percy Winterton, Commander No.2 T-Force, photographed meeting a Russian investigation team. T-Force's post-war work included the frustration of Russian efforts to obtain the services of German scientists and evacuate equipment of military importance.

(below) The skyline of the Ruhr in 1947. Germany's foremost industrial zone provided a rich hunting ground for T-Force teams in the post-war period.

captured near Hamburg. However, the equipment was found to be in perfect working order. Elsewhere, one platoon was sent to take control of a radio transmitter on the island of Borkum, but when they arrived they found they had 4,500 German prisoners to keep under control.

Despite the welcome sense of relief felt by the men of T-Force as they settled into the role of liberators, they retained a strong sense of duty brought on by the conditions in many parts of the Netherlands. In the final winter of war, forever remembered as the 'Hunger Winter', the Germans had all but starved the host population. Rations fell to a level that left the population weakened and on the brink of starvation. Among the most vulnerable – the young, the old, the poor and the sick – the death rate had risen at an alarming rate, leaving undertakers without sufficient coffins to bury the victims. With many reduced to eating flower bulbs, the RAF had made food drops but it was not enough to ward off starvation. Where possible, the liberators stepped into the breach.

In Rotterdam, the men of T-Force who arrived to liberate the city noticed that the clothing worn by the locals was threadbare. Many wore shoes whose soles had worn out and they were visibly emaciated. As the commander of the Royal Berkshire's C Company noted, the local children were 'pathetic and irresistible'.[12] To counter the sickness the soldiers set aside a portion of their own food each day. This was then distributed by the local doctor, ensuring the most malnourished children were fed first. The distribution system meant that 10 children could be fed each day with a further 40 receiving a meal three times a week.

At Delft, the detachment led by Captain Lowe supplied daily rations to several hundred hungry children. The kind-hearted soldiers could not bear to see the sad eyes of children staring at them as they ate their rations. As a result, here too the decision was taken that the soldiers would make sacrifices, offering a daily meal to the most desperate of the locals. By the time the detachment left Delft they were feeding 300 people a day. Those too sick to leave their beds to queue for food had their daily rations taken to them by the soldiers.

Similarly, at Utrecht the soldiers of the Royal Berkshires found their appetites were quelled by the sight of the starving population. As the cooks prepared their first meal in the town, they were watched by crowds of locals, all eager just to smell hot food. Once the food was distributed few of the soldiers could eat and instead handed their mess tins to the children. Even after the meal was finished the crowds did not disperse, as if they could not bring themselves to leave a location where food had been so generously handed out. For the men of T-Force, the satisfaction of seeing the joy on the faces of the children far outweighed any pleasure they got from knowing they had successfully reached another target, detained a scientist or acquired some scientific documents.

CHAPTER 8

Investigations

'. . . *secret weapons that made Jules Verne look like a small boy with a popgun.*'

News Chronicle, 16 July 1945.

The postwar phase of T-Force's operations was defined by one simple factor – the need for the western Allies to continue to search Germany and discover the Nazi regime's military secrets. Only by absorbing this research and utilizing it to their advantage could the West keep one step ahead of the Russians. If the collection and evacuation of machinery, prototypes, documents and personnel were going to continue, then it was essential to retain the use of the unit that had already been so successful in the role.

Initially, there had been a measure of scepticism among some commanders about whether a unit such as T-Force could operate successfully amidst the rapidly changing environment of a sweeping advance through Germany. The doubters had been proved wrong. As Brian Urquhart noted in his final report prior to leaving T-Force, 'It worked far better than anyone dared to hope.'[1] He stressed that military commanders had been impressed with the smooth running of the T-Force system of operations and evacuations. He attributed the success to the 'endless good temper'[2] of the officers and staff of the 5th King's HQ in dealing with a multitude of problems, the initiative shown by the officers in the field and the skill of the assessors.

With the war over and Germany occupied by the Allies, there was little time for the men of T-Force to settle down to enjoy the fruits of victory. Although they were able to carry out their duties safe in the knowledge that no one was shooting at them, there was still plenty of work to be done. Once the danger had passed increasing numbers of scientists and investigation teams arrived in Germany to continue the search for the secrets of the Third Reich. And at all times they were to be hosted by the men that had previously led the charge to find these secrets – T-Force.

During the advance into Germany few among the British Army had any idea of the role played by the unit. Most officers and men who had seen their vehicles charging around the roads of Germany merely asked themselves 'Who the hell are T-Force?' and carried on with the business of winning the war. Once the war was over, and T-Force had embarked on the mission of following up leads from earlier investigations, there still remained the necessity to draw a discrete veil over their activities.

While the soldiers got used to looking after the investigation teams, the unit received the first recognition of its wartime duties. Despite this need for secrecy that helped conceal some of their more clandestine activities, a few stories had been released to the media – albeit without revealing the perpetrators of the deeds. Having heard whispers about the activities of the unit, a well-known historian named Captain Cyril Falls, working as the military correspondent for *The Times*, requested permission to write a feature on T-Force. Despite the top secret nature of its work, Field Marshal Montgomery passed the request to Brigadier Pennycook who in turn passed it to his second-in-command, Lt Colonel Bloomfield. With little knowledge of science, Bloomfield turned to a T-Force colleague, a

Royal Navy liaison officer named Lt Commander Kenneth Goudge. Himself a scientist, Goudge was able to guide Falls on the discoveries.

Thus, June 1945 saw the first official recognition of the existence of T-Force and their role in the final battles in Germany. In *The Times* on 29 June, under the title 'Germany's Secret Weapons', Cyril Falls gave a brief insight into the events of April and May. Somewhat dramatically, it described how Germany's scientists had continued their 'feverish research' into the final days of war and the Allies had ended the war 'only just in time'. Without naming either T-Force, or the units that were its constituent parts, the writer explained how 'The British entered Germany with machinery organized to prevent the destruction or concealment of research work or plants.' As he further noted, Allied bombing had slowed the development of deadly offensive weapons 'but could not have stopped it'.

Incidents were recounted, including one in which T-Force had entered the offices of a company to find the managing director addressing a board meeting on how best to dispose of their secrets. Specific mention was made of German advances in infra-red technology, including cameras capable of taking photographs at extreme distances and high-powered searchlights designed to blind Allied tank crews. Elsewhere, the writer noted the discovery of rocket-assisted shells and a scheme to add wings to V2 rockets. Indestructible rubber tyres, air-to-ground and air-to-air rockets were also described, as were zigzag torpedoes designed to attack ships that were also zigzagging. Another fresh design mentioned was a glider that could be released from an aircraft, which in turn released a torpedo. The deployment of the glider meant the attack could take place from a greater distance, thus avoiding anti-aircraft fire from the target ship. There was little detail of the projects, since such information remained highly classified, but there was enough to amaze the reader unfamiliar with the destructive innovations emerging during the death throes of the Third Reich.

Two weeks later, on 16 July 1945, the *News Chronicle* followed up with another story of T-Force's achievements. This provided the first mention of T-Force and its commander by name, but again omitted any mention of the individual units that had taken part. Again hoping to grab the attention of the reader, it spoke of 'secret weapons that makes Jules Verne look like a small boy with a popgun'. Brigadier Pennycook was quoted as saying, somewhat optimistically, that 'Today Germany has not a single military secret left.' Further details were given of the infra-red technology, describing lenses that could pick out a ship from 20 miles and how beams could be used to project an image of an Allied tank on to a screen during night fighting. One of the most fantastical weapons noted – and one of which Jules Verne would indeed have been proud – was a flying bomb fitted with scythes that were designed to slice Allied bombers in half. As Brian Urquhart later revealed, at one point T-Force even found research documents relating to mirrors to be used in space to deflect and concentrate the sun's rays, creating an intense beam of solar energy designed to scorch the lands of Germany's enemies.

These articles omitted to record that, with the war over, T-Force remained fully engaged in supporting the ongoing investigations into what had been uncovered during the advance into Germany. Of immediate interest were the main military developments that had formed their primary targets: nuclear weapons, chemical warfare, submarines and rocket technology.

When *The Times* published its account of the work of T-Force, there was one subject that was not mentioned: nuclear research. Captain Falls did not mention atomic science, fusion, nuclear fission, heavy water or any of the other words that would become frighteningly real in the months that followed. Although the Americans were so close to unleashing previously unimaginable destruction upon Japan, atomic research remained a closely guarded secret. So much so that, although research laboratories and scientists were placed on T-Force's 'blacklists', none among the troops had the slightest idea of quite how important these targets were. Even Lt Colonel Bloomfield, who was one of the few men in T-Force who knew anything about the subject, had been told little apart from the key words. However, what he did know was enough to understand that the research was of such importance that not even the smallest detail could be revealed.

To those in the know, finding German nuclear scientists was of the utmost importance, way beyond the need to uncover high-speed submarines or new types of rocket engines. Quite simply, the most advanced conventional weapons were on the brink of being rendered obsolete by nuclear weapons. Thus, though the Nazis had not yet reached the point of constructing their own nuclear weapons, it was vital any scientists engaged in nuclear research should not share their knowledge with any potential enemies.

As previously mentioned, in the final days of the war T-Force had located and detained Dr Groth, one of the researchers whose talents could have been used to help the Russians develop their own atomic weapons. He had been rapidly evacuated to the UK. Within days Lt Colonel Bloomfield, T-Force's second-in-command, had been shocked to see Dr Groth back in Celle accompanied by two American professors. Upon returning to Germany, Dr Groth asked the newly appointed British 'Town Major' for permission to resume his experiments so that he might 'help win the war against Japan'.

It was only some time later that Bloomfield discovered what had happened to Groth upon arrival in the UK. He had been immediately whisked away where a team of Britain's foremost atomic researchers, led by John Cockcroft, interviewed him about his research. It later transpired that, within 15 minutes, Cockcroft's team ascertained that the German's research was so far behind that of the Allies that the Nazis had to be some way from developing an atomic bomb. Despite this, the Allied investigators continued to search for any targets and personnel that might help their own investigations.

Among the 106 targets investigated by T-Force in the ruins of Hamburg were some that related to nuclear research. They included the laboratory of the nuclear physicist Dr Paul Harteck, an associate of Dr Groth. In May 1945, his detention caused some controversy, since he was picked up by a specialist team with an interest in nuclear research that was working within the 21st Army Group's area. This team had been operating without notifying T-Force HQ or coordinating their activities with T-Force teams in the field. As a result, the atomic research team's work within the British zone was temporarily suspended and similar teams were withdrawn from the area. The issue was rectified when the team in question agreed to abide by existing operational orders.

Harteck's day-to-day research facilities had moved from Hamburg to a facility – later taken over by the RAF – one mile outside Celle, close to Dr Groth's underground laboratory. However, his offices and documents remained of interest as he had used an ultra-centrifuge at Celle to experiment on the separation of uranium 235 and 238. The centrifuge itself had been built by a firm based in Kiel, which in turn needed to be investigated by T-Force. The main part of the research work was done by Dr Groth under Harteck's direction. As the investigators who interviewed Groth had noted, the pair's work had included 'notable technical advances'.[3]

Upon arriving back in Germany, Dr Groth discovered that the centrifuge needed for his work was missing. Investigations carried out by T-Force HQ revealed that the centrifuge had been disassembled and sent to SHAEF for the attention of the Operation Alsos mission. It was one of the few examples of evacuations that had been unsuccessful. The hurried nature of the work and the involvement of outsiders, added to the importance of the research equipment, meant that the standard procedures had not been followed. Due to an administrative oversight, no serial number had been issued and the shipment was untraceable. Dr Harteck was later informed that the centrifuge was unlikely to be located, but was told that the British would put up half the cost of replacing his equipment but that the rest would have to be found from German sources. The plan was for his research to continue on industrial rather than military development, and focusing on protein analysis rather than isotope separation.

T-Force's work with the nuclear scientists did not end once they had been sent to the UK to be interrogated about their work. Their care once back in their homeland also fell to T-Force. In October 1945 there was some concern about the movement of ten nuclear scientists, three of whom were of particular note, back to Germany. The men had been evacuated to the UK in July 1945 at the request of General Leslie Groves, the official in charge of 'tube alloys' research in the US. General Groves believed that if the men were allowed out of custody, most would head to Russia, voluntarily or not. He was convinced they would be of the 'greatest value'[4] to the Soviet government and that, if allowed to go free, they would be kidnapped by the Russians who were eager to expand their pool of nuclear research talent. They had been removed, 'partly to enable us to get all possible information out of them, and partly to prevent their being annexed and employed by less desirable governments'.[5] No one could be certain that this was anything more than paranoia on the general's part, but no one was prepared to take a chance.

In the UK the group had lived 'on parole' on an estate in East Anglia but had soon become frustrated by their continuing detention and resented the situation they were in. Among the group were: Werner Heisenberg, whose family remained in Bavaria and were supported by the British; Walter Gerlach; Kurt Diebner, whose home was in the American zone; Otto Hahn, Max von Laue, Carl Friedrich von Weizsäcker, Karl Wirtz, Erich Bagge and Horst Korsching, all of whom were from the French zone; and Harteck whose laboratories had been discovered by T-Force. Such was the value of these scientists that General Groves was convinced they were 'superior in all-round ability to the group which had started the New Mexico laboratory'.[6]

The British suggested that Harteck should be 'shadowed' to prevent him from being kidnapped by the Russians and in November 1945 the British informed General Groves that 'special arrangements' were to be put in place to look after Harteck. The British hoped the scientists could be sent into western Germany and wanted them to be employed as a group at Bonn University. However, fears were expressed that if they were taken to Bonn they would be too close to the French zone and thus risk falling into French hands. The US and UK authorities were also concerned that the scientists could not be employed together as that would attract attention.

It was clear that if their talented minds were not gainfully employed in their homeland they would grow restless and seek employment elsewhere. This was an experience that dogged all those in T-Force concerned with the detention of scientists. For most of the scientists their work was not a means to riches but to intellectual glory. They were dedicated to the advancement of science. To many of them, politics was of little interest. Whether the Nazis or the Communists – or even the French – were their paymasters was not their concern as long as their work was published to the acclaim of their peers. Short of imprisonment, it was clear there could be no guarantee they would not escape into other zones or countries. Anxious about the implications of the scientists being lost to the western powers, Field Marshal Montgomery contacted London to insist that imprisonment would be the only way to prevent their escape to other zones.

As part of the policy of re-employing the nuclear scientists, in early 1946 Dr Groth was allowed to return from Celle to Hamburg, with T-Force transporting all his remaining equipment back from the secret laboratory beneath the silk factory. In April 1946 an officer from the 5th King's was sent to the Phoenix works at Eutin to arrange for the acquisition of a centrifuge which was under construction there and to arrange for it to be sent to Dr Harteck's laboratory in Hamburg. British interest in his work continued during the years that followed. In October 1947 extra payments were cleared by the British to ensure the completion of his project on the grounds of the importance of the work to scientific research taking place in the UK. The irony was that much of the expense was to repair the buildings in which the machinery was to be located, the damage having been caused by RAF raids.

Of the nuclear scientists that T-Force had evacuated to the UK, Otto Hahn was subject to particular interest. Such was the fame of his work that he had been awarded the Nobel Prize for Chemistry in 1944 and the Swedes wished him to visit Stockholm to receive his award. The Swedish government formally made the request, believing Hahn to be in British custody. Although the British initially stalled and avoided answering the request, it was decided that information relating to the British detainment of scientists should be released, since it already had been announced that the Americans had taken some scientists back to the US.

A formal statement was drafted on the matter of 'our German guests'. The statement referred to the close attention the British had paid to German atomic research and mentioned the raids on 'heavy water' plants in Norway: 'After the invasion of Germany a special mission was sent to make enquiries on the spot and examine all equipment and records. These enquiries confirmed the estimate already formed by our Intelligence Services that the Germans had made little or no progress towards the realisation of the project.'[7] The statement named both Hahn and Heisenberg and admitted they had since returned to Germany.

Investigations also took T-Force to Germany's Mega Volt Research Association, who described themselves as anti-military and anti-industrial, stressing their credentials as pure researchers. They were an alliance of physicists devoted to pure atomic and nuclear research who had been described as 'proceeding with very advanced research'.[8] While they were not in the forefront of German research they were of interest since they claimed to have good knowledge of the rest of the German scientists engaged in nuclear research.

T-Force also gathered a wealth of information in relation to research into chemical warfare. The unit's occupation of the various Munsterlager plants marked a significant breakthrough in the Allies' knowledge of German gas technology. While initial reports on gas technology had lumped together all gas research facilities in the Lüneburger Heide area under the name 'Munsterlager', further investigation revealed that there existed a network of camps. This included the Wehrmacht's experimental station at Raubkammer; a chemical munitions charging plant and the Luftwaffe's experimental station at Munster Nord; the Luftwaffe's chemical munitions storage facility at Oeren; and the Wehrmacht's gas storage facility at Celle. There were also additional facilities for use by smoke-screen troops.

Initial investigations also centred on why the Germans had never deployed chemical weapons. The interrogation of German officers detained at the facilities at Frankenberg and Hunstadt suggested the German High Command had never shown any desire to use the weapons they had stockpiled. During interviews they stressed that Hitler had opposed their use on the battlefield, despite his willingness to use poison gas on defenceless civilians. Later interrogations of German gas scientists suggested that Hitler had remained strongly opposed to any use of chemical weapons on the battlefield as a result of his own experiences during the Great War.

The scientists also attempted to claim that the Wehrmacht held insufficient stocks of gas to use on the battlefield. The British investigators rubbished this claim noting that they had 'made preparations for gas warfare on a lavish and costly scale'.[9] In total, the Nazis possessed 100,000 tons of gas shells and bombs. Around one-third of these were mustard gas bombs found at the Luftwaffe facilities at Munsterlager. Some of the stocks at the plant had been delivered from Poland and were due to be removed for hiding in Thuringia. They were due to be sent on 20 trains, each composed of 30 cars with 36 gas bombs per car. And this was just what was found in the British zone – an additional 16 chemical weapons depots had been located in the US zone.

Further claims were made that the Wehrmacht possessed no efficient method of deploying gas. This claim was undermined by the existence of shells and bombs that easily could have been used against the advancing Allied armies. More convincing were claims that it was considered foolish to use gas on home soil and that both German soldiers and civilians were insufficiently prepared for the use of chemical weapons.

Investigators at the Munsterlager plants considered that the German facilities were lavish and that 'no expense had been spared', allowing chemical weapons research to flourish. In the latter stages of the war, in reaction to an increasing belief that the Allies might deploy battlefield chemical weapons, the German research had increased with Raubkammer being used for testing chemical weapons to be used in close combat and against tanks. One weapon that had been developed for use against tanks and fortified positions was a hand grenade containing a glass bulb charged with hydrogen cyanide. Though these grenades were not in full production, a few thousand had been made and were considered to be excellent weapons.

It was also found that the Germans had been experimenting with anti-tank rounds filled with gas. One of the more fanciful anti-tank weapons researched by German scientists was a fast-firing machine-gun that delivered chemical rounds. Experiments had included firing these rounds at the air intakes of a tank in order to poison the crew within. The experiments had not been successful. It was particularly noted that researchers had also designed a chemical warhead, for use on the V1 flying bomb, which would deliver phosgene gas. The research had been in its early stages and no tests had been carried out by the end of the war.

As briefly touched upon earlier, the initial task of the investigators at the gas plants – seven of which had produced poison gas – was to understand the colour coding used on German chemical munitions that were all marked with a half-inch band of bright paint. They soon discovered that the white band signified tear gas, a green band meant phosgene, yellow contained mustard gas and two green bands signified diphosgene. Most importantly, the investigators uncovered shells marked with a green and yellow band. They soon realized that this was a gas they had not previously encountered.

This new gas was found by T-Force teams in 85mm and 105mm artillery shells which contained 1200cc of liquid charging with a half-pound burster charge. The liquid was a dark brown colour and had a distinct sweet smell, similar to prussic acid. These shells were carefully packed up and sent back to Porton Down for closer investigation by British scientists. At first it was believed that the shells might contain the vesicant (blister-causing) gases such as mustard gas or phosgene. Initial reports from tests on animals showed that small doses were not a problem but led to a fall in blood pressure. However, post-mortem results showed intense congestion of the liver and lungs consistent with heart failure. It was believed at first that the gas was of no immediate concern since shell distribution of the gas would not be too dense and thus not overly effective. But this optimism was countered when it was noted: 'if it were used a number of troops would be killed in a spectacular fashion'.[10]

As the tests continued, the results were shocking. When tested on animals a larger dosage of gas had an immediate and lethal effect. The scientists were surprised to see that, rather than burning the skin of the test animals, the gas paralysed them within seconds and killed them within minutes. Even more disturbingly for the scientists, it was believed that the gas-masks employed by the Allied armies would have been of little use against these gases.

Investigations revealed that the gas in question was Tabun, the first of the so-called paralysing gases to have been developed for the German military. Originally named Trilon, or T83, it was first developed by Professor Heinrich Hörlein and Dr Gerhard Schrader working for IG Farben at Elberfeld. Schrader and his assistant had noticed the chemical's power when they became exposed to it in the course of their research. They experienced a tightening of the chest that caused laboured breathing and a contraction of the pupils that forced them to shun all light. While their breathing returned to normal after exposure to fresh air, it was a further three days before their eyesight was fully restored. Early tests on dogs and monkeys − which entered Germany from Morocco via Spain − demonstrated the dangerous nature of the chemical which was an ethyl ester of dimethylaminoethoxycyanophosphine oxide. Early versions contained 5 per cent chlorobenzine, while later versions contained 20 per cent, making the Tabun more volatile.

Once the nature of their discovery was certain, the IG Farben teams transferred all the patent rights to the German military. Dr Otto Ambros, the Technical Director at IG Farben, told the teams of young scientists working on the gases that they would be exempt from military service since they would be serving their country in 'dangerous scientific work'.[11] At Dyhernfurth, Tabun was produced by these men within a large glass chamber. Inside this was a second glass chamber in which the gas was produced. The operators worked between the two, the air around pumped to a high pressure to prevent gas leaking from the central chamber to the outer one.

In total, it was estimated that more than 10,000 tons of Tabun had been produced by the German military and packed in shells and bombs, ready for use. They had a small charge fitted to either a timed or barometric fuse, reacting to pressure. These charges were designed to burst above ground, distributing the liquid on to the intended victims in small drops.

Tabun works by attacking the nervous system. Upon exposure the victim finds himself unable to concentrate. This is followed by a headache and pressure on the eyes. The pupils contract and everything around the victim grows dark. This is followed by an attack on the lungs and the victim finds breathing increasingly difficult. Next comes violent cramps, in particular of the toes. Despite its power, Tabun had little effect upon the heart which was found to continue beating even after the victim's lungs had failed. Tests revealed that it was fatal in doses of 20 milligrams of gas per cubic metre of air. Further research dispelled the notion that the gas could easily penetrate Allied gasmasks, but it was shown that a heavy concentration on the mask's filter would prove fatal and that a tiny drop of the liquid on the skin was also potentially fatal.

The second new gas to be discovered by T-Force was Sarin – or Trilon 46 – which had been the result of research by Professor Wolfgang Wirth and Dr Hans-Jürgen von der Linde.

Its effects were basically the same as Tabun, but it was discovered to be around 25 per cent as efficacious, with just 5 milligrams of Sarin per cubic metre of air being enough to kill a man. The gas was produced using two different processes – one using salt and the other using a process known as thermal rearrangement. A report of the analysis of Sarin stated that it was 'rapidly toxic through skin or eye absorption of liquid. Lethal dose possibly in order of 5 grams absorbed through skin . . . Vapour in low concentration strongly constricts pupils and causes tightness of chest. On small animals, after injection death rapid following tremors convulsions and respiratory failure. Only dangerous in field to eyes and lungs as initial cloud.'[12]

As T-Force continued its investigations requests were made to track down some of the scientists responsible for the development of Tabun and other chemicals. In late May Brigadier Pennycook telephoned SHAEF to pass on the message that a number of German gas specialists were needed for interrogation by the British authorities. Those named included IG Farben director Dr Otto Ambros, Dr Paul Hartmann, Dr Hans Henke, Dr Hilmer and Dr Gerhart Ehlers. Later investigations also took in other personalities including Dr Ambros' deputy Dr Ulrich, the managers of the Dyhernfurth and Gendorf gas plants, Professor Heinrich Hörlein, the creator of Tabun, and Dr Eberhard Gross, who discovered its antidote.

The Brigadier asked whether any of those he required were currently being 'exploited' by others teams and, if so, when they would be released. His message also noted that since they had been responsible for the research and manufacture of dangerous blister gases, they should be carefully searched upon arrest to determine whether they were in possession of chemical samples.

In addition to locating these scientists, Brigadier Pennycook had another vital task. There was an urgent need to discover what had happened to the 10,000 tons of Tabun that had already been produced. This became one of the most vital jobs of spring and summer 1945 since just a portion had been discovered by T-Force investigation teams. Much of the remainder was believed to have been removed from the production plant at Dyhernfurth and hidden in secret locations throughout Germany. Some was believed to be in storage in military ammunition dumps while the rest was thought to have been concealed in disused mine shafts, in particular in abandoned mines in the upper reaches of the River Elbe.

The only person believed to know the answer was Dr Kranz, who had been responsible for the filling and shipping of the shells from the production plant. However, he had gone missing in early 1945 and no one had been able locate him; even his former colleagues could provide no information on his whereabouts. Investigation teams made long and determined searches of the areas in which Kranz was known to have a connection but nothing was found.

The investigation teams also urgently needed to discover how much technical information had been shared between German and Japanese chemists. It was clear that the deployment of Tabun in the Far East would have terrible effects on the Allied armies. Fortunately, the eventual reports showed no evidence that poison gas technology had been shared with the Japanese. However, with the coming of the end of the war against Japan there came a new potential threat. As summer moved into autumn the interrogation of the German gas scientists progressed with one very important question in mind – how much did they know about any work the Soviets had done on these gases? When Dr Ulrich, the deputy to Otto Ambros, was interrogated he revealed that the Russians were known to have been working on similar gases but was uncertain of any further details. He did reveal, however, that he had attempted to acquire books published by Professor Alexandr Arbuzow, a Russian known to be working in the same field and who had earlier received the Order of Lenin for his research. His gas was believed to be a combination of phosphorus and fluorine, with similar properties to Sarin.

Dr Ulrich also revealed that Russian prisoners had talked of airtight cars being used to transport chemicals and that one product named anabasine, most commonly used as an insecticide, had been transported in rubber sacks. The airtight cars had all carried decontamination equipment for use against mustard gas and anabasine. From Dr Ambros – who had been responsible for IG Farben's development of Zyklon B, the chemical used in the gas chambers of Nazi death camps – it was discovered that anabasine had been extracted at Gendorf. Further understanding of Russian research was discovered from translated documents that were evacuated by T-Force from Raubkammer.

T-Force also shipped research records on another new military gas to London. This gas, using an ingredient known as azin and the chlorine adamsite, was difficult to pin down. Initial interrogations of German scientists revealed addresses outside Frankfurt where secret records of all production and shipments of the gas might be found. As a result T-Force search teams scoured private addresses and eventually uncovered card indexes and some files revealing code names, all of which were forwarded to London. The few documents that could be found showed that shipments of the gas had been sent to the filling plant at Dyhernfurth, but there were no records showing the gas had ever been fitted into any shells or bombs. Despite interest in the gas, prolonged investigation failed to reveal its exact nature or any evidence of the plant in which it had been produced.

In order to ascertain what degree of technical information might have been discovered by the Soviets, investigators quizzed the German scientists about what had been left behind in eastern Germany. The investigators were pleased to hear that German efforts to destroy or hide their work had been largely successful in locations such as Dyhernfurth, which had been ready to produce 100 tons of gas per month. All the buildings had been thoroughly cleansed and, under the supervision of IG Farben chemists, all traces of chemical processing were removed. Documents were then incinerated in large ovens. Some reports even suggested that following evacuation the plant had been bombed by the Luftwaffe to destroy any remaining evidence. The Allies were also convinced that all traces of the gas research at Spandau had also been removed leaving no trace of gas samples or research documents on Sarin. Similarly, almost the entire Falkenhagen plant had been removed. The Germans had also put measures in place to prevent chemical warfare experts escaping from the country. The authorities had confiscated all identity cards, passes and passports from the former staff of the chemical weapons plants.

During interrogations of the German scientists the investigators found the chemists attempting to distance themselves from any criminal acts. The debriefed German scientists told investigators that all their tests were carried out on animals and that no humans were subject to experimentation. They claimed their 'guinea pigs' had been cattle that had been targeted outside by artillery shells that released Tabun into the air around them. Investigators confirmed some claims of animal research, finding test facilities in which animals had been suspended from the ceiling. It was even discovered that German generals witnessed tests in which cats were placed inside captured Allied tanks and were then subjected to chemical attack.

However, the claims that only animals were subject to tests were in direct contrast to the experience of the T-Force soldiers who had occupied the Munsterlager facilities. Upon searching the offices and research areas, they had discovered test photographs that appalled them. This was proof that humans were used for testing the military gases and was confirmed during the investigations of summer 1945. It transpired that in 1943 Professor Wimmer from the University of Strassburg (Strasbourg) had travelled to Natzweiler-Struthof concentration camp where he had conducted tests on the inmates. Twelve 'habitual criminals' were selected as guinea pigs and their forearms were exposed to mustard gas. The following day their arms were examined, revealing serious blistering. The wounds were then treated to find the most effective remedy. A quarter of the guinea pigs died as a result of the exposure to mustard gas.

Similar experiments were carried out by Professor Picker, also from the University of Strassburg. He placed concentration camp inmates inside a testing chamber and exposed them to phosgene in an attempt to record the damage done to their lungs. The victims were studied over a 14-day period and all eventually recovered.

Investigators at Raubkammer noted that none of the staff at the plant admitted to any involvement in tests on humans. However, they acknowledged that around 4,000 photographs of tests, including those on humans, were uncovered at Munsterlager: 'Due to the gruesome appearance of some halfdozen fatal cases, the suggestion has been made that political prisoners might have been used in these experiments.'[13]

As the investigation teams noted, the German scientists were reluctant to discuss their research for fear of being labelled war criminals. One of the scientists who attempted to make claims that he had not been involved in research into poison gas was Dr Georg von Schnitzler, a member of the executive committee of the IG Farben board and the manager of the company's Frankfurt office. At first he claimed the company was not involved in poison gases, but then he changed his mind and gave a revised statement. He also helpfully provided details of gas-related documents that had been sent to Spain and Japan. As the investigation teams later admitted, various chemists were initially reluctant to talk but later showed a willingness to provide details about their work. The investigators found that the best way of dealing with reluctant chemists was to put them in the cells for a couple of days, after which they were more forthcoming.

The successful analysis of the gases evacuated by T-Force meant that the British and American research teams were soon able to make advances in developing counter-measures. They realized that in the event of renewed conflict the western Allies might find themselves facing the Red Army newly armed with stocks of Tabun. They were aided in their research by studying the counter-measures developed by German scientists for the very products they had so effectively produced. One counter-measure to Tabun was a drug designed to induce vomiting – in tests this had been used on a rabbit that had been dosed with the drug. Other experiments centred on maggots, from which was extracted a chemical used to inactivate Sarin.

The summer of 1945 saw T-Force, in particular the original gas staff at Brigadier Pennycook's HQ, fully occupied carrying out detailed investigations and evacuations in relation to the search for the secrets of the Nazi gas research programme. Brigadier Pennycook's staff were dealing with the evacuation of senior figures such as General Leyster, the German smoke troops commander, effectively Pennycook's German equivalent. They also examined chemical mines and a new type of flame-thrower for use by assault troops, with a range of up to 30 metres (100 feet). One of the most interesting finds for the investigation teams was German smokescreen. The experts simply could not understand how the combined chemicals could actually produce a smokescreen.

The month of July saw Pennycook visiting the War Office to discuss the disposal of German chemical weapons stocks. At the same time his staff and teams from the UK were testing CW shells at Raubkammer. The necessity for trials of the German weapons was cleared by the War Office. Despite not having ever found the need to use chemical weapons against the Germans, there was still no certainty that they would not decide to employ them in the Far East. At a meeting in London, attended by T-Force's Lt Colonel Bloomfield, the chairman of the committee organizing the trials noted that they 'must be carried out . . . to decide if any of the munitions might be of value in the remaining stages of the war'.[14]

The teams from the UK carried out full firing tests on the Raubkammer ranges in order to verify the results that had earlier been discovered in the German documentation. T-Force had to collect a number of German artillery pieces to be used to test-fire the German ordnance and to supply the necessary fuses for the shells, collecting them from German ordnance dumps. The unit also provided transport and accommodation for the teams and maintained security on the Raubkammer site. During the field trials the RAF used Hawker Typhoon fighter-bombers, whose pilots were issued with gasmasks, to spray chemicals over the ranges. Other tests were carried out using captured German Junkers Ju 88 bombers. When Lancaster bombers were used in tests, only the minimum crew was allowed on board and they were all ordered to keep clear of the bomb bay.

The field trials involved the use of live animals that were exposed to chemicals. Initially, it had been hoped to use German animals but suitable creatures were in short supply. As one member of the research team pointed out, it would have involved searching bombsites for stray cats and dogs. Instead, they used animals bred in the UK specifically for test purposes. One delivery made to the Raubkammer plant included 9 crates of rabbits and another included 40 goats. One of the tests of animals involved a man in protective clothing holding guinea-pigs' shaved bellies against bare earth that had been contaminated in chemical trials. These were later examined to check for skin damage. The reports identified how the animals died: 'Animals showed the first clinical signs within a few minutes of exposure, in the following sequence – salivation, muscular twitching, clonic and tonic convulsions, coma and death.'[15]

During this period Tom Pitt-Pladdy became involved in assisting the research when he was given the task of escorting subjects back to the UK for examination. Rather than travelling in the company of German scientists, he was flown back to the UK seated on a box full of rats that had been exposed to poison gas and were being sent to Porton Down to be examined.

The Raubkammer trials helped British scientists to identify the lethal effect of the gases, the range of the chemical clouds produced by particular shells or bombs and the effect of weather conditions. The result of the trials indicated that Tabun was effective at producing rapid death even in low dosages and was best delivered by airburst bombs or shells. Research also indicated that cluster bombs would be an effective way to deliver the gas. It was found that Tabun was best employed as a defensive weapon since it was effective against advancing troops and had sufficient persistency to prevent the occupation of territory byfollow-up troops without respirators. However, the gas's disadvantage was that its odour acted as a warning to its presence. The research teams concluded that Sarin had greater potential since it was odourless and was up to six times more effective than Tabun. Other lessons learned from the investigations at Raubkammer included the assessment that UK researchers should copy the testing towers used by the Germans in order to gain an effective understanding of the results of chemical munitions delivered by artillery. The overall result of the trials was that the British should continue research into Tabun and Sarin to identify how best they could be employed on the battlefield.

Chemical warfare teams from T-Force HQ were also sent to Frankfurt and Heidelberg to interrogate Otto Ambros and Dr

INVESTIGATIONS 251

Emmann, the former head of munitions at the German High Command. The following month saw investigators visiting the abandoned research plant at Spandau. They discovered little of value left in the plant. Most equipment had been evacuated before April and anything left behind had been destroyed in the fighting or removed by the Red Army. The only items of interest were the domed explosives testing chamber and apparatus used in the production of fluorine. In September T-Force HQ received a request for 19 gas scientists to be readied for evacuation to the UK. The message informed them: 'These personnel are in fact regarded as being of the greatest importance and essential to scientific investigation in UK.'[16]

With the assessment of Munsterlager complete, it fell to T-Force to assist the chemical weapons teams by removing all munitions from the plant for destruction. T-Force was also responsible for dismantling equipment that had been requested by teams from Porton Down. In October 1945 the evacuation was carried out with six 3-ton lorries leaving the plant every two days, and travelling via Hamburg to the UK. Included in the evacuations were the towers used to test-fire chemical artillery which had so impressed the inspection teams.

T-Force HQ also found that German bacteriological research fell under its remit. One of the scientists 'evacuated' by T-Force was Dr Joachim Mrugowsky, the head of the Waffen SS Hygienic Institute in Berlin. He was captured by the British and was initially held in a POW cage at Fallingbostel. From the interrogations of other scientists carried out in the US, it was known that Dr Mrugowsky had been concerned with bacteriological research, in particular countering attempts by the Polish underground to use bacteria against the Germans. These attempts had included waiters putting bacteria into food served to German military personnel, the poisoning of milk given to German soldiers in hospital and the unleashing of anthrax at German horse- and cattle-breeding facilities. Polish doctors had been caught carrying tubes containing typhus-infected louse droppings. Infected louse droppings were also discovered mixed with glass splinters and hidden in animal feed. Dr Mrugowsky's assistant Dr Erwin Ding-Schuler had carried out research on prisoners at Buchenwald concentration camp, infecting inmates with typhus. Another German scientist, Professor Eugen Haagen, stated that Dr Mrugowsky had been in control of his own experiments on prisoners.

While the British investigation teams had their hands full dealing with German scientists reluctant to discuss their research for fear of incriminating themselves, they also had to deal with some of their own Allies' attempts to frustrate their plans. In September 1945 the British teams were frustrated when they intended to interrogate Dr Otto Ambros. As early as May 1945 the British requested that Ambros should be transferred from the American zone so that he could be quizzed over his work at IG Farben. However, in July 1945, when he was supposed to be transferred, he was in fact diverted to Heidelberg under the care of Lt Colonel Tarr, a chemical warfare expert from the US 7th Army. While at Heidelberg, British investigators were allowed to interview Dr Ambros, but were surprised to see a suspected war criminal living in such good conditions.

It was also revealed that Lt Colonel Tarr had travelled to London to request the release of other scientists to his care. Tarr had also sent unauthorized signals requesting the release of German chemical warfare experts. The British investigation teams were then shocked to discover that Dr Ambros had even been installed as the manager of the IG Farben plant at Ludwigshafen in the French zone and was reported to be moving freely around the US and French zones. Dr Ambros, who had been shown in captured records to have been responsible for testing poison gases on concentration camp inmates, was described by investigators as 'far too dangerous and undesirable to be left at liberty, let alone employed by the Allied authorities'.[17]

However, it was believed that Tarr intended to use Dr Ambros for industrial chemical work and thus wanted to keep him away from war crimes investigators.

Indeed, Ambros was involved in a network of former chemical warfare researchers. In late 1945 one of his contacts was dismissed from his post by the Allied Military Government for continuing with Nazi activities. The scientist in question had communicated with Dr Ambros about the location of a barrel in which secret chemical warfare documents had been concealed in order to hide them from Allied investigators. It was clear that Dr Ambros had deliberately concealed his knowledge of this hidden research, despite his claims to be assisting the Allies.

While the British investigation teams were being frustrated by German, French and American chemical experts, the Royal Navy teams, who were working at the Kiel facilities seized by 30AU and the 5th King's, were able to carry out detailed investigations with full cooperation from German scientists, technicians and researchers. The wealth of research information found around Kiel stunned the investigation teams, in particular those working at the Walterwerke, keeping them fully occupied throughout the summer of 1945.

At the ELAC plant, T-Force secured all the firm's key personnel, who were swiftly put to work to produce specimens of electrical equipment for the investigation teams. They also secured the production facility used for making underwater listening devices. Outside the city, an investigation team uncovered one of the firm's key research labs hidden on a farm. In addition, a wealth of technical data related to marine gunnery, fire control and torpedo mechanisms was found at the heavily bombed marine arsenal.

Another team detained Dr Wigge who was the designer of a German naval secret, the TA550 radio-controlled torpedo, examples of which had also been secured for investigation. At a predetermined distance from the target a charge was released to home-in on the target. As it approached its quarry, the torpedo dived and struck the target ship beneath the waterline. Although the TA550 was not yet operational, investigators believed that most of the technical difficulties had been overcome and it was nearing completion.

T-Force also evacuated the entire staff of Chemische Physikalische Versuchsanstalt from Kiel. They had been responsible for chemical, physical, explosive and metallurgical research for the German navy and had proved to be cooperative, producing full charts detailing both the staff and organization of the facility. They were relocated north of Kiel to Dänisch-Nienhof, where T-Force guarded large numbers of German scientists.

However, it was the team of Royal Navy scientists and investigators based at the Walterwerke who found themselves most fruitfully occupied during the initial period of investigations. With T-Force having secured the support of Admiral Dönitz to order Dr Walter to assist the British, the scientist overcame his initial reluctance and, as the Royal Navy investigators attached to 30AU soon reported, he was soon 'proving extremely cooperative'.[18] As Lt Commander Aylen later wrote, the effect was instantaneous: 'Then ensued a somewhat breathtaking series of discoveries. The average rate of finding new weapons for the first fortnight was about two a day.'[19] In the secret report prepared at the close of investigations, Aylen reported how Dr Walter's cooperation opened up the world of 'freak weapons' that had been under development for the German military.

Torpedo combustion chambers were found concealed in the bottom of a bomb crater in some nearby woods while a complete set of microfilms for ten years of research was found in a cellar, concealed beneath a heap of coal. Lt Commander Aylen despatched a junior officer towards the Danish border to retrieve a train full of valuable parts that had left the plant a few days earlier. T-Force teams were also sent to examine the waters of the nearby Plöner See, a local lake where German naval personnel had been trained in one-man U-boats. There, they located Dr Walter's latest experimental one-man submarine.

With the capture of Dr Walter, T-Force had bagged something more than just Germany's foremost submarine-engine designer. As one Admiralty report noted, Dr Walter and his team 'are the ablest in Germany as regards the invention and development of new and improved war material'.[20] His engines were not only put to use beneath the seas, they were also making an impression in the skies above Germany. The waters of the Plöner See also provided elements of the V1 launch ramps that were reconstructed and test fired by Admiralty scientists. These tests of the V1 launch ramps were reported as 'highly spectacular', with the dummy rocket emerging from a cloud of purple smoke. The teams were also fascinated to discover designs for a vertical ramp, employing a telescopic catapult, to be used to launch jet fighters. They noted one important design fault the power of the launch would be such that the thrust would pull the catapult out of the ground each time it was fired. Even more intriguing was a similar design in which a high-pressure water jet would be employed to assist the jet fighter to get off the ground.

Since the mid 1930s the Luftwaffe had taken an interest in Dr Walter's research, noting that the chemical reactions he employed could not only be used to power a turbine, but could also create a significantly powerful thrust. Thus, from 1936 onwards the rocket physicist Wernher von Braun and his team at Peenemünde worked with Walter's engines. It was Dr Walter who designed the means to drive the turbine-powering fuel pumps in V2 rockets, with his designs then being further developed by the rocket teams at Peenemünde.

These early experiments had caused considerable interest among aircraft designers and in 1939 the Heinkel aircraft company unveiled the He 176, the world's first liquid-fuelled, rocket-powered aircraft. With a recorded speed of 346km/h (215mph) and an expected top speed of nearly 800km/h (500mph), the design seemed to be the future of high-speed fighter aircraft. However, the Luftwaffe declined to accept the design and Heinkel cancelled its development of rocket-powered fighters. But it was not the only company taking an interest in Walter's engines. Known by the designation HWK 109–509 his rocket engine was refined during the war years and eventually became the power unit for the Messerschmitt Me 163 'Kornet' rocket-powered fighter aircraft and the Bachem Ba 349 'Natter'. By mixing peroxide with hydrazine, the engine created vast amounts of heat, forcing out a stream of water vapour and nitrogen that provided the aircraft's forward thrust.

With its speed of 725km/h (450mph) at a 45-degree climb, and the ability to reach an altitude of 4875 metres (16,000 feet) in just one minute, Captain Eric Brown later said of test-flying the Me 163, 'It was like being in charge of a runaway train.'[21] Despite the comfortable seat installed for the pilot, the Me 163 was highly dangerous, with Dr Walter telling Eric Brown: 'If one bullet hit the fuel tanks it would be fatal.'[22] In total, 25 example of the Me 163 were sent to the UK for evaluation in test flights.

The Natter – or Adder – was a rocket-powered interceptor aircraft with a one-man crew, which was launched in a manner similar to surface-to-air missiles. It was among the prime aviation targets for the T-Force teams. Officially known as the Bachem Ba 349, the Natter was powered by a Walter HWK 509 A2 rocket motor and fired vertically from the ground before being piloted towards enemy aircraft. The pilot would then fire his rockets at enemy bombers before baling out. Pilot and rocket engine then landed under separate parachutes. At least that had been the intention. Only one test flight had taken place, resulting in the death of the test-pilot.

Despite this, the research remained of interest to the military. Of particular interest was the radio-control mechanism that was used to guide the rocket to the correct altitude before the pilot took over control – turning off the engine and gliding towards his target – then jettisoning the nose-cone and firing the rockets. This, in itself, was a significant advance from the original plans. At first the Natter had been designed as a virtual suicide weapon, with the pilot guiding his craft towards the tail of an enemy plane, and then ejecting at the last moment. The single example of the craft evacuated by T-Force was delivered to the RAF research establishment at Farnborough.

The engines in question were Dr Walter 'hot drive' hydrogen peroxide engines which reached temperatures of up to 3,000°F. Aircraft powered by the engine could reach a speed of 965km/h (600mph), which was – according to contemporary reports – 'an astonishing performance for an engine weighing 390lbs'. The power of the engine was 'strikingly demonstrated' in test films found at Walter's factory, in which the plane rose almost vertically into the air. In tests conducted for the RAF the engines produced a staggering noise and observers noted that, even with ear protection, proximity to the working engine, 'produced a strange physical sensation of nausea'.[23]

The doctor's relationship with Japanese aircraft developers was of immense interest to the investigation teams. He soon provided information on the HWK 509 A-1 jet unit, claiming that he had shared his design with the Japanese navy. Walter also revealed that six months earlier he had sent the design for the Me 163 rocket-propelled plane to Japan. Investigators found that he had sold the design in the closing months of the war for 20 million Reichsmarks.

In addition, Walter's engines had been put to use in another novel system developed by German aircraft engineers. Struck by the question of how to provide sufficient thrust to allow heavily laden aircraft to take off, the solution came in the form of rocket or jet engines fitted to the plane. HWK 500 Starthilfe engines were used in a system known as RATO ('Rocket Assisted Take Off') that unleashed a burst of high power to force the aircraft into the air. Once airborne, and with the fuel exhausted, the engines were jettisoned to return to the ground by parachute ready to be reused. For the Luftwaffe the system had come into its own during the later stages of the war. With German runways under attack by Allied bombers, often causing considerable damage, rocket power was used to allow aircraft to generate sufficient power to take off on short runways. Using this system a 32-ton plane could take off on a runway of just 120 metres (394 feet).

The knowledge gathered by the investigators in Kiel was vital to the simultaneous research being carried out by Eric Brown. A receiving base had been established in the British zone at which examples of captured German aircraft were collected for investigation. Since most of the aircraft arrived without any documentation, testing was both frightening and dangerous for Brown. In one case, he tested an aircraft whose engines had an operational life of just 25 hours. Since Brown had no service records for the plane he was blissfully unaware of whether the engines were brand new or due for a complete overhaul. He was lucky: just as he accelerated along the runway one engine exploded, blowing off the wing. Had the engine lasted just a few seconds longer, he would have been airborne and the explosion would have had a more dramatic impact.

During this period Captain Brown noted his surprise that so few of the German jet and rocket planes had been sabotaged, even though large numbers of piston-engine planes had been vandalized. He was certain that German pride in their developments was such that they wanted the Allies to marvel at their achievements. One example investigated during this period was the Heinkel 162 jet. Brown considered this a remarkable plane, both for having been designed and put into operation in just three months, and for its simplicity. It had top-mounted 30mm cannons so that it could fly beneath Allied bombers and fire upwards. In postwar interrogations Albert Speer claimed that, even as late as 1945, he could have put 500 of these planes a month into production. In Austria investigators found the facility where this was planned and confirmed Speer's production forecasts.

Captain Brown had the dubious honour of testing aircraft that seemed fanciful to most who examined them. One example was a craft with both forward- and rear-mounted engines. This was the first time that reverse thrust had been employed on an aircraft. It was also the first plane with hydraulically operated aerilons, something that soon became standard on all aircraft. Brown noted with relief that the plane had an ejector seat that was combined with a mechanism to blow off the rear propeller when the ejector was employed. This prevented the pilot from being shredded as he ejected.

While the Royal Aircraft Establishment investigators studied the flight capabilities of Dr Walter's engines fitted on experimental German aircraft, the teams in Kiel continued to study the marine potential of his designs. With so much information forthcoming, visitors from both the Admiralty and Air Ministry soon arrived in Kiel and spent many hours viewing the films of experimental weapons that had been shot at Walterwerke. In a single week, 31 parties of dignitaries visited the facilities, eager to find out more about the scientist who was convinced he could develop a U-boat capable of travelling underwater at the same speed as a destroyer on the open seas.

In late May 1945 Dr Walter was 'evacuated' from Kiel and sent to London for interrogation about his work. As the team who carried out the interrogation noted, Dr Walter showed every indication that he was willing to cooperate and became increasingly informative as the session progressed. He maintained that it was his political conviction that it was essential for the Anglo-Saxons to control Europe in the face of the Soviet threat.

Meanwhile, the factory was put back to work and ordered to reassemble a Type XVII U-boat and complete the construction of a Type XVIII test engine. The British also ordered the completion of hydrogen peroxide-powered torpedoes and a jet engine, and for a V1 launching ramp to be made ready for firing. Initially, the reopened factory continued to use the same Russian slave labourers that had been employed during the war, only now they received wages.

The Royal Navy teams investigated a host of what Lt Commander Aylen had called 'freak weapons', like the hydrogen peroxide-fuelled amphibious tank that was still on the drawing boards at the end of hostilities. There was also the 'Wagner Bomb', a jet-powered torpedo designed to be dropped from an aircraft, jettisoning its wings on impact with the water. Another novel invention was the Tietjens boat, effectively an explosive hydrofoil boat carrying a ton of explosive that rode above the surface and was powered by a hydrogen peroxide engine. One of the most innovative designs was the 'Cleopatra'. This was another explosive-filled boat. It had been designed to be fired from the sea to then ride on to a beach, detonating 50 metres (165 feet) inland. Its envisaged use had been to destroy beach defences. Investigators were amused to watch test films of the weapon uncovered by T-Force that showed the explosive boat rushing from the sea, then running up on to the beach, only to come to a halt amidst a group of frightened cows.

Although the 'Cleopatra' and other explosive boats were never used operationally, they did lead to plans for a flying bomb carrying 10 tons of explosives that was designed to be fired from a remote-controlled boat and used to attack coastal defences. Notable failures designed by Dr Walter included using hydrogen peroxide to increase the power of diesel engines. In this design hydrogen peroxide was directly injected into the diesel engine. The project was abandoned after a monumental explosion.

Among Dr Walter's other designs were mini jet engines to be used to deliver sea mines from aircraft. These were fitted with an interesting deceleration mechanism to prevent damage to the mine on impact with the water. Investigators also found test films showing glider bombs destroying ground targets. Similar to the Blohm + Voss 143, this jet-propelled glider bomb had been designed to be fired from shore to attack shipping. It had been installed in the Elbe estuary to defend the area from seaborne invasion. Other innovations included jet-assisted bombs and shells that had been designed for anti-aircraft use.

While aircraft and submarine engines had been the primary focus of Dr Walter's work, investigations showed that around 25 per cent of the company's research budget had been spent on torpedo design, with the developments covering both aerial and sea-delivered torpedoes. He had first become interested in torpedoes during the 1930s, carrying out his first experiments in 1935, followed by trials in 1939. While most trials had involved the use of hydrogen peroxide as a propellant, Dr Walter had also experimented with nitric acid and liquid oxygen. Tests of the weapons had been carried out at Eckenförde, so 30AU despatched a research team to the town. Of particular interest for the investigators was the compact design of the pumps used with the power units. In one design, the jet-powered torpedo used fresh water as a coolant before switching to pumping in seawater, thus saving tank space and allowing a larger charge to be carried.

Another development was a midget U-boat, which was effectively Dr Walter's hydrogen peroxide-powered torpedo adapted to take a crew. A scuttled craft was salvaged for investigation by the Allied investigators, but Walter's staff insisted the design was not safe and should not be further investigated. During interrogation Dr Kraemer, Walter's chief torpedo combustion expert, stated that he believed developments at the plant were so important that Dr Walter's name would eventually be as famous as that of Dr Diesel.

In other fields, Dr Walter's designs included remote-controlled, hydrogen peroxide-powered tanks that had been used to deliver explosive charges on the battlefield. He had also carried out research into anti-tank weapons that used his knowledge of rocket engines. One example was a new 'sticky' anti-tank charge that had been designed by Walter to overcome the problem of Russian tanks coated with concrete that had prevented earlier 'sticky' charges from adhering to the tank. In Walter's design, the charge was fitted with a small jet engine to force the charge against the tank's hull. Another innovative anti-tank weapon was the 'T-Stoff' cannon. This had begun life as a soundless and flashless cannon that was fired using compressed air rather than cordite. This developed into a weapon using Dr Walter's 'T-Stoff' propellant – a variant on hydrogen peroxide – in place of compressed air. One advantage of the design was that 'T-Stoff' was cheaper to produce than cordite. The only example of the design had to be retrieved from the bottom of a local lake.

Dr Walter had also been involved in the development of a long-range gun. This had been designed to be fired from the Pas de Calais to hit targets in England. Although the project was developed and went into production, Dr Walter played no significant role, his interest having waned since cordite was preferred over hydrogen peroxide for firing the weapon. He had, however, continued with research on using auxiliary jet propulsion for increasing the range of artillery shells.

In the months that followed the German defeat, the search for the seven remaining 'Walter' U-boats continued. By September

1945 they had all been found. However, there was one prob-lem for the British and American investigation teams. Under the terms of the Tripartite Naval Commission – through which the Americans, British and Soviets had agreed to register and control the German naval booty – the Russians had the right to expect Dr Walter's designs to be handed over to them, at least in part. However, the western Allies had no intention of sharing all of the advanced technology. Three of the prototype U-boats were found to be badly damaged and could offer little help to the Allied investigators. Four others (two sunk in the Kaiser-Wilhelm canal and two in the waters near Cuxhaven) were discovered almost intact. All four were salvaged and taken to the Walter factory for further investigation. The boat found at Eckenförde bay was left unsalvaged for fear that it might have to be handed over to the Soviets. Instead, its discovery was left unreported until it could later be safely removed and broken up. The Russians did not attempt to claim the missing submarines until December 1945 – and they did not receive a satisfactory reply from the western powers.

Although it had been decided at the Potsdam Conference of 17 July to 2 August 1945 that the western Allies would share all their naval booty with the Soviets, there was little political or military will to adhere to the agreement. Instead, the British and the Americans had decided that only they would share the wealth of technological research discovered at Kiel and within the salvaged submarines. As a result, in August 1945, U-Boat U1407 left Kiel and sailed for the Vickers-Armstrong subma-rine yards at Barrow-in-Furness in the UK and, a few weeks later, U1406 left for America, carried on the deck of a troop-ship. At the same time all available machinery and spare parts – mostly salvaged from the wrecks of the other Walter sub-marines – were also sent to western shipyards. With them went vast supplies of the highly dangerous hydrogen peroxide fuel needed to power the engines of Dr Walter's craft.

At the conclusion of investigations at the Walterwerke, Commander Aylen submitted his report. This gave a clear indication of the value of securing Dr Walter, his staff and his facilities by T-Force. There was no doubt that the doctor had been central to the technological advances made by the German military in the latter stages of the war. Jet fighters, flying bombs, missiles and high-speed submarines – all areas in which the German scientists had outstripped those at work in the UK and the US – had all been reliant on the efforts of those at the Walterwerke. As Commander Aylen noted, 'undoubtedly the firm's achievements were great. They were responsible for developing an entirely new technique using a new medium, and designing weapons or parts of weapons which were to prove most deadly, of which the ME163 engine, the V1 launching gear, the Walterboat, the V2 and similar devices were probably the most important.'[24] He further noted that only the Allies development of the atom bomb and radar – both war-winning developments – were greater technical achievements than Walter's designs.

The potential of the weapons under development was noted in the commander's report: 'It is admitted that many of the weapons were of quite freakish nature, but had the war continued for one more year, the devastation that the more important ones would have caused would have been very great.' The report also emphasized the necessity of utilizing the talents that had been acquired when T-Force had occupied the Walterwerke, noting that 'Walter himself remains an enigma. He was undoubtedly a good Nazi, but at the same time he is an extremely capable technician . . . It is logical to assume that the continuation of the employment of the brains of the key men of the Walter team by the Allies should yield equally important and unforeseen results.' Although he could not have known it at the time, one of Commander Aylen's final comments was to have particular resonance in the years ahead, when he wrote, 'It lurks constantly in the writer's mind that he [Dr Walter] may even yet prove to be one of the sinister crooks of international fame who features so often in films and fiction.' Once in the office of the Director of Naval Intelligence, the report was seen by Commander Fleming who, either consciously or subconsciously, was already storing up information to be used in his future fiction.

In the winter of 1945 the Type XVII submarine testing plant was dismantled and shipped to the United States, while the testing stands for the hydrogen peroxide engines were shipped to the UK. In 1946, the U1407 was relaunched as HMS *Meteorite* – a fitting name for a submarine that could travel at previously unheard of speeds. It remained in service as a testing unit for four years and was broken up in 1950.

It was not only the Admiralty that had an interest in the developments underway at the Walterwerke. Dr Walter's research into aircraft engines resulted in an interest from the RAF. A team from the Royal Aircraft Establishment at Farnborough was therefore sent out to Kiel to investigate the plant. They noted that by the time of their arrival in late summer, their US equivalents had already made numerous visits to Kiel and put in requests to evacuate equipment. While the primary interest of the Farnborough team was the use of Walter's engines for rocket propulsion, assisted take-off and missiles, they were also interested in the metallurgical and chemical processes that had been developed by Walter's research teams. Another particular interest was in the highly advanced wind tunnels employed by the Luftwaffe to test their innovative aircraft. Reports showed that German wind tunnels were far in advance of any similar equipment in use in both Britain and the US. Once again it was found that Dr Walter's engines had been utilized in the wind tunnels to simulate high speeds.

By the close of investigations at the Walterwerke as many as 50,000 microfilms had been sent to the UK for further investigation, giving British military scientists a clear idea of the research projects that had driven forward the German development of weapons in the latter stages of the war. In July 1945 there were concerns over the possible switchover of the Walter factory to civilian production. This received great attention from the Admiralty which resisted the request, stressing that the plant should be fully exploited by the British, and – in language chosen to reflect the Nazi underground movement – described the attempt to 'civilianize' its work as a 'werewolf in sheep's clothing'.[25] Of greater importance than the plant was the staff, who were described in one Admiralty report as being the ablest scientific brains in Germany, who 'should not be left free with their wealth of knowledge and inventiveness'.[26] The prospect of switching the plant from military to civilian production also raised the concern that Walter's top designers and researchers might seek employment elsewhere, potentially with the Russians. In the end, it was discovered that there had been no intention of 'civilianizing' the main plant. A request to reopen in order to produce civilian machinery came from one of Walter's other concerns, a torpedo facility that had previously been an agricultural works. However, this request was also refused.

It was decided that Walter and 15 of his staff should be evacuated permanently to the UK by T-Force. They were expected to take essential furniture, including bedding – although as the Admiralty noted, only one of the party actually had full household possessions since the others had all been 'bombed out' in the final months of the war. In total, 14 men, 13 wives and 24 children were selected to make the journey to the UK. In the end only a number of the men travelled in the first batch, with the others and the wives moving to the UK during 1946. Professor Walter and his team of seven engineers were given contracts commencing in January 1946 to continue their work on behalf of the British.

With investigations complete the decision was made to destroy parts of the Walterwerke. By the end of November 1945, with the staff evacuated, all remaining weapons were removed for further investigation in UK while those that had been fully exploited were taken for scrap. Submarine parts were crated and removed to the Vickers submarine facility at Barrow-in-Furness. Next all chemicals were evacuated, the V1 test launch ramps were destroyed and the hydrogen peroxide storage bunkers were blown up. What remained of the plant was then handed over to the military government to be used as a machinery store.

As part of the process of moving Walter and his staff to the UK to continue their work, security checks had to be carried out. The findings did not make for good reading. Dr Walter was described as having an 'unsatisfactory political background'[27] while both Schmidt, an expert in gas turbines who had worked on the Me 163 fighter, and Dreyer, a U-boat electrician, were considered undesirable. The security report noted: 'They were active Nazis, and would, it is considered, become so again given the opportunity.' In addition, the wives of seven of the men, including both Schmidt and Dreyer, were found to be of security interest. As a result of the security checks, Dreyer was deemed to be non-essential and remained in Germany while Schmidt was re-employed on British V2 rocket trials at Cuxhaven. It was later noted that Dr Schmidt's background meant that once his employment with the British was completed he would need to face a 'denazification court', the results of which would destroy any hope of a career in research.

There were no restrictions put on the evacuation of Dr Walter to the UK, despite his close links with the Nazi regime. As one October 1945 report explained, Dr Walter was an ardent Nazi who had been a party member since 1931, holding the rank of Amsleiter. He was also a scientist and technician of the 'highest order' who was 'regarded locally as a complete

Nazi'.[28] However, as the Admiralty stressed, here was the leader of a highly efficient team of scientists 'whom it is far better to have with us than against us . . . we would be most blameworthy if we fail to take full advantage of the practical experience of these men's brains'.[29] It was also pointed out that if Britain did not accept Dr Walter they would spend the next few years having to watch over him to ensure he did not sell his ideas to other nations.

Investigations carried out during late 1945 revealed that T-Force had been right to be concerned about Russian interest in Dr Walter and his staff. Hans Lüthje, the manager of the Walter factory at Eberswalde in the Russian zone, had earlier fled to Kiel and continued his employment at the Walterwerke. In November he reported that he had received a mysterious visitor. This man claimed that all technicians previously employed in the east would soon be returned to their old positions. In order to secure his safety, the man suggested Herr Lüthje return home immediately and hand himself over to the Russians. He stressed that the Russians had a particular interest in Dr Walter's work and were keen to secure the employment of any of his senior staff. The visitor also explained that he could secure Herr Lüthje all the necessary paperwork to make the journey to Eberswalde. The man left him to think over the offer, instructing him not to speak to anybody about what they discussed, and promised to return a week later to get Herr Lüthje's answer. Keen not to return to his former factory, Lüthje reported his mysterious visitor to the British authorities. Other former employees at the Eberswalde plant reported that they had received letters from former colleagues pointing out the benefits of employment within the Soviet zone.

The Russian interest spurred the British on, making sure that Walter and his team were not lost to the potential enemy. As the Royal Navy's representatives in Berlin noted: 'The consequences of the loss to us of the services of such men as Walter and his entourage are incalculable . . . they should be given reasonable assurance of future employment by us on a long term basis.'[30]

The British and American desire to utilize German technological advances, and to keep them hidden from the Soviets, was extended to other sites. Concentrated at Cuxhaven and Trauen were a number of rocket scientists whose earlier work had rained down on London in the form of V1 flying bombs and V2 missiles. Among them were specialists in missile guidance, stabilization systems, rocket fuel and radio control. These were men who had previously worked at the Peenemünde research plant or the Nordhausen rocket production plant, whose experiments and innovation had been at the expense of thousands of slave labourers who toiled and died in appalling conditions – something that would never be forgotten by witnesses such as Reg Rush of 30AU.

There had been considerable interest in German rocket technology throughout the campaign in northwest Europe. Back in summer 1944, when Dalzel-Job had reached rocket launching sites on his dash through northern France, investigators had been swiftly despatched to analyse the sites. The same had happened as the British and Canadian armies had advanced along the French, Belgian and Netherlands coastlines. During the operational period SHAEF had ordered that all V1 and V2 rockets should be protected and preserved for analysis or evacuation. In May 1945 General Eisenhower ordered the carrying out of test firings of V2 rockets, stressing that successful trials would save many years of development work by Allied research teams, allowing them to cash-in on the work carried out by the Germans. Following the disbanding of SHAEF in June 1945, the responsibility for such research test firings became a national, rather an Allied concern. As a result V2 research came under direct control of the War Office which established

'SPOG', the Special Projectiles Operations Group, to direct the tests. On 5 June 1945 the project was given the name of 'Operation Backfire'.

In order to carry out test-firing of rockets it became necessary to locate sufficient complete examples of V2 rockets and firing equipment. It was initially hoped that 30 complete rockets could be made ready for the tests, expecting at least 50 per cent to be unsuccessful. The site selected for the tests was the Krupps testing ground six miles south of Cuxhaven in northern Germany. This was the site to which Wernher von Braun's research facilities had been relocated following Allied bombing of Peenemünde.

Once more T-Force, having the most experienced search and evacuation units, came into the picture. Between 31 May and 10 June investigation teams scoured 21st Army Group's area of operations. On 15 June orders were issued for the 'freezing' of all V2 components within Germany, ensuring that nothing could be evacuated, moved or destroyed. Large numbers of rocket components were discovered around the towns of Celle and Fallingbostel, where former prisoners of war were able to provide intelligence on where rockets might be found. As one report noted, missile components were collected from 'farms, holes in the ground, railways sidings'.[31] Shortages of necessary working drawings and wiring diagrams meant that document teams were also despatched to various locations to find the necessary documentation. Investigation of documents uncovered at this time revealed the Germans to have been planning a long-range missile carrying a pilot in a pressurized cabin. The rocket was to have retractable wings that would be extended towards the end of the journey, allowing the rocket to glide to earth – effectively this meant that the rocket was capable of being reused, in many ways similar to NASA's Space Shuttle, itself the heir of the space projects initiated by German scientists following their employment in the US after 1945. The

British investigators noted this rocket would take a mere 40 minutes to cross the Atlantic.

As examples were uncovered, all equipment was labelled by T-Force and prepared for transit to the rocket testing sites. On 25 June, the 5th King's element attached to 30 Corps was issued orders for its role in 'Operation Backfire'. The lists despatched from T-Force HQ included 87 different target items needed for the operation. As these items were discovered, T-Force arranged the transit of equipment ready for use at Cuxhaven. A detachment of Kingsmen was sent to Wismar to collect a trainload of V1 rockets. From the fire station at Oldhau, T-Force collected heavy ground equipment forming part of the launch system. Most V2 components came from the 18 miles of underground facilities at the Mittelwerk rocket factory near Nordhausen. The US military was eager for British assistance in evacuating the plant since the entire area was due to come under Russian control. They had no intention of leaving anything behind for their former allies. For the men of T-Force there were more personal concerns, as Jack Twining-Davies, 5th King's Regiment, recalled: 'After experiencing the destructive powers of Hitler's V1s and V2s in London and Antwerp, it gave me great pleasure to tow a stripped down body of a "Doodle Bug" to the docks.'[32]

During the summer of 1945 orders were issued for the raw materials needed to complete the project, with responsibility for location and transport again falling to T-Force. The main necessity was fuel, the highly combustible hydrogen peroxide which was stored at the Walterwerke. Detachments from T-Force used a road tanker supplied by the Royal Navy to transport the fuel from Kiel to Cuxhaven. T-Force veterans recalled the tension of transporting a substance known to be highly volatile across a landscape already scarred by war. As they recalled, the vehicles had to stop at regular intervals while temperatures were monitored for fear of the hydrogen peroxide overheating and exploding. It was clear to all that care had to be taken to prevent accidents: it was a foolhardy man who dared to smoke a cigarette while transporting hydrogen peroxide.

Despite the warnings, not all among the T-Force personnel displayed caution while they were handling rocket fuel. Some of the soldiers found a novel use for the V2 rockets they were sent to guard. If the rocket's fuel tanks had been emptied it was possible for the soldiers to put their heads into the empty space. The lingering odour of hydrogen peroxide had an immediate effect upon them, inducing the light-headed symptoms of drunkenness. Others used captured rocket fuel to mix with coffee, creating a potent alcoholic brew. Such was the danger of this drink that one corporal died after drinking it, while others were rendered temporarily blind.

Two train loads of equipment were moved from Kassel in the US zone to Cuxhaven via Bremen. From Mittelwerk, five trains of 55 wagons each – carrying 640 tons of equipment – were sent north to Cuxhaven. The combined length of the trains was more than five miles. From Antwerp came six complete tail units. Requests had to be made for the Americans to supply propulsion units, since many examples had already been evacuated by the US for tests.

At Cuxhaven, 570 German technicians and other staff, including military mechanics, were employed on the project. Among them were former members of V1 and V2 launching crews who were taken from POW camps. Finding sufficient experienced staff was complicated by the rivalry between the US and the UK rocket projects. The staff of the American project, Operation Overcast, requested that 27 of the German personnel be sent to the US. The British agreed to release 14 of them due to the importance of research, noting that the Americans might soon have rockets ready to be employed in the war against Japan. Effectively, the British authorities decided that long-term collaboration with the US on missile projects was far more important than rivalry over the allocation of scientists.

It was during this period that some among T-Force came into contact with Germany's most notorious rocket scientist, Wernher von Braun. Although few records were kept of von Braun's movements while in the custody of the British, members of T-Force had him in their care. Tom Pitt-Pladdy recalled how von Braun spent two days at the former Luftwaffe airfield at Völkenrode, guarded by elements of T-Force. The rocket scientist also made a visit to Kiel during the summer of 1945. George Lambert recalled how von Braun had demonstrated chemicals as used in rocket propulsion:

> I was taken to a Scientific Building and in one of the labs, Wernher von Braun gave us a demonstration of one of his famous rocket fuels. He had a beaker containing what he called X stuff, and another beaker containing what he called Y stuff. When he mixed X and Y there was a loud explosion and a shattering of glass. At that time I had no idea who von Braun was and what a high reputation he had as a rocket-man, or how much damage he had done to England with the V1 and V2.

Despite the original ambitious plans to assemble 30 complete rockets ready for testing, the operation was gradually scaled back. With winter approaching the operation had to be kept basic. Quite simply, the weather conditions of autumn, with its increasing rains and winds, were not conducive to rocket tests. Furthermore, the impact of the weather on missiles that had not been produced for long-term storage resulted in many components being too rusted to be safely used. The British also made the decision that American research, using missiles copied from V2 plans, would actually provide superior results for analysis than tests carried out on rockets hastily assembled from spare parts.

Operation Backfire commenced on 1 October 1945, but the first test-firing was a failure. The following day a second test was carried out, with the missile landing within 3 miles of the aiming point. On 4 October another successful launch was made. The rocket fell short of its target but on the correct trajectory. On 15 October a final launch was made before an audience of 100 spectators. At the end of the project T-Force was again employed, transporting 180 tons of rocket equipment from Cuxhaven to the evacuation facilities at Hamburg ready to be sent to the UK.

With the project finished, there were widespread concerns about the technicians being released with the likelihood that they would be picked up by the Russians for employment. There was little that could be done with lower-level technicians – the British already had large numbers of significant scientists to interrogate, without being concerned with people with limited knowledge.

Although Operation Backfire had been carried out on a scale much reduced from that originally planned, certain basic principals were noted. The report's author might have been speaking about numerous examples of the research seized and secured by T-Force when he noted: 'For the sake of their very existence, Britain and the United States must be masters of this weapon of the future.'[33]

CHAPTER 9

Cold War

'It is desired to restrain the Russians from using German brain-power and technical skills to build up their war potential.'

Top secret report, January 1947.[1]

With the war over, the occupation of Germany began. For most of the British Army this signalled the beginning of the end; getting ready for parades and inspections and counting off the days until demob. Yet for the men of T-Force, it seemed that every day brought more and more investigation teams into Germany to search the targets they had secured in the final days of war.

Although the work of the soldiers continued as before, T-Force's organizational structure changed as the military adapted itself to peacetime conditions. On 31 May 1945, on orders from the Supreme Headquarters of the Allied Expeditionary Force, a new body was formed under the title of 'Field Intelligence Agency, Technical'. FIAT was set up to 'co-ordinate, integrate and direct the activities of the various missions and agencies interested in examining, appraising and exploiting all information pertaining to German economy'.[2] FIAT was given the power to freeze all targets of interest to the group, to send its representatives to any location under SHAEF's control and to carry out the 'arrest, internment and removal' of any Germans believed to be of interest. In the coming months it would play an important role in the work of T-Force.

At the same time CIOS, the organization that had guided T-Force's operations, was wound down. As an international organization it was no longer necessary – combined operations were the child of wartime conditions, and once SHAEF had disbanded so were all the bodies it had commanded. Thus, in peacetime the responsibility fell back to the individual nations. From July 1945 T-Force took its instructions from BIOS, the British Intelligence Objectives Sub-Committee. Similarly, FIAT was moved from the command of SHAEF and began to take its instructions from the Allied Control Commission. Under these new arrangements, T-Force continued to work to a set of instructions little different to those used in wartime, searching for 'Any material of whatever nature and wherever situated, intended for war on land, at sea, or in the air, or which is or may be or has been at any time in use by, or intended for use by the armed forces, civil defence, or any other formation or organization.'[3]

The legal justification of T-Force's continued work came under article 12 of the terms of surrender:

The United Kingdom, the United State of America, and the Union of the Soviet Socialist Republics shall possess supreme authority with respect to Germany. In the exercise of such authority they will take such steps, including the complete disarmament and demilitarisation of Germany, as they deem requisite for future peace and security. The Allied Representatives will present additional political, administrative, economic, financial, military and other requirements arising from the surrender of Germany. The Allied Representatives, or persons or agencies duly designated to act on their authority, will issue proclamations, orders, ordinances and instructions for the purpose of laying down such additional requirements, and of giving effect to the other provisions of the present instrument. The German Government, the German High Command, all

German authorities and the German people shall carry out unconditionally the requirements of the Allied Representatives, and shall fully comply with all such proclamations, orders, ordinances and instructions.[4]

With investigations going on throughout the British zone, T-Force was rapidly allotted duties from the Ruhr to the Baltic. With the HQ of 21 Army Group – renamed as the British Army of the Rhine in August 1945 – established at Bad Oeynhausen, HQ T-Force also relocated to the area. For the next two-and-a-half years the HQ would remain in the area, using it as the base from which the uniformed investigation teams were sent out across Germany to assess the targets on the blacklists. To cope with the incessant demand for shipping equipment back to the UK, the unit also established a new base at Hamburg as a crating and despatching centre. In addition, T-Force increasingly offered travel, accommodation and messing facilities for investigation teams. As one T-Force officer noted, they offered services that were a combination of Thomas Cook travel agents, the freight company Carter Patterson and a Lyons Corner House.

In the initial postwar period the men of T-Force were unable to immediately forget the wartime emotions that had caused so much enmity towards the population of Germany. Les Goodwin, a despatch rider with the 5th King's, recalled the situation:

Many of the local people, particularly the children and the old would hang around our billet hoping to pick up scraps of food. They would come to dining room windows at mealtimes to watch us eat and at first we were not concerned with their plight having just recently been exposed to the horrors of Bergen-Belsen. After we left the dining area we dumped whatever was left in our mess tins into a garbage bin and the civilians would hold their hands inside the garbage bins hoping for anything that they could catch that would stave off their hunger.[5]

With war over, the men in T-Force soon found opportunities to relax. Despite the feeling of antagonism shown by some of the soldiers towards German civilians, others soon found comfort in the arms of German women. As Harry Bullen remembered, he and his mates obeyed the non-fraternization orders 'for about five minutes!' His mate Bob Brighouse recalled: 'You'd see the local girls walking along and about five yards behind would be one of the lads, with his rifle over his shoulder. You knew what was going on!' One member of A Company, 5th King's, recalled that he would sit in bars and watch the locals walking past. Whenever he saw a young woman that he liked the look of, he would leave the bar and approach her, offering cigarettes for sex. It was rare for such offers to be refused. Harry Bullen also recalled: 'I was in the woods one night with a girl. I heard someone shout "Redcaps!" We all came running out pulling our trousers up. There weren't any MPs there, someone was just having a laugh.'

Despite these initial mixed emotions, many of the men in T-Force were soon engaged in tasks that ensured the resurrection of Germany from the ashes of defeat and gave employment to the very scientists who had been responsible for so many of the weapons that had blighted the soldiers' lives. In addition to the primary targets, such as gas production facilities, nuclear scientists and the Walterwerke, T-Force investigation teams continued to search a myriad of smaller, less consequential targets related to the German war machine. Although 30AU were no longer charging off into the unknown, their duties continued to be of vital importance. Throughout the summer teams from 30AU, minus those sent to the Far East, continued the search for maritime secrets. At Priwall, near Travemünde, divers attached to the unit searched the seabed where torpedo casings and warheads had been used to hide secret documents. Following leads from the Walterwerke, a team from 30AU was sent to southern Germany to search for additional records of torpedo research. One of their finds was an experimental closed-cycle diesel engine that was found in a railway siding in Stuttgart. Other successful discoveries included stocks of gold, bearer bonds and secret seaplane research that had been buried.

Following leads picked up in Hannover, 30AU sent a team to the Harz mountain region. They located a Professor Wagner and obtained from him a number of documents related to 'V' weapons. In total, they examined 26 targets in the Harz. Their targets included the town of Blankenburg where documents were found relating to the assembly of prefabricated hull sections in U-boats. Elsewhere, they discovered an underground store containing radar components including the latest 'Berlin' sets, complete with their magnetron valves and precision wave guides. Other finds included high-speed Morse code transmitters and intelligence on U-boat anti-ASDIC devices and snorkel battery recharging systems.

Elsewhere a team was sent to find certain documents that were missing from the library they had uncovered at Schloss Tambach, as previously described. In the end, the entire war diaries of the German navy were actually discovered buried under the doorstep of a naval HQ at Plön. The continuing search of Schloss Tambach – an operation in which Ian Fleming oversaw the Royal Navy's role – saw the evacuation of 50 tons of documents to the UK.

Not all of the work in this period revealed military secrets. Continuing their work in Kiel, the Kingsmen found that some Germans continued to obstruct their work. Major George Lambert was called to one factory where the staff refused to open the safe. A safe-breaker was called up from the Royal Engineers who soon put paid to the German resistance. Inside the safe, they discovered a packet of industrial diamonds. Colonel Wreford-Brown soon took possession of the diamonds, but not until after Major Lambert had made him sign a receipt for them.

Other T-Force units in Kiel took on routine duties. Although the war was over, there was no let up in the ever-dangerous work of the bomb disposal engineers. It made little difference to them if there was a war on or not – as long as there were bombs to be defused, there was work to be done. When they had first arrived in Kiel the engineers had little choice but to take on guard duties at T-Force targets. There were simply too many targets that needed to be secured. With just 500 men under his command, Major Hibbert had been unable to spare troops for anything other than the primary targets. After all, for Hibbert the occupation of Kiel's targets was first and foremost to prevent the Red Army attempting to steal the city's secrets first.

Once the rest of the army had caught up, the engineers set about fulfilling their primary function. The last week of May saw the engineers spreading out across the countryside around Kiel in an attempt to uncover hidden stores of weapons and ammunition. The desire to secure any such dumps was hastened by the fear that they might fall into the hands of any Germans intent on continuing with armed resistance. The minds of the High Command was full of thoughts of the so-called 'Werewolves', dedicated bands of SS men, Hitler Youth and ardent Nazis who Hitler had promised would unleash a violent insurgency, revitalizing the spirit of the seemingly defeated Reich. Though few such attacks ever took place – and those that did were sporadic and disorganized – the fear was genuine, ensuring vigilance from all the British soldiers and plenty of hard work for the T-Force engineers.

On 26 May the 5th King's, along with two companies of Pioneers, were given orders to move into the zone occupied by 30 Corps. With the main targets, as identified in the blacklists, already under investigation, T-Force moved on to those that had been given lower priority. These were the so-called 'grey targets' that had originally been identified by CIOS and opportunity targets that had been spotted during the final advance into Germany. These were added to the original targets that had been bypassed as a result of the unit's limited capability in the initial phase of operations.

As Germany settled down to adapt to a world without war, it soon became clear to the men of T-Force that their work would not be over for some time. One month after VE Day, 803 Smoke Company was moved to Hamburg to continue T-Force duties at the Blohm + Voss factory. They gathered secret documents related to 'special' aircraft, crated equipment and protected the premises from unwanted intruders. Nearly three months later, they were still in the same location, continuing to sift through reams of documents related to aircraft research.

One of the targets assessed by T-Force during this period was a salt mine located in the village of Hulsea, north of Magdeburg. According to the blacklist, the mine was in use as storage for 'ammunition of a special kind'. It fell to T-Force to discover the meaning behind this vague description. What they found was even more unusual. Upon arrival at the mine, which had been worked by slave labourers who had been housed on site, the soldiers discovered the whole place had been ransacked. At war's end the slave labourers had turned on their guards, killing most of them, then smashing up machinery and buildings at the mine. Lt Ken Davenport was in the first party to descend into the darkness:

> With the aid of a makeshift winch we managed to descend to the first level work area, the large bucket 'lift' being let down rather bumpily, squelching on the bodies of German soldiers who had been thrown down the shaft by the D.P.s. The stench was indescribable, but with the aid of torches we were able to find our way down a short passage into a huge cathedral like chamber which was stacked with storage boxes.[6]

Much of what they found was of little interest. The 'special ammunition' appeared to be boxes of 'dum-dum' bullets – deadly hollow-pointed bullets that were banned by international law.

For the engineers of T-Force's bomb disposal company, June 1945 began with the news that they would soon be leaving to continue their duties in a different formation. However, in their final days in the unit, their work continued unabated as they joined the Kingsmen on innumerable searches for German technology. They travelled to Peenemünde and Warnemünde in search of rocket technology and were sent to Leck to deal with a large number of highly advanced HE 162 'Salamander' jet fighters. The nature of T-Force's investigative role meant that the bomb disposal staff faced the greatest dangers in the immediate postwar period. At Haningsen they were detailed to investigate an underground ordnance store that was accessed via a lift. However, prior to entering they were warned that a large explosive charge had been set to go off when the lift reached the bottom. The subaltern in charge of the detachment decided to descend in the lift himself, to discover if the charge actually existed. He was lucky: when he reached the bottom there was no explosion. However, he soon discovered the charge was actually in place but the detonator had not been connected. Another task of the engineers was to don diving suits to recover items of interest dumped underwater by the enemy. At Embsen the target was a quantity of platinum that had been thrown into the river by fleeing Germans.

Through the summer and into autumn, the work of T-Force continued with hardly a break. The troops searched anywhere that intelligence suggested might have been used for hiding documentation. In one of these searches a unit of T-Force discovered three lorry loads of Krupps documentation hidden at a colliery. During this period, many of the targets may not have been as vital as secret aviation projects or nuclear research but they still retained a military purpose. The evacuation lists covered all manner of military materials, great or small. T-Force located and evacuated items as seemingly irrelevant as .22 rifles or, from Krupps at Essen, data as vitally important as four cases of files, drawings and documents related to tank design – a field in which the Germans had consistently proved themselves to be far in advance of the Allies. Of particular interest were plans and items of machinery used to harden the steel used in the construction of armoured vehicles. They were also sent to scour the countryside in search for serviceable Panther and Royal Tiger tanks that were needed for investigations by tank designers. At Clausthal-Zellerfeld T-Force detachments investigated a factory, which had been moved from Köln to escape Allied bombing, and found gyros for use in airborne torpedoes and, more interestingly, a high-speed oil-diffusion pump.

During this period a team from T-Force uncovered secret German plans for anti-aircraft rockets for use against formations of bombers. The rocket had a circulating path, so that if it missed its target it would turn in a circle to potentially strike another plane in the formation. This was similar in thinking to torpedoes that were set on a timer to turn around if they had missed their target. There was also the Typhoon rocket for use against formations of bombers. Each rocket was designed to break up into 60 to 100 separate bombs. In early 1945 the German military had ordered 2 million of these rockets, but problems with the ignition system meant it had never gone into production.

At Wesermünde T-Force searched a subsection of Wernher von Braun's Peenemünde rocket-building facility. Large amounts of equipment were evacuated and 35 scientists made available for interrogation. Investigations at a naval research station at Neustadt uncovered Admiral Dönitz's chief adviser on electronics. He was put under guard and soon provided fruitful information on marine radar research and torpedo fire systems to his interrogators. The torpedoes in question were rocket-propelled and capable of travelling at up to 70 knots. The plant had also been researching rubberized anti-ASDIC fittings for use on submarines. Close investigation of the facility revealed that Germany was at least two years behind the British and US in radar development.

While offensive military equipment remained the prime focus of attention, all products with a military application were investigated. Two scientists, Dr Lorsbach and Dr Taute from the Record Rubber Works, were evacuated to the UK since their work was considered extremely valuable. They had devised a new plastic about one-fifteenth the weight of cork. It had efficient heat insulation properties and could be produced in varying weights. As investigators noted, it could be either as soft as sponge or as heavy as wood. The interior of the product consisted of closed cells of an inert gas, which led investigators to believe its ideal use would be to produce puncture-proof tyres, lifebelts and diving suits. The materials were found to be in use at a plant in Rodenburg where life-saving maritime equipment such as rafts and lifeboats were in production. Elsewhere, targets included new types of springs for use in vehicle suspension and even special types of tarpaulin.

For Tom Pitt-Pladdy the postwar work of T-Force ran the risk of being boring, until he was handed a job perfectly suited to an ex-gunner: 'There was no question of which was the most interesting. When HQ moved to Munsterlager I moved to the Unterlüss gun range.' As an experienced gunner, he was ideally suited to the job and could converse with the German staff with an air of authority. Despite having been lightly bombed the plant was fully operational, with all the personnel in place. Pitt-Pladdy was impressed by the quality of the German field guns.

While at the plant he was contacted directly by Brigadier Pennycook and told to take three of the Germans to HQ T-Force. When he got there, he was then told to take them to the UK. He was on the plane before anyone even had a chance to inform his company commander. Before the Germans could be moved, though, Pitt-Pladdy had to ensure all the correct paperwork was filled in. He recorded their names, addresses, a reference number, the date of evacuation, the name of the conducting officer, the date of hand-over in the UK and the name of the interested agency on whose behalf the evacuation was taking place. Only then could the group depart:

> I flew back to London and was greeted by eight big black limousines and about 20 policemen, all waiting to take these Germans away. They were gun designers who specialized in automatic weapons who'd worked in Spain during the civil war. There was also the senior designer who was retired but still lived at the range. He was a fountain of knowledge and they wanted him in London. After I handed them over I was sent on a weekend leave.

His return to Germany gave a stark indication of the nature of T-Force's work and how disparate were the jobs the troops were employed on: 'When I got back to Germany no one even knew I'd been in England.'

For Pitt-Pladdy, Unterlüss was an ideal situation. He had a 30-mile artillery range to test guns on and could run his own firing programmes. His favourite weapon was an automatic 35mm gun on a hydraulic platform that had been made in Brno in Czechoslovakia. Despite Pitt-Pladdy's own enthusiasm for his gunnery experiments, he found it difficult to raise interest amongst those detailed to inspect the German weapons developments:

> We were visited by a party from the Boulton-Paul works in the UK – they also made guns on hydraulic platforms. I put on shoots with this Czech gun for the chap. But he didn't even

want to see it. He told me that Boulton-Paul did everything better. But it was sent back to England. We photocopied all the
plans and sent them back to Fort Halstead. But I understand
most of it just stayed in the cellars and remained untouched –
even though most of it was equipment they could never have
dreamed of having!

While undertaking a range of investigation duties that were
becoming increasingly routine, T-Force also became involved
in some operations which were deemed so secret that no official records of the operations were kept. Even more than 60
years after the end of the Second World War, some of documentation related to T-Force operations in the second half of
1945 remains classified. In the early months of peace, T-Force
was soon put to work locating and 'evacuating' German scientists from the Soviet zone.

Effectively, this was the beginning of the Cold War. As had
been made clear by the insistence that T-Force should forestall
any Russian attempts to seize intelligence from the vital military targets in the port of Kiel, any idea of a continuing
alliance was over. If, during this period, the eastern and western blocs were not yet enemies, they were certainly already
fierce rivals. It was obvious to all involved in the demilitariza-
tion of Nazi Germany that the British and Americans were not
prepared to accept the loss of German scientific knowledge to
the Russians. Thus T-Force became central to the policy of
ensuring that many scientists in eastern Germany were
brought west to continue their research.

At first it was a relatively simple process. The lists compiled
by CIOS gave the names and locations for many scientists
deemed to be of interest. In the early days of summer 1945,
prior to the strict settlement of the demarcation lines, it was relatively easy for the T-Force detachments to drive into the
neighbouring zone and carefully avoid Red Army patrols to

reach their targets. By studying their maps, sticking closely to the country lanes and avoiding towns, it wasn't difficult to reach their destination without encountering a problem. Often the main issue was that the startled local population seemed unsure of the true identities of the men who, though dressed in British uniforms, were openly operating in the Soviet zone. Though the men of T-Force did not yet realize it, their targeting and enticement of scientists to the West was the beginning a process that would continue throughout the Cold War.

One early operation involved contacting a Luftwaffe pilot at his home to collect scale drawings of new German aircraft. Jack Twining-Davies recalled this 'evacuation' visit:

> Our task was to pick up an important civilian who lived in a country house. The Intelligence Officer disappeared and did all the talking. When they appeared the civilian carried a suitcase and was followed by a tearful woman and a small boy. I was totally unaffected by the touching scene. It was pouring with rain at the time and when I was told he was to travel in the cab with us I refused to move, so he had to get in the back of the truck. I wonder did he help put man on the moon or was his science of a more human type?

The understandably cold-hearted attitude towards the Germans, as shown by many among T-Force in the early days, did not last forever. Les Goodwin, the Kingsman who had happily watched civilians search through dustbins for waste food explained the change in attitudes: 'As the days passed we weakened and gave them our leftover scraps. Then we began to save a bit of food to help the poor souls, as we now saw them, to survive. They were now the victims of war rather than the perpetrators.'[7]

It was while working at the Unterlüss artillery range that Pitt-Pladdy found that a humanitarian response reaped its own rewards:

Dr Ross – a doctor of gunnery who had worked on the flak towers in Hamburg and Berlin and had even had books on the subject published in English – appeared and told us he was willing to work for us for a few cigarettes. All he asked was for us to remove his family from the Russian zone. I waited until after dark and went in to get them. There were no problems. So he worked for us.

Though this was a relatively simple operation, it was just a taster for what would soon become an integral part of T-Force's postwar work. The military realities of the final days of war had resulted in a number of unforeseen situations. The British may have feared that the Russians would exceed the agreed limits of their advance – a fear that had inspired T-Force's hasty advance on Kiel – but they themselves occupied territories that were not allotted to them. Two major areas, the 'Schwerin Pocket' and the 'Magdeburg Bulge', both officially within the Soviet zone, had finished the war under occupation by the western allies. The Schwerin Pocket was the area to the north of the River Elbe between Lübeck and Wismar, while the Magdeburg Bulge was the area up to the River Elbe that the British had occupied.

To resolve the issue, a date of 21 June 1945 was agreed for the British and Americans to begin their withdrawal over a ten-day period, but the western Allies wanted to make sure that they did not leave too many valuable targets behind. Thus, in early June SHAEF sent instructions to the newly formed Enemy Personnel Evacuation Section (EPES) to prepare lists of scientists and technicians whose skills were desired for exploitation by the British and Americans. In the following months EPES had compiled a card index of 15,000 names of scientists and technicians of interest to the British and Americans, with an average of 500 being added each month.

The evacuation lists were issued to T-Force via FIAT on 18 June 1945, with priority targets marked with an 'X'. The lists stressed that the targets 'should' be brought west, rather than 'should be asked' to come west. The wording was open to wide interpretation and later resulted in confusion and accusations about how the 'evacuations' had been carried out.

The lists were prepared at an interrogation facility named 'Dustbin', based at Kransberg Castle. Although near Frankfurt-am-Main in the American zone, Kransberg Castle was guarded by members of the Ox and Bucks and British Military Policemen. During the postwar period the officers and men of T-Force became regular visitors to the American zone, transferring scientists to the 'Dustbin'. The purpose of the facility was to house surplus scientists held by the British since there was an official limit to how many could be detained within the British zone. At Kransberg Castle, EPES received the assistance of inmates such as Albert Speer, formerly the German Minister for Industrial Supply, and Professor Werner Osenberg, formerly the head of the Planning Office of the German Research Council.

The need for the British to comb the area of the 'Bulge' for military secrets prior to the handover meant that T-Force had to be positioned to exploit the zone. As a result the 5th King's Battalion HQ and Major Lambert's A Company were sent to the town of Goslar where they established their HQ. The town, untouched by war, was perfectly positioned in the Harz mountains, just miles from what would soon become the frontline in the Cold War.

The target lists included a wide variety of names and occupations, such as the technical staff of three universities. Among other targets were specialists in fields that were vital to military research such as researchers into machine-tool development, jet engine designers, aircraft engineers, gun-site designers and specialists in aircraft mass production. Some of the names included on the lists were the families of scientists who had already been taken into Allied detention and whose cooperation was ensured by being reunited with their kin.

The importance of family reunion was shown by the fact that lists even included the grandchildren and sisters-in-law of important scientists. Some on the targets brought their secretaries with them and one even brought his domestic servant. There were rocket engineers, members of Albert Speer's former ministry and the directors from a factory making ME 262 jet fighters. At opposite ends of the spectrum were experts in plywood and a Waffen SS general named Kangler. T-Force teams were also sent out to find people who made claims of inventions, even if their worth had not yet been proven. One example was a man who claimed he had designed a tank track allowing safe movement through a bog. Mathematicians, chemists and physicists were all included on the lists, as was a doctor with specialized knowledge of internal organs. Others from less exciting fields included dentists, botanist, vets and even glassblowers.

At the Mittelwerk plant near Nordhausen, occupied by the Americans and earlier investigated by 30AU, the entire underground rocket production factory was detailed for evacuation. The facilities belonging to Rheinmetall-Borsig were of particular importance, with military timing devices being included on the lists along with scientific staff. One IG Farben plant had seven chemical warfare scientists that were to be evacuated. From Plauen came Dr Horn, a specialist in missile control. Factories producing insecticide were also swiftly examined to see if they yielded any new products.

Evacuations were carried out in both the British and the American zones. Some targets received particular attention. US Army T-Forces transported vast amounts of equipment from the world famous Carl Zeiss optical works, and also took its specialists in gyroscopic gunsights. Others in the facility were specialists in fire control equipment, lens manufacture, periscope production, binoculars, rangefinders and all manner of optical instruments. As any soldier who had used the binoculars issued to the British Army knew all too well, German binoculars were far superior. As one officer had commented, British binoculars were only suitable for a night at the opera, and even then only if you had good seats. Even trainloads of personal effects, including furniture belonging to the employees of Carl Zeiss, were moved west. The majority of the equipment from Carl Zeiss was then transported to North America by the US Air Force.

Elsewhere in the American zone large numbers of scientists and technicians were moved from the Junkers factory at Dessau and from plants belonging to IG Farben at Bitterfeld, Leuna and Wolfen. Complete professional staffs moved westward from the universities at Leipzig, Jena and Halle. At Wolfen the AGFA Werke, one of Europe's foremost producers of photographic films and equipment, was subject to considerable attention. Orders were issued that the entire plant, along with its technicians, should be evacuated in advance of the Russian takeover.

On 8 July, T-Force HQ reported nearly 50 scientists and their families had been successfully withdrawn from the zones due to be occupied by the Russians. The following week a further 9 were evacuated, including a specialist in locks. One brought with him 30 boxes of documents on biology from the Brunswick Technical University. On 10 July T-Force units in 30 Corps zone reported on the scientists who had been removed from the Magdeburg Bulge, noting that some brought their household effects. Realizing the likely permanence of their move, many brought share certificates and details of their bank accounts. Others were less well-prepared and many technicians brought little more than the tools of their trade. From the Hillersleben artillery testing range came 9 gunnery specialists, out of more than 30 that had been on the original list. In addition to personnel evacuations, T-Force removed Junkers aircraft engines from Halberstadt, radar equipment from Werben and anti-tank mines from a store located in a salt mine. In total, around 250 German scientists and their families were moved by T-Force into the British zone, while ten times that number moved into the American zone.

George Lambert later explained the way that most scientists were collected:

> The head Scientist was given the option of moving further west – out of the area which would become the Russian Region. None of these facts were mentioned – he was asked the straight-forward question – 'Would you and your immediate family like to move further west?' They understood why they were given the option! They were allowed to put as many clothes, furniture, books and documents etc. into a three ton truck and then take them to the village of Bad Gandersheim about 10 miles west of Goslar. It was taken over by the British Army and the new inhabitants came on my ration strength.

The evacuations to Bad Gandersheim caused immediate problems as the scientists' own bank accounts were held in the east and any western accounts were frozen, thus the burden of feeding them fell to T-Force alone. Further problems were discovered by the evacuees who wanted to make sure their families found out about their new location. In particular, those with children currently held in POW camps were concerned that messages should be forwarded to them to ensure they did not return to the Russian zone upon release.

John Longfield was sent into the Soviet zone on an evacuation mission that had been specifically designed to solve this problem. He was ordered to enter the Soviet zone to collect a scientist named Dr Katter. Accompanied by a driver, Longfield embarked on the 200-mile round trip behind what would soon be known as the 'Iron Curtain': 'I had to do one odd job. I was given a truck and a driver and told to go fast, get to this place and pick up a scientist. They told me to stick as much of his furniture into the back of the truck and bring him back.'

Longfield found such orders were outside of the expected tasks for an ordinary infantryman: 'My concern was, what if the Russians object? So they told me "Just act stupid and hope for the best!" As someone else was told "If you get problems with the Russians when you are bringing scientists out just hand over your watch and they'll let you go." Luckily the Russians took no notice of me and my scientist – they just stared at me as we drove past.'

With the doctor safely in the British zone, Longfield was then given an unusual follow up task: 'Then I was to go to the Baltic coast, where all the German prisoners were being held. There I had to ask for this German officer. It turned out the scientist was the father of this officer. The scientist had told the British he was only willing to come out of the Russian zone providing he was reunited with his son.' The son was located and extracted from the POW camp, but not before Longfield had the unnerving experience of walking along through a POW compound surrounded by thousands of German soldiers.

Fortunately for T-Force, not all of the incoming scientists were marooned at the central facility at Bad Gandersheim. Specialists in certain military fields began to be relocated at research establishments under the control of the occupying armies. In Hamburg scientists with interest in X-rays and infrared research were brought together. Torpedo specialists, in particular those who specialized in homing systems and echo control, were housed at Eckenförde. The research investigated included acoustic GNAT torpedoes and the LUT zigzagging torpedoes. The latter were intended to be fired in salvos of three, thus making avoidance action extremely difficult. Some of Germany's top submarine researchers were sent to Priwall and Kiel, including hydrogen peroxide specialists, the designers of homing torpedoes and experts in underwater ballistics. The

Focke-Wulf factory at Detmold once again became home to
aviation experts, men whose previous efforts had terrorized the
skies above Europe.

The concerns related to the concentration of scientists and
technicians at Bad Gandersheim went beyond the issue of
feeding and housing. In August 1945, HQ T-Force requested
that the scientists be removed from the location with greater
speed. The problem was that few of them were of sufficient
military interest to be taken to the 'Dustbin' facility for interrogation. Brigadier Pennycook also asked SHAEF whether
they could ask the Russians to allow the scientists to access
their bank accounts and stressed the need to quickly find out
how many of the scientists were needed for 'Dustbin'. The
reply was that just 9 out of a total of 250 were required for
interrogation and that it was not thought advisable for a
request to be put to the Russians for access to the bank
accounts. However, fully realizing the implications of leaving
so many eminent scientists and technicians unemployed,
Pennycook requested that the process be speeded up so that
the scientists might know their fate as soon as possible. In particular, he was concerned about the impact of inactivity upon
his charges, with great brains being unable to work on any of
their research projects.

A further issue for Brigadier Pennycook was that 'Dustbin'
had been designed to hold just 90 scientists. However, by
September 1945 around 5,000 specialists and their families had
reached the US zone and the castle was overflowing. There
were so many scientists of interest that, although the British had
evacuated a large number to the UK for interrogation, were
employing some in research facilities within Germany and had
filled the official accommodation within their own zone,
'Dustbin' in the US zone was still over-flowing. As was clear to
all at T-Force HQ, there were more German scientists than
anybody knew what to do with.

While this should have been an issue for the central policy-makers, it was T-Force HQ who had to deal with the burden. In September Lt Colonel Bloomfield complained that, from June onwards, a steady stream of American officers had been presenting themselves at T-Force HQ asking what should be done with the surplus scientists. He reported that the situation was so acute that the Americans were threatening to turn all the scientists loose: 'This would mean that some would find their way back to the Russian zone . . . I am informed that the Russians are offering strong financial inducements to return, which may account for some of the restiveness.' Bloomfield went on to point out that, while it was clear the technical qual-ifications of the German evacuees would be of great use to the British and Americans, 'It seems quite impossible to get anyone to indicate any interest in the matter.'[8]

Within months it was reported by the Scientific and Technical Research Board of the Allied Control Commission that there were around 500 German scientists within the British zone who would constitute 'a serious danger in the hands of a potentially hostile Power'.[9] The Control Commission noted that only some of these could be taken to the UK for employment, and the remainder could not all be given suitable employment within the Allied zones of Germany. Therefore, there was little that could be done to assist those who found themselves unem-ployed: 'These will, however, find a ready market for their services with the Russians, and to a lesser degree with the French.'[10] To deal with the problem it was therefore mooted 'to remove as soon as possible from Germany, whether they are willing to go or not, those whom it is considered vital to deny to other powers.'[11] In reaction to this report, further examina-tion was made of the situation. One of the conclusions reached was that it was not just the danger of the Soviet war machine that faced the western powers. In addition there was the fear that German scientific and technical prowess could be employed by the Soviets to swamp western markets with cheap, mass-produced goods, thus undermining western economies.

It was not just the Control Commission and the Americans who complained to T-Force about the situation of scientists held in limbo. Brigadier Pennycook's requests for assistance were made in response to an increasing sense of disquiet among the scientists. One of the evacuees wrote to complain about her lack of money: 'I beg for a sum of money to have my subsistence. The deportation happened so suddenly and unexpected that I could take with me the money that I have had just at home.'[12] Another complained that she had been promised financial help at the time of her evacuation but that nothing had been forthcoming. Some had been given just five hours to pack what they needed and to make any arrangements to settle their affairs. Some described their evacuations as 'well intentioned' but 'forced'.[13] One who was moved west by the Americans complained that he had lost nothing in the course of the war but had lost everything he owned – his home, his library, his furniture and his savings – since being moved west.

Complaints were made about many of the evacuations, in particular those carried out by the Americans, with some Germans describing themselves as 'forced evacuees'.[14] One group evacuated by the Americans from a Junkers factory claimed they had all decided to remain in the east but had been ordered west by US officers and were unable to refuse. In the course of the move to Stockstadt on the Rhine, two of the 54-strong party – an old man and a child – died. Another in the American zone noted that he had been told there was a strict limit on personal luggage – two suitcases and one rucksack – but that any technical equipment could be crated for evacuation. He was also told that if he refused he would be removed by force. The Leipzig group had been called to a police station and told their journey was 'top secret'. One of the scientists complained that he was physically impaired after a beating by stormtroopers during the 1930s and that he had to support his ageing parents who had been ruined by the Nazis as a result of his father's membership of the Freemasons. When forcibly evacuated he and his wife lost all their property.

The charge of widespread strong-arm tactics levelled against T-Force was balanced by the reaction of many other evacuees. Instead of being upset by their change in circumstances, many of the scientists immediately made strenuous efforts to continue their research in western Germany. Upon arrival in Bad Gandersheim some of the scientists requested that their offices, research labs and factories should be added to the list and evacuated westwards in order to ensure continuity of their research. In addition, some of the staff formerly employed by the evacuated scientists made their own way west in order to be able to continue employment with their previous bosses. It was also noted that some of the target scientists had already left their homes when the evacuation teams visited them. Many had voluntarily made their way west in search of employment, causing a noticeable rise in the numbers of eastern scientists applying for jobs in western universities.

Disgruntlement over the evacuations carried out by T-Force also came from other sources. The British Foreign Office complained that the dismantling of 450 tons of aircraft manufacturing equipment, of which the largest piece weighed 8 tons even after dismantling, would provoke a furious reaction from the Russians when they discovered the loss. However, the Ministry of Aircraft Production argued that the advantage of securing the equipment would outweigh the embarrassment that its removal would cause. The evacuation was cleared to proceed.

Following the completion of the handover of the Schwerin Pocket and the Magdeburg Bulge, the Russians did issue a formal complaint about the behaviour of the British. They noted the mass removal of equipment from their zone, in particular the removal of 100 tons of gold taken from a medical supplies store. The British were also accused of removing a large quantity of rolling stock, including 15 railway engines and more than 1,200 goods wagons, nearly 40 of which were reported to have been filled with goods being 'evacuated' from the Soviet zone.

With the Russians about to take over the areas formerly occupied by the western Allies at the beginning of July, it was not only technology and research scientists that came to the attention of T-Force. Their targets also began to take a human angle. With an increasing gulf emerging between the former Allies, it was decided that some former enemies should be evacuated rather than be left to the mercy of the Red Army. In some cases the evacuations were entirely unofficial, with individual members of T-Force transporting those it felt in need of protection.

Dutch interpreter Willy van der Burght was sent to translate for a detachment of Kingsmen who were detailed to evacuate wounded German soldiers from a hospital:

> When we had evacuated the hospital the lady doctor asked 'Are you taking me with you?' The captain said 'She looks ok', so we took her back to Goslar. When we got there she asked me 'Where can I stay?' I said she could use my room but she said she had a baby, a two-year-old daughter and her old mother with her! So I let them have my room and I slept elsewhere. The next morning the captain asked where she was. I told him she was in my room. He said 'You lucky boy!' But then I explained that she had her family with her. So he told me to drive her to the camp where we kept the scientists. He said no one would notice the extra people there.

On the final day before the Red Army was due to occupy the Schwerin Pocket and the Magdeburg Bulge, T-Force received an unusual request. Orders had been sent out that all British units should pull out of the area. These orders, which had been carefully obeyed, left the local German population anxious about what might happen next. However, while all civilians could expect some change to their lives, some knew the change would be extreme and were in the privileged position of being able to do something about it.

One of those in a position to help was a German nobleman, the Duke of Brunswick. Concerned about his friends in the Stolberg family, whose ancestral home was to become part of the Soviet zone, he approached the British Army for assistance. The Stolbergs were one of Germany's most senior princely families and had played a notable role in the old German empire. Mindful of the Soviet's antagonism towards royal families, the British agreed to assist by evacuating the family westwards.

The headquarters staff approached the ever-busy and highly experienced T-Force to assist the evacuation of the Stolberg family. The operation had not been officially sanctioned, but that had never previously stopped them.

On the morning of 2 July 1945, 7 Platoon of A Company, 5th King's Regiment, left their base in Goslar and headed towards the Harz mountains. In charge was Lt Stan Taylor, driven by Private Harry Henshaw in a requisitioned Mercedes sports car, with six 3-ton trucks to carry the family and their luggage westwards. There was no time to spare: all troops had already left the areas to be handed over and there was a two-day ban on troop movements. To speed up the process, Lt Taylor and Private Henshaw raced ahead of the column to give the family notice of the move. It was an eerie journey; the roads and streets were empty, not a single civilian was to be seen. Wary of the Russians, the civilians had expediently hung red flags from their windows to greet the imminent arrival of their future oppressors.

Approaching through the valley, the Kingsmen took in their surroundings. Martin Luther had once described the town of Stolberg as appearing to look like a bird: the castle was its head, the narrow alleys leading from the market place were its wings, the market place the body, the Gothic church its heart and the long valley road its tail. Like so many towns in northern Germany, the streets of Stolberg were crammed with half-timbered medieval buildings. Yet unlike so many others, the town was untouched by war. The twelfth-century Knight's Gate still stood proudly to welcome visitors – whatever their nationality. The stone church towers and the rounded walls of the thirteenth-century smelting house were intact, rather than in the familiar piles of rubble that had greeted the Kingsmen in so many of the towns they had passed through. The City Hall still displayed the badges of the local craftsmen. Though the guilds and their historic emblems had survived, the same could not be said of the craftsmen – like so many German towns and cities there were few local men left to greet the British soldiers. That morning, the only things that moved in the town were the red flags fluttering from windows as the car moved towards the castle.

If the forests and town had seemed like a fairy-tale landscape, the castle only helped to deepen the impression. Perched high above the picturesque town that nestled in the bottom of a beech tree-lined valley, the castle towered over the houses. Originally built in 1201, then added to through the centuries, Castle Stolberg was typical of the medieval homes of German princes. The heavy stone walls of the original structure had become the base for an elegant palace, with white walls and a steeply sloping roof. But this was not a sightseeing tour; instead, there was plenty of work to do.

Arriving at the castle, Lt Taylor introduced himself to the Prince, who showed him the crates of possessions that were to be moved. The British soldiers were shocked. They had expected to move the family and their personal belongings, but they discovered the family intended to move as much of the treasure contained within the castle as was possible. Included inside the crates was a priceless library of over 24,000 books and manuscripts dating back to the twelfth century. This was a slice of Germany history, one that the Stolberg family had no intention of sacrificing. The soldiers were soon hard at work filling their trucks with the family heirlooms.

As soon as the trucks were full they descended into the town and hurried back towards Goslar. As they drove through Stolberg the soldiers noticed an immediate difference about the town. The streets were still deserted, but the red flags had disappeared. Believing the British had returned to stay, they had replaced the red flags with white ones – mostly bedsheets that hung from upstairs windows – to signal their lack of aggressive intention.

Arriving back at Goslar, the trucks were driven to the local museum where the Stolberg family's treasures were unloaded for safekeeping. Some soldiers were surprised to see that the family was not with them. They had remained behind, preferring to see their possessions safely evacuated than to save themselves. Lt Taylor then informed his men that he was going to take three trucks back to the castle to bring out the family and anything else that could be carried.

As they drove back into Stolberg the troops noticed that the civilians had been active during the intervening hours – all the white flags had been removed and once again replaced by red ones. But still there was no one in the streets. At the castle the family and more of their possessions were loaded into the trucks. The soldiers were also given presents and were able to take anything they wanted from the castle, as a gesture of thanks from the Prince. All the furnishings had to be left behind and the walls were still hung with weaponry from battles throughout German history. Paintings of German and British kings seemed to fill every space on the walls, yet they could not be moved – there was simply no space in the trucks. As he left the castle, Harry Henshaw picked up one of the antique books that there had been no room to remove during the original trip. There was just time for the Prince and his family to take one last look back at their ancestral home. It was a sad moment since they had been told there would be little chance of ever returning there. As they left for the last time they knew that within hours their home would be occupied – and most probably looted – by the incoming occupation force.

As they drove down the hill – with the family safely hidden behind the soldiers in the lorries – Lt Taylor told Harry Henshaw that he believed the Russians must be near and that they would have to remain alert. He was right. Just a mile after leaving the castle they encountered a Russian patrol in the town's market square. There was no alternative route and, as such, no way to get past them. Telling his driver to stop and ordering the troops to remain in their trucks, Taylor went forward to negotiate with the Russians. It was a tense time. The Russian insisted on searching the trucks but Taylor refused. As they talked, the soldiers watched in fear, expecting at any moment to be arrested and sent to Siberia. Eventually Lt Taylor returned to his car – he had convinced the Russian to allow them to pass. And so they continued on their journey to Goslar, passing numerous Russian military patrols and convoys. As Stan Taylor later recounted, he had driven back 'saluting every Russian I saw'.[15] Arriving safely at Goslar, the Stolberg family were taken to a hotel used to accommodate German VIPs. It would be many years before they would return to their ancestral home.

After the operation, the Princess offered two pieces of silverware from the family's collection as a gift to interpreter Willy van der Burght. He accepted these and also agreed to take a note from her to Prince Bernhardt of the Netherlands. He delivered the note, only for the Prince to admit he was not in a position to offer assistance to the Stolberg family.

The unofficial Stolberg evacuation was not the only operation carried out by T-Force on the final day. The 5th King's Intelligence Officer, Lt Ken Davenport, was detailed to fetch a German scientist from a village to the north of Magdeburg. Again, the fluid situation within Germany meant that the operation was a hasty one, needing to get the scientist out before the Russians located him. Davenport was given a truck, a driver and an interpreter for the task.

Arriving at the target, the German scientist – a specialist in chemical warfare – was, in the words of Lt Davenport, 'a very willing abductee, preferring the British devil he knew to the Russian ogre he didn't'.[16] He was told to pack whatever possessions he could into the truck and then, with wife and child inside, they set off on the return journey. The return to Goslar was not to be as simple as the outward journey. Lt Davenport soon discovered that the area had been re-boundaried, and allocated to the Russians. Moreover, a Russian checkpoint had been set up. It was obvious that the Russians would not take kindly to a German scientist being spirited out of their territory under their noses.

Fortunately, Lt Davenport had with him a Czech-born interpreter, serving in the British Army under the name of Williams. Sergeant Williams could speak a total of 11 languages, including Russian. He descended from the truck and approached the checkpoint, explaining to the guards that he had lost his way and was trying to reach the British zone. Unconvinced, the Russians insisted they be allowed to search the truck. Knowing the result of such a search, the British acted swiftly. From the cab, Lt Davenport produced a carton of cigarettes and half a bottle of schnapps. The scientist was then persuaded to 'donate' his expensive wristwatch to the Russians. This did the trick and, after much expressing of goodwill and Allied solidarity, the British

were allowed to safely continue their journey. The relieved
German scientist was then safely delivered, ready for interrogation about the chemical warfare projects he had worked on.

While the men of the 5th King's were deeply engrossed with
carrying out the orders of T-Force HQ – orders that had come
from the High Command – it seemed to some that the battalion's own senior officers were growing less interested in the
unit's duties. The relationship between the King's Regiment
and T-Force did not sit comfortably for everyone. While Tom
Pitt-Pladdy saw the King's as little more than a cap badge, others were protective of the name and – so it seemed to
Pitt-Pladdy – were more concerned with the regiment itself
than its T-Force duties. In many ways, he felt, the tremendous
success of T-Force was in spite of some senior King's Regiment
officers, rather than because of them. This conflict of interest
meant that Pitt-Pladdy found that he and his company commander, Major Frank Denton, did not see eye to eye. When
Pitt-Pladdy was sent from his beloved gun range at Unterlüss to
take over a role in a 'Cave Exploration Team' in the Harz
mountains, he felt sure it was simply designed to get him as far
away from the rest of the company as possible. Pitt-Pladdy
found himself working closely with Major George Lambert and
the rest of A Company at their base in the town of Goslar.

The role of the 'Cave' teams was to search through the
Harz mountains to locate whatever equipment might have
been concealed from the prying eyes of the Allies in the final
days of the war. Most of the time the finds were anything but
spectacular. Some caves contained basic machinery, but many
were simply used for storing wine that the locals believed –
quite rightly – would otherwise be looted by the occupation
forces or displaced persons.

While in Goslar, Tom Pitt-Pladdy gained a solid understanding of life in an occupying army. In particular he recognized

the fondness for alcohol displayed by some of his comrades. Lt Ken Hardy, serving with A Company, was responsible for the smooth running of the town's brewery and distillery, something that relied on the supply of coal by the British Army. In return, the officers received a constant supply of drink. As Hardy later recalled, during this period he began to drink heavily, often starting the day with a glass of water – followed by a glass of gin. He would then drink both beer and gin steadily through-out the day, a process he repeated day after day. This routine was his way of dealing with the aftermath of a conflict that had seen him witness awful horrors, including watching his best friend die and seeing half his platoon wiped out in just minutes.

Just 22 years old, with seven months experience of front-line action and a serious psychological breakdown as the reward for his endeavours, Hardy felt he deserved the opportunity to relax. One night Tom Pitt-Pladdy witnessed the effects of this overindulgence: 'I was called out from my room. There was a commotion in the street and I could hear German voices. I went out to find a group of German civilians pushing a pram – in the pram I found Ken Hardy, dead drunk.' As Hardy later admitted, he had gone to war as an innocent 21-year-old, only to return home on leave just over a year later to shock his mother with how much he had changed.

At first, the officers and men of T-Force were so engrossed in carrying out their tasks in isolation that they were unaware that their work was being replicated by the other Allied nations. The active involvement of American assessors in the teams of experts that had travelled with them into northern Germany revealed an American interest. Some, including liaison officers like Majors Hibbert and Urquhart, had been given clear warn-ings that the Soviets intended to seize naval intelligence from Kiel, but on the whole there was an initial ignorance of the burgeoning rivalry with the Russians. Lt Colonel Bloomfield,

Brigadier Pennycook's second-in-command, became aware of the situation on a trip to Berlin. On a visit to Hitler's bunker he noticed a large piece of machinery on the ground just outside the bunker entrance. It had clearly been prepared for despatch to the Soviet Union, with a destination stencilled on the side in Cyrillic lettering. Bloomfield was certain that this was the handiwork of the Red Army's equivalent of T-Force.

Intelligence sources soon revealed that the Soviets were actively competing with T-Force to acquire scientists and military secrets. Within Berlin, from 1945 onwards, the Russians operated a number of research organizations. The 'Soviet Technical Commission' worked through a German organization known as Deutscher Normenausschuss, based in the British sector of Berlin. This had established around 30 to 50 subcommittees covering a wide range of scientific studies. These committees were primarily staffed by individuals from German official scientific bodies based in the US and British sectors. They received a substantial wage from the Soviets of up to 5,000 Marks and were also in receipt of the same food rations as Soviet officers. The organization worked by requesting scientists from various fields to contribute to reports on the research they had carried out in the preceding 15 years. Many German scientists were eager to add to the reports compiled for the Russians since, by bringing together a range of research into one concise report, it actually benefited their own research.

The Soviets also utilized members of the scientific branches of 'The People's Commissariat', part of the Soviet Communist Party. Many of those employed were former Nazi party members who had been dismissed by their previous employers. The wide range of Soviet organizations with overlapping interests was related to the sense of mutual distrust between Communist Party scientists and those working for the Red Army. In one case two separate teams attempted to view a library of books on chemistry. The second team arrived to find that the previous visitors, their supposed comrades, had removed the entire library to the Ukraine.

Just as the Allies had done, the Soviets soon set to work on reopening military research facilities within their zone. The main Russian targets were specialists in radar, rockets, missile guidance systems, electronics and aircraft design. At Peenemünde, where the Germans had developed the V1 and V2 rockets, the Soviets tested artillery rockets. Rocket research also continued elsewhere, in particular near Magdeburg, and the offices of FIAT noted that the conditions of work and pay offered by the Soviets had proved very attractive to the German scientists. Reports continued to reach the western Allies of Russian attempts to induce scientists and technicians to move east for employment. Included among them was a BMW researcher from West Berlin who was asked to work on Russian rocket research. Another of those approached by the Russians was Dr Heinrich Gorbrecht, reported as a senior figure in German atomic research, who was approached by Marshal Georgi Zhukov and asked to go to Russia. He accepted a post in Moscow but reported to the western powers that he would have preferred employment through them – but like so many others, he had found that there were more German scientists than the western Allies had positions. Some of those who left the Carl Zeiss plant at Jena, only to find themselves 'frozen' in the US zone, were also approached by the Russians with the prospect of re-employment.

One scientist who was targeted by the Russians for employment reported how he went to the Russian HQ at Karlshorst in Berlin on routine business. After passing through the sentry point, he was led into a room and was closely scrutinized by a Russian soldier who drew a sketch of him; he was then taken into a large room at one end of which sat a Russian official. The official proceeded to harangue the scientist about why he refused to go to Moscow. At the end of this intimidating, if bizarre, meeting the German was allowed to leave and return to the American sector. The scientist had been unnerved by the encounter but reported that no direct pressure had been applied and no attempt had been made to force him to work for the Russians.

While some reporting suggested the Russians had forced scientists to work for them, top secret documents showed that most were attracted by the high salaries, good rations and working conditions offered in Russia and thus went voluntarily. One Berliner, who provided information to the Allied authorities, pointed out that he knew of no examples of German scientists being forced to relocate to Russia. In the main, it seemed, their primary aim was to be allowed to continue their research – something that was generally denied to them by the western powers, which had closed their laboratories and placed scientists in detention or suspended animation in camps like 'Dustbin' or villages such as Bad Gandersheim.

One scientist from Jena who was held by the Americans admitted that both the Russians and British had expressed an interest in his work but that the Americans had left him idle. This treatment made it difficult to ensure that scientists did not move east. Reports also circulated that Professor Hermann Oberth – inventor of long-range rockets – had been held by the Americans at Dustbin but released in October 1945 to live in Nürnberg. He was on a list of scientists required for employment in the UK but instead he was attracted by offers from the Russians. Another technician named Veith, who was wanted for employment by the Admiralty, was allowed to leave the US zone and enter the Soviet zone. He was soon relocated, apprehended and put into custody in Dustbin.

The difficulty of keeping hold of experts was shown by the departure of a number of men who had acted as assistants to German professors. Being younger than their employers, they were more inclined to take their chances and accept employment with the Russians. In one case, a doctor accepted an offer of employment in the Soviet zone on the promise of a good salary, double rations and the agreement that he would not be quizzed on earlier links to the Nazi Party. The understanding that the junior research scientists were the future professors and world experts resulted in EPES noting the importance of keeping such people in work and 'in good will towards us'.[17]

Even after the closing of the borders in July 1945, it fell to T-Force to undertake a number of covert operations to bring German scientists out of Berlin. Although the city was divided, it was simple enough for civilians to move from the Soviet zone of occupation into the British zone. Once again, T-Force's experience in evacuating men and machinery made them the obvious choice for carrying out operations of which no official records were to be kept.

Former artillery officer Tom Pitt-Pladdy commanded the evacuation of a German scientist from Berlin in late 1945. He had been called by Brigadier Pennycook, who told him he was to pick up a German physicist who was going to bring out all his papers with him. Pitt-Pladdy was sent to Goslar to organize the operation: 'The company commander at Goslar was absolutely ace – Major George Lambert – he really looked after his chaps. He told me a White Scout Car had been sent for me to use. It had no rear entrance, only an extra door behind the driver. The cargo section could be completely covered by a tightly laced tarpaulin cover; it had very restricted vision and its weight made it a pig to handle.' To ensure anonymity, all iden-tification marks, including tactical signs, were painted out. The interior was filled with kitbags and a small 'nest' was left in the rear in which the scientist was to be hidden. Some 20 jerry cans of petrol, cartons of cigarettes and a few other 'goodies' – intended for bribes – were also loaded into the vehicle.

Prior to departing for the operation, Pitt-Pladdy made a careful study of the area he would be returning through. By sneaking into the Soviet zone through areas of the unpatrolled border in the Harz mountains, he was able to work out exactly what he might face. He simply drove around, keeping an eye out for Soviet troops and observing their movements:

> I spent a few days scouting around in the Russian zone and discovered that the Russian units opposite us were orientals. They had no motor transport, just horse and carts. If I had any trouble I could simply put my foot down and speed away from them. They were right up on the Brocken mountain. I'd also discovered it took two days for any orders from their officers to actually reach these troops. So I decided I would come back through the lines there. I had no intention of using the official border.

The mission Pitt-Pladdy and his team were about to embark upon was the essence of a 'Cold War' operation. The operational orders for the Berlin trip were only ever communicated verbally. The lack of written orders served to create a sense of what might now be termed 'plausible deniability'. Essentially, if Pitt-Pladdy and his unmarked vehicle were arrested by the Russians there would be no paperwork connecting them to official British policy. However, as a result of this secrecy, T-Force first had to get out of the British zone without attracting attention from the intermediate authorities. As was noted at the time by Pitt-Pladdy, 'We couldn't drive around the British zone in an unmarked Scout Car loaded with cigarettes – the MPs would pull us in.' Thus, a representative from HQ T-Force paid an unofficial visit to commander of 5 Brigade, who kindly arranged for Military Police under his command to turn a 'blind-eye' to the movement of the unauthorized and unmarked vehicle. He also suggested that a visit was made to the Assistant Provost Marshal in Berlin – effectively the second-in-command of police in the British zone of Berlin – to seek assistance. However, it was stressed that once they had passed the final British checkpoint at Helmstedt they would be on their own.

Despite not expecting to meet much traffic on his journey, Pitt-Pladdy soon learned why the unmarked White Scout Car was essential for their operation: 'The place was stiff with vehicles including tanks. There were a few times when they pointed their big guns at us, but they just let us go on. That was because the Russians also used White Scout Cars – they had also got them from the Americans. So we didn't look out of place.'

Reaching Berlin without difficulty, Pitt-Pladdy made his way to the arranged pick-up point near to the Brandenburg Gate. The gate acted as the border between the British and Russian zones and would mean that the scientist could be taken into the vehicle and moved immediately westwards out of the city. The timing was tight. The pick-up was scheduled for 3.30 p.m. in order that they could be safely out of Berlin by 4 p.m. and cross back into Helmstedt, in the main British zone of Germany, by nightfall. As they drove into the city Pitt-Pladdy realized they would have to work swiftly since snow flurries had begun to fall that would slow their return, risking missing the deadline to leave the Soviet zone:

> We reached Berlin and made the rendezvous near the Brandenburg gate. An unmarked military vehicle could not hang about in plain view, so it was tucked into a side street. The crew consisted of myself, one escort, a driver and a Dutch interpreter. The escort had said to me 'What do I do if the Russians stop us?' I told him we would worry about that if it happened. The rendezvous was stiff with Russians, but I went off to do a recce and look for the scientist.

While he was away the driver and the escort, Ken Moore, went into a local bar where they sat down, ordered a drink and sold their rations to the locals. At the end they had a packet of sugar left over and kindly handed it over to a Red Cross nurse who was also seated in the bar. On the way back to their vehicle they met a Russian soldier who attempted to tell them they should not be in the area. Pretending not to understand they quickly returned to their vehicle and awaited the return of Lieutenant Pitt-Pladdy.

Upon returning to the side street, Pitt-Pladdy was shocked to see a crowd near his vehicle. At first he was certain that the Russians had discovered them. The reality was less dramatic but no less irritating. A tram was parked beside his vehicle and people had dismounted to form a queue. The queue led to Pitt-Pladdy's Dutch interpreter who was selling cigarettes to the eager civilians. To avoid attracting any further attention a new position had to be found and Pitt-Pladdy swiftly told the interpreter that his time with T-Force was over.

They waited until the scheduled meeting time but the scientist failed to show up at the rendezvous. The delay was unfortunate. With the snowfalls getting heavier, and little chance of reaching the British zone before nightfall, they set off on the return journey having failed in their mission. Eager to make haste to Helmstedt, their car twice skidded off the road, at one point demolishing a Russian signpost. Their only consolation was that the falling snow meant the roads were clear. Driving on an icy road, in almost zero visibility, they eventually reached the border – long after the official closing time. Fortunately, the guards were not concerned by what was happening on the road – they were more interested in sheltering from the weather: 'Luckily we didn't meet any Russian patrols. At the border there was no sign of any life so I knocked at the door of the sentry post. A Russian officer appeared and I thrust a jerrycan of petrol and a carton of cigarettes into his hand. He took them, slammed the door and we drove off across the border.' It was not until midnight they arrived safely back at Goslar.

Two days later, while repainting unit signs on to the Scout Car, Pitt-Pladdy received news of why the mission had failed. It turned out the physicist had been carrying an empty suitcase. He had been on his way home to pick up the research papers that he had buried in his garden. The Russians had picked him up because they thought an empty suitcase meant he was a black marketeer. So he spent the night in the cells and was released next day. When he was released he went to the British Provost Marshal in Berlin who then contacted Goslar to inform him that the 'target' was safely in British custody. From there, while disguised in a British Army uniform, he was eventually smuggled from Berlin in a large military convoy. As Tom Pitt-Pladdy later recalled: 'I don't know why they didn't think about doing that in the first place.'

The clandestine methods used by T-Force had proved unsuccessful on this occasion, but the authorities remained determined to keep such operations under wraps, as Tom Pitt-Pladdy soon realized. Annoyed by the actions of the interpreter, who had jeopardized the entire operation and risked the arrest of evacuation team by the Russians, he was keen to see a reprimand: 'I wanted the Dutchman charged when we got back. But I was told he couldn't be charged since nothing was to appear in writing about the operation.'

Ken Moore recalled how it felt to be travelling back from Berlin, seated close to a concealed German scientist, on a similar journey. Surprisingly, he did not experience any tension: 'Ignorance is bliss – and we were a blissful lot. We didn't have any instruction on what to do if we were stopped and were discovered.' As Moore explained, he was seated in the back of a Scout Car unable to see the Russian soldiers they passed on the return journey. He freely admitted that, had he seen how many Russians were in the area, he might have been more concerned:

We didn't know if we were supposed to fight our way out. There
was a certain sense of apprehension as you got near the check
points but we might be forgiven for our ignorance because we
didn't realize what we were doing was anything extraordinary.
Of course they could have caught us and sent us to the Gulag –
but we didn't realize that at the time. We had nothing to measure it by. It was a serious job but I was ignorant of the
circumstances and the dangers.

Such scenes, taking place long before Winston Churchill made
his fabled 'Iron Curtain' speech, were like something from any
number of Cold War spy novels. With scientists evading the
Russians, black market dealings and covert military operations
in unmarked vehicles, T-Force had become the first of the
'Cold Warriors' and set the standard for the fiction of the years
ahead. But the heroes were not secret agents, spies or dashing
James Bond-type secret agents. It was more as if *The Third Man*
was being played out by members of an ordinary British
infantry battalion.

While these covert operations were being carried out by
T-Force within the Russian zone, the unit was also engaged in
operations that kept up the facade of cooperation between the
former Allies. Throughout 1945, relations with Russia
remained reasonable on the outside, with both sides officially
feigning cordiality. However, despite the veneer of cooperation,
the British were only prepared to allow Russian access to scientists and research facilities on a strictly reciprocal basis. In
turn, the Russians offered constant excuses that the targets the
British wished to visit had been destroyed during the Red
Army's advance. Both sides played the same game, with the
Russians trying to send more inspection teams than officially
agreed and the British refraining from being too vocal in their
complaints in the knowledge that there were T-Force teams
unofficially heading east to extract scientists of interest. When

reciprocal visits were agreed it was officers from T-Force who escorted the Russian teams, meeting them at the border control post at Helmstedt. T-Force also provided drivers and escorts for the British teams that visited IG Farben plants in eastern Germany.

As a counter to the Russian policy of limiting access to industrial plants in eastern Germany the British instituted a 'reservation policy'. Under this policy they established lists of research subjects that were to be withheld from the Russians. Sites that were to be kept away from Russian inspection included the Rheinmetall-Borsig facility and the torpedo research plant at Eckenförde. In general, it was believed at T-Force HQ that it would be more efficient to 'reserve' particular subjects of interest rather than entire plants. Thus, Russian investigators would not be denied access to plants; instead, they would simply be kept away from certain areas within them. At Raubkammer, it was decided the Russians should be allowed access to the plant since there is little that they could from learn from viewing the facilities. However, no discussion of the gases Sarin or Tabun was allowed. One of the subjects on the reserved list was anti-radar equipment for use on submarines, which the Russians were known to have an interest in. As a result, 14 days' notice of a visit was requested by naval officers in charge of German ports, allowing such equipment to be dismantled and hidden in advance of any Russian visits. As one Royal Navy report stressed, the Russians should only be allowed access on a reciprocal basis since: 'Past experience has shown that Russians are prepared to take everything and give nothing.'[18]

The list of subjects that were not to be shared with the Russians was expanded to cover numerous fields including: ship-to-ship guided missiles; nuclear physics; radar and counter radar measures; U-boat aerials; encryption technology; high-voltage electrical research; infra-red night-vision equipment;

biological warfare; long-range smooth-bore weapons; ultra-violet equipment for blinding the enemy in battle; and research on supersonic aerodynamics. The Admiralty also requested that hydrogen peroxide submarine engines, German submarine detection equipment and acoustic torpedoes be included on the restricted list. Interestingly, these restrictions were not only applied to the Russians; the French were also to be excluded from certain areas of interest although, it was noted, their requests were to be treated 'more liberally' than those received from the Russians.

The British used this restricted policy despite the misgivings of their American allies. Conscious of the Russian attitude to reparations, the British were concerned that US policy was too lax. They were pleased when the Americans introduced a policy to deny intelligence graded any higher than restricted to either Russia or France. The British element at FIAT raised concerns that if the Americans allowed Russians access to industrial plants, it could raise complaints about the UK being uncooperative. In particular, the British expressed concern about the US's unilateral release of intelligence related to British research projects.

Hand-in-hand with the evacuation operations from the Russian zone, T-Force was requested to carry out investigations of Luftwaffe facilities within the British zone. With some British politicians fully aware of the potential for conflict against the Russians, there was a drive for the work of T-Force to continue unabated. In July 1945, Ernest Bevin, the new British Foreign Secretary – long aware of the Soviet threat through his prewar activities in the trade union movement – requested complete intelligence reports on all Luftwaffe research facilities located within the British zone. He was eager that these should be exploited for fear that they might eventually be claimed by the Russians as reparations. Bevin and other like-minded politicians were aware that work had to be carried out swiftly, in particular in those areas due to be handed over to the Russians.

Inspections carried out during this period resulted in the assessment that the Germans had been more advanced than the Allies in some areas of aircraft research, but not in all fields. Of particular interest to the investigators were German wind tunnels that both the British and Americans admitted were far superior to any they were currently operating. During 1945 the British established 'Operation Surgeon', designed to acquire equipment for the RAF college at Cranwell. This included the evacuation of an entire experimental laboratory from the Focke-Wulf facilities at Detmold.

This evacuation coincided with increasing concern over the legality of such operations. With the British sweeping through their zone for any examples of what might fit the description of 'war-like stores and booty', some among the Americans tried to insist that prototypes could not be classed as 'booty'. They argued that anything still under development should be 'frozen' in Germany and be open to all the Allied powers under the forthcoming reparations scheme.

Undeterred, the British continued to claim all military prototypes as booty and allowed T-Force to continue with evacuations. The men who had been bombed and strafed by the Luftwaffe through 1944 and 1945 had little interest in concerns about the fate of either the facilities or the men who worked in them. All that mattered was that they should never again produce weapons to attack the United Kingdom. They had no desire to see Germany using peacetime to benefit from the military research that had brought so much misery to the world and disruption to their lives.

In stark contrast to the secret operations carried out by many members of T-Force through 1945, or the evacuations of so-called 'freak weapons', some areas of the unit were increasingly encumbered with less glamorous duties. As the year progressed, a sense of change emerged. No longer working under threat, the soldiers noticed the change in their duties that eventually resulted in a focus on reparations as opposed to the pursuit of technology and war booty. The equipment and commodities that were to be evacuated to the UK bore little relationship to the items that T-Force had been established to find. Instead, efforts were increasingly concentrated on gathering machinery and technical equipment to help rebuild British industry and equip it for the postwar production of civilian goods.

Just six weeks after the end of the war the HQ of the British Army of the Rhine requested that T-Force put its resources at the disposal of the Board of Trade Reparations Assessment Teams – the less than charmingly named BOTRATS. To cope with the changing demands on their resources it was necessary to expand accommodation facilities. A new transit camp was opened in a luxurious villa (reports do not give a precise location) that had formally been home to a wealthy industrialist. For some in T-Force the house was most notable for its well-stocked library of pornography.

With the East–West alliance having disintegrated at the end of the war, and the Soviets no longer perceived as liberators, the postwar period should have been the springboard for unrivalled new levels of cooperation among the western Allies. Indeed, there were many official contacts between the Allies, with T-Force assisting both French and Dutch academics to acquire documents and books from German universities and technical institutes to replace those stolen during the Nazi occupation. Yet while the politicians continued to promote fraternal relations and most soldiers within Germany had a good relationship with their allies, there were some who deliberately undermined the harmony. As military operations wound down and the T-Force operations increasingly concentrated on civil reparations, the spectre of industrial competition arose.

The discussions that arose over the question of what should be classed as booty and what should be shared out as reparations was just the beginning of a new rivalry, much of which was not played out across the international negotiating tables.

It was not long before the staff of T-Force began to notice this rivalry impeding their work. Back at the Unterlüss Rheinmetall-Borsig plant – where so much important research on weapons design and construction had previously been uncovered – Tom Pitt-Pladdy became aware of the changing situation. Initially, everything had run smoothly. However, he was to encounter a problem relating to a full range of Hollerith punched-card machines that had been marked for evacuation to the UK. As Pitt-Pladdy recalled, 'The Labour government was thinking about the National Health Service and had got its eyes on the Hollerith machines and some machines that were used for addressing envelopes.'

The Hollerith machines, an invention of the American company IBM, had been sent to Germany in the prewar years. The machines had come to the fore during the Holocaust when the Nazis used the card indexes to record their victims. Having been used for genocidal bureaucracy, the British had no qualms about removing them to the UK – regardless of who actually owned the machines. As Pitt-Pladdy recalled: 'The government wanted the machines sent back straight away. But I got a message to say we were not allowed to move them since they actually belonged to an American firm and the Americans had claimed them. They had only been licensed to the Germans.' Ignoring the American opposition, the machines were swiftly removed and sent to the UK: 'This drew the first overt attempt at sabotage from the Americans. This American officer arrived and everything at the factory slowed down and stopped. My photocopying department started running into delays. The whole operation began to develop "gremlins".' Alerted by a change in German attitude, Pitt-Pladdy contacted Brigadier Pennycook.

His message worked and some new visitors soon arrived at the plant. One of them took Pitt-Pladdy aside and produced credentials to show that he was from the Special Investigations Branch of the Military Police:

> He told me not to worry, he would look into it and sort it out. He came back later and told me it was the American who was causing the problem. It turned out that as a civilian he worked for Du Pont. He had told all the Germans that because of contracts between Du Pont and the German firm they were to hand nothing over until he had screened it. So he was quickly sent on his way – and we kept the Hollerith machines. That was the end of the interference.

Despite the success of the Military Policeman in thwarting the American attempts to hinder T-Force operations, Pitt-Pladdy again found himself in trouble with his superiors in the 5th King's. He was reprimanded for having called in the Military Police directly through T-Force HQ rather than contacting his battalion commander.

Such issues were not limited to this one factory. Records created by FIAT show that within the American zone there were problems with accredited investigators who had long-standing, prewar business connections with Germany. They were found to have a greater interest in the affairs of their own firms rather than in their duty of carrying out investigations for the benefit of all. FIAT also reported on investigators requesting permission to remain in Germany once their work was complete, in order to attend to private business matters.

These offences occurred despite strict rules issued by CIOS on cooperation between investigation teams and T-Force. Under these instructions investigators were supposed to report to CIOS representatives at T-Force HQ, and then meet with the relevant group leader who would organize the details of their visit, including organizing their accommodation, food, travel and escort. To prevent unauthorized disposal of intelligence, all investigators were bound to provide a summary of their final report to T-Force HQ and to report to the relevant CIOS group leader on what they had found.

Despite these rules, there were numerous attempts at unauthorized evacuations. Although historical documents pertaining to such events focus on offences by Americans, there was little doubt British industrialists were engaged in similar attempts to gain an advantage over their rivals. One particular incident reflected the way T-Force's role appeared to be heading. A perplexed junior officer delivered a British civilian to T-Force HQ and took him to see Lt Colonel Bloomfield. The civilian, Mr H.L. Muschamp, was in Germany on behalf of the Ministry of Supply as an expert in textile manufacturing machinery. He was travelling through the Ruhr valley assessing factories related to his own branch of industry. In one factory he had found some machinery that was of interest. This was normal – after all, that was the role of the assessors: it was their job to find suitable machinery to revive Britain's worn out industries. However, what had startled the officer was Mr Muschamp's request that the machine tools were to be dismantled, crated and despatched to H.L. Muschamp Ltd, Widnes, Runcorn, Cheshire.

Surprised by such a brazen attempt to gain personal advantage, Lt Colonel Bloomfield explained to Mr Muschamp that T-Force was a military service, operating upon the orders of the British government, not acting on behalf of individual businesses. Bloomfield said, in no uncertain terms, that shipments could only be made to government ministries. The rather disgruntled Mr Muschamp left and Bloomfield telephoned BIOS in London to alert them of the situation. Just 48 hours later T-Force HQ received a message from London: 'Consign the machinery tools to Ministry of Supply, c/o H.L. Muschamp Ltd, Widnes, Runcorn, Cheshire.'[19]

This was a sure sign that the old T-Force role would soon be a thing of the past. The changing nature of T-Force's duties made a distinct impression on many of the soldiers. Those who had fought the enemy for years had been happy to play such an active role in dismantling the war research plants that had been responsible for so much misery in the previous five years. If they detained scientists who had designed the aircraft which had blasted the streets of their home towns, or dismantled the factories whose production lines had turned out the guns that had taken the lives of so many of their friends, it gave a sense of achievement born of the genuine feeling that they were doing good by disarming Germany. As Lt Colonel Bloomfield later wrote: 'It was not for T-Force to wonder if the British government had forgotten the economic and political lessons learnt from the reparations policy followed at the end of the First World War. Nor was it our job to speculate on the destinations or consequences of what we were dispatching, and whom we were sending, to in UK.'[20] However, as their work changed to a more overtly civilian role, questions were raised.

Tom Pitt-Pladdy became eager to leave T-Force and return to his former regiment, the Royal Artillery. He had never fitted in with the old guard of the 5th King's Regiment. Arriving just before the advance into Germany, he had not got to know many of his fellow officers. His experience with his company commander – who had told him he didn't want T-Force work interfering with the day-to-day business of the King's Regiment – had not made a good impression on him. Pitt-Pladdy noted that this officer seldom left his office since he believed that T-Force work was beneath him. Nor was the former gunner pleased by the discovery that it would be the original officers of the regiment who would get the recognition for the successes of the unit. He had even heard Colonel Wreford-Brown say that the original King's officers would get medals – not the incomers, who were thought of as interlopers.[21] However, as discussed in the next chapter, it was really the changing nature of T-Force duties that inspired Pitt-Pladdy's desire to seek new employment. As he recalled, 'Some of the reparations work was quite dubious.'

For many in T-Force there was a genuine sense that, by dismantling Germany's research facilities and destroying her offensive capabilities, their work was making a genuine contribution to the future security of Europe. However, the policy came at a price. In a secret report issued by T-Force HQ, the nature of German scientists who were cooperating with the British, and who were being employed on defence projects for British firms, was examined. In the eyes of some at T-Force, it was one thing to steal the ideas of the men whose weapons had attacked the UK, but quite another to offer them shelter, employment and security.

The report noted that it had caused great difficulty for many British and American scientists to 'overcome their repugnance to lending their talents to the evolution of lethal weapons'.[22] This was contrasted with the attitude of German scientists: 'There is no question that many of their German opposite numbers have delighted in the application of their gifts to such a purpose.' In particular, it seemed the Germans had enjoyed the lack of financial restraint put on their research in wartime. It was not just their morality that concerned the author of the T-Force report: 'Furthermore, there is abundant evidence that the mentality of these scientists remains martial to a degree, even when they are not unrepentant Nazis.'

A prime example of this issue was Dr Walter who was described as being cooperative, yet 'a professed Nazi'. He was reported to be frustrated by the end of war, which had curtailed his research, in particular on 'Ingolene' – a high strength version of hydrogen peroxide that he had named after his son – which was believed to be too expensive for peacetime use as a propellant. Similarly, Dr Draeger – a specialist in oxygen

breathing apparatus – stated under interrogation that he hoped
the war against Japan would continue for two more years to
give the Allies the opportunity to bring into use the German
closed-cycle diesel submarine engines. He enthusiastically noted
that in two years of war he had made more progress than in
twenty years of peace. In making these statements Draeger had
shown himself more interested in his personal research than in
the suffering of those who actually had to fight the war.

The report also noted the arrogance shown by some scientists and researchers who believed they should be allowed to
continue their work without censure by the Allies. Among them
was Dr Groth, the scientist T-Force had discovered working on
isotopes of uranium and heavy water in his secret laboratory
hidden beneath the silk factory in Celle. He was described as
showing a 'naïve innocence' in requesting that the Allies return
all his equipment in order that he might continue his research.

The T-Force report on German scientific research highlighted how, 'at the end of the war in Europe, Germany was on
the eve of some very remarkable developments in many fields,
particularly those connected with the propulsion and control of
projectiles.' It emphasized that T-Force could not be certain
that the scientists could be trusted to work unsupervised and
not develop dangerous weapons for a resurgent Germany:
'Even if these individuals can be made to bring their talents to
bear on the production of twentieth century ploughshares
instead of twentieth century swords, no power on earth can
ensure that they will not, in secret, continue at the very least
the theoretical design of war weapons.'

It was also pointed out that interrogations carried out by
British weapons experts might have given the German scientists new ideas and that when held together in detention
centres they might have shared information on how best to
develop their weapons. The writer was unequivocal about how
the problem should be dealt with: 'It appears that the only

solution of this problem is to deport all these individuals from Germany and from Europe.' His proposal was for them to be employed in the UK, the Dominions or the US, where their gifts 'might be employed in the service, and not the destruction, of mankind'.

CHAPTER 10

The Spoils of War

'The right of the Allies to use information collected by Allied investigating agencies is one of the consequences of Germany losing the war. The Allies are entitled to use this information as they see fit . . .'

Control Commission for Germany, 25 January 1947.[1]

As history has shown, the Russians were unashamed about their plunder of Germany in the aftermath of war. Whole factories were dismantled, down to the last nut and bolt, and shipped back to the 'Motherland'. As one T-Force officer later recalled, he watched as Russian technicians removed urinals ready to be sent to Russia along with the factory's complete machinery. The scale of the Russian 'rape' of German industry was often compared with the physical rape inflicted on Germany's women by the conquering Red Army.

The Russians used their wartime sufferings as justification for the systematic plunder of German industry. But they were not alone. As many in T-Force remembered, the British were not slow in joining in with the plunder of Germany. Indeed, there was widespread hypocrisy over the British role, with the true scale of British efforts to acquire German machinery, equipment and prototype technology never fully revealed to the public. Instead, within the UK, a lie was fostered that the British had concentrated on aiding Germany's recovery. Yet the truth was that for the first years of occupation, T-Force had systematically worked through Germany to acquire whatever was required for rebuilding British industry.

While it was true that the British did not asset strip Germany to the same degree as the Russians, T-Force carried out similar operations throughout the British zone. As one T-Force officer later noted: 'It was all a question of scale.' It was clear to those 'in the know' that the British were not prepared to sit back and watch its former ally take a considerable advantage from the plunder of Germany. Consequently, German industry paid the price of military defeat.

From January 1946, with the slow recovery of Germany underway, the work of T-Force was increasingly channelled to the directives of the Inter-Allied Reparations Agency (IARA). Careful negotiations carried out in Paris had resulted in an agreement between 18 Allied nations to divide available compensation between the victors. The spoils of war fell into two groups: Category A comprised German gold reserves and foreign assets; Category B covered plants and machinery, including merchant shipping. The need for reparations from Germany was acute. British industry had been hard-pressed by the demands of the war economy, with much industrial equipment being worn out or in need of redevelopment for civilian use.

One company that illustrated the desperate need for assistance from the reparations scheme was rubber production company Revertex. In August 1946 it approached the Board of Trade to request rubber testing equipment. Its own equipment had been destroyed during the occupation of Malaya by the Japanese. Furthermore, technical drawings of the equipment had been destroyed during the Blitz. The only source of machinery and technical drawings was Germany; if the firm was to restart rubber production in Malaya, it would need reparations and, thus, the assistance of T-Force.

The United Kingdom was to be allotted 27.8 per cent of the total reparations available to the western powers. In the words of one representative of the Ministry of Supply, this was the end of 'the days of piracy'.[2] T-Force could no longer officially swan around Germany removing whatever was desired by BIOS. Instead, apart from itemsof military equipment, all materials to be evacuated as reparations by T-Force had to be directly cleared through the local offices of the Control Commission for Germany. Only once they had issued a 'Form 80G' could evacuations of non-military goods or equipment take place.

Although the official reparations programme did not come into effect until 1947, by which time T-Force was winding down, for the final 18 months of its existence the unit was responsible for guiding teams from Britain, France, the US and the Soviet Union around industrial targets in Germany. Their investigations would result in the various nations submitting requests to remove equipment under the reparations programme.

Before the official reparations policy began, there remained plenty of opportunity for T-Force to continue to acquire whatever was required by UK authorities but all evacuations of non-military materials had to be recorded. These reparations were officially to be treated differently from the military booty that was removed from Germany. Despite the supposedly clear definition between reparations and booty there continued to be grey areas in which the legality of operations was less than certain. As was admitted by one government department, 'It is next to impossible for us to produce detailed lists of items which we have taken even though they are now to come under the heading of reparations, since as already stated we have not hitherto thought it necessary to keep itemised lists of each transaction.'[3] Among the goods that had originally been handled as booty were 102 aircraft, delivered to the UK for civilian use, and trucks and signals equipment that had been handed over freely to Allied nations.

Effectively, the lack of clarity existed because there was confusion over the definitions of military and non-military goods. During 1945 the removal of many of the materials by T-Force was, arguably, legally defensible. Officially, booty was given the broad classification of 'warlike stores and booty', which was taken to mean any movable enemy property found on the battlefield. In September 1945, the legality for any operations to remove such materials to the UK was given by Proclamation No.2 of the Allied Control Council, agreed between the Four Powers – the US, the UK, the Soviet Union and France. This document, known as the 'Additional Terms of Surrender', gave the Allies complete control over all research, design, development and production facilities 'directly or indirectly relating to war or the production of war material, whether in government or private establishments, factories, technological institutions or elsewhere'.

During 1945, all the goods that had fallen under the gaze of the investigators from CIOS, BIOS and associated bodies were treated as booty by the British and Americans, rather than being classed as reparations. Aircraft, guns, tanks, ships, machinery, technical documents and the results of scientific interrogations were all thrown together into this category and were never counted against the total value of reparations. As a result, any attempt to put a figure on the economic value of the work of T-Force becomes impossible. Yet there were many products that fell into a grey area. For example, the advanced rubber production techniques that had been so important to the German war effort could still be classed as booty despite the widespread utilization of the products in civilian industry. Similarly, BIOS investigators had uncovered the formula for Analgetica, a highly powerful painkilling drug developed in Germany. This was designed for use by the military to alleviate extreme pain in frontline casualties. The drug had serious side effects and development had been slowed for fear of how it might be used if it fell into the wrong hands. Although this design was evacuated as part of the postwar booty due to its military use, it was clear that it had a wider purpose, one that would possibly be of great financial reward to anyone developing the drug for clinical use.

The dubious nature of such evacuations as booty did not unduly concern the British authorities. Indeed, some in Whitehall, foreseeing the incoming rules on reparations and increased scrutiny of evacuations, had used it as an excuse to remove non-military materials from Germany as booty prior to the introduction of the revised interpretation of policy. By treating non-military, or dual-use materials, as booty – therefore not declaring them to the other Allies – the British were able to increase their share of postwar reparations.

The year 1946 began with some signs of change for T-Force operations, but many of the earlier problems faced by Brigadier Pennycook and his staff had not gone away. Despite his repeated requests to speed up the processing of the scientists, large numbers continued to languish in holding camps. In February 1946 Pennycook wrote to the Board of Trade to express his concern that the treatment they were receiving would make it unlikely any would want to come to the UK: 'I must say that the more I think of it the more convinced I am that unless there is a definite change of heart and of treatment being meted out to those we already hold, we shall in fact get none.'[4]

The Brigadier pointed out that it was not T-Force that was responsible for the problems of the scientists, but the UK authorities which had failed to interrogate or employ them within a reasonable time. With reference to a party from Bad Gandersheim detained by T-Force, he noted that the order for their detention had come from SHAEF, under instructions from the US State Department and British ministries. This party was held for eight months doing nothing, only to be finally cast adrift and told to find their own employment. One scientist complained that he would not be receiving his pension since the terms of it were that he should have been resident in the British zone as of 8 May 1945. However, at that point he was resident in Magdeburg, a town occupied by the British but not technically within the British zone. After that, he was taken by T-Force to the British zone and then abandoned, without either employment or a pension. His only hope was to return to the Soviet zone and seek work.

The AGFA scientists detained by T-Force at the Central Hotel in Goslar faced a similar situation. Their families' expenses were paid through the local military government, which then billed the town authorities. This was entirely unofficial and the locals objected to the payments being made for the families. The British had made promises to the families when they were first evacuated but these promises could no longer be met.

The disquiet expressed by the scientists was officially reported in March 1946. A top secret FIAT report revealed how Germans evacuated from Jena by the Americans the previous summer had failed to find employment. A total of 450 scientists, along with their families, had been 'evacuated' and then 'frozen' at Heidenheim while the Allies decided what to do with them: 'They seem to be unanimous in the opinion that their scientific and technical talents have been completely wasted, and that many who have technical information of interest and value have not even been interrogated.' The report went on to stress that, by failing to exploit the talents of the evacuated personnel, the Allies were 'failing in their occupational duties'.[5] To deal with the underemployment of these individuals, FIAT suggested they should be put to work collating and translating technical data that had been amassed by the various T-Forces since the crossing of the Rhine. The idea was that there could be an entirely German staffed and operated 'FIAT Technical Institute'.

For T-Force itself, major changes occurred during 1945 as the veterans of the wartime T-Force slowly left to pastures new. There had been a steady drain of personnel from the units that had raced through Germany in the final weeks of war. Many of those with long service had been demobbed, heading home to their families ready to rebuild their lives in the peace they had secured. In June 1945 Major Brian Urquhart, who had played such a vital role in both planning the wartime investigations and liaising between T-Force HQ and the forward units, was one of the first to leave, his place being taken by Major Young. In October that year, command of the 5th King's passed from Colonel Wreford-Brown to Lt Colonel Percy Winterton. Late 1945 also saw the departure of T-Force's chief staff officer, Lt Colonel Bloomfield, with Lt Colonel David Edwardes arriving to replace him. Then, in early 1946, Brigadier Pennycook also departed to be replaced by Brigadier William Edward Grylls, known as 'Ted'. Following his departure, Pennycook continued to play an active role in determining evacuation policy by acting as the War Office's representative on BIOS.

The biggest sign of the new rules under which T-Force was to work came in spring 1946 when the unit was reorganized. The 5th Battalion King's Regiment was detached from T-Force and returned to 'line duties' prior to being disbanded. However, although the battalion was no more, the work of the soldiers was far from over. Many of the Kingsmen did not leave with their regiment. Instead they stayed behind to provide continuity in the new T-Force detachments as part of 'No.2 Research, Restitution, Reparations (T-Force) Unit'. Similarly, the 1st Buckinghamshire Battalion of the Ox and Bucks was detached from T-Force, leaving behind a nucleus of officers and men who would form the 'No.1' T-Force unit. These two

T-Forces consisted of an HQ and four detachments. No.2 T-Force covered the north and east of the British zone with what had been A, B, C and D companies of the 5th King's becoming 21 to 24 T-Force Detachments, based at Goslar, Peine, Lübeck and Hamburg respectively.

From June 1946 the entire T-Force organization was moved from the British Army of the Rhine and instead came under the control of the Control Commission Germany (CCG). From August, T-Force HQ, consisting of a brigadier, 13 officers and 34 NCOs and based at Bad Oeynhausen, became responsible for briefing investigators and arranging their visits around Germany. Under this were two investigators' camps at Löhne and Herford which accommodated the specialists visiting from the UK. Each of the two T-Forces also operated seven or eight 'hotels' and messes in which investigation teams were housed and from where transport could be arranged for them. In addition to these units, T-Force continued to maintain the equipment evacuation depot at Hamburg staffed by 3 officers and 30 NCOs. In total the unit consisted of 116 officers, 2,207 other ranks and 88 British civilians who were employees of the British element of the Control Commission.

In the period up to the end of 1946 the new T-Force was responsible for escorting over 6,000 investigators, 4,470 of whom were British while the remainder were French and American. T-Force also played host to 1,400 reparations teams and took experts on visits to more than 7,300 targets in the British zone, covering an estimated 1 million miles on their travels. More than 6,590 tons of equipment was shipped to the UK and 3,600 German scientists and technicians were investigated, 415 of whom were evacuated to the UK between March and October 1946.

Ted Grylls later described his officers as 'a combination of industrial agent, Intelligence Officer, and agent of Thomas Cook or Carter Paterson. They must provide technical and industrial information. They keep track of civilian German persons. They brief all visitors, and direct their activities while in the area. They also have to act as, or provide interpreters for the visitors, the majority of whom cannot speak German.'[6]

A new generation of young soldiers, most of whom had not experienced the full fury of war and whose military careers were just beginning, arrived in Germany to staff the newly reorganized unit. One of these new arrivals was Lieutenant Michael Howard. A newly commissioned 19-year-old, Howard was a keen young man who had volunteered for service on his 17th birthday. He had been inspired by a radio broadcast telling of the heroism of members of the Rifle Brigade at El Alamein that he heard while still at Rugby School. The story had an immediate impact on him: 'I thought – If I'm going to have to serve, I would like to serve with men like that.' He enjoyed his training, being surrounded by people just like himself, all of whom shared the common bond of wanting do whatever they were called upon to do. However, the duration of his training meant he had missed the fighting. He had still been at an officer cadet unit when he noticed that, during tactical lectures, the swastikas had been replaced by the Rising Sun to reflect the likely enemy. As Howard later recalled, 'The sight of these flags put a chill over us all. I don't think any of us much fancied going out to fight the Japs.' Fortunately, by the time he was commissioned in September 1945, even the threat of Japan had been extinguished – swept away by the fruits of the atomic research that had been such a concern to T-Force the previous summer.

Arriving in Germany in March 1946, Michael Howard was to play a central role in the activities of T-Force for the next 21 months. He was posted to Germany due to his knowledge of the language, and found himself at a reinforcement holding unit in Osnabrück. Having been told by a friend with family connections at the Control Commission that T-Force was engaged in interesting and important work, he requested a posting and was soon despatched to the HQ of 1st Bucks in the town of Kamen: 'There, my affirmative answer to Colonel Nicol's question in the bar, ten minutes after my arrival, as to whether I played contract bridge elicited the response that in that case I should be the Intelligence Officer . . . I got the "plum" job. They thought they were fitting me in where I couldn't be a nuisance.' Within weeks Colonel J.W. Nicol had left, to be replaced by Lt Colonel E.H. 'Peter' Brush, a regular Rifle Brigade officer who had been captured at Calais in 1940 and had spent five years as a prisoner of war. During the battle for Calais he had been wounded three times – including being shot through the throat by a French sniper – but each time had risen from his stretcher to resume his command, before he was captured by the Germans.

When Colonel Brush asked Howard where he might find sub-alterns for T-Force, the young Lieutenant suggested he select them from the surplus officers of the Rifle Brigade who were 'kicking their heels' at the reinforcement holding unit. As Michael Howard later noted, these were young officers from some of the country's top public schools. Most of these schools had both their own Home Guard unit and a Junior Training Corps. The years of training in these units had produced officers with a confidence that had proved critical to their being prepared to accept respon-sibility, despite their youth and junior status.

One of the beneficiaries of No.1 T-Force's selection of Rifle Brigade subalterns was Lt John Bendit. He was another keen young man who had volunteered for service at the age of 17, joining the army in October 1942. He had selected the Rifle Brigade after his school, Charterhouse, had been visited by two officers of the regiment, who had toured some of the major public schools to select the best young men available. Commissioned in August 1943, Bendit was posted to another regiment and spent much of 1944 working in a specialized unit established to create scale models of the D-Day landing beaches. These were later used for briefing officers in preparation for the invasion. In the days immediately before D-Day, Bendit travelled around southern England delivering the maps to be issued to the officers of the units due to land in France.

In August 1944 Bendit finally arrived on the continent and joined his regiment in Belgium the following month. He recalled his first attack: 'I watched my men making a flanking move. Suddenly behind this bush I saw a German helmet. I said "This one's mine!" I took careful aim and fired. Eventually we rounded everybody up – including the fellow who'd been behind the bush. He started hobbling and I though "Ah! That was my shot" Then one of my chaps said "No sir, that was my shot, I saw him move his foot when I fired."' Bendit watched as his men loaded the prisoners into a truck to be taken from the battlefield. He noticed that the German who had been his target refused to sit down, telling his captors, 'I can't sit, I've been shot in the backside.' Bendit allowed himself to smile: 'I thought "That's mine! First blood!" My first action, I'd shot a German in the bottom.'

After a few months in action Bendit contracted jaundice and was evacuated to hospital. Following treatment, he was posted as an instructor at a training battalion and missed the rest of the fighting. He remained there until late 1946 when he joined the T-Force detachment based in Leichlingen. The job was a surprise to Bendit, who had no idea what was expected of him: 'It was most extraordinary. In the evenings we'd be acting as hosts in the T-Force hotels, looking after these teams that had come to visit factories. The next morning we'd get a list of places and off we went to collect people and machinery.'

Another of the new arrivals at T-Force was John Bayley, who would later become known as the husband of the novelist Iris Murdoch. As his friend and colleague Michael Howard recalled, Bayley had been 'like a fish out of water' in the Grenadier Guards, where he had been assigned the task of writing a regimental history for the Second World War. Howard also noted that Bayley was certainly not Guardsmanlike in his appearance, bearing, behaviour and inclination. As a result, he had been transferred to No.1 T-Force, where he found a niche as an evacuation officer at Kamen. He soon earned the admiration of his peers for his social and intellectual virtues – exactly the qualities that had failed to endear him to some in the Grenadier Guards.

At first, much of T-Force's work remained focused on military matters, with BIOS attempting to retain tight control over sites openly accessible to outsiders. Military research plants, such as the Rheinmetall-Borsig munitions facility at Unterlüss, were kept on a 'restricted access' list until British investigations were completed. As detailed in the previous chapter, the Joint Intelligence Staff also listed a wide range of technological developments that remained under restrictions and were held back from release to non-British or non-American parties.

Despite the creation of these lists, in some instances the tangled web of bureaucracy surrounding the investigation teams resulted in unwanted visits being authorized. In one case clearance was given for an Allied team to visit the ELAC plant in Kiel without BIOS being informed. As a result, urgent efforts had to be made to remove items of interest, placing them under lock and key in areas which the investigation teams were unable to access. The technology in question was German infra-red 'Fasan' and 'Nibelung' equipment. In response to this incident, the Admiralty requested that all foreign reparations teams should be discouraged from interviewing scientists and technicians. If interviews were unavoidable then they should only take place in the presence of a British officer. Particular concern was raised that the French military was known to have an interest in the equipment.

As the emphasis on evacuations changed from military to industrial targets, so too did the burden of work. During wartime and initial postwar operations the 5th King's had carried the burden of evacuations. This had been caused by their geographical location. Many of Germany's military training grounds and development facilities had traditionally been in the area to the south of Hamburg, in which the Kingsmen had been operating. Furthermore, the northern coastline was home to the ports of Bremen, Hamburg, Kiel and Lübeck, all of which had been home to naval research facilities. Once most of these had been fully investigated and evacuated, the burden of their work for the newly designated No.2 T-Force was considerably diminished. By 1946 the research facilities which had been reactivated in the immediate aftermath of war began to wind down. The German scientists who had been set to work to continue with the most important areas of their research had been interrogated and assessed and the most talented among them – men such as Wernher von Braun and Hellmuth Walter – were enjoying lucrative employment with their former enemies. With the main military researchers no longer working in T-Force's zone of operations, the workload had diminished.

However, the area of operations of No.1 T-Force, formerly the 1st Buckinghamshire Battalion, was centred on the Ruhr, Germany's economic powerhouse, so its workload greatly increased when the focus shifted to industrial materials. At the HQ at Kamen, Michael Howard soon found himself at the centre of T-Force operations: 'We worked like bastards – it was months before we had a Saturday or Sunday off.' However, the war had its rewards:

> It was interesting and engaging. We had absolute priority on transport and accommodation. The job stood out as something that could keep you out of trouble for a long time. The officers in the field didn't have the whole picture. They would say 'We've got to go to a factory and pick up some blueprints.' So they didn't get much of a broad picture of what was happening.

> Also none of the senior officers knew much since I was running the intelligence function and answered directly to HQ T-Force without going through my own colonel.

As Howard later noted, all operations carried out by T-Force in Nordrhein-Westphalia were handled by his office, either personally or by the highly efficient and capable Intelligence Sergeant, Bob Wigg. Sergeant Wigg could recall vast amounts of the equipment handled by T-Force if someone simply quoted the evacuation serial number to him. Howard also noted that, following the departure of Colonel Peter Brush, not all of those who followed him in command of No.1 T-Force were so interested in the unit's work. He noted in his diary, 'one of the Staff Officers from HQ T-Force came down to tell us that it was realized that the new CO wouldn't be interested in the work'. As he recorded in a letter home, Colonel P.C. Grant, one of the subsequent COs had 'not an idea in his head, but, I believe, a considerable aptitude for fly-fishing'. Howard considered Grant to be a 'positive nuisance and a hindrance' whose main contribution was to spoil relations between No.1 T-Force and the local population. In his first week with the unit, Colonel Grant only entered the Intelligence Office once – and that was to see if the floor was dirty. On his next visit to the office, he asked what their role was but left before they could answer.

Grant was not the only officer who took no interest in T-Force's work. Three of the majors acting as detachment commanders were charged with offences including misuse of women, liquor and official transport. As Michael Howard later recalled, these officers had signed on for further service in Germany 'because they simply could not face going home to be deprived of the delights of wine, women and song, so freely available to them'. Tony Lucas, a contemporary of Michael Howard, was unimpressed by his first experience at T-Force. Having known Howard from prep school, Lucas also became a

Rifle Brigade subaltern and arrived in Germany in early 1946. There, he had been told that, if he was not intending to stay on as a regular officer, he should find himself an interesting position elsewhere. This took him to C Detachment of No.1 T Force at Ratingen. He was unimpressed by the officers of the Pioneer Corps running the operation, including a major who was operating an unofficial mess, effectively a 'private knocking shop' in which nudity was *de rigueur*: 'It ended up in scandal when a girl was found dead.' A German woman had gassed herself after she discovered her boyfriend, a Pioneer Corps Company Sergeant Major, in bed with another woman. The officer was swiftly demobbed to evade the Military Police and avoid a scandal. Realizing his old friend's situation, Michael Howard arranged for Lucas' transfer to B Detachment where he was able to play an important role in evacuation duties.

With so little interference from senior officers, Howard was left to his own devices and found there was certainly no shortage of work for the staff of the Intelligence Office. At BIOS's insistence, No.1 T-Force set about an investigation of the vast network of factories in the Ruhr. Their targets could be as small as a single roll of blueprints or as large as an entire foundry, with all machinery needing to be dismantled, numbered, crated and evacuated for reassembly back in the UK. As he wrote to his mother in May 1946: 'The pressure of work is unparalleled . . . At the moment I am in the throes of evacuating some 150 tons of mining machinery from all over the shop, having evacuated 250 tons of miscellaneous stuff this last fortnight. Not to mention the fact that we are removing to the UK an average of 5 Germans per week.' The burden of their work was such that Howard soon heard through Colonel Brush that, although No.1 T-Force was handling 80 per cent of T-Force operations, he – a junior lieutenant – was doing a job that was handled by three captains at No.2 T-Force. This led to Brush requesting Howard's promotion to captain.

Some of the tasks given to No.1 T-Force recalled earlier operations. One night the newly promoted Captain Howard was awoken by a phone call and given an unfamiliar codeword. After much explanation, he discovered that he had been given a highly sensitive task: 'It was to be 11,000 kilos of highly refined uranium ore in the cellars of Widia Werk at Krupps, to be packed into suitable containers and flown from Bückeburg to Northolt in the UK for the atomic research programme. This material was normally referred to as "Yellow Cake".' The reason for the sudden phone call was also explained to the sleepy captain – a Russian reparations team was due to visit the factory and would be free to lay claim to the uranium if it was not swiftly relocated. No.1 T-Force soon swung into action:

> The detachment under Tony Lucas packed it, unweighed – there was no accessible weighing equipment – into empty three-inch mortar bomb boxes, loaded on to a 10-ton Mack truck and delivered to me at Kamen. The truck's springs and suspension seemed to be all right, so I told Cpl Weatherall to draw a Sten Gun and a couple of magazines, sit on the cargo, take it to Bückeburg, and 'if any bastard tries to take it away from you, shoot him'.

With the cargo safely loaded he gave the corporal one final order: 'Get a receipt.'

When the valuable uranium cargo was delivered to the UK it was found to weigh just 6,000 kg. The missing 5,000 kg sparked an immediate scare, with the Special Investigation Branch of the Military Police launching an immediate investigation. This was to last six months, without locating a single kilo of the missing uranium. As Captain Howard soon realized, the weight of the original consignment in the pile had simply been an estimate and it had never been weighed until it reached the final destination. Despite the concern, what really mattered was that 6,000 kg of uranium ore – vital to the nuclear research programme – had been denied to the Soviet Union by the quick work of T-Force.

The new T-Force seemed very different to the one that had driven through the ruins of Germany securing factories and scientists. While the civilian visitors were fascinated by the targets they were sent to investigate, the routine nature of the work during this period was far less interesting to those within the organization who recalled the excitement of the earlier investigations. The new T-Force had six particular tasks: looking after visiting businessmen; accommodating and transporting BIOS teams; guiding reparations and restitution teams; securing reparations for the British authorities; dealing with commercial buyers; and taking care of quadripartite evaluation teams. All of these groups needed to be housed and fed, transported to and from 'targets', and then have their reports typed up. Once all that was complete, it was T-Force that ensured that all machinery, equipment and documents reached their intended destination.

In all, T-Force operated 15 transit messes within the British zone and had over 1,000 beds available for reparations teams in a number of 'hotels' and messes staffed by NCOs who supervised German civilian staff. The largest number of visitors the unit dealt with at one time was 500. Between June 1945 and October 1946 a total of 6,084 BIOS investigators were catered for. In addition, between March and October 1946, 900 Allied Reparations and Restitution Teams were accommodated, while the visits of 1,600 British teams making visits to targets in the American and French zones were also organized by T-Force.

The Allied Nations Reparations and Restitutions Teams would submit requests for goods to be removed as reparations. They came from a total of 19 countries, including such unlikely locations as Brazil and Uruguay. T-Force was responsible for the accommodation and escort of these teams and did not allow them free movement within the British zone. Instead, T-Force's 'conducting officers' ensured that they only had access to specific locations, thus preventing their investigation of restricted sites of military interest.

Even though some targets could be as small and sensitive as glass lenses, during 1946 evacuations amounted to an average of 500 tons per month. Between March and December 1946, T-Force also evacuated a total of 65 German scientists to the UK for employment while a further 350 were sent for interrogation. Clerks working for T-Force also maintained a card index of more than 3,600 names of scientists and technicians of interest.

By December 1946 visits from businessmen were running at around 60 per month. For 1947 it was anticipated that, while BIOS investigations would wind down to a nominal level, the visits of reparations teams were expected to quadruple. In 1947, they also expected a total of 200 visits by commercial buyers from the UK. BIOS, via T-Force, also handled requests from nations of the Empire and Dominions for the British to release scientists. Australia, Canada, Pakistan, India and South Africa all requested to sponsor German scientists to work in their countries.

If the soldiers found their work increasingly routine, T-Force officers discovered that the new rules increased their concerns. No longer could they turn up and remove whoever or whatever they desired with impunity. Instead, the work, which had originally been simplified by the fact that it answered only to CIOS, became increasingly complicated. As discussed, under the new policy, BIOS had to notify the Allied military government for permission to remove items of interest from Germany. As such, they had to compete with the conflicting purpose of military government, many of whose executive staff were more interested in rebuilding Germany than in ensuring the western powers maintained the advantage in the burgeoning Cold War.

THE SPOILS OF WAR

Along with the increasing industrial nature of T-Force investigations came an increasingly civilianized staff. As of December 1946 it was expected that T-Force would continue to operate for two further years, but it was expected to become almost entirely civilianized within that period. One of the proposed methods of civilian recruitment was to find jobs for suitable officers and men being demobilized from the occupation forces in Germany. Lt Ken Davenport, who had earlier served as the 5th King's intelligence officer, was demobbed in January 1947. Rather than returning home to 'civvy street' he took up employment with a Local Administrative Unit (LAU) in the village of Löhne, just five miles from the T-Force HQ at Bad Oeynhausen. His new civilian role was to provide transport to the visiting Consolidated Advanced Field Teams, transporting them between hotels that had been commandeered for the use of the occupation forces and the targets they were detailed to visit.

One of those who arrived as a civilian worker with T-Force was Jean Hughes-Gibb.[7] By the time she arrived in Germany in 1946, she had already experienced all the tragedy and uncertainty of war. A prewar debutante, she had been widowed in 1942 when her husband Frank Vogel – a British brigadier who had been on General John Gort's staff in France in 1940 and later joined General Eisenhower's staff in London – had been killed in a plane crash. She had heard the tragic news of his death while working in military intelligence at the War Office. A second marriage had failed, leading her to seek a change of scenery and so she travelled to Germany to work with the British Element of the Control Commission. Finding the work boring, she had soon made friends with a number of officers at the Army of the Rhine HQ. While there she became reacquainted with Brigadier Ted Grylls, who had introduced Jean to her first husband back in 1939. As the new Commander, T-Force, Brigadier Grylls soon offered her a position, and she became the only civilian at HQ T-Force at the time, and also the only female member of the staff. She had taken on the work of an army captain who had been posted elsewhere and each morning an army car arrived to take her from her quarters to the unit's HQ: 'Ted Grylls told me my job would be what I made it. No organization like this had existed before and there were no precedents to follow.'

The changing policies had a profound effect upon the men of T-Force. One recalled how he had previously been locating and evacuating scientists, V1 flying bombs and important aviation data, yet by the end of his time with the organization he was detailed to 'evacuate' sacks of flower seeds. As he put it, 'the bottom of the German barrel was being scraped'. Yet some of the old figures remained within the organization. Harry Henshaw had taken part in the occupation of Kiel and helped evacuate the family of Prince Stolberg in the face of the Russian threat. In 1946 he settled down into the new routine, working as a clerk in an evacuation office: 'After the scientists had visited their prospective targets and found the equipment they wanted, they would list all they required and forward a list to the evacuation office where the necessary documents would be completed and an identification number would be provided which then remained with the equipment until it arrived at its destination. There had to be six copies of these forms for every item and these had to be translated into German.'

The work was endless. His office moved addressograph machines, trainloads of highly unstable hydrogen peroxide, electrical equipment belonging to Siemens and over 1,000 tons of tungsten steel warheads. One of the most notable targets for which Henshaw spent many hours laboriously typing out the necessary forms were sets of railway signalling equipment – one set for each of the UK's railway companies. The work continued late into the night, seven days a week, for three whole weeks. Not only was the work boring but, as Henshaw recalled, they were still expected to behave like soldiers: 'we didn't receive any overtime for doing this. We were expected to parade for P.T. the next morning and failing to appear meant being put on a charge!'

Another vast industrial target that had to be evacuated was a complete blast furnace and kiln weighing 2,300 tons, taken from a steelworks in Salzgitter. Piece by piece, the equipment was taken apart, with T-Force staff following the instructions of technicians and numbering each part, ready for Harry Henshaw to type out six copies of the necessary documents for every single component. Once this long process was completed, the equipment was packaged and transported back to the UK to be reassembled in a plant belonging to the firm of Dorman Long in County Durham.

While much of the equipment was heavy industrial machinery, some elements of the work were of a more experimental nature. One such operation gave Henshaw a break from his mundane desk duties, taking him to a factory in the American zone to get hold of a newly developed piece of equipment: 'It was an encephalograph, an instrument that measures electrical potentials on the scalp and generates a record of the electrical activity of the brain. It was requested by a hospital in Middlesex and was one of the first ever made. It was needed urgently for a patient who had a tumour on his brain.'

Mindful of the delicate nature of this target, Henshaw arranged for an ambulance belonging to the Royal Army Medical Corps to transport the machine to its destination. It was then flown to the UK and swiftly put to use. The evacuation office soon received a letter of appreciation, telling them it had arrived safely and thanking them for their careful assistance.

Although there was a genuine necessity to the seemingly never-ending clerical work and the organization of transport and hotels for visiting scientists, it could not compare to the earlier period. Even life within Germany held less attraction as society began to settle down after the war. T-Force now had a London office, shared with BIOS, which was responsible for the travel and welfare of British scientists heading out to Germany and which also organized the reception of German scientists arriving to be employed in the UK. Their tasks included meeting scientists at the airport or at Liverpool Street railway station, then taking them to the London office. Their documents were checked and overnight accommodation was arranged ready for their journey to their new employment. Rather than driving around Germany searching for elusive nuclear scientists or checking U-boats for booby-traps, the men of T-Force were filling in railway warrants, issuing food coupons, checking passport photographs and arranging foreign visas.

The new investigation teams made requests for a broad range of industrial technology, such as the patents for fountain pens and electrical cable connectors, or the radio calibration of tuning forks. Samples despatched to the UK via T-Force during 1946 included scissors, razors, crepe fabric for use in 'High class ladies goods', woollen stockings and animal hair clippers.[8] As one officer noted, 'It was so varied. The evacuations didn't fall easily into categories.' Michael Howard even recalled a British team arriving in Germany to investigate dome-headed drawing pins. It was all a far cry from Lt Colonel Wreford-Brown's intentions for his Kingsmen when he had lobbied for their employment in the frontlines.

Former Royal Artillery officer, Tom Pitt-Pladdy, soon began to realize T-Force was no longer the same organization he had joined back in March 1945. There had undoubtedly been great worth in the duties he had earlier been engaged in, but life had changed. He had been struck by the nonchalance of some of the investigators who had arrived from the UK. He had initially become disillusioned when he had attempted to demonstrate a rapid-firing, Czech-made artillery piece to a

uninterested investigator. As someone who had served throughout the Normandy campaign as a gunner, Pitt-Pladdy knew
what he was talking about – after all, he had unleashed enough
high explosive on the enemy and seen the horrific effects of
concentrated firepower to realize when a weapon was of interest. But the investigator simply brushed him aside without
bothering to examine the gun, telling the astonished Pitt-Pladdy
'We have far better weapons at home.'

Also the process of helping civilian investigators find
machinery for their own factories began to irritate Tom Pitt-
Pladdy, who felt that he was being used to help make
industrialists get rich. He had no interest in copper smelting,
the German lamp industry, the use of pulp in paper production, dairy farming, wool spinning or plywood production.
After five years of war, this was not the role he expected, nor
one that he relished.

Despite his misgivings about the work, Pitt-Pladdy continued
with his duties but noted how there was increasing opposition
to the work of T-Force. As the Control Commission began to
flex its muscles over the government of Germany and others
became increasingly confident of their position, he found some
in authority were prepared to challenge T-Force. In one case
he found himself confronted by an irate RAF Wing
Commander: 'I was finding it extremely difficult to get my
hands on the "addressograph" machines. People just wouldn't
give them to me.' When this was reported back to London
immediate measures were taken to ensure that the machinery
was handed over:

> So HQ managed to get me a letter from the Minister of Supply,
> Stafford Cripps. I had a telegram from him stuck in my back
> pocket. I went back to one place and they told me 'I thought we
> said we weren't going to let you have the machines.' So I pulled
> the letter out. He went purple – I'd never seen anything like it.

So he rang T-Force HQ and said 'I've got an officer here and he's trying to bully me.' HQ told him it was genuine and so he just waved me out of the room. I got my machines.

Increasingly unhappy, Pitt-Pladdy made the decision to seek employment elsewhere. Discovering that the Royal Artillery was experiencing a shortage of officers willing to take a regular commission, he returned to the regimental HQ at Woolwich and signed on for further service. He was to remain with the Royal Artillery for the rest of his service life.

The lack of cooperation Tom Pitt-Pladdy had experienced during some investigations and evacuations was not unusual, as Michael Howard noted: 'there were occasional challenges to our authority, some by Germans and rather more from officers of the Control Commission'. One example was when the CCG prevented No.1 T-Force from evacuating a consignment of mining equipment in April 1946. The reason given was that the machinery was needed to increase German coal output. In another case, the CCG attempted to prevent the evacuation of a number of gun-barrel boring machines, despite the fact that these were clearly items of military equipment and could be classed as booty.

Michael Howard also recalled one incident in which he was forced to use the original T-Force pass, although its validity appeared to be obsolete due to the fact it was authorized by HQ 21st Army Group – a formation that no longer existed. Regardless of the circumstances and the legitimacy of the pass, it gave the junior officer significant power: 'I used it once to keep off the premises a full colonel from HQ Control Commission Düsseldorf, who put in an appearance to try to prevent the evacuation of some high-grade alloy tanks designed and used to store hydrazine hydrate – used in the production of V2 fuel.' The colonel's argument was that they were needed for the storage of milk: 'I thought "Balls to that!" I told him they were "warlike stores" and "booty" and that he would have to bring on Brigadier Barraclough, the Deputy Regional Commissioner, if he really wanted to countermand my order. Otherwise, I had the authority to keep him off the premises. He told me that I was the rudest young officer it had ever been his misfortune to meet. In that he was probably quite right.'

As Howard noted at the time, the situation showed how the parameters for the definition of 'booty' had been expanded from the battlefield to the industrial sphere to include anything that had been used to promote the waging of war. In Howard's case, he justified the removal of the fuel tanks with his own memories of the awful effects of the rocket attacks on London. He thought of the civilians rendered unconscious by a rocket blast in South Kensington that had burst a water main. As they lay unconscious in the gutter they had been drowned by the torrent of water flooding from the shattered pipes. He also thought of his friend who had been blown from a taxi by the blast of a V2 explosion. When he came round, he found a lady's severed hand resting upon his chest. In Howard's mind, rocket fuel storage tanks were without doubt military equipment and could be removed from Germany without qualms: 'Milk storage? Not this time, not in the aftermath of total war!'

Once the industrial teams had made their initial assessments and prepared their reports decisions were taken over whether research scientists and technicians were needed for interrogation in the UK. Those selected for evacuation were asked by T-Force to make themselves available for travel to the UK. In her new position at T-Force HQ, Jean Hughes-Gibb had entered a strange world. It was a far cry from her job at the Control Commission whose purpose, she recalled, was to 'help the German people build up their economy and restore institutions that had been shattered by enemy action'. Effectively, Jean operated as a liaison between the BIOS office in London – at

whose meetings she sometimes acted as the representative of
T-Force HQ – and the German scientists and technicians who
were wanted for interrogation or work in the UK or the
Commonwealth. For each target scientist she was given a name
and their last known address. Checking her maps for the individual's proximity to T-Force units, she then allocated the job to
a particular detachment. As she later recalled, 'Some of the scientists were found quickly but others had to be searched for.'

Once the Germans had been located by the search teams,
escorting officers were detailed by Jean Hughes-Gibb to accompany them to London where they were taken to an
interrogation centre in Wimbledon, based at the premises of
Beltane School. From mid-1947 the detainees were housed at
Spedan Towers, a large house in Hampstead, north London,
which had been the home of John Spedan Lewis, the founder
of the John Lewis chain of shops. The BIOS reception centre
had no barbed wire, no guards and was operated by an
unarmed military staff. Despite their status as detainees, the
Germans housed there were allowed to leave the centre and
travel up to five miles away. As Michael Howard described it,
the function of the interrogations was to discover whether the
scientist in question had any 'valuable intellectual property' that
could be exploited for the benefit of the UK and – most importantly – be denied to the Soviet Union.

The activities of T-Force increasingly generated complaints.
Some came from within Germany, raising fears over the treatment of scientists being interrogated in the UK. There was
particular concern over the conditions at Beltane School which
had acquired a 'bad name and was inclined to make German
scientists nervous of proceeding to England',[9] something that
caused Brigadier Grylls (like Brigadier Pennycook before him)
to raise the fear that, unless the situation improved, T-Force
might find it difficult to get scientists to sign contracts to take
employment in the UK.

However, rather than coming from the locals, it was competing elements of the British authorities within Germany that saw fit to raise the most effective criticism of T-Force. In one case, a senior civil servant employed by the Control Commission complained that T-Force was using 'Gestapo' methods to abduct and kidnap scientists. This was a claim that raised the ire of those within T-Force. When the accusations were first published in 2007, T-Force veterans were both confused and angry at the claims. As Ken Moore noted, as part of the generation that had lived through and witnessed the crimes of the Nazis, to be compared to the Gestapo was particularly offensive. As others were quick to point out, most of the operations to collect scientists in the postwar period were carried out by unarmed officers and NCOs in daylight. Furthermore, as Michael Howard observed, most of the German scientists he dealt with were eager to come to the UK. If nothing else, the opportunity to work – or simply to be clothed, fed and housed in heated accommodation – was better than a meagre existence amidst the ruins of Germany.

It appeared to the T-Force veterans that these complaints and accusations had arisen from the conflict of interest between those; such as T-Force, whose role was to investigate and dismantle German industry and those in the Control Commission whose role was to return stability to Germany, and to get its industry back working at prewar levels in order to prevent it being a drain on Allied resources. Michael Howard became aware that accusations had been made by a Mr Bearder, the Controller of the Chemical Industry Branch of the Trade and Industry Division within the Control Commission. Howard believed the attacks on T-Force were the result of the evacuation of a group of eight scientists from IG Farben's plant in Leverkusen. One of this party had 'defaulted', that is, he failed to turn up for his appointment to be transported to the UK. The man in question, a Dr August Wingler, was discovered to have attempted suicide rather than face interrogation in the UK. Howard later discovered that Dr Wingler had been involved in IG Farben's research into Acridine and Rutenol, drugs that had been used in fatal tests on inmates at Auschwitz. As Howard noted, the suicide attempt was less a symptom of T-Force's methods and more a result of his fear that he was to be investigated for his role in the Holocaust. In Howard's view, the accusation that the other seven IG Farben scientists had been abducted was groundless. If anything, Bearder's accusations were deliberately made in an effort to undermine T-Force's activities in an attempt to allow the Control Commission to aid the recovery of German industry.

Following completion of investigations into any particular branch of German industry, reports were published by His Majesty's Stationery Office (HMSO). In addition, BIOS held exhibitions to show what was available via reparations. At one exhibition, held in London in December 1946, 2,500 visitors attended and nearly 600 reports were sold to representatives of industry. Similar numbers attended exhibitions in Glasgow, Bristol and Birmingham, and more than 4,500 attended the event in Manchester. Thus, information on a wide range of German industries began to be freely available within the UK.

While T-Force's evacuation work had been designed to bring economic advantage to the UK, the publication of results was not only to the benefit of British industry. As summaries of German research became available, there were no restrictions as to who could purchase them. As a result, German firms were also able to acquire the results of research carried out by their rivals. Effectively, a German company that had diligently researched in a particular area could do nothing to prevent the fruits of their research being available to anyone who bothered to purchase a publicly available report. When complaints were received by BIOS about IG Farben's research into insulin being made available, including to other German companies, their answer was simple: 'Under the terms of surrender all German firms were obliged to hand over all their information to the Allied governments, it was no concern of the Germans themselves what use was made of such information.'[10] After all, the men of T-Force were more than acquainted with some of the more sinister chemical research the firm had previously been engaged in.

Such was the mass of information arriving at the Board of Trade and Ministry of Supply via T-Force that many reports – on such subjects as tungsten carbide, raw plastics, microscopes, metal testing equipment, crank presses, synthetic rubber, gear production lathes, map tracing equipment, dried milk for use in baby food production, recording equipment and gas detection equipment – languished unread for long periods. The Control Commission's research branch reported having received a report on electromagnetism that no one bothered to look at for over a year.

There was also the question of how western scientists were going to absorb the vast amount of research that had taken place in Germany through the war years. Researchers in the field of electron microscopy discovered that five books had been published on the subject. In addition over 180 technical articles had been published in journals. All needed to be translated before their contents could be fully examined by the West.

The scale of the assessment of German industrial and military research was just part of a problem encountered by the authorities in Germany. In addition, large numbers of German scientists were desperate to find favour with the British. In the hope of registering new patents, hundreds of scientists and inventors – some genuine, some cranks – inundated the offices of the Control Commission with their inventions. Unfortunately for those receiving the letters, there was no way of distinguishing between major new developments and ridiculous claims.

Even the most important invention might be heralded by a letter written in tortuously bad English, seemingly making it worthy of nowhere but the litter basket. One 'crank', who submitted his ideas to the British, claimed to have invented a death-ray which could be used against a wide range of targets including mosquitoes, fleas, lice, rats, gangsters, terrorists and demonstrators. One observer noted that the man was 'quite convinced that he has succeeded where thousands of others before him have failed. This office regards him as just another mad inventor.'[11]

A similar problem was also experienced by one of the investigators tasked with interrogating scientists when he assessed the claims made by one German who approached the British to offer his services:

> This man is a typical, incipient schizophrenic, thwarted in a probably genuine idealistic approach to scientific investigation in early life. There are . . . many of this variety in Germany, who dabble in the ideas of physics; they are known as Pathologers. The man's story was of course a farrago of nonsense from beginning to end. The man may or may not be deliberately deceiving the English authorities; he has certainly, as a schizophrenic, been deceiving himself for twenty years.[12]

Although there was some criticism of the British policy towards German scientists, there remained plenty who were eager to be embraced by it. Correspondence sent to the British element of the Control Commission, and forwarded to T-Force, revealed the desperation of those offering their services. One 70-year-old inventor wrote to the British requesting to be allowed to find a British partner to develop his products:

> I agree to the condition that my joint partner pays to me for the licence to give him merely as long as I am alive and my wife is

alive . . . Of course we wish to live still some time, but I think
the time will be short on account of the actual shortness of food.
For this reason I trust, the joint partner will send me a number
of care parcels, containing flour and lard or other good fat for
kitchen use.[13]

As Jean Hughes-Gibb recalled, such were the circumstances
endured by vast numbers of Germans that even the manager of
a cigar factory close to T-Force HQ had been reduced to living in a wooden hut.

The reason behind this desperation to work for the British
was explained by Michael Howard:

When I first arrived in Germany it was still winter. The country
was frightfully bust. Life was very meagre and people were hungry, cold and dying. At one point the rations for Germans were
about 850 calories a day – that was about the same as we had for
breakfast. In Essen I saw people walking in the street who were
stumbling and weaving as if drunk. I realized they were weak
from hunger and cold. They were dying on their feet. The scientists had often lost their factories, or had no raw materials to work
with. They were working in cold, unheated offices. The idea that
people living in those circumstances would object to be pulled
over to Wimbledon to be interrogated just doesn't work out.

When letters arrived from researchers in search of employment,
it was impossible for the readers to be certain whether a man's
claim to talent was genuine or whether it was simply a desperate plea to be removed from Germany and offered work abroad.
Sometimes it took little more than some basic research among
those acquainted with the topic to discover that the writer was
indeed respected in their field. A letters from a scientist which
included a list of commercially available products, along with
details of manufacturers or clients, was always certain to garner

more attention than a letter introducing itself with the words, 'I have an idea for a new . . .'

Regardless of content, the letters needed to be sifted, with some others sent for further investigation. Those bodies who passed the letters on to the research branch of the Economic Sub-Commission of the Control Commission received replies informing them of how they should respond to the German applicant, such as 'the matter has been considered, but that we find his invention is of no interest to us. Incidentally, it is a variation on the "perpetual motion" theme, and is quite impracticable.'[14] Staff sifting through these letters were increasingly frustrated by their contents, described as 'the usual half-baked schizophrenismus'.[15] On first viewing a writer might appear to be offering information of great value, only to reveal little more than a basic knowledge of their subject, as one British scientist replied to a proposal from the Control Commission on the subject of a 'Method for Deriving Atomic Energy': 'I cannot think how the paper you sent me with your note of March 1st could ever have come to be described as above. It is merely an elementary essay on radio-activity and makes no proposals of any kind whatsoever. Please smother.' In another case one British scientist noted that 'Herr Peuser's contribution to the science of atomic energy is worth rather less than the paper it is written on.' A similarly terse reply was made on a claimed cure for cancer: 'as you may guess, many people have claimed to have discovered cures for cancer, which on close examination are often discovered to be founded on enthusiasm rather than on scientific observation'.[16]

Some found it hard not to make fun of some German claims about technological breakthroughs. When presented with a letter on the subject of beer bottle caps, the director of the Scientific and Technical Intelligence Branch (STIB) replied to the Control Commission:

The officers of STIB are renowned for their knowledge and experience in dealing with any type of stopper for bottles. Should, therefore, any of our officers be passing through Dresden on their way to Siberia, we will arrange for them to deal adequately with this German national . . . it is with some concern that we note that this German national does not claim to have a store of Atom Bombs in his cellar . . . You may rest assured that vigorous action will be taken in proportion to the supreme importance of this matter to the Imperial Economy.[17]

Of course, not all of the enquiries were from those presenting outdated, worthless or fantastical developments. Some came from genuine sources, such as from a former Luftwaffe photography specialist who had made night flights over London during the Blitz, photographing the scenes below, who now wished to discuss his proposals for improved night-time aerial photography. His proposal was taken seriously and he was asked to prepare a detailed report on the subject.

For those scientists selected for evacuation, the process of their removal to the UK was handled by the officers, NCOs and men of T-Force. The procedure for evacuation was that T-Force received the names of the scientists from the British element of FIAT. It was then the responsibility of T-Force to locate and 'freeze'[18] the scientist while awaiting the necessary paperwork to clear them for evacuation. In cases where the scientist was being offered employment, T-Force then awaited the arrival of a representative from the relevant ministry who delivered the contract of employment. Once all paperwork was in place the subject would be transported to London by a T-Force evacuation officer. Only when all relevant paperwork was completed would clearance be requested for exit from Germany. In some sensitive cases, the names of scientists were not revealed to the international element of the Control Council on security grounds.

Although some records appear to show T-Force aggressively detaining scientists during this period, Michael Howard recalled that in his experience there was no need to force the scientists to cooperate. Accusations that T-Force detachments had been waking up scientists in the middle of the night and forcing them to leave at gunpoint were described as 'arrant nonsense'. As he noted, he only actually wore his side-arm – a German Luger pistol given to him by his father – on one occasion in two years, when in the company of Russian officers who insisted on carrying their weapons. John Bendit recalled an operation in which he had to deliver two Germans to London for interrogation by Military Intelligence in London. When his car broke down on the autobahn and his driver went off to find help, he was struck by the fear that the two Germans might run away. Since he was not armed, he realized he would be unable to stop any escape attempt.

His colleague Tony Lucas, with the T-Force detachment at Heisingen, outside Essen, was equally certain of the willingness of German scientists and industrialists to cooperate with the British:

> I flew back people from Germany on about three occasions and delivered them to an address in Wimbledon. You just handed them over. You weren't told anything about it. Initially when you contacted people they were a little fearful. But once they were convinced they were going to be safe, they were happy to go. I had no feeling that I was kidnapping people. They would ask us questions about what was going to happen in London.

He noted that the majority of Germans he met in the factories of the Ruhr were well disposed towards the occupying army. Of the accusations that T-Force used 'Gestapo' tactics, he was certain it was 'absolute rubbish'. Lucas saw no evidence that German firms were being bullied:

They were always so polite and helpful. They were prepared to give us whatever we wanted because they wanted to use the British as protection against the Russians. The Germans were basically cowed – and we were the last line of defence against the Russians. The whole of Germany was haunted by the spectre of a Russian invasion. Lots of Germans were refugees from the east and they knew exactly what would happen if the Russians came in. The attitude was 'If you want anything, take it away.' They wanted to rebuild if we would help them. They wanted our investment to get their industry going again. They told me 'You put money into the Ruhr and we'll get it going again.'

Michael Howard described the scientists detained by No.1 T-Force detachments as accepting their position meekly and quietly, acquiescing to the request that they present themselves for evacuation. He also recalled just three occasions, out of the thousands of visits made by T-Force during this period, in which factory owners resisted T-Force's attempts to remove equipment and documents. In one case an elderly German man attempted to bribe Michael Howard to say that the documents had been destroyed. Another factory owner tried to claim the documents being searched for had been destroyed in a bombing raid back in 1943. Furthermore, it was German factory staff who actually crated up equipment ready for evacuation to the UK. As Howard noted, the attitude of subservience displayed by the local population was such that, following restrictions being lifted on industrial action, one German political leader actually came to his office to ask permission to hold a strike meeting.

An additional series of evacuations that employed the resources of T-Force was Operation Bottleneck. Since many British firms needed specialist staff to fulfil contracts, yet were unable to find suitable personnel due to the constraints caused by mass mobilization and the employment of specialists on military projects, the scheme was designed to ensure a smooth flow of German technicians to undertake short-term contracts in the UK. The name possibly derived from a letter sent to the Board of Trade from Simon Carves Ltd of Stockport. Written in August 1946, the letter explained how there were 'bottlenecks' in their production of coke ovens for export due to a shortage of drawing-office staff. They had already identified a suitable company in Germany whose staff were currently idle and wished to use their experienced draughtsmen as they realized it would take at least a year to find enough similarly skilled draughtsmen in the UK. Despite the benign nature of this pro-gramme, effectively a mechanism to employ Germans who might otherwise remained unemployed, Operation Bottleneck was the subject of criticism within Germany, with claims made by the head of the German journalists' union that those who travelled to the UK were in some way forced to participate in the scheme.

Under this operation T-Force despatched the Germans to the UK and took them to Spedan Towers. There, they were processed and received identity papers. The sponsoring firms were then responsible for all wages, accommodation and food for the contracted staff. For T-Force this was a very routine job, as the targets were very ordinary German workers rather than the experts whose genius had driven the German war effort.

While operations to use vital technicians continued, T-Force remained in the awkward situation of still holding scientists of a far higher potential who had been detained during 1945. Despite repeated requests from T-Force HQ, little was done to alleviate the situation. As it became increasingly difficult to hold all of the specialists who had travelled west, lists were issued to T-Force by BIOS and FIAT giving the names of any scientists who should continued to be detained rather than be allowed to travel home to eastern Germany and thus fall into the hands of the Soviets.

With the question of the scientists evacuated from the Soviet zone during 1945 still unsettled, the British opened a new facility named 'Matchbox' to interrogate scientists and other experts arriving in the west. It was stressed that FIAT needed to take swift action in Berlin since scientists arriving at their offices risked arrest upon returning to Russian controlled areas. This policy of removing scientists to the west was in contrast to the policy of the Americans, who made no effort to remove scientists from Berlin unless they appeared on the list of top 1,000 names. The British policy increased the burden on T-Force who had the responsibility for their evacuation and accommodation. Despite this burden, the organization was able to cope. As Jean Hughes-Gibb recalled, the scientists at Matchbox lived well, being fed and clothed and living in heated accommodation. It was a far cry from the living conditions endured by so many Germans at that time.

In addition to this scheme, the British authorities in Germany also had to cope with the fate of German scientists who were gainfully employed within the British zone. It was clear that, just as the western powers had retained their interest in the Germans, so too had the Russians. During 1947 and 1948 there arose a number of concerns regarding the possibility that German nuclear scientists might be abducted by the Russians. In particular Professors Otto Hahn and Werner Heisenberg were believed to be under threat. Heisenberg was living openly in Göttingen and had refused to move into protected accommodation. The area was considered to be dangerous due to its proximity to a number of 'black crossing points' into the Soviet zone. Just as the British had made unauthorized cross-border trips to locate scientists of interest, the threat of retaliatory Russian moves was considered to be very real.

In early 1948 the Cabinet Defence Committee reported on Russian efforts to recruit scientists from within the British zone. Although much of the active recruitment of scientists had diminished, the Russians attempted to secure the services of unemployed technicians who had previously worked in plants now in Russian hands as part of the reparations process. It was believed that eight scientists on the T-Force lists had gone to work in the Soviet zone and one was also reportedly employed in Yugoslavia. These included specialists in remote control, radar, rocket fuels, engines, weapon design and gun sights. As a result, Operation Scrum Half commenced and a number of covert intelligence teams were established to watch over scientists of particular interest, while mail and telephone intercepts were used to monitor any communications between the scientists and anyone attempting to lure them away.

The burgeoning Cold War and the constant fear that the Russians would be able to gain a military advantage over the western Allies continued to dominate thinking within T-Force. As Intelligence Officer of No.1 T-Force, Michael Howard was intimately involved in operations designed to frustrate the Russians: 'The Russians were deeply suspicious. Just as much as we were suspicious that they were not to be trusted – they were suspicious that we were similarly untrustworthy. They saw their ploys as defensive, rather than aggressive measures. It was the same on both sides.' The suspicious nature of the Russian teams was soon revealed to Michael Howard:

> Now and again we had a Russian team in one of our messes. They were not allowed to speak English or German – we knew that most of them spoke German and many would have spoken English. We also knew that one out of every team of four was there simply to keep an eye on the others. Sometimes the same 'expert' would come back in another team as a supposed expert in a different technology – one time he might be an expert in drawing pins, the next in gas turbines. But we always knew which one the spy was because he was the one that the rest of his team kept looking at nervously.

The soldiers of No.1 T-Force became actively involved in the attempts to undermine Russian reparations teams. Michael Howard was woken one night by a telephone call. Given a coded message that meant nothing to him, he asked the speaker to explain in clear language. It transpired a quadripartite reparations team – including Russians – was due at Krupps in Essen in three days time. At the works were three enormous pieces of experimental ordnance, two field guns – one with an 18-metre (60-foot) barrel – and a huge howitzer. These were required by the research arm of the Royal Artillery.

With the Russians likely to lay claim to the experimental guns, T-Force was unable to take any chances – they had to be removed, and quick. The problem was that the guns were stored amidst a sea of rubble, with at least 110 metres (120 yards) of wreckage separating them from the nearest viable road. It fell to Captain Howard to find a solution. He contacted his friend Tony Lucas at Essen, who was despatched to Krupps to find a way out: 'We had to bulldoze an exit through the rubble and ruins, and get the people at Krupps to lash up jury-rig gun carriages to allow the guns to be towed.' On the final day, with just hours to spare, the guns were finally removed from the ruins and, pulled by vehicles normally used for towing tank transporters, they set out in a column led by Captain Howard riding a motorcycle. He led the column to the back streets of Kamen, where they were safely hidden until the reparations team had departed. Once the coast was clear, the guns were transferred to the evacuation depot in Hamburg and sent to the UK for further evaluation.

It was not only physical strength that was used by T-Force to frustrate the attempts of the Russian teams to investigate plants in the Ruhr. Despite the legality of the Russian visits, T-Force officers were happy to engage in subterfuge in order to hide materials and equipment from them. When it was found that a Russian reparation team was to visit the

Vereinigte Aluminium-Werke at Lünen, it was expected they would lay claim to a specific section of the works. However, this had already been requested by British Aluminium for their factory at Monmouth. Only T-Force's heavy workload had prevented the earlier evacuation of the equipment. If 110 tons of equipment were to be denied to the Russians it would require some careful administrative work. Once again the Intelligence Office at No.1 T-Force came up with a solution. As Michael Howard remembered, 'The only thing for it was to see that these items were not included in the inventory, and that the only way to achieve this was, we concluded, to ensure that at the signing ceremony – always a convivial affair – no one would be sober enough to notice.'

At the conclusion of their inspection, the Russian team, including the obligatory KGB officer, agreed to celebrate the success of their mission with the British officers. The Russians brought a crate of vodka to the party, which the British officers matched bottle-for-bottle with German brandy: 'These ingredients were mixed in a one to one ration, and the unholy brew – which could itself have fuelled a V2 – was served in half-pint beer mugs.' As the party continued the unsigned inventory rested innocently on a table in the corner of the room. The increasingly inebriated Russians were introduced to the game of darts, all the time being urged to drink-up by Charles Middleton, the group's conducting officer. Himself increasingly unsteady, Michael Howard managed to remain focused on their task at the end of the party. Once the Russian eyes were 'glazed and unfocusing', Howard dragged them away to a table to sign the inventory, from which the equipment had been carefully omitted. The document was quickly spirited away, and fingers were crossed that the Russians never noticed they had signed an incomplete inventory. Within about a week, the contested section had been entirely dismantled and shipped to Hamburg ready for transport to the factory in Monmouth.

During this period, such parties regularly became part of the Cold War battlefield. Michael Howard also recalled how he and Tony Lucas had to watch over the Russians to prevent them from attempting to influence local elections around Heisingen. They were expected to be present at the polling stations, trying to intimidate the Germans into voting Communist: 'So the night before the elections, at a party in the mess where they were staying, we went and peed into their petrol tank.' They then stuffed orange segments into the tank, hoping this would further spoil the fuel. The next day the Russians spent their time cleaning out their petrol tank and were unable to reach the polling stations.

As it became increasingly clear that the Russians had now replaced Germany as the enemy, German attitudes reflected the changing status. This was shown when one man walked into the offices of No.1 T-Force and approached Michael Howard, telling him: 'I have come to enlist.' Stunned by the German's words, Howard told him not to be so impudent. Still the German persisted: 'He told me "But you will be needing me. I am a pilot of the Messerschmitt 262 jet. You will need me to fight against the Russians." However, at that stage I still had to show solidarity with our gallant Russian allies. So I told the corporal to throw him out. However, I knew perfectly well that what the German had said was probably true.'

As the evacuation operations continued, it became clear the value of what was being dismantled and removed to the UK was diminishing. Tony Lucas recalled his latter days with No.1 T-Force, taking a team from the Port Sunlight soap manufacturers to visit the premises of their German rivals. He felt this was wasting everybody's time. He also watched as the Russians continued their dismantling work in the Ruhr: 'The Krupps steelworks was being solidly dismantled by the Russians down to the last nut and bolt. The Germans watched them and said to us "It's all out of date and as soon as we can we are going to replace it." The fact that the Russians were moving it just saved the Germans from demolishing it.' Their words made him think there was little point in continuing with the process: 'Certainly by 1947 T-Force seemed like a bit of an "empty box". Most of what we were bringing out was totally worthless.'

He was right. From 30 June 1947, investigations were terminated and towards the end of 1947 T-Force evacuations began to wind down. There was less and less interest in what Germany could offer to the UK and more emphasis on how Germany could begin to pay for itself as it became re-established as a functioning state. Increasingly, the work of T-Force was handled by civilians, including locally employed staff. There was little to do except await requests for machinery. These calls became less and less frequent as it became clear that everything of real value had already been picked over.

Another sign that operations were winding down came in August 1947 when it was decided that no more documents were to be removed to the UK. Michael Howard questioned this policy, noting that since T-Force was still having to remove documents to be sent to other countries, it made sense for copies to be retained for possible future use by British industry. Despite the rule change, Howard made the decision to continue copying documents, such as a batch that had been requested by Czechoslovakia. When he attempted to obtain other documents that had already been sent to foreign powers so that copies could be sent to the UK, he faced opposition from the military government. This prompted a letter to T-Force HQ in which Captain Howard noted 'We were faced with the ludicrous situation of officers of Military Government refusing to deliver to the accredited representatives of HM Government documents and drawings which they had released to allied governments without a murmur.'

He further noted that in the preceding two years the broadest interpretation had been placed on the term 'booty'. However, while the British had acquired many 'civilian' items under this broad interpretation, under the new policy T-Force was unable to acquire documents of a genuine military value: 'It is not understood how the present policy as regards equipment and as regards documents can be reconciled.' The reply he received from HQ T-Force in November 1947 was a sure sign of the changing world that the unit was operating in:

> I am afraid there can be no question of raising the whole matter again, since we have no support from BOT (Board of Trade) and MOS (Ministry of Supply) . . . I should explain that T-Force is under fire from influential quarters at home and in Germany and we have necessarily to tread very carefully. You can see the trend of high policy in Germany and it is, clearly, at any cost to put Germany back to work so that we can be repaid some of our current expenses – the future apparently will look after itself. In this light T-Force activities in the document and equipment fields are obviously a hindrance and they must be terminated willy-nilly at the earliest opportunity.

It was clear that T-Force's days were numbered.

Soon after this, Michael Howard – who had been central to postwar T-Force reparations evacuations – returned home to attend university and complete the education war had interrupted. When he was demobbed in December 1947, he recorded that T-Force had handled the evacuation of 6,000 equipment 'serials', around 6,000 sets of blueprints and technical documents, and some 650 'personalities'. When he departed there were just 6 'serials' left for evacuation. Furthermore, through BIOS and T-Force, a total of 170,000 pending patents submitted in Germany had become available to UK firms. As Howard noted in a letter to his parents, T-Force was 'the only unit in Germany which is not a liability to the taxpayer in that the consequences of the work have a considerable and direct bearing on our economic recovery'.

Captain Howard later recorded that the work of No.1 T-Force had not gone wholly unrecognized. He discovered that in parliament, Sir Peter MacDonald, the member for the Isle of Wight, had asked of Sir Stafford Cripps: 'Who are these bright young men?' Although Cripps's answer went unrecorded, Howard felt the question was not out of place. He felt the junior officers that served with him had perfectly fitted that description:

> By 1948 five of us had left the army to take up places at Oxford or Cambridge, two of them as scholars. And two of them were later to become known to the literate public – Robin Smyth for a number of years as the *Observer*'s senior correspondent on the continent. And John Bayley as the distinguished literary critic and Wharton Professor of English at St Catherine's College, Oxford – and as the husband of the philosopher and novelist Iris Murdoch.

Indeed, Bayley used his service with T-Force as the barely concealed background for his novel *In Another Country*, published in 1955.

By the end of the final two years of its existence, with so many of the soldiers having been demobbed, T-Force was a primarily a British civilian organization whose duties revolved around documenting and valuing the items that had been evacuated between April 1945 and December 1947. One thing was clear, it had been a substantial haul, both industrially and intellectually, and much of what T-Force had sent home was already in use within British industry or being used in military research projects. The job was over, but the legacy remained.

CHAPTER 11

Aftermath

'I have never thought that what I did as a soldier had any significance to the outcome of the conflict, but then who did? However, what we did as a unit in T-Force did, I am confident, make a very significant contribution to the security of the British Commonwealth of nations, and the freedom that we all enjoy today.'

Les Goodwin, 5th King's Regiment, No.2 T-Force.

'When all the profits and losses of victory, and of the occupation of Germany, come to be weighed up there is one item which will deny an estimate. That is knowledge. The secrets of German industry and science. I put it at £100,000,000.'

Daily Express, 9 October 1946.[1]

History has managed to forget T-Force. Not even the veterans of the conflict recall anything about them. As the 'official' occupation force sent into Kiel exclaimed in May 1945, 'Who the hell are T-Force?' Whatever the reason, the work of T-Force – of the 5th King's Regiment and their infantry colleagues, the Royal Army Service Corps drivers, the safe-crackers and bomb disposal experts of the Royal Engineers and the Pioneers who crated up everything that was found in Germany – has never received public recognition. Except for the few hundred words published in 1945, nothing was heard again of their exploits for many years to come. As Les Goodwin, who had taken part in the Kiel operation, recalled, 'Much of our exploits were not exposed to me until some fifty years later when we came together at a meeting of the Old Comrades Association.'

It will take a long time to be able to fully understand the entire role of T-Force. In the 1980s Michael Howard tried to discover how much information was still available on the organization; the answer was very little. The records of the British element of the Control Commission had ended up in the archives of the Foreign Office. He discovered that, between 1948 and 1956, 90% of all its documents had been destroyed – a total of 103 tons of paper. Between 1956 and 1984, a further 90% of the remainder had been shredded, leaving just 1.5 tons of paper from the original 114 tons. He was convinced that what was left could never possibly tell the complete story of the British policy towards German armaments and industry in the postwar years. Howard even offered his services to the Foreign Office to help them edit their files on the subject prior to them being placed in the National Archives. His intimate knowledge of the reparations process gave him a clear understanding of the importance of the amassed documents. Without that knowledge he feared vital parts of the puzzle would be lost, not least documents revealing the real value of both reparations and booty acquired in the aftermath of war.

His offer was rejected, helping contribute to the inevitable confusion over the history of T-Force. It transpired that even the official Treasury report on the value of reparations was missing from the records. Furthermore, the complete files on German chemical warfare remain closed and those documents that have been released do not include examples of the 4,000 photographs of German gas tests uncovered by T-Force, including those showing the chemical warfare tests on live subjects. Even in late 2008 the government refused to release the entire files to the public.

The few records and reports that had been kept remained hidden for many years. Just prior to demobilization at the end of 1945, Lt Colonel Bloomfield wrote the official record of the T-Force operation. The report was printed and then given a restricted category, which he thought was absurd since the *The Times* article had already revealed the essence of their activities. As he later recalled, 'This history is doubtless now buried in the archives of the Ministry of Defence or the Imperial War Museum.'[2] For Lt Colonel Bloomfield the memory of the active role was important, describing the wartime period as 'wonderfully vigorous and rewarding, and in fact enjoyable'. However, he believed the spirit of T-Force had been tarnished by the postwar roles imposed upon it.[3]

Certainly, many of the Kingsmen admitted they had long believed that the nature of their work meant they should not reveal it to anybody. Others felt they had little idea about the true nature of their employment and chose to forget what had happened. Whatever the case, T-Force had been involved in and around a number of the twentieth century's most notable scientific advancements. Yet they had done it all with an air of detachment that belied the importance of their work. When Brigadier Grylls passed away in 1994, his obituary in *The Times* erroneously described him as the commander of T-Force, which it said was a clandestine organization set up to rescue German scientists and research work from the path of the approaching Soviet Army. This was inaccurate since he had only taken over in the postwar period. When this discrepancy was pointed out it was explained that Brigadier Grylls had always regarded his activities as 'Top Secret' and had never fully explained his role to outsiders.

While most among the T-Force personnel soon left the army and forgot all about their role, some among them retained an interest and later became fully aware of the vast scale of their labours. Years after leaving T-Force, Tom Pitt-Pladdy found

himself visiting the Royal Artillery research facility at Fort
Halstead. This was the very location to which he had sent so
much of the research material – including samples of German
artillery pieces – he had personally evacuated from Germany.
While serving at German gun ranges in the postwar period he
had sent back numerous test result tables and technical drawings to be assessed by the specialists at Fort Halstead. However,
the staff there told him the shocking truth: Fort Halstead had
been so overwhelmed with the sheer volume of documents,
technical data and samples sent by T-Force that much of it
remained untouched in the cellars.

Somehow, the involvement of T-Force remained well hidden
from the prying eyes of historians. At Buxtehude, a detachment
from the 5th King's had taken control of the records of the
headquarters of the German navy, yet postwar histories gave
the credit to the 7th Armoured Division, which was the main
British unit operating in the area. The secretive nature of the
T-Force role, and its continuing purpose in the postwar period,
ensured that attention was kept away from the unit.

Thus, somewhat curiously, T-Force became the most secretive of all of the elite British forces of the Second World War.
They were, by anyone's definition, a special force, but their
involvement had lacked the sense of swashbuckling abandon
that pervaded the other special forces of the day. Instead,
T-Force was a quintessentially British unit. Although it was
required to carry out a job that would be essential for the
future security of the UK, its empire and the western Allies, the
men selected for the task were an ad-hoc collection of soldiers
deemed unfit for service in the frontlines and surplus men from
units that had been broken up after the fighting in Normandy.
This was a curious mixture of shellshock cases, men released
from hospital after being wounded and teenagers fresh from
training. Add in a selection of safe-crackers released from
prison, and a liaison officer leading the advance with his leg in

plaster, and one has a 'special force' that might at first seem to be a fictional creation.

And that is where T-Force's legacy becomes particularly interesting. The work of T-Force and 30AU was to resurface in literature during the 1950s and 1960s. The series of books, short stories and films featuring Commander James Bond were closely related, and sometimes directly descended, from the story of T-Force operations in the final months of war and the first months of peace. These stories came from the pen of Ian Fleming who, as Commander Fleming, had been the driving force behind the creation of 30AU, which then become the inspiration for T-Force. Then, in turn, both T-Force and 30AU had advanced through Germany in pursuit of targets as selected for them by the Combined Intelligence Objectives Sub-Committee, as identified by the Combined Intelligence Priority Committee, both of which had featured Fleming in a prominent role. In Fleming's first novel, *Casino Royale* (1953), Bond even describes himself as being like a boy playing at being a Red Indian – 'Red Indians' having been Fleming's wartime nickname for 30AU.

Fleming's role in CIOS has been widely neglected by biographers. One recent book that focused on his wartime activities made no mention of Fleming's connection to the organization. Instead, there has been much speculation about where Fleming gained the target intelligence he fed to 30AU, with one writer concentrating on supposed links to the French Resistance. While this speculation has created an aura of mystery around Fleming, the truth is less dramatic. As a member of both CIOS and CIPC, Fleming was sitting at the heart of the scientific intelligence community. These sub-committees handled all intelligence relating to targets needed for investigation by both the US and the UK, not just for the navy, but also for the army and the air force. Since CIOS was the Allied intelligence hub during 1944 and 1945, it was little wonder Fleming was well

informed, which aided both his work at the Admiralty and his
James Bond novels.

The connection between Fleming and CIOS may also be the
source of another mysterious operation claimed to have been
carried out by the British in 1945. The 1996 book *OPJB: The
Last Great Secret of the Second World War* by Charles Creighton
(published by Simon Schuster) claimed that Fleming played a
role in 'Operation James Bond', the supposed evacuation of
Hitler's deputy, Martin Bormann, from Berlin. The claim,
widely dismissed by experts in the field, was mostly based
around a combination of rumour and the misreading of real
events that took place in 1945. However, even critics of the
book admitted there was something behind the story – it was
just unclear what the truth might be.

What is certain is that, as a member of CIOS, Fleming was
most likely involved in – and had knowledge of – the planning
and selection of targets for the intended T-Force operations in
Berlin. These were to have been carried out in the event of a
sudden German collapse. In the event, these operations never
took place since the Nazis resisted until Berlin had fallen to the
Russians. Most likely, the writer of *OPJB* has conflated frag-
ments of knowledge about Fleming's involvement with the
planning for T-Force operations in Berlin with his known
involvement in the creation of a commando unit in the form of
30AU. This in turn appears to have been conflated with real
operations carried out by T-Force to extract German scientists
and personalities of interest, preventing them from falling into
Russian hands. Indeed, since no written records exist of
T-Force's operations to extract German scientists from the
Soviet zone, it is unsurprising that rumours of them have been
twisted into high drama.

While some writers have taken rumours of Fleming's role in
secret operations and woven these into their accounts, there is
little doubt that Fleming himself plundered his recollections of

the top secret files that passed across his desk in Room 30 of the Admiralty. Although it went widely unnoticed, Fleming managed to insert essential elements of the T-Force story into his 1955 novel, *Moonraker*. In this, the third book in the Bond series, Fleming described Bond's defeat of Hugo Drax, the benefactor of a British nuclear missile system named Moonraker. This was being constructed in Kent by a team of German scientists, among them dedicated Nazis – just like the real scientists evacuated by T-Force ten years earlier. The 50-strong team was described in the book as the Nazi's top experts on guided missiles – the best of those that the Russians 'didn't get their hands on'. Indeed, Drax is revealed to have been a Nazi who had formerly been employed by the armaments giant Rheinmetall-Borsig, a company whose facilities had been such a prominent target for T-Force back in 1945. He is also revealed as a former member of a commando unit formed by Otto Skorzeny, who had been famous for his daring operations, including the rescue of Benito Mussolini from captivity in 1943. In earlier years Skorzeny had been responsible for the German intelligence-gathering operations that had inspired the creation of 30AU.

Yet the connection to the T-Force story was not just revealed in subtle hints. There were echoes of Operation Backfire, the early British efforts to launch V2 rockets that had utilized large numbers of German personnel and for which T-Force had located and transported the equipment and fuel. However, the connection went deeper. Instead of building a loose cover identity for one of his characters, Fleming directly used one man who had been a pivotal figure in the work of 30AU and T-Force in 1945.

In the novel, Drax's assistant on the Moonraker rocket project is named as Dr Walter, an expert on hydrogen peroxide and rocket engines. As described, the real Dr Hellmuth Walter – Germany's foremost expert in hydrogen peroxide rocket propulsion – had indeed come to the UK to work on defence projects. In his case it had not been missile systems but on the hydrogen peroxide-powered submarines that had made him such an important figure during the war. No doubt Fleming had absorbed the prophetic words of Commander Jan Aylen in his report on 30AU's activities in Kiel when he had written of Dr Walter: 'It lurks constantly in the writer's mind that he may even yet prove to be one of the sinister crooks of international fame who features so often in films and fiction.'

The novel also alludes to the infamous instability of the fuel used in the missiles, with Bond planning to destroy the prototype rocket by suicidally standing beneath it with a cigarette lighter. The danger of the fuel was something well known to all those former T-Force soldiers who had transported tanks of it across Germany to be used in Operation Backfire.

Elsewhere in *Moonraker*, Bond fears that a Russian suicide squad will come from the sea to carry out an attack on Dr Walter's missile. Once again art and life were carefully intertwined. Back in 1945, when Major Tony Hibbert had been told to rush to Kiel, it was the fear of a Russian amphibious operation to seize Dr Walter and his submarine research that had been one the most important catalysts behind the operation.

Of course, the real Dr Walter had willingly cooperated with the British. Just like his fictional counterpart, he helped build-up teams of specialist scientists and technicians to be employed by the western powers. On trips back to Germany he used his connections with other scientists to help extract information on Russian research projects taking place within Germany. In particular, he acquired documents and intelligence from a German turbine specialist who had made an unauthorized journey into the Soviet zone to visit a research establishment in Dresden. The intelligence acquired was exactly what the Admiralty had hoped to find out about Russian turbine development and, as was noted by Dr Walter, the technology could be used for driving super-heavy tanks. It appeared that the Russians had encouraged the plant's staff by allowing them freedom to carry out their research without political interference. In particular, they did not care about the Nazi past of the research staff and technicians, deflecting criticism by the German Communist Party who felt their earlier tormentors should not be rewarded. This lack of concern for the political past of the scientists was something that tempted many Germans with dubious backgrounds into employment in the Soviet zone.

Of course, Russia was not the only power willing to ignore the Nazi background of a scientist as long as he was prepared to work for them. Most famously, the US faced criticism for its employment of Wernher von Braun, whose V1 and V2 production had relied on slave labour. Many more dedicated Nazis had been transferred to the US to continue their research, their crimes deliberately concealed from the American public. Though on a smaller scale, the British also gave employment to other Nazi scientists, as well as Dr Walter, despite the teams interrogating them noting that 'there is abundant evidence that the mentality of these scientists remains martial to a degree, even when they are not unrepentant Nazis'.[4]

The connection between the T-Force/30AU operations and Fleming's Bond novels is further revealed in *Thunderball* (1961). In the novel a rogue group steals nuclear warheads and attempts to hold the world to ransom. The theft of the bombs is carried out through the activities of an Italian pilot who was revealed to have been involved with handing over developmental aircraft to the Allies during the war in Italy. Of course, Fleming's 30AU were active in Italy during the war – searching for intelligence targets such as experimental aircraft. Furthermore, the group travels in a high-speed hydrofoil, the nose of which raises out of the water as it gathers speed. Once again, this provides a direct link to Commander Aylen's 1945 report on the designs under development at Walterwerke. Included in the report was the Tietjens boat, a hydrofoil carrying one ton of explosive. Photographs of the hydrofoil, rising from the sea to ride across the waves, were included in the report that passed to the Directorate of Naval Intelligence – and therefore Fleming – in 1945.

More direct links were revealed in the 1966 short story, 'Octopussy'. The character of Dexter Smythe is revealed as having been a Royal Marine attached to a unit named the 'Miscellaneous Objectives Bureau' or 'MOB Force'. This unit is shown, just like the real 30AU, to be under the command of the Combined Operations HQ and to have been involved in intelligence-gathering, escorting specialists into their targets. The targets include locating confidential reports and information on concealed weapons dumps. Just like the real 30AU or T-Force, the fictional 'MOB Force' is organized in small detachments operating independently all over Germany. Furthermore, 'MOB Force' receives its target intelligence from a variety of sources, reflecting the role of CIOS to collect the information that had guided both 30AU and T-Force.

'Octopussy' specifically reflects Fleming's own involvement in 30AU's capture of the records of the German navy at Schloss Tambach. In the months immediately following the end of hostilities the Director of Naval Intelligence had appointed Fleming to oversee the examination and investigation of these records.

There were other connections to be made. As some in 30AU recalled, the unit's main link with the Admiralty was through Margaret Priestley, a female member of the Admiralty staff who worked in Room 30, which had given 30AU its name. It was she who handled documents arriving from the continent and passed on those deemed necessary to be seen by Fleming. However, in latter years she made it clear that she had no intention of allowing her personal role to be highlighted by, or indeed known to, any researchers. When one writer prepared a manuscript on the history of 30AU she insisted that all references to her should be deleted. Her request was complied with. However, her name was revealed in the book, *Attain By Surprise: Capturing Top Secret Intelligence in WWII*, written by David C. Nutting (published by David Colver, 2003), a former member of 30AU.

It is not clear why Margaret Priestley remained so guarded about her role. One possible explanation was that her connection with Fleming and the Admiralty might have resulted in her being seen as the inspiration for Miss Moneypenny. As the link between the active unit and Ian Fleming, her position reflected the literary one between Bond and his senior commander, 'M'. Furthermore, her name shares some similarity with 'Moneypenny'. Furthermore, in 'Octopussy' one of the female staff at 'MOB Force' HQ is called Mary Parnell, a name that also may have been derived from Margaret Priestley's initials. Whether this was her reasoning, or simply that she had no desire to be the subject of speculation, remains uncertain since her thoughts died with her.

The secrecy surrounding the operations carried out by 30AU resulted in a glamorous veneer covering their work. Later historians, unable to discover all the facts about what was one of the most secretive British units of the Second World War, have overplayed elements of the unit's activities. As one writer noted: 'They were the James Bond characters who would locate the secret base – the German HQ – attack it, arrest the information from it and stop the world being blown up by a madman.'[5] Such claims are exaggerated, perhaps reflecting Fleming's desire for the way that 30AU should be used rather than its real operational methods. In Germany, 30AU was never involved in the type of serious fighting characterized by such commando operations as the raid on St Nazaire. Their activities in Normandy, though undoubtedly daring, did not involve the losses experienced by the average infantry battalion. Their work was exciting and essential. It was carried out with considerable initiative and was highly effective, resulting in vast amounts of intelligence being collected for use by the Allies – both on the battlefield and for future development projects. But they were never an assault unit and – like the rest of T-Force – their operations within Germany were always tempered by their primary duty: to collect intelligence and pass it to the correct authorities.

In later years it was revealed that one of the inspirations for James Bond was Patrick Dalzel-Job, who had played a leading role in 30AU's wartime activities. An expert skier, a keen yachtsman and linguist, he was active in undercover operations in Norway – Commander Bond is revealed to have earned his '00' prefix by carrying out the assassination of a Norwegian Nazi. Just as Bond is often seen as Fleming's alter-ego, Dalzel-Job was the active commando officer carrying out the type of operations that Fleming longed to take part in, but was prevented from undertaking due to the importance of his role at the Admiralty.

Others have seen potential inspiration for Bond in Patrick Dalzel-Job's fellow officers in 30AU, including the heroic Dunstan Curtis, while Reg Rush has suggested the former commander of B Troop, Lt Commander Jim 'Sancho' Glanville. He was the officer who carried the 'black books' containing target lists, as Reg Rush remembered: 'He was a knowledgeable fellow. He had as big a part as anybody. The senior officers were great, but "Sancho" was at the "sharp end". He was feeding intelligence back to the senior commanders. He was a wonderful character.'

The connection between 30AU, in particular Dalzel-Job, and Fleming's creation of James Bond resulted in earning the Royal Marines a strong reputation. They were not forgotten like their counterparts in T-Force. What little was written about T-Force was not always accurate. When Dalzel-Job came to write his memoirs he was less than complimentary about T-Force. He claimed 30AU had been hampered by its relationship with T-Force, failing to understand that he himself was effectively part of the unit he was criticizing. John Bradley – the metallurgist who took part in the Kiel operation – always referred to T-Force in his letters to his family. This was despite the fact that he was part of the Royal Navy detachment and worked with 30AU, travelling into Köln with Dalzel-Job. His personal records reveal his involvement with the overall organization rather than the specific wing.

Despite the criticisms Dalzel-Job made of T-Force, it is useful to compare operations carried out by the two units. Tom Pitt-Pladdy's T-Force assault on the farmhouse at Bomlitz was a feat of arms comparable to 30AU operations carried out by Dalzel-Job during this period. In similar circumstances Dalzel-Job's men had attacked a farm occupied by German officer cadets. His men had dismounted their vehicles and assaulted the farm, killing one German and capturing 13 others. Dalzel-Job later recounted how the Germans felt they had been captured honourably by commandos. In that incident the assaulting force had been a unit of highly trained commandos – all volunteers – backed up by armoured cars. At Bomlitz the assaulting troops had been medically downgraded infantrymen, led by a former artillery officer. The two incidents were virtually the same, yet the commander of one assault later dismissed the other force as looters who methods were too slow to have any effect. The defeated German marines at Bomlitz would hardly have agreed with this criticism.

Instead of praising the work of T-Force, Dalzel-Job wrote: 'It was indeed quite satisfied to enter its targets behind the first troops, and its function was to look after whatever documents and material remained at that stage, rather than attempting to forestall removal or destruction. In practice, T-Force usually arrived too late to do much good, and (like most non-fighting soldiers) their guard-troops were often more interested in private looting than in securing enemy intelligence.'[6] When Dalzel-Job wrote of the fall of Bremen he noted that his own detachment had shaken off the 'retarding influence' of T-Force to enter the city centre. Yet in reality, as the marines moved into the city centre, T-Force was already at its target, Bremen's main post office, while under persistent sniper fire.

The frustration felt by members of 30AU was probably a result of the changing role they had been allotted in Germany. They were no longer free agents, allowed to roam wherever they liked acting on behalf on the Royal Navy. Instead, they were part of a formalized establishment to ensure the fair distribution of military intelligence – in all its forms – between the British and Americans. Moreover, their new masters had insisted that '30 Advanced Unit combat personnel will not be allowed to operate as a combat element of T-Forces.'[7] As documents prepared for an official history of the unit put it:

> The operations of 30AU were hampered during this period by a number of competing organizations, mostly of an inter-service nature, and composed mainly of non-combatant troops, which tended to generally slow up and generally impede the movements of 30AU. It was further found that the large inter-service organizations set up to handle intelligence targets were slow and cumbersome compared with the small and workmanlike unit consisting of properly trained men, and on this account were not very successful.[8]

If these words were intended as a criticism of T-Force they were unfair.

30AU's official history records that:

> The Army (British and Allied) counterpart of 30AU were termed 'T' Forces. The essential difference between 'T' Forces and

30AU was that the former expected to be called forward when a target had been secured while, on the other hand, 30AU were prepared to fight to get at their targets as early as possible . . . the cooperation and coordination of the 'T-Forces' and 30AU were not always entirely easy, especially as 30AU's desire to press forward to their target was frequently misunderstood as lack of desire to cooperate fully with T-Forces.[9]

Although the report went on to describe the two units as having an amicable relationship, these words are unfair. It suggests that T-Force was unprepared to fight for its targets, ignoring the point that 30AU itself did not have to fight for its targets in Germany. Just like the rest of T-Force, it encountered obstacles that prevented its advance to certain locations but – like T-Force – it did not have to attack individual targets. When called upon, though, T-Force carried out its active duties, such as at Bremen under sniper fire and when it entered Kiel, shoulder-to-shoulder with 30AU. Indeed, had it not been for the efforts of Tony Hibbert as the commander of 'T-Force Kiel', clearance would not have been forthcoming for the advance to the city. Thus, without his role, the Admiralty might have lost the intelligence that was uncovered at Walterwerke and other targets.

Of course, the rivalry was not one way. Members of the infantry element of T-Force were also critical of their marine counterparts. As one officer later recounted:

30AU were 'prima donnas', they always behaved with a certain élan . . . When these sailors, the 'senior service', took to dry land, they felt they had to show they were brighter and better than the 'brown jobs' alongside whom they worked, and felt themselves to be in competition with. They were particularly riled when T-Force took certain of the naval targets, in Kiel and elsewhere, before they did, and had to bad mouth them in their own defence.

It is natural for all the soldiers and sailors to have remained proud of their own regiment and its role, but the criticism of T-Force seems unfair; 30AU was not hampered by transport shortages, nor were any of their men transferred to the unit after suffering from shellshock or wounds that made them unsuitable for frontline service. Any criticism that they were lesser fighting men than the marines is unjustifiable. After all, so many of the Kingsmen – such as Vic Woods and Bob Brighouse – were veterans of D-Day, having landed in the first waves. Then there was Ron Lawton, who had been a Royal Marine himself back on D-Day, taking landing craft on to the Normandy beaches. Others like Ken Moore and Tom Pitt-Pladdy had manned artillery positions throughout the Normandy campaign, with Pitt-Pladdy serving in the frontlines as an artillery observer. Similarly, John Longfield had fought in Normandy as a Bren gunner, witnessing death on a daily basis, and Ken Hardy had led an infantry platoon for seven months before finally succumbing to battle exhaustion. In one day in the summer of 1944 he had seen half his platoon killed or wounded in less than an hour. Leading T-Force into Kiel was Tony Hibbert who had first fought in France in 1940, and then won the Military Cross at Arnhem Bridge four years later.

Many among T-Force had probably seen as much action as the Royal Marines since D-Day. Add to the equation the bomb disposal engineers whose role in T-Force had been so vital. What of their perilous experiences? Day after day, week upon week, for five years, they disarmed bombs, mines and booby-traps. Should they be regarded less highly than the Royal Marines? Were these the 'non-combatants' described in the history of 30AU? For Tom Pitt-Pladdy it was always important that the Pioneers working in T-Force should also be recognized for their contribution. As he recalled: 'They were "unflappable" – they were old soldiers who were unfazed by either danger or hard work.' As Kingsman Jack Twining-Davies later wrote:

'I personally took great offence at our "secret army" being described as looters by an ex-Royal Naval officer, who emphasized his own heroism, while overlooking the veterans amongst us of Dunkirk, Norway, the Western Desert, Italy and many other places, including Normandy.' To treat these as lesser soldiers than the Royal Marines of 30AU was unjustifiable. After all, what mattered most was that, in April and May 1945, they had carried out their duties as ordered, had surpassed expectations and succeeded in their mission. Surely, that was the mark of a soldier and worthy of praise.

Regardless of arguments over whether the men of T-Force were 'real soldiers', one thing was certain. Their work, both in wartime and after, played a vital role in the postwar economic recovery of the UK and in its long-term military security. In particular, the organization was central to the UK's reparations programme. What is most difficult to calculate is the financial value of the materials evacuated from Germany both as reparations and as 'booty'. Such is the paucity of study on the subject of British postwar economic and military exploitation of German industry that even those with a deep understanding of the economic aspects of the programme have failed to grasp the depth of effort made in the final days of war and early days of peace.

In a 1997 article for the *Journal of Contemporary History*, John Farquharson – an academic expert in British reparations policy – stated that 'It is a fairly well known fact that for various reasons the western Allies failed to extract very much in the way of tangible gains in their reparations programme.'[10] Despite the depth of his research, Farquharson made one simple error: he put the date of T-Force's creation as July 1945, a full four months after the unit became operational within Germany. It was as if its entire wartime role was forgotten and the connections between the collection of 'booty' and the acquisition of reparations were missed. However, he made the important assessment of T-Force's role that 'no one really knows how much industrial equipment fell under the heading of booty'. He further noted that, quite simply, before January 1946 no one had kept records of the value of what T-Force had evacuated from Germany.

He was right. When the value of reparations was calculated, it did not include items that should not have been classed as 'war booty' but which nonetheless had been acquired by T-Force and sent back to the UK in the early operational phase. For example, when Tom Pitt-Pladdy ensured the cooperation of a German factory owner by poking the barrel of an anti-tank gun through the man's window, it had not just been research information that the detachment had found. In the cellars a large quantity of ball and roller bearings had been discovered. These were essentially civilian items that should have been classed as reparations rather than booty. However, the bearings were swiftly crated and sent back to the UK for the use in domestic industry during a period when no one was calculating the value of reparations.

The nature of the technical equipment also defied valuation. As one meeting in January 1946 concluded: 'in some cases of highly specialized equipment, valuation in money may be difficult or impossible'.[11] Furthermore, taking scientists to the UK for interrogation was described by one researcher as 'hidden reparations'.[12] It was a fair description. It remains impossible to quantify the fruits of their knowledge, meaning that any advantage gained could not be offset against the total sum allowed for reparations to the UK.

In his study of the UK's role in acquiring 'booty' and reparations from Germany Farquharson wrote, 'it is difficult to find a time when reparations or booty was granted precedence in the UK zone'. Again, his assessment missed the period in the final weeks of war in which T-Force had a virtually free role to go where it wanted, securing whatever facilities it desired and detaining any scientists it needed. In the final days of the Second World War even the 'Stop Order' issued by General Dempsey, the commander of the British 2nd Army, could not prevent T-Force from advancing on Kiel.

By spring 1947 the British admitted that BIOS had registered some 70,000 patents in London, all of which had come from original German scientific and technical research. When the work of BIOS came to an end in July that year it was revealed that between 3,000 and 4,000 investigation teams had been despatched to Germany, carrying out more 12,000 investigations. From this around 2,000 reports had been published by HMSO. In just one year, nearly 20,000 summaries of investigations had been distributed in the UK to official bodies and trade associations. Furthermore, more than 200 German scientists had been interrogated in the UK following evacuation by T-Force. What value could be put on the fruits of these interrogations? In the postwar period vast amounts of BIOS reports were published while a touring exhibition was used to publicize what had become available from German sources. Advertisements were taken out, posters distributed and circulars despatched to firms likely to be interested in the available technical information.

While the long-term economic value of technical information cannot be calculated, there exist certain estimations for the value of equipment removed from Germany. One set of final figures for the value of 'booty' gives the low figure of £85,000. Such a figure cannot accurately reflect the physical value of the numerous submarines, tanks and aircraft that were located and delivered to the UK by T-Force. Add to that the construction price of the V2 rockets located for Operation Backfire and one can safely see that the figure belies the truth. In reality, 'booty' was impossible to put a price on. Indeed, in 1945, a CIOS report put the value of German radar equipment evacuated by the British and American T-Forces as totalling £1 billion.[13]

Similarly, the figure for official reparations is also difficult to calculate. The UK's receipts total for official reparations was just over £30 million. However, this figure does not reflect the values that were calculated at the time. As previously noted, a *Daily Express* journalist put forward a possible value of £100 million. This figure had been mentioned to someone in authority within Germany who admitted it was as good a figure as any. The long-term value of all the information, distributed by HMSO following the BIOS investigations, must have made a significant impact on postwar exports, as British firms became capable of matching the techniques developed by their German rivals.

In September 1947, a document was sent to BIOS to show the importance of T-Force's work. This information was then passed on to Brigadier Grylls at T-Force HQ to express thanks for the unit's work. It revealed that the British fabric manufacturer Courtaulds was in the process of constructing a factory copied from the IG Farben plant at Dormagen, but the Courtaulds facility would be five times the size. Similarly, another British company had reported signing a contract to the value of £400,000, based on information gained from German industry. It was reported that technology acquired from Germany for use in the production of rayon would result in British fabric manufacturers being able to compete favourably with its foreign competitors.

The question of the financial gains resulting from T-Force's work has long fascinated Michael Howard. As a central figure in the postwar evacuations he wanted to find out what his work had meant for the UK. He made his first tentative enquires not long after being demobbed from the army. In 1949, accompanied by his former T-Force comrade Tony Lucas, Michael Howard drove through Germany on holiday to attend a music festival in Salzburg. On the return journey he visited the last remnants of No.1 T-Force. At this point his former comrades were in the process of cataloguing and valuing all the items that had been evacuated since commencing operations in spring 1946. The figure given to Michael Howard was £2 billion. He felt it sounded astronomical – in today's money he later calculated that it would amount to £80 billion. He was also uncertain of how his former colleagues, and the accountants that were working with them, had been able to make the calculations: 'What value do you place on a prototype machine or a new process for deriving gasoline from lignite?' However, he further noted that later writers had claimed the Russians removed equipment to the value of £20 billion from Germany and that the British had taken equipment to the value of one-tenth of the Russian haul. That would result in a figure of £2 billion. Whatever the accuracy of these figures, it was clear that the real value of reparations and booty acquired by the British from Germany far exceeded the official figures.

Some assessments of the exploitation of German scientists have been negative, pointing out how the Allies – in particular the Americans – lost the moral high ground as a result of employing men who had been so inextricably linked to the atrocities carried out by the Nazi regime. Other assessments have been more balanced, such as those made by John Gimbel, the notable American expert on postwar Germany. He found that American exploitation of German personnel and technical know-how resulted in the creation of an extensive network of scientific, business and industrial cooperation between the two former enemies. Gimbel's research showed that former FIAT investigators acknowledged the very real benefits they gained from contacts in Germany once they returned to their businesses in the US. The argument was that this provided the bedrock upon which the success of the Marshall Plan and Germany's postwar economic regeneration was built. Some Americans working in reparations even made the claim that by removing research information from plants it would benefit German industry by stimulating fresh research. Despite these claims, some German firms reported holding back from fresh research for fear of losing it to their competitors around the world.

From his research, Gimbel concluded that Allied scientists from all areas of industry had been exposed to the successes of German industry. Once these men had completed their war work they returned to their former employers with a detailed understanding of research that had been carried out in Germany. This encouraged them to both exploit the research carried out by their former enemies but also to work with German firms to market the wealth of knowledge they had uncovered. Most importantly, the Americans had reported major technical advances found within Germany, both in military and civilian products. They had discovered wind tunnels far superior to those in use in the US, textiles that were unmatched by the output of American mills and revolutionary sound recording devices that set the standards for the years ahead.[14]

While detailed analysis of the impact of the reparations schemes remains important, one T-Force veteran summed up how the effect of reparations and the British removal of German equipment influenced postwar economic development. For Tony Lucas it was clear that the real benefit of reparations was gained by Germany rather than the UK. He felt that, in the 1950s, Germany had one great advantage. Yes, they had their secrets 'sucked dry' by the British, with their industrial plants emptied and their plans and blueprints removed, but this gave the German scientists and researchers something new to focus on:

> They had lost the prototypes they had been working on. We had taken the blueprints for their work. The parts had been sold. When you have lost your best machines to your commercial and industrial rivals, you sit down and design the next

generation of machinery. Which is what gave Germany an advantage in the 1950s, because their intellectual property was handed over to exhausted British businessman who said 'By God, that's marvellous. Thank God we can copy it.' Not realizing that the Germans were saying 'Right, we've lost that. We'd better get on with designing the next machine.' They moved the next step forward.

There was another strong argument to support the importance of T-Force's role in the postwar economic success of West Germany. During 1945 T-Force had been detailed to enter areas of Germany soon to be handed over to the Soviet Union, areas that would eventually form part of East Germany. These areas were stripped clear of both military research equipment and industrial materials. More importantly, hundreds of scientists and technicians were removed westwards. This became a vast pool of scientific and intellectual talent that would be essential in the redevelopment of West Germany. Effectively, by denuding East Germany of some of its most talented researchers, T-Force and its American equivalent ensured West Germany maintained an advantage over its neighbour in the years ahead.

For one T-Force veteran there was another question that occupied his mind. For Tony Hibbert the controversy surrounding his advance on Kiel continued to fascinate him. After all, his actions had resulted in him spending VE Day under open arrest. While most of the emphasis had been placed on the need to secure the Walterwerke and similar research facilities, Hibbert remained convinced T-Force's role had been far more important. He believed that the orders that had resulted in his arrest on VE Day had not been a result of a misunderstanding, as claimed by some unit historians. Instead, he was convinced that he had been appointed to command the operation to help cut off any Russian advance on Denmark. Why else would such a risk be taken? He recalled:

> When you think of it, it was just bloody stupid. Why risk it? You could say, if you give the Germans too much time they will destroy everything. But we were risking a lot of key people. We had scientists and experts in all sorts of fields. To bung them through the German lines when the Germans were still fighting, doesn't make sense. It still doesn't. But we did it, and it worked. If I'd waited for the duty officer to give me permission the column would have run straight into the SS. But on paper, it was a stupid order.

The fact that he had never received any written orders only served to underline the sensitive nature of this operation. History has recorded that the advance of the 6th Airborne Division to Wismar ended the Russian advance towards Denmark. However, Hibbert was unconvinced and started to examine the reasons for the unrecorded orders for his advance on Kiel. What he uncovered made him even more certain his orders had been genuine. It seemed that commando raids by the Russians to seize naval intelligence and research materials were believed to be imminent.

In latter years, the more he delved into the situation – speaking to veterans from the ships that had sailed for Copenhagen, his former comrades in the upper echelons of T-Force and the paratroopers who had taken part in the Wismar operation – the more it appeared clear that the Russian intention had been to seize at least the Kiel canal, and at most the entirety of Denmark. It became obvious to Hibbert that the British occupation of Wismar had not been considered to be the end of the Russian threat. Rather, by cutting off the immediate thrust of the Russian advance, the 6th Airborne Division bought the British time to consolidate in the north.

And seizing Kiel was part of that consolidation. At the Supreme Commanders HQ there remained serious concerns about the future of Denmark and northern Germany. Theories about the Russian intentions abounded. If they seized Kiel and the canal, would they be used as a bargaining tool to get a grip on Denmark? Conversely, with the Russians in Denmark, would they only relinquish control on the condition that they receive free access to the Baltic via the Kiel canal? The options, it seemed, were endless.

To learn more, Hibbert travelled to Denmark and soon realized how deeply the civilians had feared – and expected – occupation by the Red Army. Many had even begun studying Russian, in particular learning to say phrases like 'Please don't hurt my daughter.' The strongest indication of Moscow's plans Hibbert could discover was the occupation of the Danish island of Bornholm on 9 May 1945. The most likely intention of the occupation was shown in Foreign Office documents of 1946 revealing a conversation between the first UN Secretary General, the Norwegian Trygve Lie, and a Foreign Office employee. After his meeting with the Soviet UN delegation, Lie believed that the Russians would leave Bornholm only when the question of access to the Kiel canal and Baltic Sea had been resolved. In later years Hibbert travelled to Bornholm and spoke to the locals about the intentions and behaviour of the Russians who had occupied the island for 18 months.

Above all else, Hibbert recalled the verbal orders from his friend Brian Urquhart who had informed him of the very real Russian threat, both on the ground and from the sea. Whatever the history books might now say, Hibbert had been told that the Allies had intercepted signals stating the Russian intentions. It was also clear to Hibbert that the Russians preferred the idea of holding Denmark and linking it to its possessions in Eastern Europe via Schleswig-Holstein. Thus Wismar, Lübeck and Kiel were vital to the Russians to keep a land route open. To this

day, Hibbert remains convinced that the threat was genuine
and that failing to stop the Russian advance would have
changed history.

T-Force's work to acquire technical information for military use
was perhaps the most vital of all the organization's roles. In
many areas, Germany had been at the very forefront of military development during the Second World War. In 1945
CIOS issued a report detailing the research uncovered by
T-Force that it considered to be of significant interest. In the
field of weapons manufacture the report noted: 'The capture of
practically all the German experimental firing range records is
expected to provide data of the highest importance and will
greatly assist weapon and projectile research in the United
Kingdom and in the United States.' The rockets and guided
missiles seized for investigation were also perceived to be of
vital importance: 'The despatch of large numbers of completed
V weapons for shipment to development centres in the United
Kingdom and in the United States will greatly assist in research
in this type of weapon.'[15]

Other areas in which CIOS determined that significant
advances had been made were jet propulsion, aerodynamics,
the production of synthetic fuel and rubber, and chemical warfare, reporting: 'the discovery of new war gases which have
proven more lethal than any chemical warfare agents hitherto
known'.

In August 1945, the Admiralty reported that a series of submarine technical 'handbooks' captured by 30AU at Bremen
had been vital in understanding the operation of Type XXI
U-boats. Without these books, the U-boats themselves were
deemed worthless. These books were estimated to have a value
of £1 million because of the time and effort they saved.
Otherwise experts would have spent vast resources recreating
the books by dismantling entire craft and studying them down

to the final rivet. Without the books it would have been impossible for the UK or US navies to carry out sea trials.

Even in fields where German technology was inferior to that used by the Allies, research materials uncovered by T-Force were still deemed to be of vital importance. Although German radar equipment was less well developed than that in use by the western Allies, CIOS concluded that the discovery of a marine archive warehouse, containing documents relating to German naval radar, was invaluable. Furthermore, the radar equipment retrieved from Germany was estimated at having a monetary value of $1 billion. This indicated that it was not only the technical advances made by researchers that were important, but that all research needed to be examined. If the Germans had attempted to develop a new system that resulted in failure, it highlighted areas that the British and Americans no longer needed to examine. In itself, such information could save thousands of hours of research and development time.

That said, German radar research did actually play a major part in the development of the radar systems later used by the US. The system in question was the 'Wullenweber', a circular antenna system used to triangulate radio signals. The system was developed by the German navy. An example of the apparatus – with 40 vertical elements built in the arc of a 120-metre-diameter (394-foot) circle – was operated from Skisby in Denmark. Escorted to the facility by T-Force teams, British experts in radar examined the Wullenweber equipment, taking notes on the operational system. The equipment was then destroyed. However, that was not the end of the Wullenweber. Using technical information gained from the analysis of the equipment and following the 'exploitation' of the team responsible for its design, the US military developed its own version of the system. This was the FLR-9. Installed in nine sites worldwide, the FLR-9 formed the backbone of 'Iron Horse', the American's worldwide network of early warning radar systems. Throughout the Cold War this was used to keep the western powers informed of all movements through the skies around the world.

The technological advances seized by T-Force continued to have an impact long after its soldiers had been demobbed and returned to 'civvy street' to settle down and raise families. Most notably, Wernher von Braun, the designer of the V1 and V2 rockets, whose transit to the UK for interrogation had been facilitated through T-Force, became world famous for his role in the American space programme. The rocket samples, blueprints and fuel samples seized by T-Force and 30AU and then sent to the UK and the US for further development were also vital for postwar missile development. The 'Waterfall' rocket, which had been designed in Germany for anti-aircraft use, played a significant role in future American projects, leading directly to the development of the American Hermes-A1 missile.

The significance of the developments in German aviation research that were studied by the British in the aftermath of war were not lost on Captain Eric Brown. As Britain's foremost test pilot of the postwar years he was closely connected with aviation research. He had been responsible for bringing back 26 aircraft researchers to the UK where they worked for a year, with two of them remaining in permanent positions. As Brown recalled, the British wartime jet – the Gloucester Meteor – seemed pedestrian by comparison to the Me 262 and other German experimental craft. Brown was unequivocal in his judgement that the whole of British postwar aviation research was copied from the Germans. In particular, Brown noted that the British DH108 and GAL/56 (a tailless swept-wing experimental glider), the Russian MIG15 and the American F86 Sabre all owed their origins to wartime German research.

One particular incident stuck in Captain Brown's mind. In the autumn of 1947 he attended a meeting at which the idea of designing a supersonic airliner was first discussed. In attendance was Dr Karl Doetsch, a German aerodynamicist and test pilot, and Dr Dietrich Küchemann, a German expert in wind tunnels. Both were former employees at the German aviation research plant at Völkenrode, which had been occupied by T-Force in 1945. Dr Küchemann made a vital contribution to the meeting, explaining that the best wing configuration for such an aircraft would be a slender delta wing. As Captain Brown noted, this led to the development of the delta-winged HP115 and eventually to the creation of Concorde, the world's first supersonic passenger jet.

In 1956 the Royal Navy launched its new submarine, HMS *Explorer*, followed in 1958 by HMS *Excalibur*. These hydrogen peroxide-powered submarines were the latest examples of the wartime research carried out at Kiel by Hellmuth Walter. This was the culmination of ten years of research at the Armstrong-Vickers shipyards at Barrow-in-Furness. Even after a decade of hard work, the Explorer-class submarines were still not ready for service. The 'Walter' engines were fitted into the hulls of 'Porpoise' class submarines with a modified superstructure to improve their streamlining. The first of the two craft was little more than a test submarine that was used to help prepare for the later launch of HMS *Excalibur*. In trials HMS *Excalibur* was initially a success. It achieved the impressive speed of 25 knots submerged – the same speed that was believed to have been achieved by the U-boats originally produced by Professor Walter for the Kriegsmarine.

By this time Walter was no longer working with the British. He returned to Germany in 1948 where he had formed the Paul Seifert Engine Works. Then in 1950, taking advantage of the job offers that were made to so many of the most notable Nazi scientists, he emigrated to the United States, joining the Worthington Corporation in Harrison, New Jersey.

The initial results made the submarine highly prized for assisting the Royal Navy on training exercises in which surface

ships searched for fast-moving submerged targets. At first, the
new submarines had been nicknamed 'Blonde Class' as a result
of the fact that hydrogen peroxide was most famously used as
hair dye. The second nickname they acquired was more worrying. The highly unstable fuel was unpredictable, causing a
number of explosions. His led to the nickname of 'Exploder
Class' becoming attached to the submarines. Despite the years
of research, there were just too many accidents caused by the
fuel. An accident with a hydrogen peroxide-powered torpedo –
known as a 'Fancy' – caused the loss of HMS *Sidon* in 1955.
Twelve submariners died and seven were seriously injured in
the incident.

Although the dangerous nature of hydrogen peroxide led to
its abandonment as a submarine fuel, experiments with 'air-
independent propulsion' – first explored in the shipyards of
Germany in the early twentieth century – have continued with
liquid oxygen replacing the original fuel.

Other pieces of technology developed from equipment
uncovered by T-Force continue to appear from the design
boards of the military. In 1998 the United States military
announced the development of a new weapon that could fire
around corners – an updated version of the German weapon
that T-Force first acquired 53 years earlier.

Perhaps the story of Britain's 'Target-Force' might have been
completely forgotten had it not been for the efforts of one
man. Ken Moore, a veteran of Normandy with the Royal
Artillery, who – like so many of his colleagues – had been
transferred into the infantry in the winter of 1944, never forgot his time with the 5th King's Regiment. In the postwar
period he had been the editor of the unit's newsletter, *Freelance*,
which had been the only source of regimental information for
the men whose detachments were spread across northern
Germany. In the 1990s, Moore decided to attempt to relaunch

his publication as a newsletter for the veterans of the 5th King's, who he had assembled to form an Old Comrades Association. He has long remained convinced of the importance of the work carried out by him and his comrades: 'Infra-red rays? What the hell was that? Science wasn't as well developed in those days. Reel-to-reel tape recorders were amazing, they were one of the things we found. They were incredible – the "Blackberry" of their day! Now you might think anything of it – but back in 1945 they were "state of the art".'

In 2006 the author joined a party from the 5th King's Regiment as they returned to Kiel. Still every bit the 'old soldiers', they took up residence at a British mess based within a German military base – old enmities are clearly forgotten. It seemed odd to see Tony Hibbert, nearly 90 years old, walking through the busy streets where 61 years earlier he had been in complete control. Upon visiting the Naval Academy, Major Hibbert was interviewed by a local film crew. He posed on the very same steps from where Kapitan Möhr had greeted him by pointing a machine-pistol towards him. T-Force's legacy was plain for all to see. Somewhat appropriately for the men who had helped restore democracy to Kiel and the surrounding area, the steps are now within the chamber of the parliament of the federal state of Schleswig-Holstein.

By day the veterans of T-Force spent their time with their local hosts, visiting old bases in Denmark and northern Germany and laying wreaths in memory of the wartime dead, regardless of nationality. By night they congregated in the bar of the British Army's yacht club. Moored outside the window was a yacht that had formerly belonged to Hermann Göring. The boat was a permanent symbolic reminder of T-Force's role in dismantling the Nazi regime – it had been seized by the British in 1945 and has remained in the army's possession ever since.

What of the T-Force targets now? As Jean Hughes-Gibb recalled, the work of T-Force was important in that it was morally correct for Germany to pay the price of its aggression: 'We knew that we were helping in a way that was unique. It was a measure of compensation for all the horrors and suffering of the war. Compensation was probably a better word than reparations. It was to make the Germans put something back.'

Some of the technical equipment acquired through the reparations programme remained in use for many years. One engineer recalled collecting German lathes for use at his workplace during the 1950s. The lathes in question, found in a vast store of reparations equipment, were far in advance of anything available to him in the UK and could be operated without the hours of recalibration usually needed on British equivalents. A large amount of German equipment ended up in use at the College of Aeronautics at Cranfield, later to become the Cranfield Institute of Technology, and now Cranfield University. Based on a Second World War RAF airbase that had become a test-pilot training centre, the facility became a leading aviation research and development centre in the postwar years. Throughout those years, German equipment, acquired through reparations, was widely available for use by engineers employed there. Only at the close of the twentieth century did they finally get rid of some of the German equipment that had arrived in the postwar years. How can any estimate be put on the value of equipment that remained in use for so many years?

However, for the veterans of T-Force, it was the disarmament of Germany and rebuilding of western military power to counter the Soviet threat that was T-Force's lasting legacy. They were right. Germany no longer presents the military threat it once did. Even the Soviet threat has now gone, to be replaced by a new menace in the form of terrorism – a conflict in which the enemy does not wear uniforms or advertise its existence to the West. For the veterans of T-Force, this is not their fight – their job was to save technology and intelligence for Britain and its allies to use in the Cold War that gripped the world for nearly 50 years. Those years of peace were their epitaph. It was with a knowing sense of irony that a detachment of T-Force veterans returned to Kiel in 1997. They visited the Walterwerke factory – the descendent of the wartime H. Walter Kommanitgesellschaft, once the producer of the world's most advanced submarine propulsion systems – and discovered its fate. It was no longer at the cutting edge of military technology; instead, the factory was producing machinery for manufacturing ice-cream cornets and wafers. Revenge is sweet.

Perhaps the final words should come from T-Force liaison officer Major Brian Urquhart, who would rise to become the Deputy Secretary-General of the United Nations. In June 1945 he wrote a report on T-Force. His words summed up everything the veterans of T-Force continue to feel about their work: 'It is to be hoped that all the energy and skill expended by so many people in these last three months may make some contribution both to the shortening of the present war and the prevention of wars in the future.'[16]

Notes

Chapter 1: The Birth of an Idea

1. Lt Colonel R.D. Bloomfield, quoted in *The T-Force Story*, 5th King's/No.2 T-Force Old Comrades Association.
2. National Archives ADM 223/500.
3. Ibid.
4. National Archives DEFE2/1107.
5. National Archives ADM223/500.
6. Ibid.
7. Ibid.
8. Ibid.
9. National Archives WO204/795.
10. Ibid.
11. National Archives FO935/20.
12. National Archives DEFE2/1107.

Chapter 2: Normandy and Beyond

1. 'The Ways of a Kingsman', unpublished memoir by Ken Davenport.
2. National Archives ADM223/500.
3. National Archives WO171/1317.
4. *From Arctic Snow to Dust of Normandy*, Patrick Dalzel-Job, Sutton,1991.
5. National Archives ADM223/500.
6. Ibid.
7. Ibid.
8. National Archives WO171/742.
9. National Archives WO219/551.
10. Ibid.
11. Ibid.

Chapter 3: The Birth of T-Force

1. *The T-Force Story*.
2. National Archives DEFE2/1107.
3. National Archives ADM223/500.

4. Ibid.
5. National Archives FO935/20.
6. National Archives FO1031/49.
7. *A Life in Peace and War* by Brian Urquhart, Harper Collins, 1987.
8. National Archives WO171/3865.
9. Ibid.
10. Lt Colonel R.D. Bloomfield, quoted in *The T-Force Story*.
11. National Archives WO219/818.
12. *The Kingsman*, regimental newsletter, 10 August 1944.
13. National Archives WO171/1316.
14. National Archives WO171/5161.
15. *The T-Force Story*.
16. Ibid.
17. Ibid.
18. Ibid.
19. Ibid.
20. Ibid.
21. National Archives WO171/5161.

Chapter 4: Operation Plunder and Beyond

1. National Archives WO171/5161.
2. Ibid.
3. National Archives WO205/1049.
4. *The T-Force Story*.
5. Ibid.
6. Ibid.
7. From an online biography of Jack Heslop-Harrison by Professor Brian Gunning, 2001.
8. *The T-Force Story*.
9. National Archives WO171/3865.
10. Ibid.
11. *The T-Force Story*.
12. Ibid.
13. National Archives WO219/1668.
14. National Archives HW8/104.
15. National Archives WO205/1049.
16. National Archives WO171/3865.
17. Les Goodwin quoted in *The T-Force Story*.
18. *The T-Force Story*.
19. National Archives WO171/5161.
20. *The T-Force Story*.

21. Ibid.
22. Interview with Ted Tolley, C Company, 5th Battalion, the King's Regiment.
23. *Arctic Snow to Dust of Normandy* by Patrick Dalzel-Job.
24. National Archives WO205/1049.
25. National Archives WO171/3865.

Chapter 5: To the Bitter End

1. *Rutland Mercury*, 22 August 1997.
2. National Archives WO171/5161.
3. Ibid.
4. Lecture, Royal Hospital, Chelsea, 25 November 2008.
5. *The T-Force Story.*
6. 'The Ways of a Kingsman' by Ken Davenport.
7. *The T-Force Story.*
8. National Archives WO208/2183.
9. National Archives WO171/3864.
10. *The T-Force Story.*
11. Ibid.
12. Ibid.
13. Ibid.

Chapter 6: Kiel – Into the Unknown

1. National Archives WO285/12.
2. *The T-Force Story.*
3. National Archives WO205/1049.
4. *The T-Force Story.*
5. Ibid.
6. *Kiel, May 1945: British Troops Occupy the German Naval City* by Renate Dopheide, Kiel City Archives, 2008. English translation by Margrete Thorsen-Moore.
7. National Archives WO205/1049.
8. The ship that Major Gaskell boarded was the *Monte Rosa*, a prewar liner that had been converted into a troop transporter and, later, a hospital ship, but had been badly damaged. She was in Kiel being used as a floating barracks. Vic Woods looked up and realized it was the very same ship he had seen in Wallasey Docks during the 1930s when his brother had asked him to accompany him to the ship in order to practise his German on the crew.
9. National Archives WO205/1049.
10. *The T-Force Story.*

11. *Kiel, May 1945: British Troops Occupy the German Naval City* by Renate Dopheide.
12. Ibid.
13. National Archives ADM223/500.
14. *The T-Force Story.*
15. The young marine Jurgen Hakker settled back into his home city, eventually becoming a doctor of literature. He had experienced an interesting war. As a teenager he was one of the so-called 'Swing Kids', German youths who expressed their anti-Nazi nature through their devotion to American jazz music and Americanized clothing. It was not an easy life for Kiel was a military town and the population seemed to be resolute supporters of the Nazi party. After the Allied bombing of Kiel, he was forced to join the Hitler Youth in Lübeck, but was able to continue some level of defiance by keeping his hair long enough to offend Nazi sensibilties.

Chapter 7: Liberators – T-Force in Denmark and the Netherlands

1. *Freelance*, the newsletter of the 5th King's/No.2 T-Force Old Comrades Association.
2. The Freedom Council of Denmark: The Local Committee of Haderslev. Quoted in *The T-Force Story.*
3. National Archives WO205/1049.
4. *Freelance.*
5. *The T-Force Story.*
6. Ibid.
7. Ibid.
8. Nederlandse Binnenlandse Strijdkrachten (Netherlands Forces of the Interior).
9. National Archives WO171/5161.
10. *The T-Force Story.*
11. National Archives WO171/5161.
12. *The T-Force Story.*

Chapter 8: Investigations

1. National Archives WO205/1049.
2. Ibid.
3. National Archives FO1032/205.
4. National Archives FO800/565.
5. Ibid.
6. Ibid.

7. Ibid.
8. National Archives WO171/3865.
9. National Archives WO171/3864.
10. Ibid.
11. National Archives FO1031/86.
12. National Archives WO208/2183.
13. National Archives WO208/2951.
14. National Archives WO188/2072.
15. National Archives WO189/2615.
16. National Archives FO1031/81.
17. National Archives FO1031/86.
18. National Archives WO171/3865.
19. National Archives ADM199/2434.
20. National Archives ADM178/392.
21. Lecture, Royal Hospital, Chelsea, 11 November 2008.
22. Ibid.
23. National Archives ADM199/2434.
24. Ibid.
25. National Archives ADM178/392.
26. Ibid.
27. Ibid.
28. Ibid.
29. Ibid.
30. Ibid.
31. National Archives WO219/5335.
32. *The T-Force Story*.
33. National Archives WO33/2554.

Chapter 9: Cold War

1. National Archives FO1031/67.
2. National Archives WO219/1003.
3. Quoted in 'Governed or Exploited? The British Acquisition of German Technology, 1945–48' by John Farquharson, *Journal of Contemporary History*, vol.32, 1997.
4. National Archives CAB121/430.
5. *The T-Force Story*.
6. Ibid.
7. Ibid.
8. National Archives FO1031/20.
9. National Archives FO1031/65.
10. Ibid.

11. Ibid.
12. National Archives FO1031/132.
13. Ibid.
14. Ibid.
15. *The T-Force Story*.
16. Ibid.
17. National Archives FO1031/75.
18. National Archives FO1031/5.
19. *The T-Force Story*.
20. Ibid.
21. Despite Tom Pitt-Pladdy's lack of regard for some in the 5th King's Regiment, he was highly complimentary towards Captain George Lambert, saying 'God Bless Him' for the care and attention he showed towards all the men of A Company.
22. National Archives WO171/3865.

Chapter 10: The Spoils of War

1. National Archives BT211/19.
2. National Archives FO1057/53 and 'Governed or Exploited? The British Acquisition of German Technology, 1945–48' by John Farquharson.
3. National Archives FO1034/33.
4. National Archives WO171/8633.
5. National Archives FO1031/67.
6. National Archives FO1031/1.
7. In 1951 Jean Hughes-Gibb married distinguished jurist Professor Gerald Draper, who was a colonel in the British Army and served as a war crimes investigator in postwar Germany. He was later part of the team that drafted the updated Geneva Convention. Jean Hughes-Gibb is now known as Julia Draper.
8. National Archives BT211/14.
9. National Archives BT211/24.
10. National Archives BT211/167.
11. National Archives FO1031/62.
12. National Archives FO1032/159.
13. National Archives FO1032/153.
14. Ibid.
15. Ibid.
16. Ibid.
17. Ibid.
18. National Archives WO171/8633.

Chapter 11: Aftermath

1. National Archives BT211/24.
2. *The T-Force Story*.
3. Ibid.
4. National Archives WO171/3865.
5. *Ian Fleming's Secret War* by Craig Cabell, Pen and Sword, 2008.
6. *Arctic Snow to Dust of Normandy* by Patrick Dalzel-Job.
7. National Archives WO219/1668.
8. National Archives HW8/104.
9. Ibid.
10. 'Governed or Exploited? The British Acquisition of German Technology, 1945–48' by John Farquharson.
11. National Archives FO1034/33.
12. 'Governed or Exploited? The British Acquisition of German Technology, 1945–48' by John Farquharson.
13. National Archives FO1032/330.
14. 'The American Exploitation of German Technical Know-How after World War II' by John Gimbel, *Political Science Quarterly*, vol.5, no.2, Summer 1990.
15. National Archives FO1032/330.
16. National Archives WO205/1049.

Bibliography

Published Sources

The Paperclip Conspiracy by Tom Bower, Michael Joseph, 1987.

Wings on My Sleeve by Captain Eric 'Winkle' Brown, Weidenfeld & Nicolson, 2006.

Ian Fleming's Secret War by Craig Cabell, Pen & Sword Books Ltd, 2008.

OPJB: The Last Great Secret of the Second World War by Christopher Creighton, Simon & Schuster, 1996.

From Arctic Snow to Dust of Normandy by Patrick Dalzel-Job, Sutton, 1991.

To the Victor the Spoils by Sean Longden, Constable, 2007.

Attain by Surprise: Capturing Top Secret Intelligence in WWII by David C. Nutting, David Colver, 2003.

A Life in Peace and War by Brian Urquhart, Harper Collins, 1987.

The T-Force Story: A Short History of T-Force Operations in North West Europe During the Second World War produced by the 5th King's/No. 2 T-Force Old Comrades Association.

Unpublished Sources

The National Archives:

I have consulted numerous files held at the National Archives. It is noted that this subject is so broad that each avenue of research opened up a complex and sometimes perplexing web of subject matter. To read every relevant document would be an impossible task for any author. As such my research was concentrated within Foreign Office, War Office and Admiralty documents.

The following list contains a selection of those documents viewed during the research for this book:

The Foreign Office (FO Series):
935/51–52–53–54 – FIAT Accession Lists
936/160 – London Office
936/303 – T Force

940/106 – Equipment Correspondence
944/964 – T Force Hotels
1031/65 – Personnel to be Denied to Russians
1031/66 – Scientists Taken by Russians
1031/67 – Scientists from Russian Zone
1013/852 – Reparation Duties
1031/1 – T Force Working Party
1031/4 – Termination of T Force
1031/5 – Liaison with Russians
1031/6 – Liaison with Russians
1031/17 – Disarmament of German War Research
1031/49 – History of T Force
1031/72 – FIAT policy
1031/20 – Exploitation of Scientists
1031/28 – Evacuation of Electrical Equipment
1031/52 – General Reports
1031/227 – General Reports
1031/73 – FIAT Policy
1031/76 – FIAT Reviews
1031/78 – Allied Investigators
1031/87 – General Reports
1031/88 – General Reports
1031/77 – FIAT Review of Metallurgy
1031/236 – Captured Documents Lists
1031/237 – Franz Hayler Documents
1031/238 – Dr Glassman
1031/89 – Dr Lautenschlager Interrogation
1031/101 – Dr Nold Interrogation
1031/100 – Hartmann Interrogation
1031/241 – Dr Osenberg Interrogation
1031/160 – Lose Blatter
1031/185 – Lose Blatter
1031/84 – Personnel Exploitation
1031/99 – August Dorken Reports
1031/131 – Reports on Individuals
1031/228 – IG Farben Reports
1031/230 – IG Farben Reports
1031/231 – IG Farben Reports
1031/232 – IG Farben Reports
1031/233 – IG Farben Reports
1031/134 – IG Farben Reports

1031/135 – IG Farben Overseas Reports
1031/137 – Scientist Interrogation Reports
1031/90 – Interrogation Reports
1031/132 – Evacuees from Russian Zone
1031/141 – Interrogation Reports
1031/144 – Interrogation Reports
1031/142 – Interrogation Reports
1032/1470A & B – Policy on Technical Targets
1032/1459 – FIAT
1032/1471 – Access to Technical Targets
1039/57 – Functions of T Force
1039/83 – T Force Disarmament Teams
1050/1422 – Berlin Targets
1062/435 – FIAT Intelligence on Tank Production
1065/12 – Future of FIAT & T Force
1071/3 – Reorganisation of T Force
1031/106 – Misc. Papers
1031/219 – Luranil Gendorfer Programme
1031/75 – Personnel Exploitation
1031/63 Interrogation Reports
1031/145 – Interrogation Reports
1031/151 – Interrogation Reports
938/3 – Professor Hahn
942/546 & 288 – Hahn in Stockholm
1031/12 – Von Braun Interrogation
938/3 – Hahn & Heisenberg
1046/540 – Otto Hahn
1031/69 – Dustbin
1031/70 – Dustbin
1005/1602 – Final Reports
1032/470 – Subcommittee Teams
1032/475 – Subcommittee Teams
1050/1419 – Black List
1078/56 – Speer Reports
935/20 – CIOS Minutes
935/21 to 24 – Black List
935/28 – Grey List
935/51 to 54 – FIAT Evacuation Lists
943/404 – Mining and Metallurgy
1031/86 – Poison Gas
1031/87 – Chemical Warfare Interrogation Reports

1031/81 – Operation Dustbin
1031/82 – Operation Dustbin Chemical Warfare
1031/83 – Dustbin & Bacteriological Reports
1031/89 to 91 – Major Tilley Chemical Warfare Reports
1031/239 – Dustbin & Dr Schrader Reports
1031/104 – Professor Wirth Interrogation
1031/105 – Dr Schrader Interrogation
1031/107 – Dr Ehman Interrogation
1031/85 – V Weapon Personnel
1031/219 – Pennemunde Reports
371/65168 to 72 – Dismantling of Goering Steelworks

The War Office (WO Series):
171/1316 – 5th King's War Diaries 1944
171/1317 – 8th King's War Diaries 1944
171/5211 – 5th King's War Diaries 1945
171/11094 – Equipment Evacuation Depot
205/1048 – Organisation and Policy
205/1049 – Activities in 2nd Army
205/1050 – Activities with 1st Canadian Army
219/551 – Special Force to Seize Intelligence
219/1028 – Misc. Papers
219/1003 – Establishment of FIAT
219/1630A & B – T Force Planning
219/1631 – Targets for Berlin
1050/1422 – Targets for Berlin
219/1985 – List of T Force Targets
219/1986 – Collection of Documents
219/1987 – Reports
219/2549 – Operation Eruption
219/2460 – Operation Eclipse
219/2461 – Operation Eclipse
219/2694 – Berlin Planning
267/614 & 615 – Reparations and Restitution
229/60/3 – T Forces
229/5/17 Ashcan & Dustbin
205/828 & 829 – Kiel Reports
309/198 – U Boat Destruction Orders
309/645 – U Boat Destruction Orders
208/2183 – Reports on Tabun & Sarin
195/9222 – Production of Sarin

219/5334 – Special Projectile Operation Group
219/5335 – V2 Firing Trials
219/3365 – Firing Trials
229/9/38 – Trials of Captured Rockets
219/1668 – Info to CIOS
204/11445 – S Force in Italy
204/907 – S Force in Italy
204/9917 – S Force in Italy
204/6321 – S Force in Italy
204/795 – S Force in Italy
204/6692 – S Force in Italy
204/796 – S Force in Italy
219/1251 – Reparations & Planning Reports
258/80 – Reparations Policy
106/4456 – Reparations Commission

The Air Ministry (AIR Series):
51/378&379 – T Force Policy
51/424 – T Force and Eclipse
40/2832 – Interrogation of Herman Zumpe
40/2534 – Hydrogen Peroxide
40/2536 – Peroxide Storage
40/3063 – Infra Red Detection
20/5625 – Kiel Interception
20/1694 – Kiel Apparatus
20/5807 – Kiel Apparatus
48/170 – Deutsche Werke
48/172 – Krupps
40/2005 – Blohm & Voss Reports

The Admiralty (ADM Series):
1/18328 – Submarine Trials
1/22336 – Synthetic Rubber in Submarines
213/557 & 645 – Torpedo Reports
204/586 – Instrument Illumination in Subs
213/883 – Underwater Explosion Tests
199/2434 – Walterwerke
178/392 – Walterwerke
265/71 – Walterwerke
281/25 – Walterwerke
281/142 – Walterwerke

213/53 – Kiel University Research
213/247 – Walterwerke
213/910 – Infra Red Aircraft Detector
283/1 – Walterwerke Hydrogen Peroxide
290/285 – Dr Walter Interrogation
1/19025 – Diesel Engines for Warships
1/16396 – German Design to be Used in UK Subs
1/18380 – Use of Captured German Subs
1/18621 – Exchange of Info on Subs
1/16493 – Walter Boote

Miscellaneous Files:
CAB79/32/7 – Kiel Canal & Baltic Entrance
CAB80/93/72 – Kiel Canal & Baltic Entrance
INF2/44/653 to 655 – Dempsey etc in Kiel with Hipper
DSIR23/14897 – Walterwerke
DSIR23/15067 – Walterwerke
AVIA6/10782 – Walterwerke
AVIA28/849 – Propulsive Duct Development at Walterwerke
AVIA49/120 – Interpretation of War Plants
AVIA15/2507 – Report on Reparations
AVIA15/3845 – Policy on Reparations
AVIA49/124 – Hydrogen Peroxide
DEFE2/1107 – 30AU
DSIR36/2014 – Aircon in German Subs
TS62/66 – Sale of Reparations

Appendix

Major Tony Hibbert MC

Left: Tony Hibbert in his Royal Horse Artillery uniform, 1946. *Right:* Hibbert in Kiel in May 2006. Sixty-one years on, Hibbert is seen on the steps of the former Naval Academy where he had accepted the surrender of the city's garrison.

After leaving school in the early 1930s, Tony Hibbert seemed destined for a career as a wine importer, before a visit to Germany convinced him that war was inevitable. Returning to London, he joined the Royal Horse Artillery and served in France in 1940. After returning via Dunkirk, Hibbert joined the commandos and then the fledgling Parachute Regiment. As the Brigade Major of the 1st Parachute Brigade, he served at Arnhem Bridge during Operation Market Garden, where he won the Military Cross. Following capture by the enemy, he was able to escape and go into hiding. After crossing the Rhine and returning to Allied territory, he broke his leg in a car accident. This injury resulted in his eventual transfer to T-Force, where he led the Kiel operation.

Major Hibbert was discharged from the army in 1946 and entered what he called 'the cut and thrust of commercial life'. In 1981 he retired and moved to Trebah Gardens in Cornwall. He soon discovered he had purchased one of England's most important and beautiful gardens. Since then he and his family have devoted their lives to restoring the gardens – now visited by more than 100,000 people each year – which have given Tony Hibbert what he described in 1995 as 'the happiest 24 years of my life'.

Captain Tom Pitt-Pladdy

Left: Tom Pitt-Pladdy as a newly commissioned artillery subaltern. *Right:* Pitt-Pladdy photographed at his home in York, October 2008.

Upon leaving T-Force in 1946, Tom Pitt-Pladdy discovered there were opportunities for artillery officers. Returning to the UK, he decided to stay on in the army to build a career. He took on an intelligence role and soon found himself operating radars on the Greek–Turkish border. This was followed by a posting to Palestine, where he operated six observation posts in Jerusalem, working in conjunction with the Palestinian police and living in the CID mess. In total, Pitt-Pladdy spent 24 years in the army, leaving in the early 1960s. He then went into the Territorial Army as an administrative officer and eventually worked in York as a recruiting officer for the Royal Artillery.

Michael Howard

Left: Michael Howard in Germany during summer 1946. *Right:* Michael Howard photographed at his home in January 2009.

Following demobilization from the army in late 1947, Michael Howard studied modern languages at Peterhouse College, Cambridge. Graduating in June 1949, he stayed on for a further year, 'nominally reading Economics but in fact having a jolly good time (at the expense of his late Majesty and a grateful nation)'. From 1950 he worked as a merchandizing manager for an American company, working in the UK, El Salvador and Guatemala, where he was joined by his wife, Ann, and his three children were born. Returning to the UK in 1963, he worked for Lloyds Merchant Bank until retirement. Michael now lives in Kent and retains a keen interest in T-Force. Like Ken Moore, he has striven to ensure the unit's work is not forgotten. He has collected vast amounts of documentation related to T-Force, without which this book might never have been written.

Reg Rush

Left: Reg Rush in Minden, Germany, May 1945. *Right:* Reg Rush photographed at his home in Norfolk, summer 2008.

Reg Rush had never planned on joining the army and only made the decision to leave his reserved occupation after seeing the effects of German bombing in 1940. As a Royal Marine Commando he served with 30 Advanced Unit in France and Germany. He first became involved with 30AU reunions during the late 1970s. It was only then that he learned about the connection to Ian Fleming and James Bond. As one of his wartime comrades told him: 'I didn't realize we were famous!' Yet there was a darker side to the period. The reality of having been one of Fleming's 'Red Indians' left a number of veterans of 30AU prey to mental illness. Whilst Rush himself was fortunate not to fall victim to psychological problems, many of his former comrades suffered significant mental damage, with a number eventually being confined to psychiatric hospitals. That was the true price of war. Rush remains staunchly proud of his service as a Royal Marine and has never lost his connection with the sea, having settled in Norfolk, where his home overlooks a harbour.

Ken Moore

Left: Ken Moore photographed in 1945. *Right:* Ken Moore at a 5th Kings/No.2 T-Force reunion in Sheffield, October 2008.

In the post-war period Ken Moore was the editor of *Freelance*, the regular magazine that was distributed to members of the 5th King's/No.2 T-Force. This work took him all over Germany, giving him a freedom that was enjoyed by few of his comrades. Following demob he lived and worked in both Germany and Denmark, before eventually settling in his native Norfolk. He was the driving force behind the creation of the 5th King's Old Comrades Association. His aim was always that T-Force should be recognized for its role in the peace and security enjoyed by the West since 1945. This book is effectively the culmination of Ken's efforts to provide a lasting reminder of the achievements of T-Force.

Major George Lambert MC

Left: George Lambert in 1943. *Right:* George Lambert in 1998 holding a photograph of the *Admiral Hipper*.

Major Lambert was awarded the Military Cross for the leadership he showed when T-Force occupied Kiel. He was one of the most popular officers in the 5th King's and was highly respected for the concern he showed for his men. Following demob from the army, Lambert returned to his job at Hurstpierpoint College in West Sussex, where he became the senior maths master. He remained at the college for the rest of his working life. George Lambert died in June 2001.

Clockwise from top: **Anthony Lucas** (left) and **John Bayley** photographed in the Officers' Mess at HQ No.1 T-Force. In the postwar years Anthony Lucas qualified as a barrister and for many years worked for ATV. John Bayley later found fame as a writer and poet, notably marrying Iris Murdoch in 1956. He was Warton Professor of English at St Catherine's College, Oxford University, between 1974 and 1992, and was awarded the CBE in 1999. His novel *In Another Country* drew heavily on his memories of Germany in the postwar years, and his experiences as a junior officer with T-Force.

John Bendit. Seen here as a young subaltern with the Rifle Brigade, Bendit served in north west Europe in late 1945. He still recalls how the first shot he fired 'in anger' hit a German soldier in the backside. He later served with No.1 T-Force in the Ruhr.

Robin Smyth worked with Michael Howard in the intelligence office of No.1 T-Force in Kamen. He was the younger son of Brigadier Sir John ('Jackie') Smyth, Bt., VC, MC, MP. Postwar he became Senior History Scholar of Trinity College, Oxford, and was ultimately the *Observer*'s senior correspondent on the Continent, based in Paris.

John Longfield. Following service with T-Force, Longfield served with the Army Education Corps in Berlin. Demobbed as a sergeant, he returned to the UK, went to university to study economics and then trained to be an accountant. Unenthusiastic about spending the rest of his life as an accountant, he found a job as a lecturer in economics. Upon retirement, the rest of the staff admitted that, behind his back, they referred to him as 'Long John Field' – a suitably piratical name for a former T-Force soldier. Looking back on his military service, Longfield sees service with T-Force as a pleasant period compared to his time in Normandy, of which he says 'It was the most intense two months of my life. When I look back it is like a dark green blot on my life. The green is the fields and trees and Normandy – the darkness because it was a dark period of my life.'

Clockwise from top-left: **Lt Colonel Guy Wreford-Brown**, commanding officer 5th Battalion The King's Regiment. Throughout autumn and winter 1944, Wreford-Brown campaigned to see his battalion employed in an active role. It was his persistence that saw the battalion given its T-Force role.

Ron Lawton had originally served in the Royal Marines, taking part in the D-Day landings as a member of the crew of a landing craft. He was later transferred to the 5th King's Regiment and served in T-Force.

Vic Woods was one of the first Kingsmen to land on Sword Beach on D-Day. Following demob in early 1946, Vic Woods returned home to Merseyside, eager to forget the war and settle down with his wife, who he had married in 1941 and then been apart from for five years. Despite the desire to forget his experiences, in particular the morning of D-Day, it was not that easy: 'One thing that lingered with me for years was the smell of diesel. It was from the landing craft – when the tanks started up. That was combined with the gunfire. It stayed with me. After I came out of the army I had a spell of what they'd now call severe stress. I couldn't stay on a bus because of the smell of diesel. The fear came back to me. My wife told me I was crying out in the night. I'd shout "Get Down!" When the Cold War was ongoing there was talk of being recalled to the army. I found that worrying – I didn't ever want to go through that again. I felt I'd done my bit. I never wanted to talk about war. Also the T-Force business was so far out no one would ever believe it. People would have thought "what a load of nonsense" – so I never mentioned it.'

Commander Ian Aylen, 30AU. Aylen, commonly known as 'Jan', was an engineer officer in the Royal Navy. After service at sea in the early war years he was appointed to a shore role in Bath. Desiring a return to active service, he transferred to 30AU. He led the investigations at the Walterwerke in Kiel, where he was fascinated by Dr Walter's 'freak weapons'. He was awarded the OBE for his work in Germany in 1945. He retired from the Royal Navy in 1962 with the rank of Rear Admiral. Jan Aylen died in 2003.

Top left: Bob Brighouse. *Top right:* Tom Wilkinson. *Middle:* Harry Bullen. *Bottom left:* Harry Henshaw. *Bottom right:* Jack Chamberlain.

Veterans of 5th Kings/No.2 T-Force photographed at their annual reunion, Sheffield, October 2008.

Clockwise from top-left: Soldiers of D Company, the 5th Battalion The King's Regiment, enjoying life in Germany, summer 1945.

Freelance, the unit magazine of the 5th Battalion The King's Regiment and No.2 T-Force. It was edited by Ken Moore who later resurrected the magazine as the journal of the battalion's Old Comrades Association.

Officers of No.2 T-Force at a party to mark the closing down of the unit. Lt Colonel Percy Winterton, Commander No.2 T-Force is on the right.

Ken Moore enjoying the company of a Danish girl, 1945.

Index